We made it to volume 20! This is *Shonen Jump*'s longest-running romantic comedy, thanks to your support! I am truly grateful! There's more still to come, so please stay with us. I'm still hanging in there!

Naoshi Komi

Wow! Second time already?

NAOSHI KOMI was born in Kochi Prefecture, Japan, on March 28, 1986. His first serialized work in *Weekly Shonen Jump* was the series *Double Arts*. His current series, *Nisekoi*, is serialized in *Weekly Shonen Jump*.

NISEKOI:
False Love
VOLUME 20
SHONEN JUMP Manga Edition

Story and Art by
NAOSHI KOMI

Translation ✐ Camellia Nieh
Touch-Up Art & Lettering ✐ Stephen Dutro
Design ✐ Izumi Evers
Shonen Jump Series Editor ✐ John Bae
Graphic Novel Editor ✐ Amy Yu

NISEKOI © 2011 by Naoshi Komi
All rights reserved.
First published in Japan in 2011
by SHUEISHA Inc., Tokyo.
English translation rights arranged
by SHUEISHA Inc.

Printed in the U.S.A.

Published by VIZ Media, LLC
P.O. Box 77010
San Francisco, CA 94107

10 9 8 7 6 5 4 3 2 1
First printing, March 2017

www.shonenjump.com   www.viz.com

You're Reading the WRONG WAY!

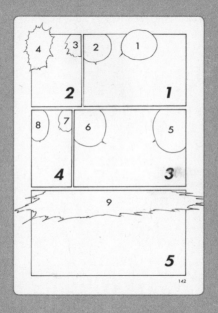

NISEKOI reads from right to left, starting in the upper-right corner. Japanese is read from right to left, meaning that action, sound effects, and word-balloon order are completely reversed from English order.

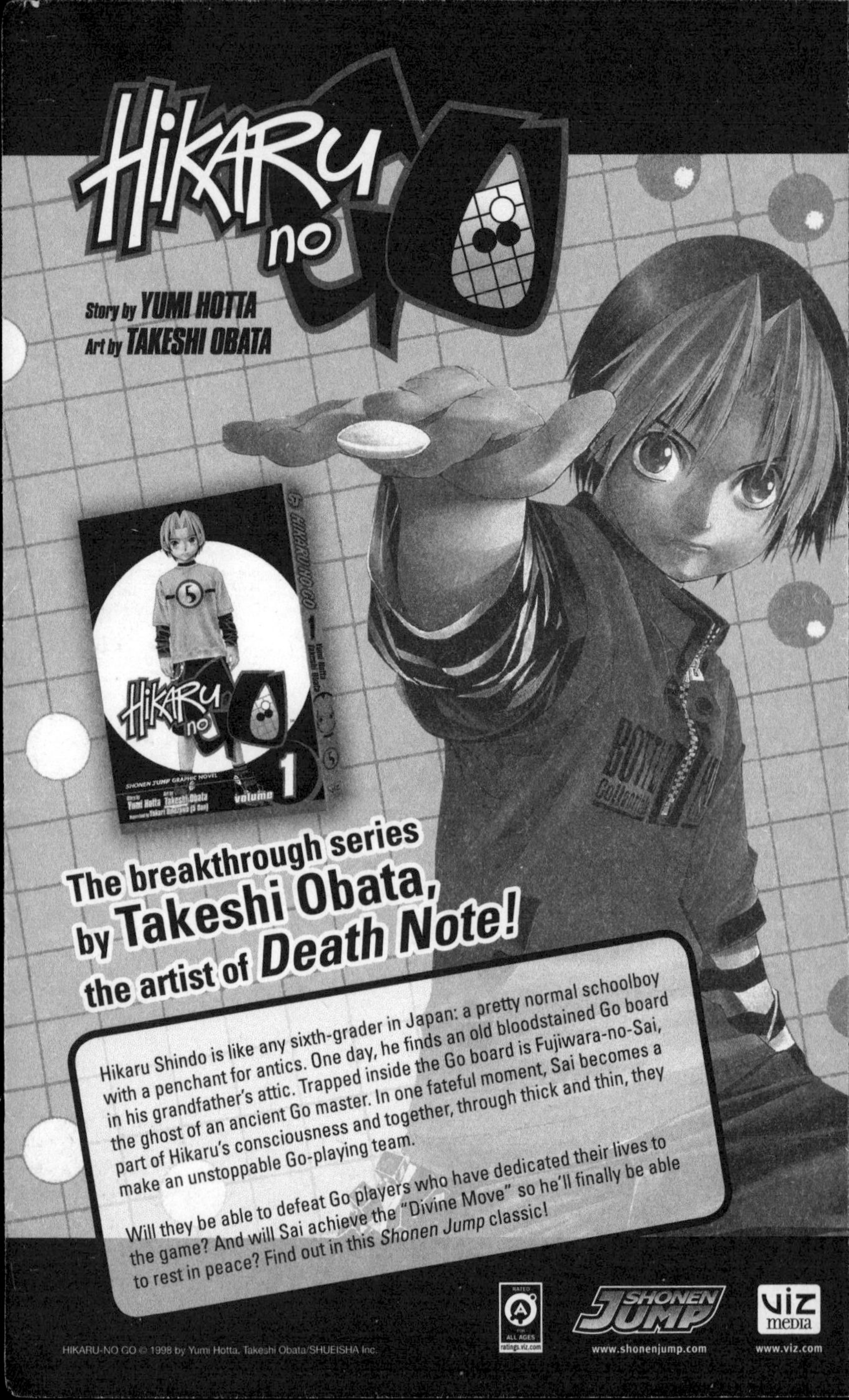
HiKARU no GO
Story by YUMI HOTTA
Art by TAKESHI OBATA
HiKARU no GO
SHONEN JUMP GRAPHIC NOVEL
volume 1
The breakthrough series by Takeshi Obata, the artist of Death Note!
Hikaru Shindo is like any sixth-grader in Japan: a pretty normal schoolboy with a penchant for antics. One day, he finds an old bloodstained Go board in his grandfather's attic. Trapped inside the Go board is Fujiwara-no-Sai, the ghost of an ancient Go master. In one fateful moment, Sai becomes a part of Hikaru's consciousness and together, through thick and thin, they make an unstoppable Go-playing team.
Will they be able to defeat Go players who have dedicated their lives to the game? And will Sai achieve the "Divine Move" so he'll finally be able to rest in peace? Find out in this Shonen Jump classic!
HIKARU-NO GO © 1998 by Yumi Hotta, Takeshi Obata/SHUEISHA Inc.
RATED A FOR ALL AGES
ratings.viz.com
SHONEN JUMP
www.shonenjump.com
VIZ MEDIA
www.viz.com

Story and Art by
NAOSHI KOMI

NISEKOI
False Love
vol. 20: Order

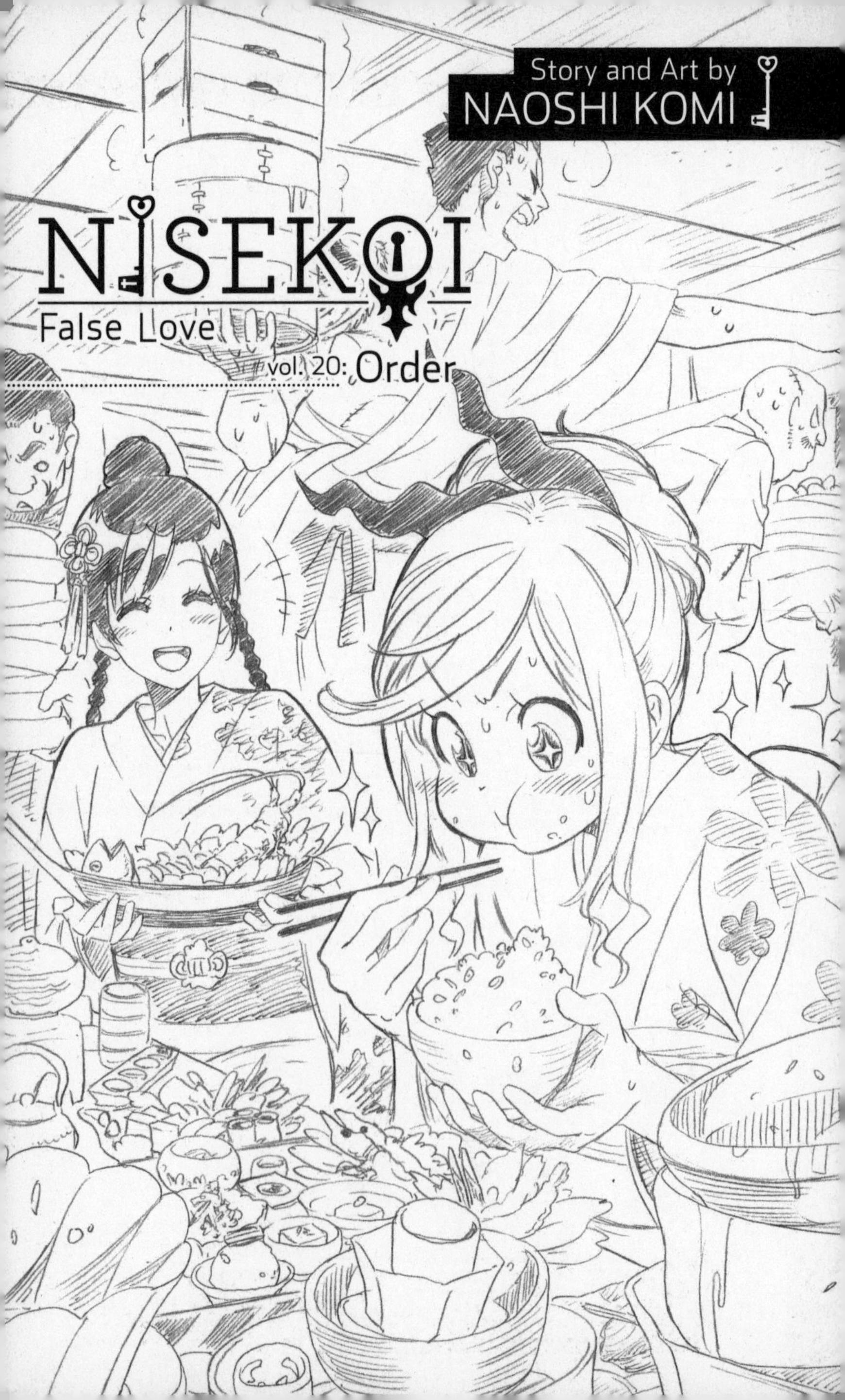

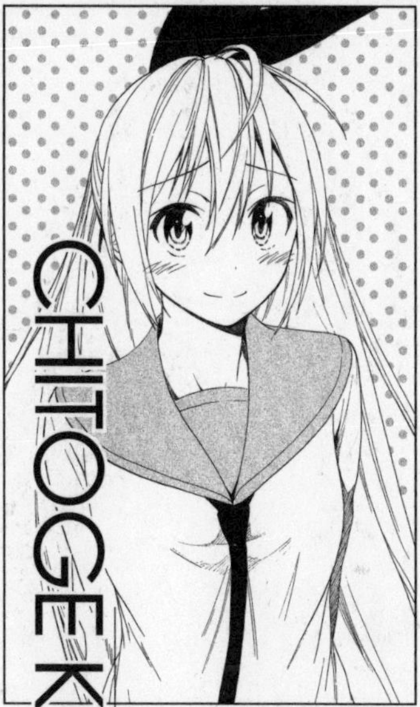

CHITOGE KIRISAKI

A half-Japanese bombshell with stellar athletic abilities. Short-tempered and violent. Comes from a family of gangsters.

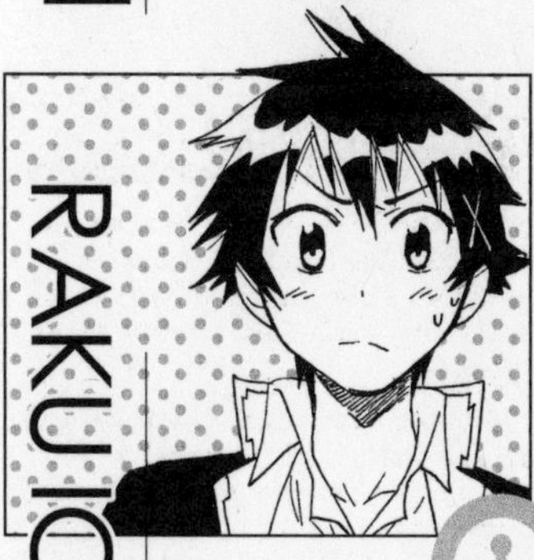

RAKU ICHIJO

A normal teen whose family happens to be yakuza. Cherishes a pendant given to him by a girl he met ten years ago.

KOSAKI ONODERA

A girl Raku has a crush on. Beautiful and sweet, Kosaki has no shortage of admirers. She's a terrible cook but makes food that *looks* amazing.

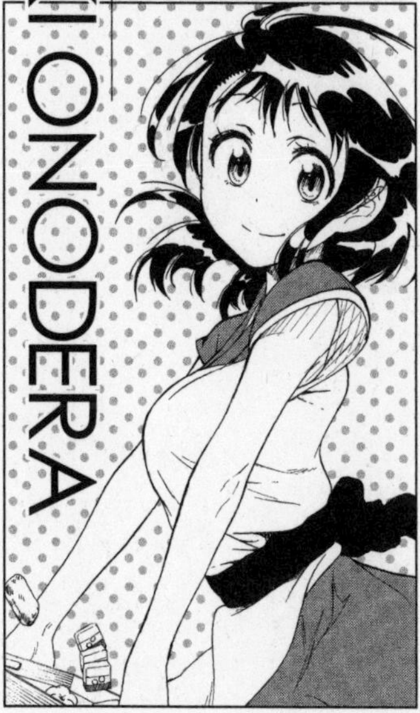

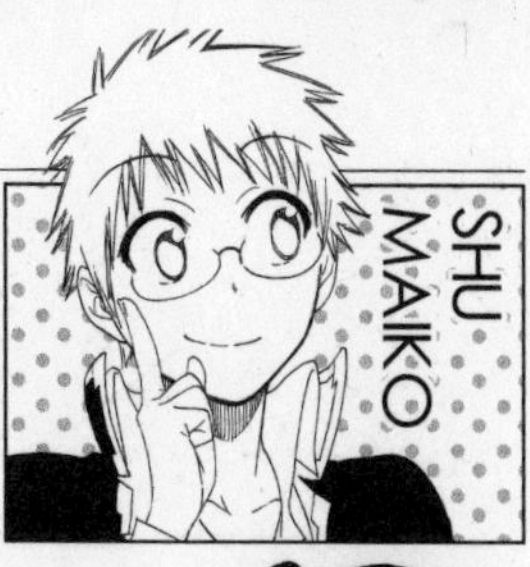

SHU MAIKO

Raku's best friend is outgoing and girl-crazy.

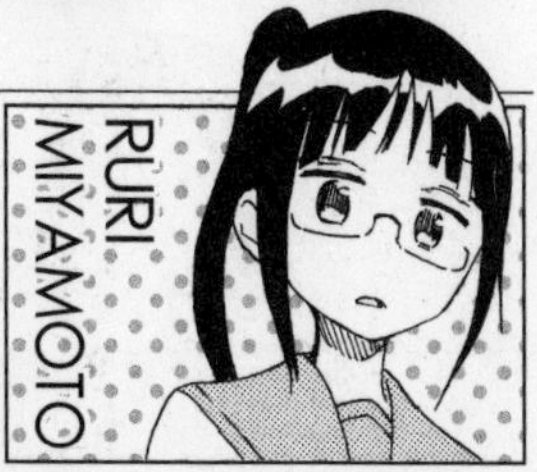

RURI MIYAMOTO

Kosaki's best gal pal. Comes off as aloof, but is actually a devoted and highly intuitive friend.

YUI KANAKURA

A childhood friend of Raku's, Yui is the head of a Chinese mafia gang and the homeroom teacher of Raku's class at his school. She is currently staying at Raku's house and also has a special key linked to some kind of promise...

MARIKA TACHIBANA

Daughter of the chief of police, Marika is Raku's fiancée, according to an agreement made by their fathers—an agreement Marika takes very seriously! Also has a key and remembers making a promise with Raku ten years ago.

CHARACTERS & STORY

Ten years ago, Raku Ichijo made a promise with a girl he loved that they would get married when they met again...and he still treasures the pendant she gave him to seal their pledge.

Thanks to his family's circumstances, Raku has to pretend he's dating Chitoge Kirisaki, the daughter of a rival gangster. Despite their constant spats, Raku and Chitoge manage to fool everyone. Chitoge also has a token from her first love ten years ago—an old key. Meanwhile, Raku's crush, Kosaki, also has a key, as do Marika, the girl Raku's father has arranged for him to marry, and Yui, a childhood friend who's their homeroom teacher. On New Year's Eve, Marika takes action and abducts Raku so they can watch the first sunrise of the year together. But the two of them wind up stranded alone on a deserted island!

SEISHIRO TSUGUMI

Trained as an assassin in order to protect Chitoge, Tsugumi is often mistaken for a boy.

HARU ONODERA

Kosaki's adoring younger sister. Has a low opinion of Raku.

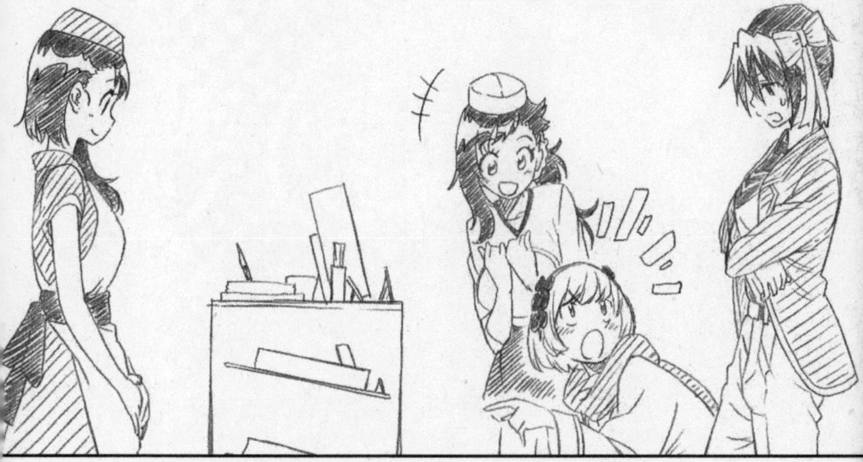

NISEKOI
False Love

vol. 20: Order

TABLE OF CONTENTS

Chapter 171: Heart

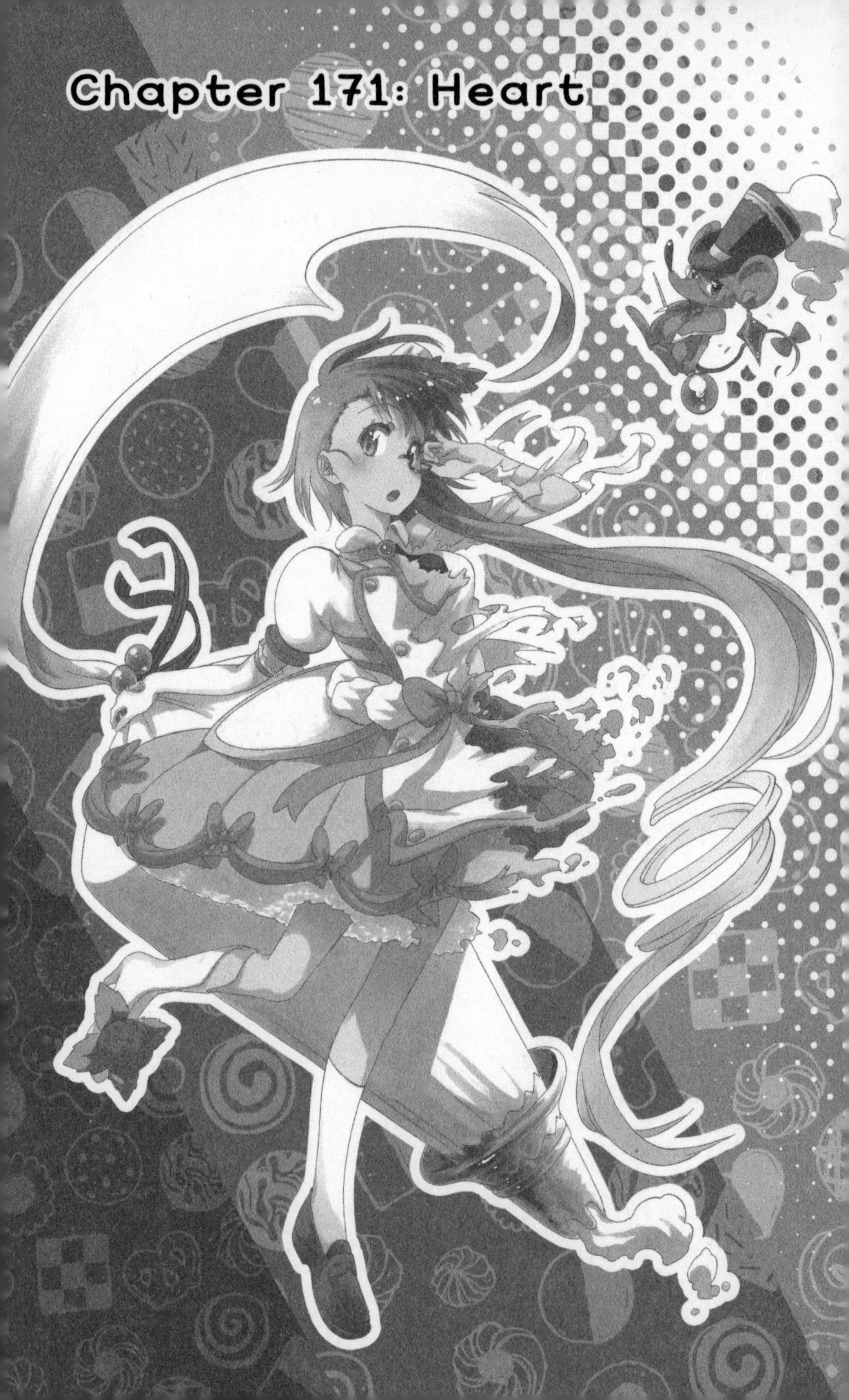

NISEKOI
False Love

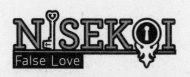

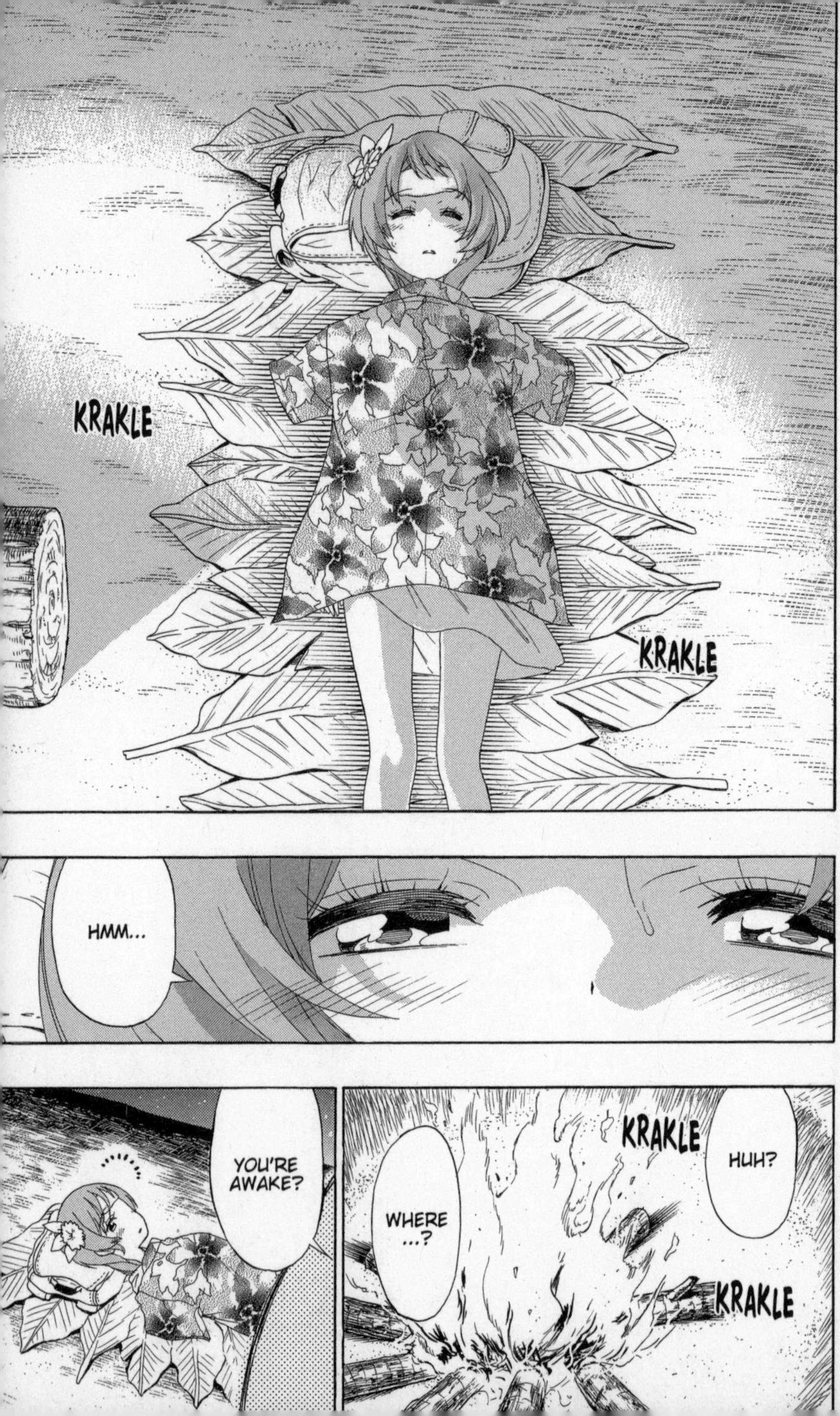
KRAKLE
KRAKLE
HMM...
HUH?
KRAKLE
WHERE ...?
KRAKLE
......
YOU'RE AWAKE?

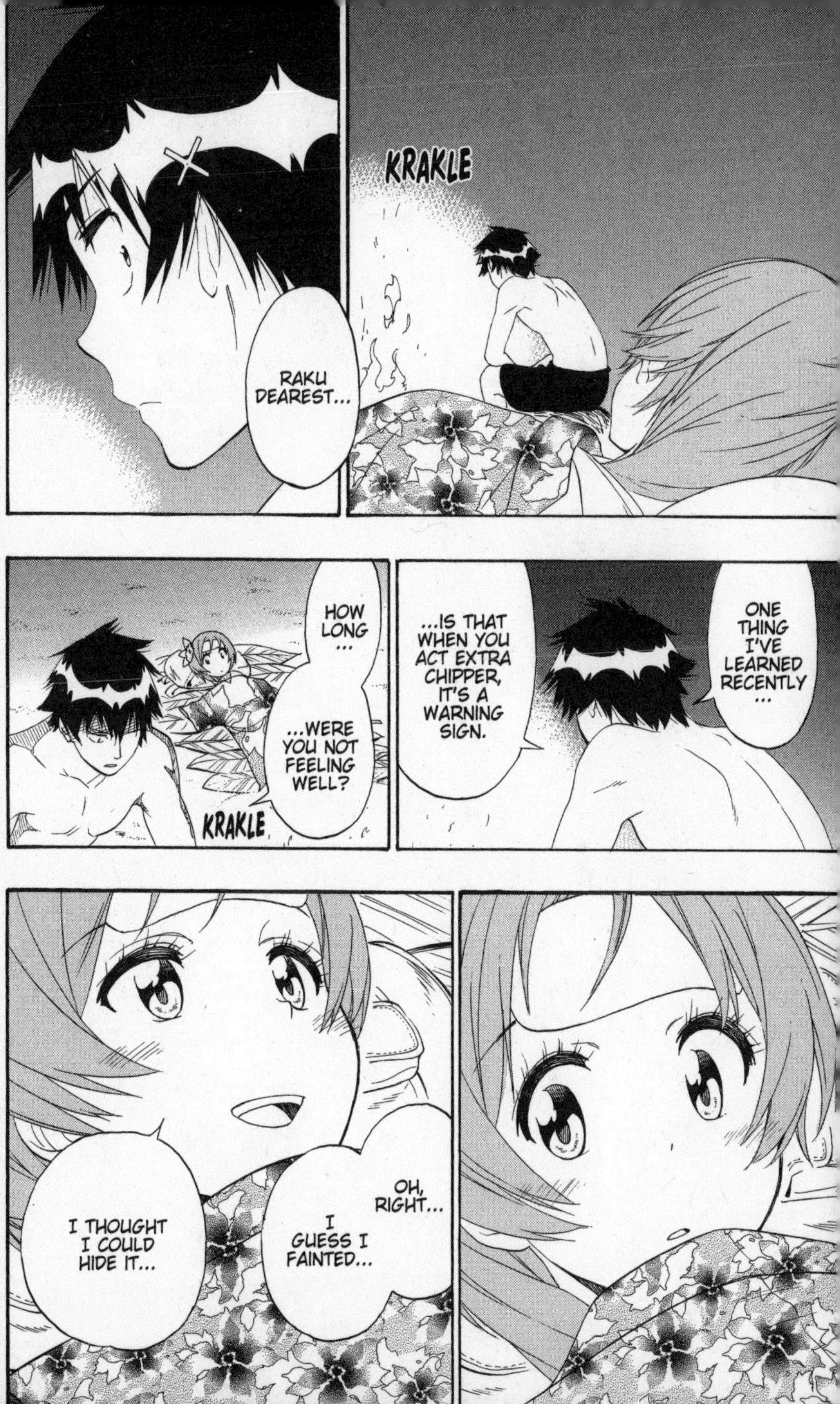
KRAKLE
RAKU DEAREST...
ONE THING I'VE LEARNED RECENTLY...
...IS THAT WHEN YOU ACT EXTRA CHIPPER, IT'S A WARNING SIGN.
HOW LONG...
...WERE YOU NOT FEELING WELL?
KRAKLE
OH, RIGHT...
I GUESS I FAINTED...
I THOUGHT I COULD HIDE IT...

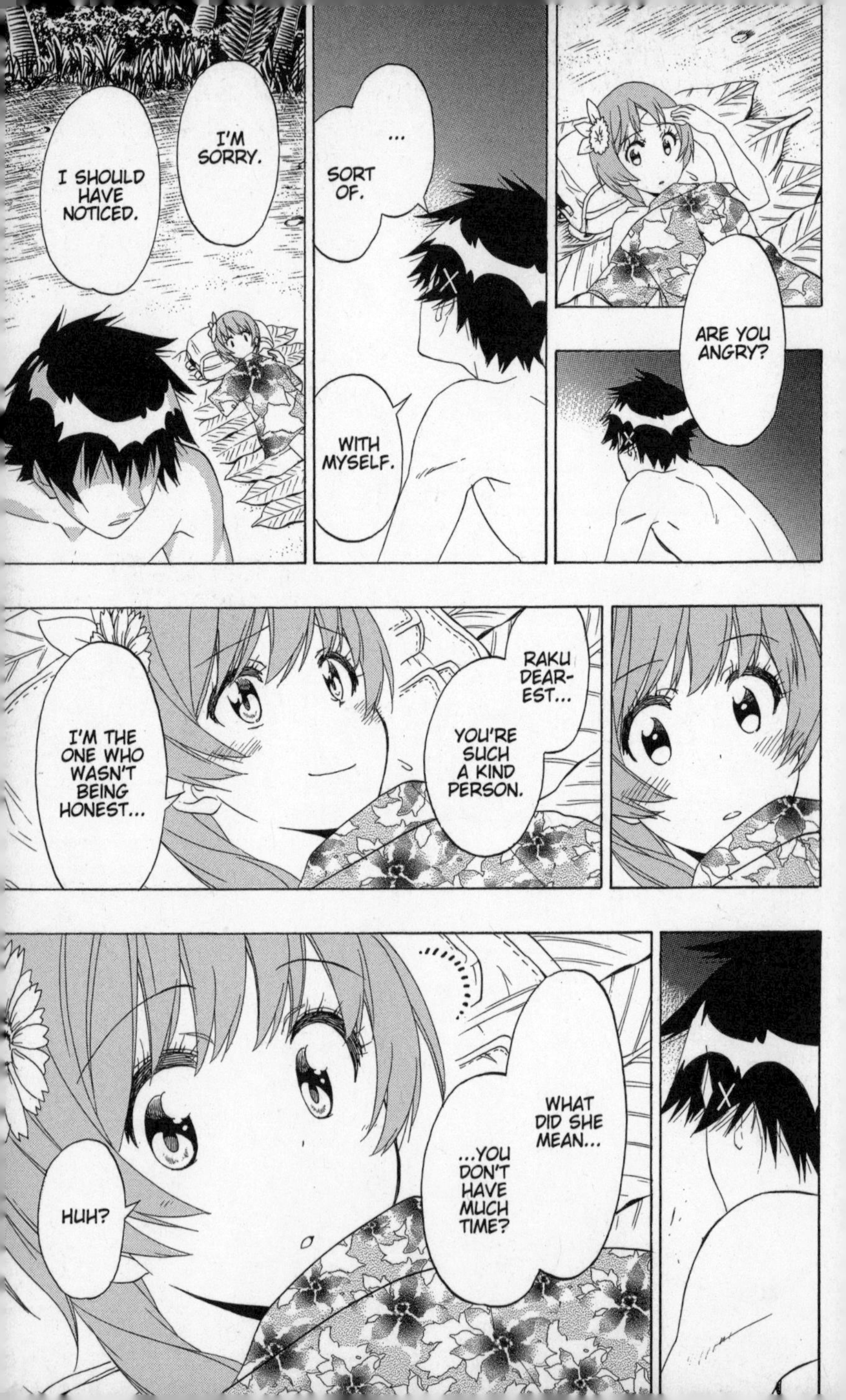
ARE YOU ANGRY?
...
SORT OF.
WITH MYSELF.
I'M SORRY.
I SHOULD HAVE NOTICED.
RAKU DEAREST...
YOU'RE SUCH A KIND PERSON.
I'M THE ONE WHO WASN'T BEING HONEST...
...
WHAT DID SHE MEAN...
...YOU DON'T HAVE MUCH TIME?
HUH?

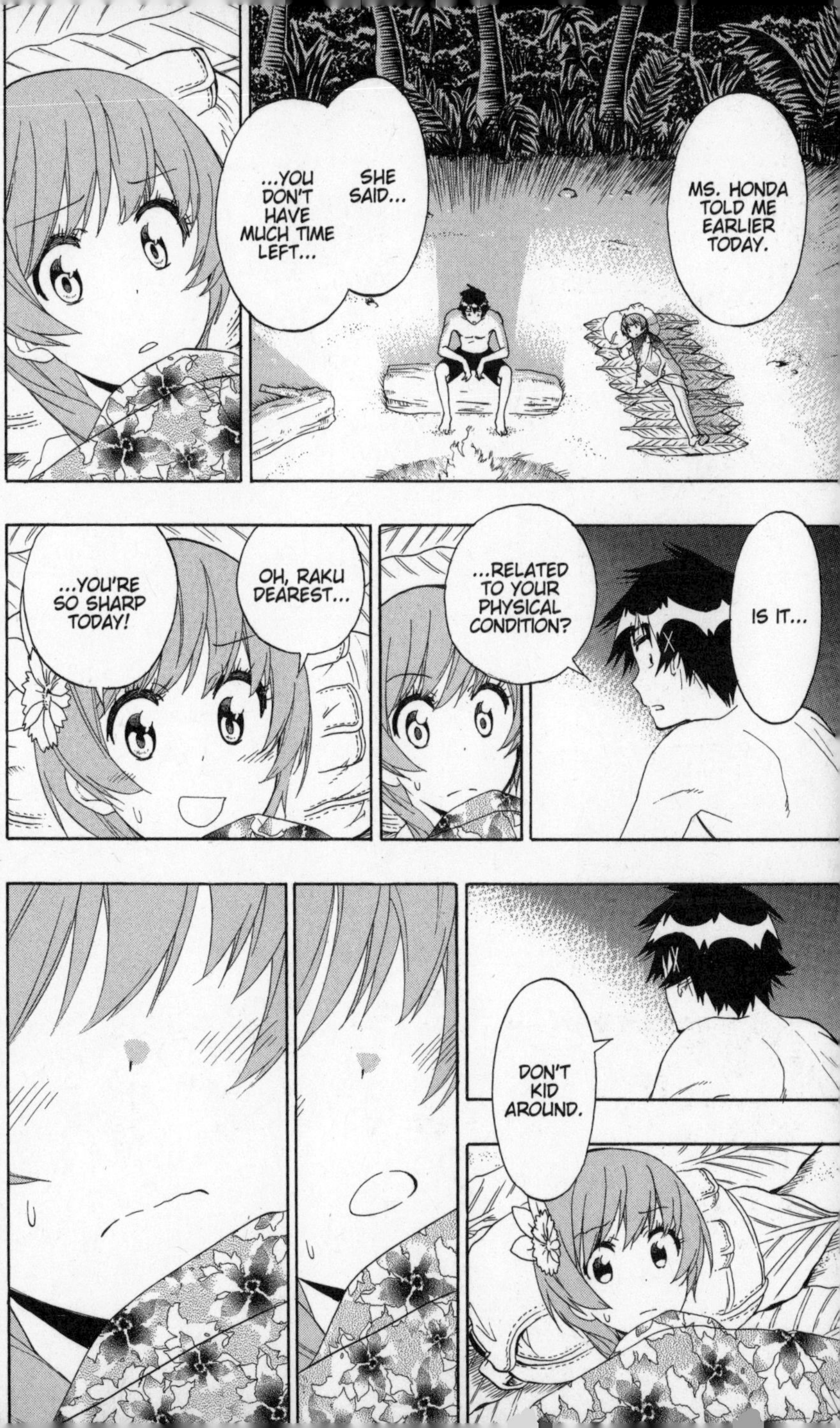
MS. HONDA TOLD ME EARLIER TODAY.
SHE SAID...
...YOU DON'T HAVE MUCH TIME LEFT...
IS IT...
...RELATED TO YOUR PHYSICAL CONDITION?
OH, RAKU DEAREST...
...YOU'RE SO SHARP TODAY!
DON'T KID AROUND.

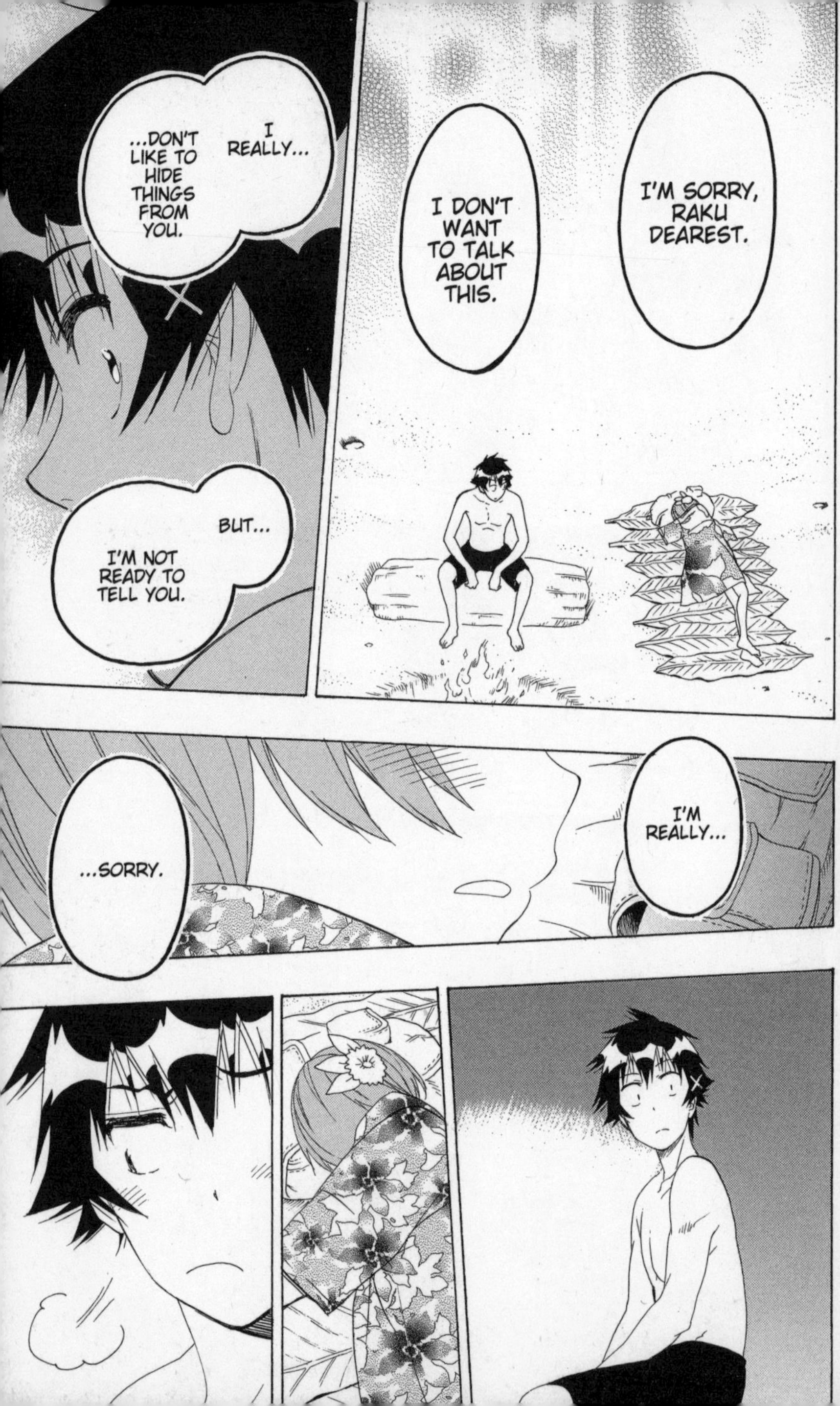
I'M SORRY, RAKU DEAREST.
I DON'T WANT TO TALK ABOUT THIS.
I REALLY...
...DON'T LIKE TO HIDE THINGS FROM YOU.
BUT...
I'M NOT READY TO TELL YOU.
I'M REALLY...
...SORRY.

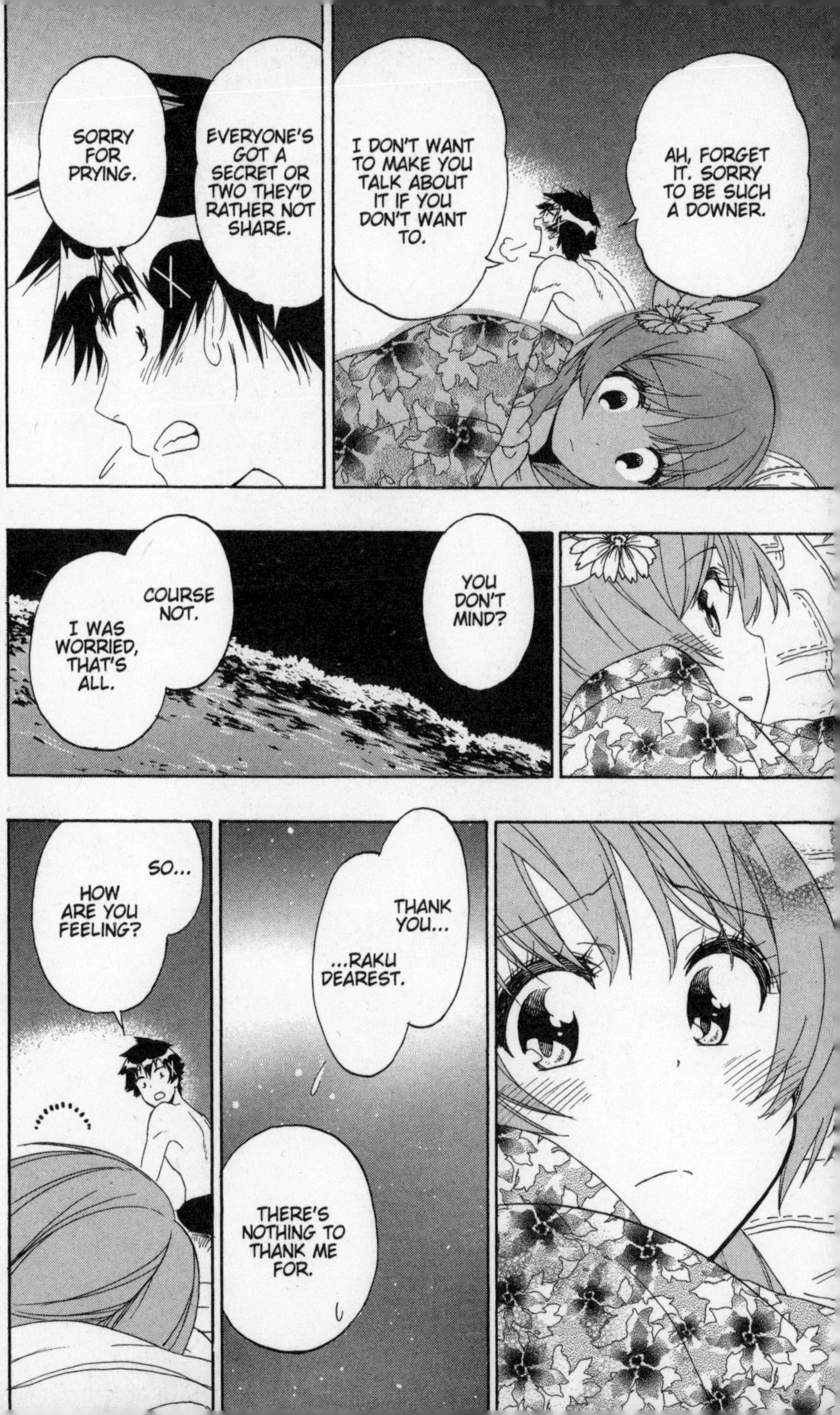
AH, FORGET IT. SORRY TO BE SUCH A DOWNER.
I DON'T WANT TO MAKE YOU TALK ABOUT IT IF YOU DON'T WANT TO.
EVERYONE'S GOT A SECRET OR TWO THEY'D RATHER NOT SHARE.
SORRY FOR PRYING.
YOU DON'T MIND?
COURSE NOT.
I WAS WORRIED, THAT'S ALL.
THANK YOU...
...RAKU DEAREST.
THERE'S NOTHING TO THANK ME FOR.
SO...
HOW ARE YOU FEELING?
......

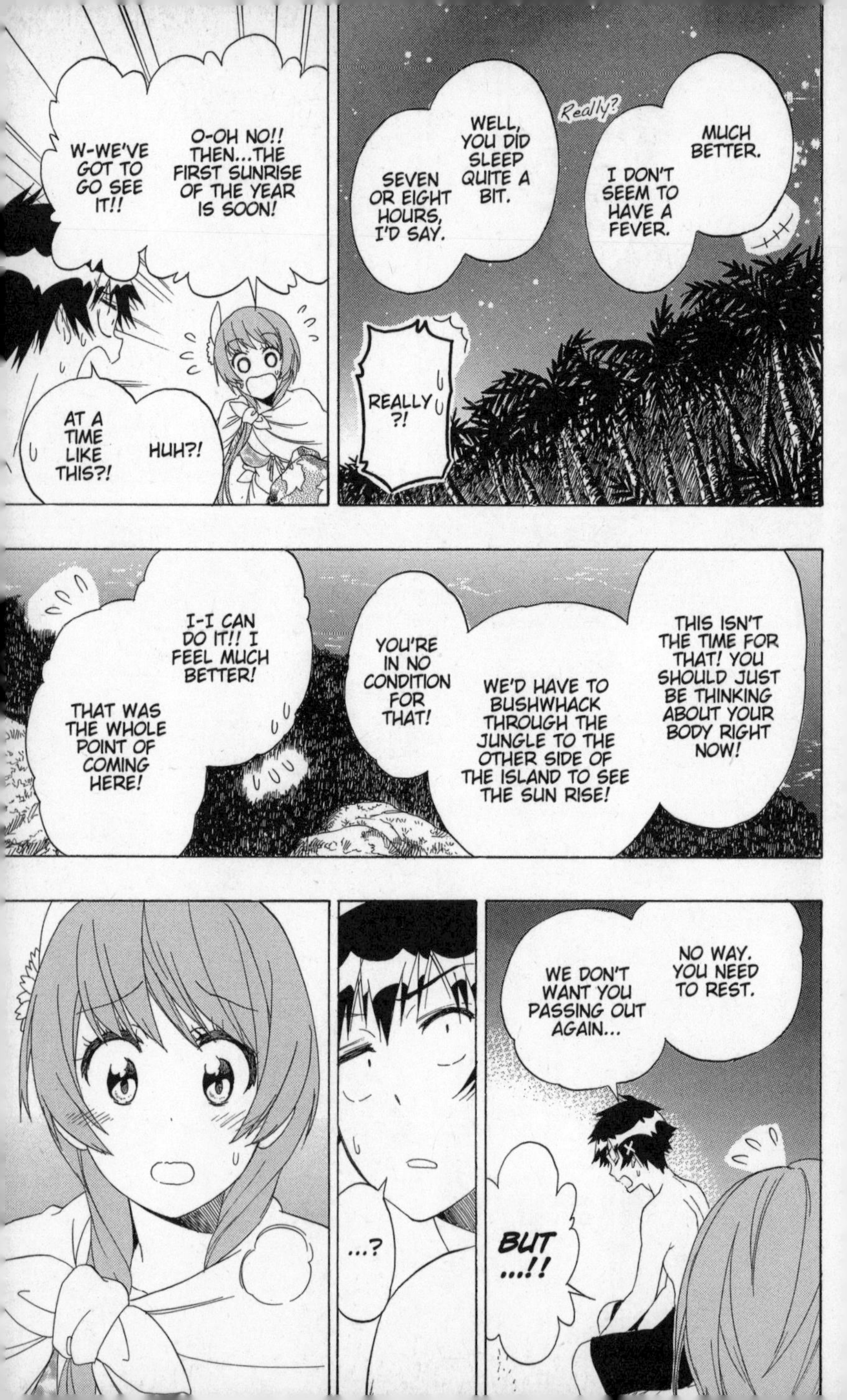
MUCH BETTER.
I DON'T SEEM TO HAVE A FEVER.
Really?
WELL, YOU DID SLEEP QUITE A BIT.
SEVEN OR EIGHT HOURS, I'D SAY.
REALLY ?!
O-OH NO!! THEN...THE FIRST SUNRISE OF THE YEAR IS SOON!
W-WE'VE GOT TO GO SEE IT!!
HUH?!
AT A TIME LIKE THIS?!
THIS ISN'T THE TIME FOR THAT! YOU SHOULD JUST BE THINKING ABOUT YOUR BODY RIGHT NOW!
WE'D HAVE TO BUSHWHACK THROUGH THE JUNGLE TO THE OTHER SIDE OF THE ISLAND TO SEE THE SUN RISE!
YOU'RE IN NO CONDITION FOR THAT!
I-I CAN DO IT!! I FEEL MUCH BETTER!
THAT WAS THE WHOLE POINT OF COMING HERE!
NO WAY. YOU NEED TO REST.
WE DON'T WANT YOU PASSING OUT AGAIN...
BUT ...!!
...?

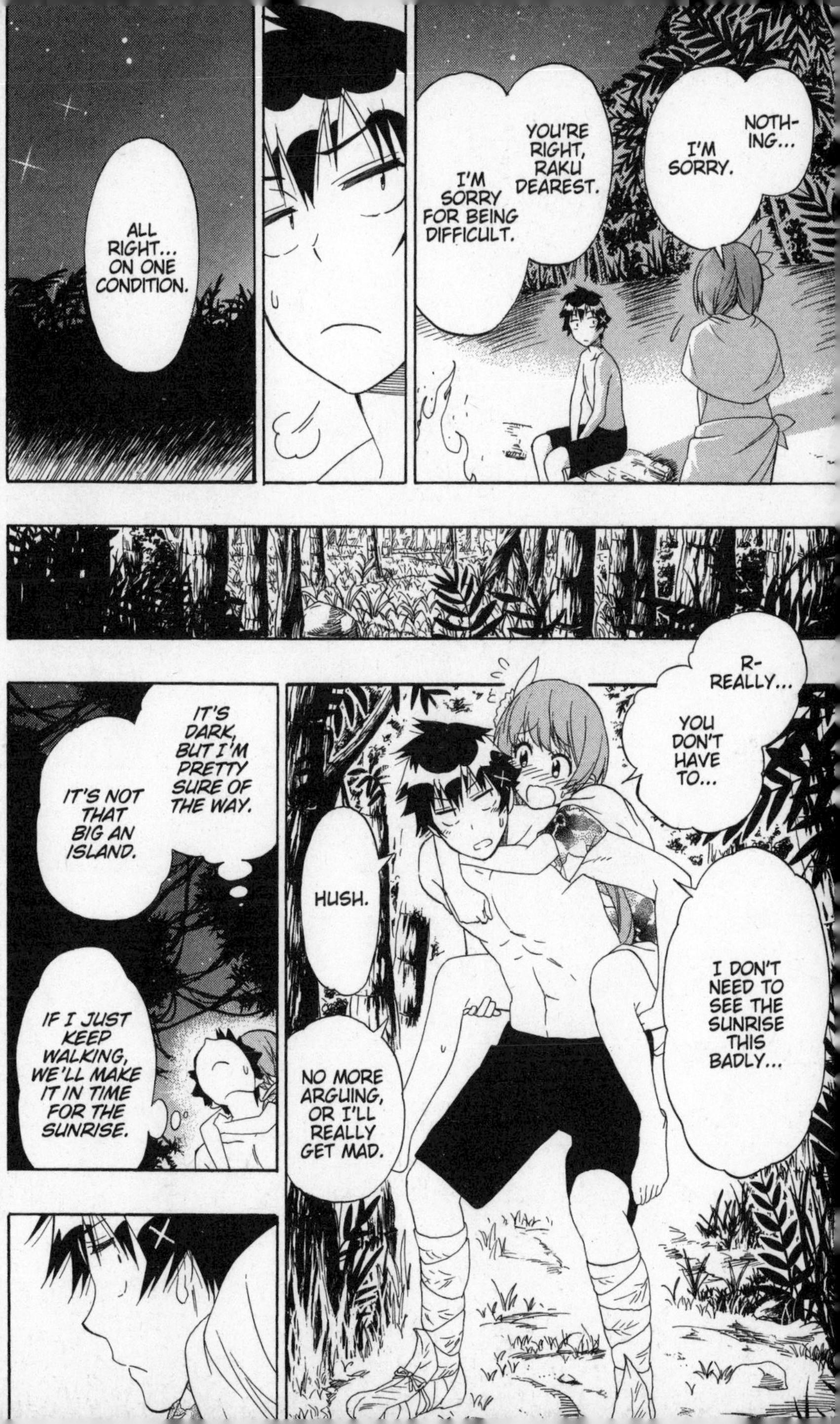
NOTHING... I'M SORRY.
YOU'RE RIGHT, RAKU DEAREST. I'M SORRY FOR BEING DIFFICULT.
ALL RIGHT... ON ONE CONDITION.
R-REALLY... YOU DON'T HAVE TO...
I DON'T NEED TO SEE THE SUNRISE THIS BADLY...
HUSH.
NO MORE ARGUING, OR I'LL REALLY GET MAD.
IT'S DARK, BUT I'M PRETTY SURE OF THE WAY.
IT'S NOT THAT BIG AN ISLAND.
IF I JUST KEEP WALKING, WE'LL MAKE IT IN TIME FOR THE SUNRISE.

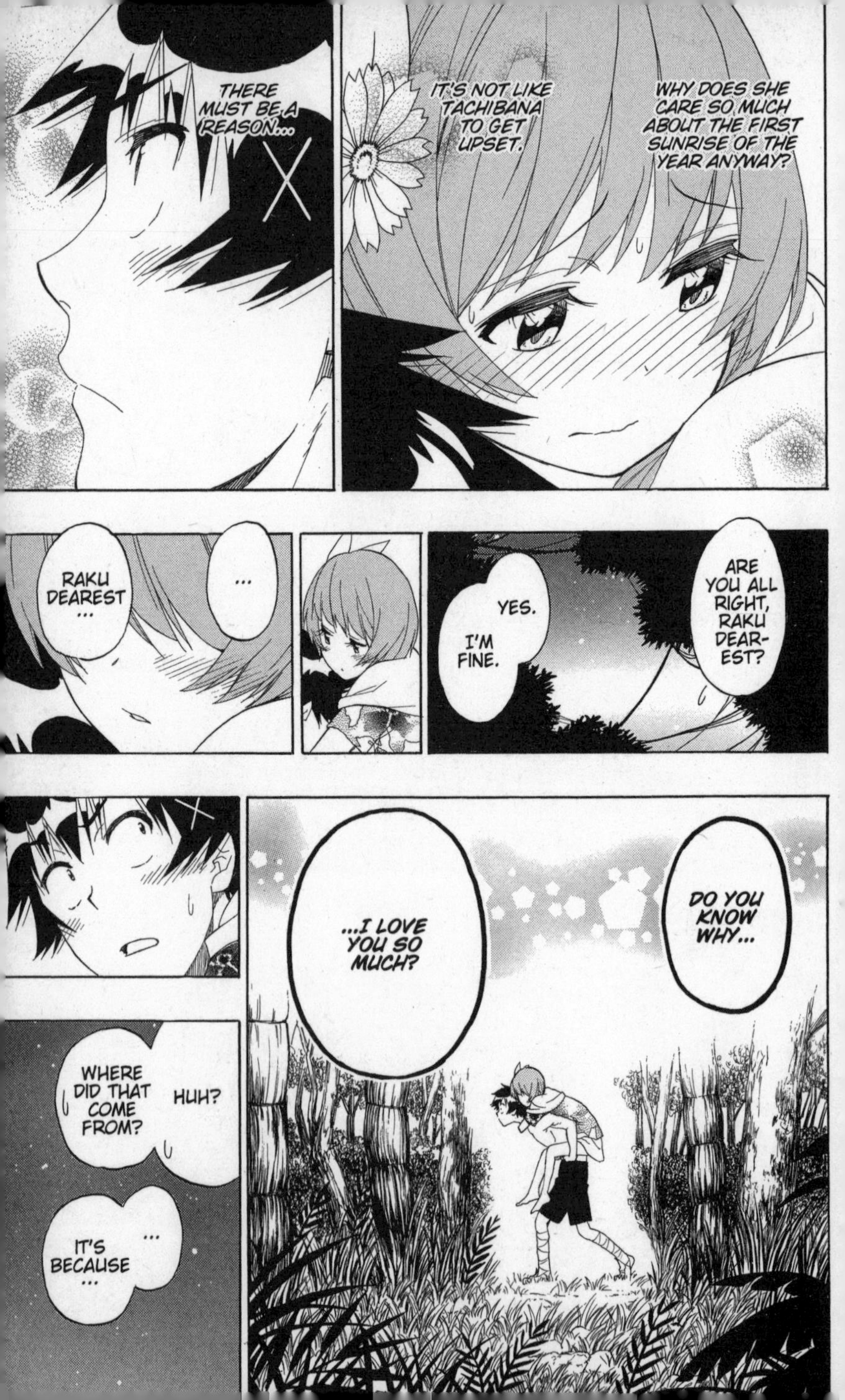
WHY DOES SHE CARE SO MUCH ABOUT THE FIRST SUNRISE OF THE YEAR ANYWAY?
IT'S NOT LIKE TACHIBANA TO GET UPSET.
THERE MUST BE A REASON...
ARE YOU ALL RIGHT, RAKU DEAR-EST?
YES.
I'M FINE.
...
RAKU DEAREST...
DO YOU KNOW WHY...
...I LOVE YOU SO MUCH?
HUH?
WHERE DID THAT COME FROM?
...
IT'S BECAUSE...

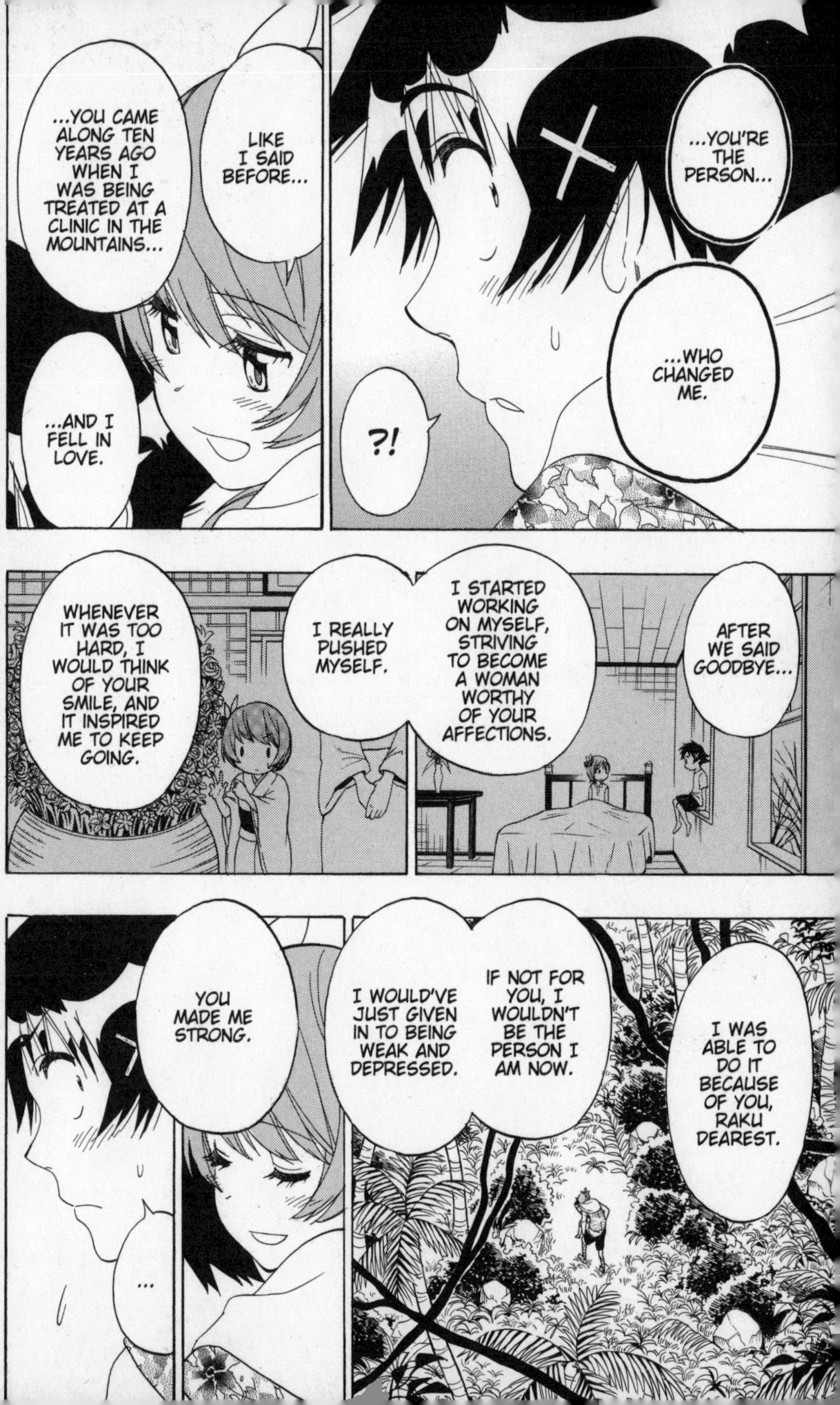
...YOU'RE THE PERSON...
...WHO CHANGED ME.
?!
LIKE I SAID BEFORE...
...YOU CAME ALONG TEN YEARS AGO WHEN I WAS BEING TREATED AT A CLINIC IN THE MOUNTAINS...
...AND I FELL IN LOVE.
AFTER WE SAID GOODBYE...
I STARTED WORKING ON MYSELF, STRIVING TO BECOME A WOMAN WORTHY OF YOUR AFFECTIONS.
I REALLY PUSHED MYSELF.
WHENEVER IT WAS TOO HARD, I WOULD THINK OF YOUR SMILE, AND IT INSPIRED ME TO KEEP GOING.
I WAS ABLE TO DO IT BECAUSE OF YOU, RAKU DEAREST.
IF NOT FOR YOU, I WOULDN'T BE THE PERSON I AM NOW.
I WOULD'VE JUST GIVEN IN TO BEING WEAK AND DEPRESSED.
YOU MADE ME STRONG.
...

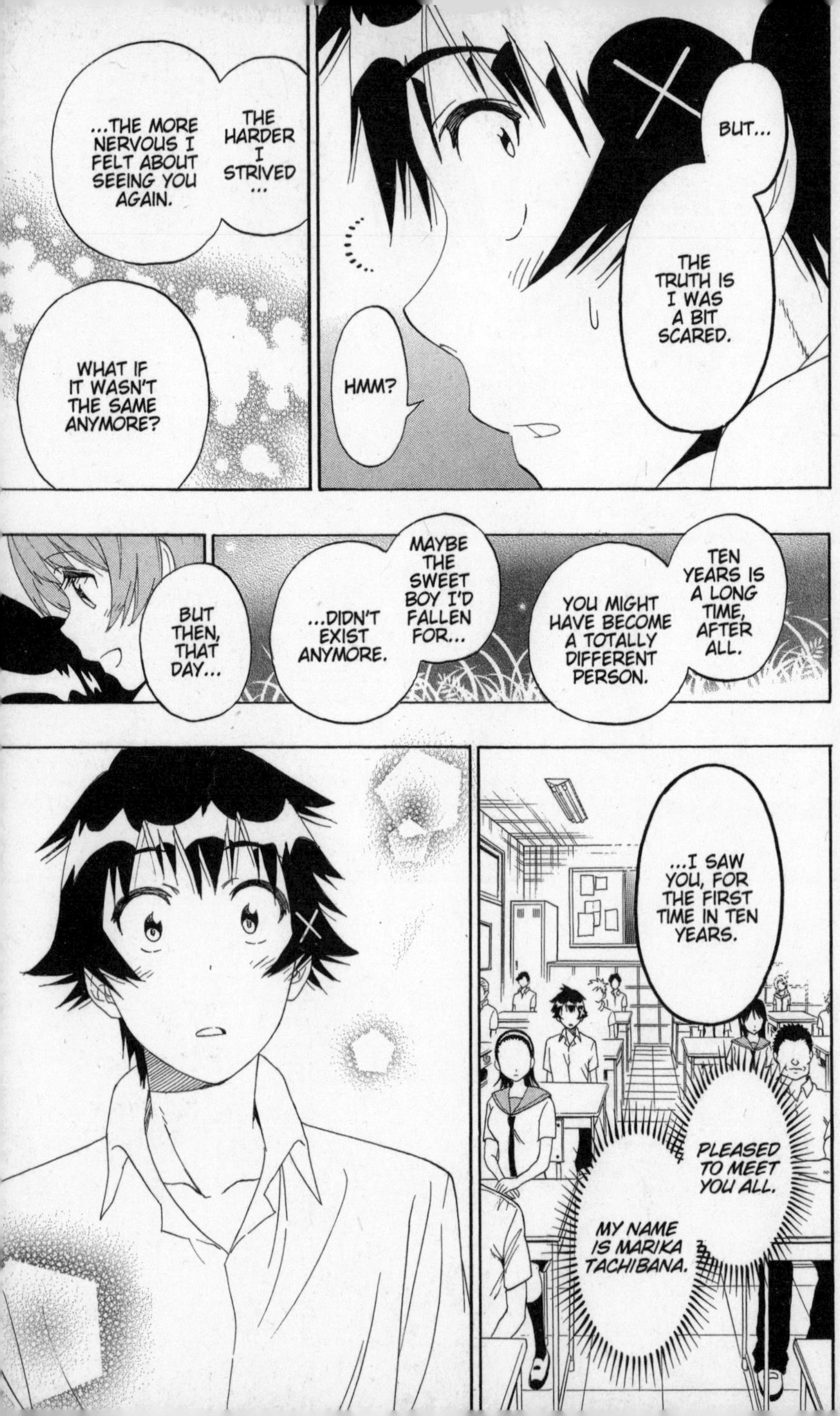
BUT...
THE TRUTH IS I WAS A BIT SCARED.
HMM?
THE HARDER I STRIVED...
...THE MORE NERVOUS I FELT ABOUT SEEING YOU AGAIN.
WHAT IF IT WASN'T THE SAME ANYMORE?
TEN YEARS IS A LONG TIME, AFTER ALL.
YOU MIGHT HAVE BECOME A TOTALLY DIFFERENT PERSON.
MAYBE THE SWEET BOY I'D FALLEN FOR...
...DIDN'T EXIST ANYMORE.
BUT THEN, THAT DAY...
...I SAW YOU, FOR THE FIRST TIME IN TEN YEARS.
PLEASED TO MEET YOU ALL.
MY NAME IS MARIKA TACHIBANA.

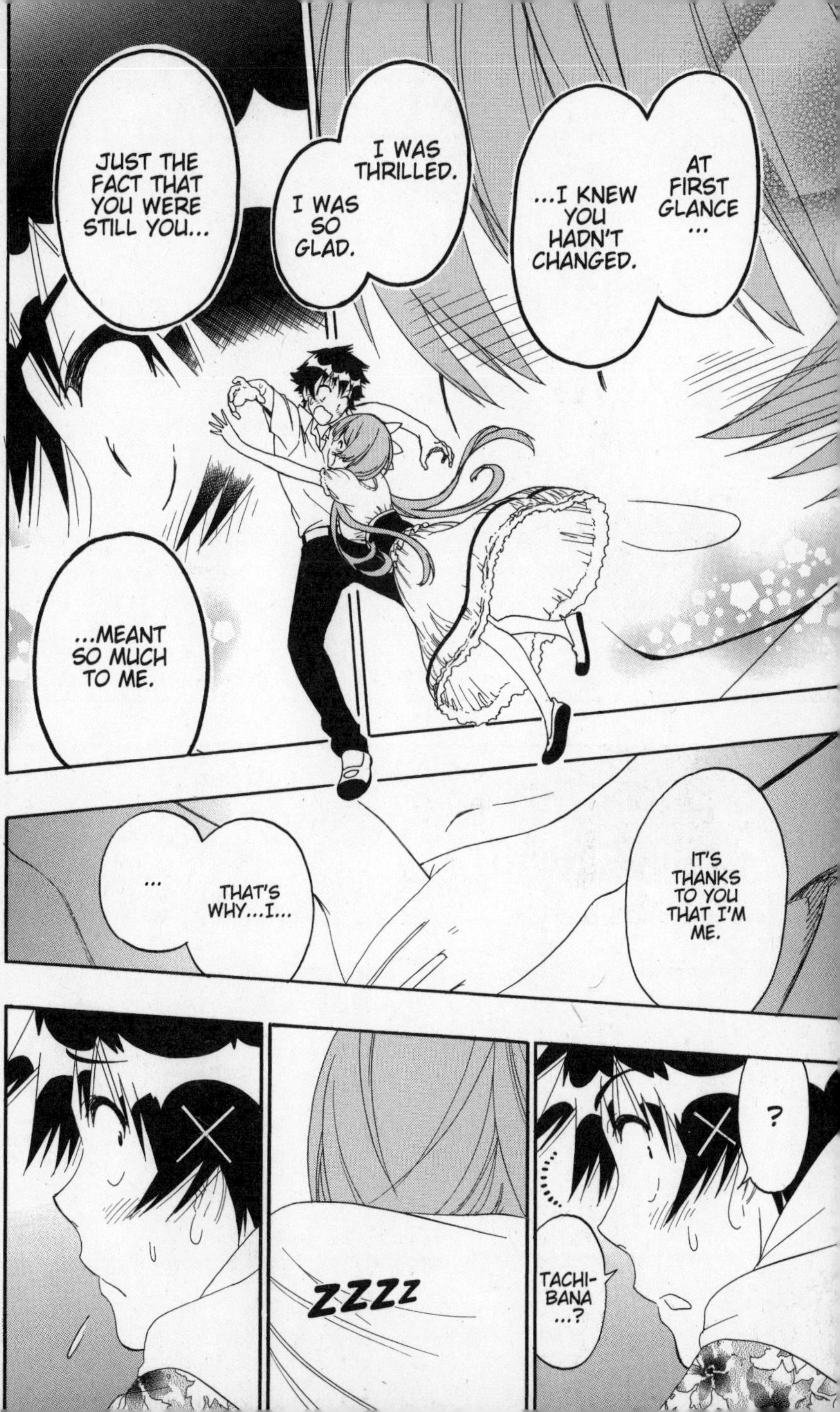
AT FIRST GLANCE...
...I KNEW YOU HADN'T CHANGED.
I WAS THRILLED.
I WAS SO GLAD.
JUST THE FACT THAT YOU WERE STILL YOU...
...MEANT SO MUCH TO ME.
IT'S THANKS TO YOU THAT I'M ME.
THAT'S WHY...I...
...
?
TACHI-BANA...?
ZZZZ

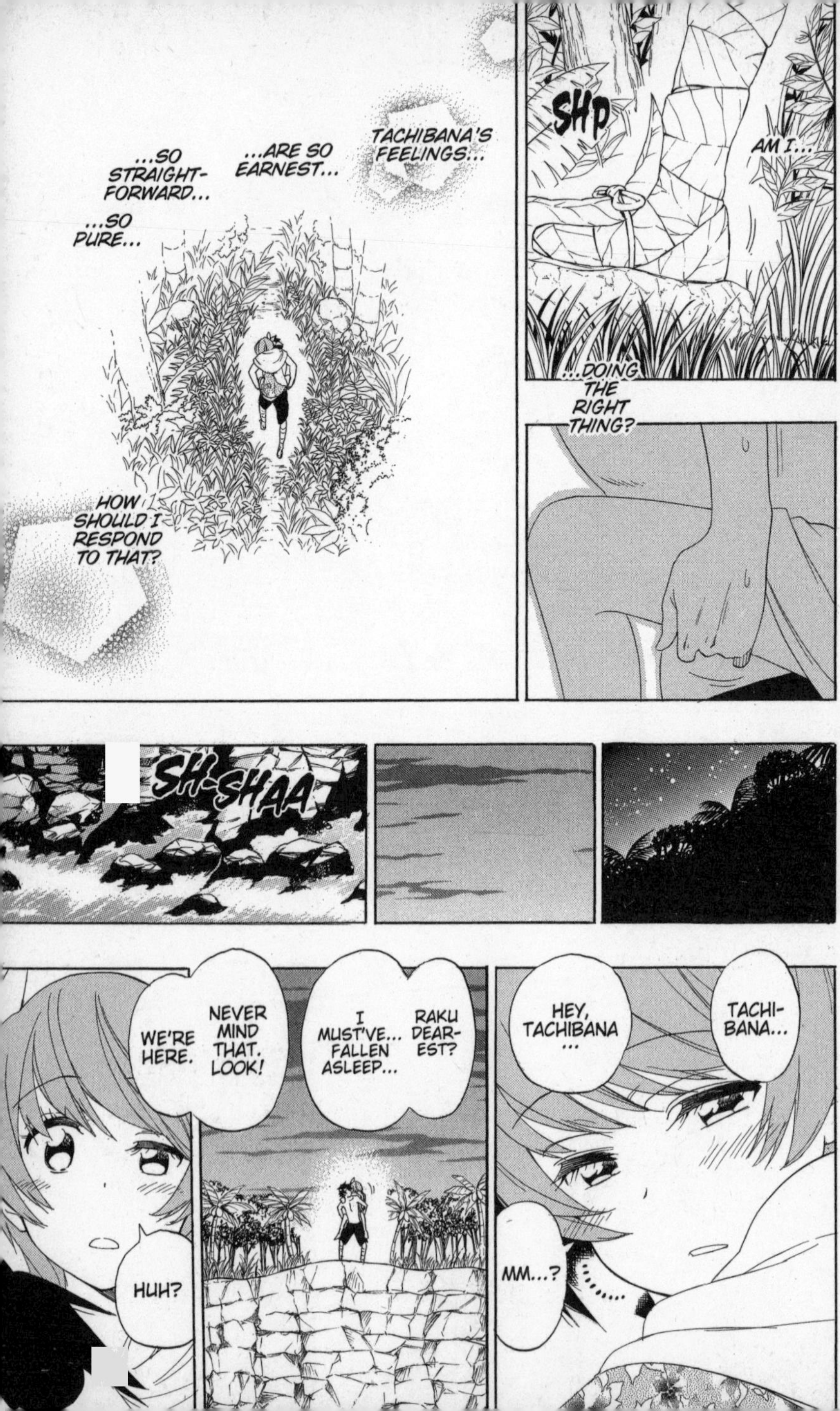
SHP
AM I...
...DOING THE RIGHT THING?
TACHIBANA'S FEELINGS...
...ARE SO EARNEST...
...SO STRAIGHT-FORWARD...
...SO PURE...
HOW SHOULD I RESPOND TO THAT?
SH-SHAA
TACHI-BANA...
HEY, TACHIBANA...
MM...?
......
RAKU DEAR-EST?
I MUST'VE... FALLEN ASLEEP...
NEVER MIND THAT. LOOK!
WE'RE HERE.
HUH?

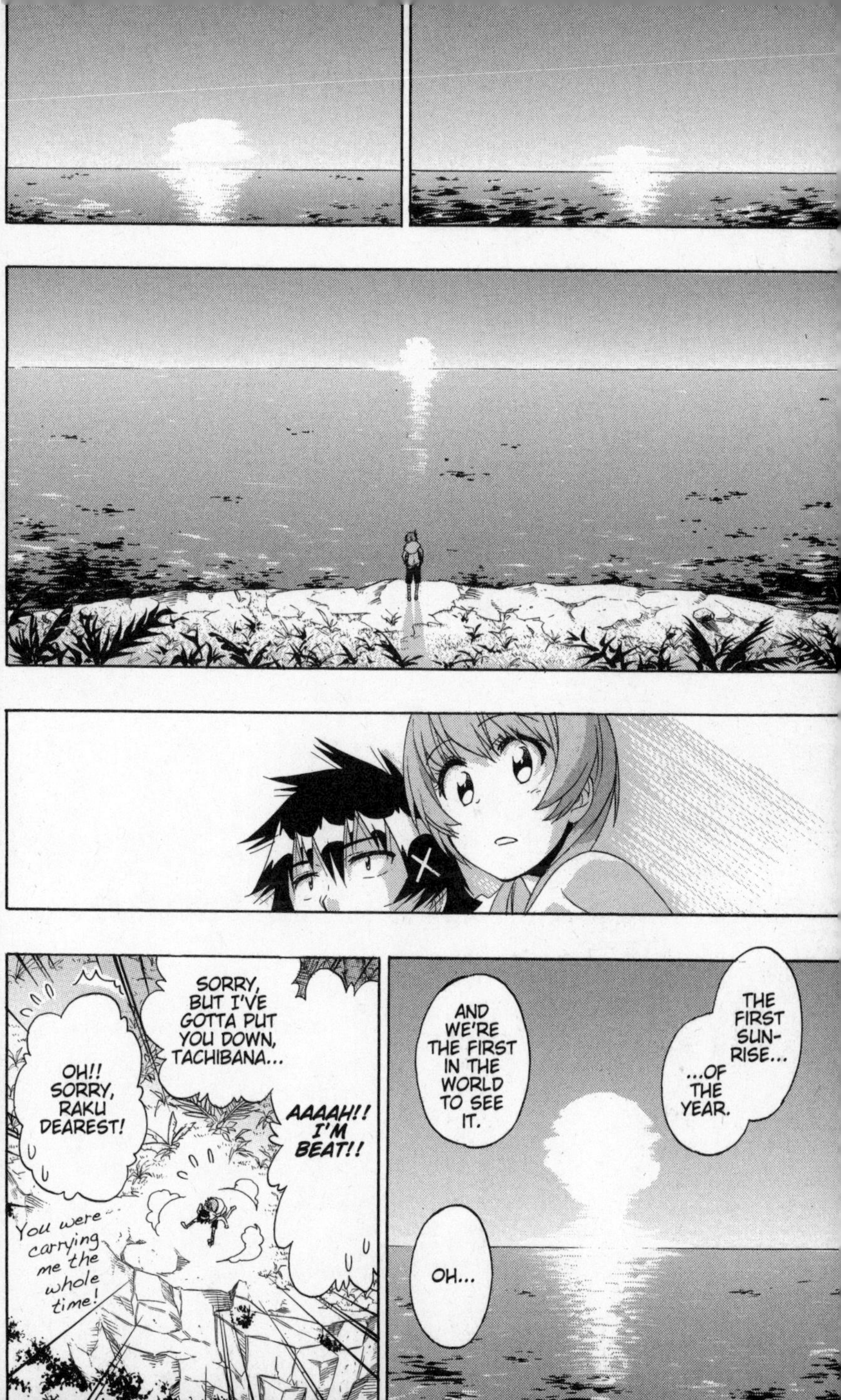
THE FIRST SUN-RISE...
...OF THE YEAR.
AND WE'RE THE FIRST IN THE WORLD TO SEE IT.
OH...
SORRY, BUT I'VE GOTTA PUT YOU DOWN, TACHIBANA...
AAAAH!! I'M BEAT!!
OH!! SORRY, RAKU DEAREST!
You were carrying me the whole time!

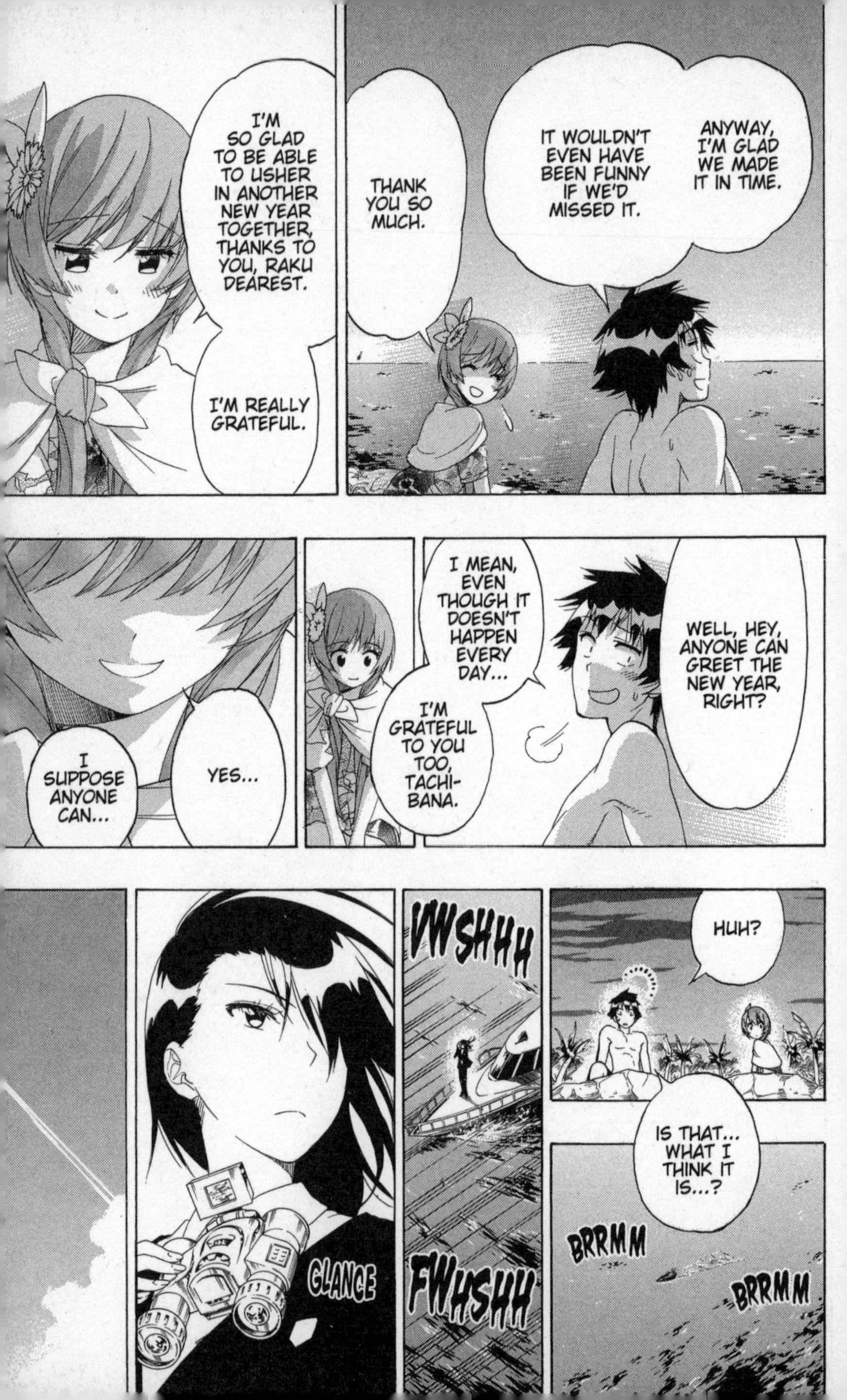
ANYWAY, I'M GLAD WE MADE IT IN TIME.
IT WOULDN'T EVEN HAVE BEEN FUNNY IF WE'D MISSED IT.
THANK YOU SO MUCH.
I'M SO GLAD TO BE ABLE TO USHER IN ANOTHER NEW YEAR TOGETHER, THANKS TO YOU, RAKU DEAREST.
I'M REALLY GRATEFUL.
WELL, HEY, ANYONE CAN GREET THE NEW YEAR, RIGHT?
I MEAN, EVEN THOUGH IT DOESN'T HAPPEN EVERY DAY...
I'M GRATEFUL TO YOU TOO, TACHIBANA.
YES...
I SUPPOSE ANYONE CAN...
HUH?
IS THAT... WHAT I THINK IT IS...?
BRRMM
BRRMM
VWSHHH
FWHSHH
GLANCE

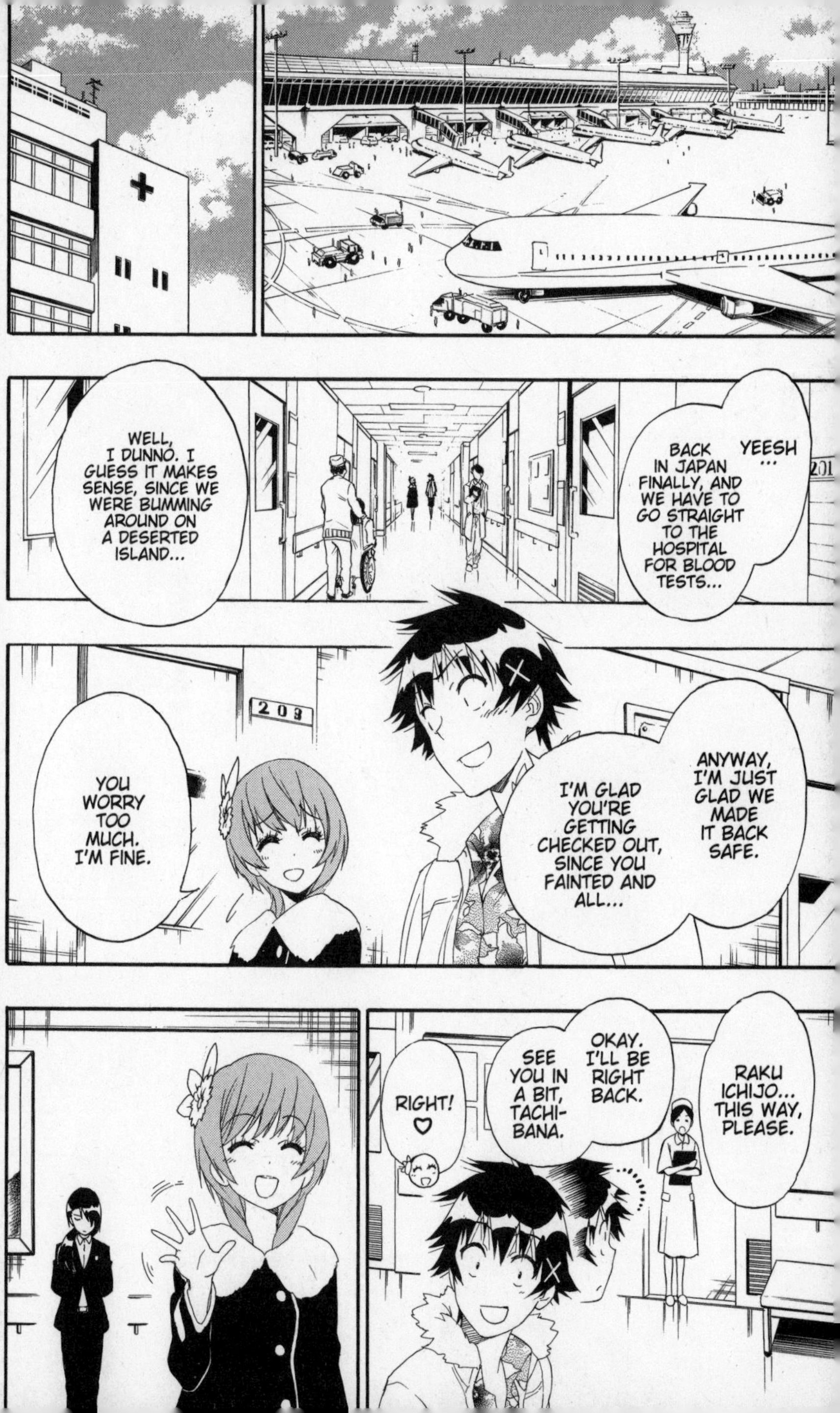
YEESH... BACK IN JAPAN FINALLY, AND WE HAVE TO GO STRAIGHT TO THE HOSPITAL FOR BLOOD TESTS...
WELL, I DUNNO. I GUESS IT MAKES SENSE, SINCE WE WERE BUMMING AROUND ON A DESERTED ISLAND...
201
ANYWAY, I'M JUST GLAD WE MADE IT BACK SAFE.
I'M GLAD YOU'RE GETTING CHECKED OUT, SINCE YOU FAINTED AND ALL...
203
YOU WORRY TOO MUCH. I'M FINE.
RAKU ICHIJO... THIS WAY, PLEASE.
OKAY. I'LL BE RIGHT BACK.
SEE YOU IN A BIT, TACHIBANA.
RIGHT! ♡

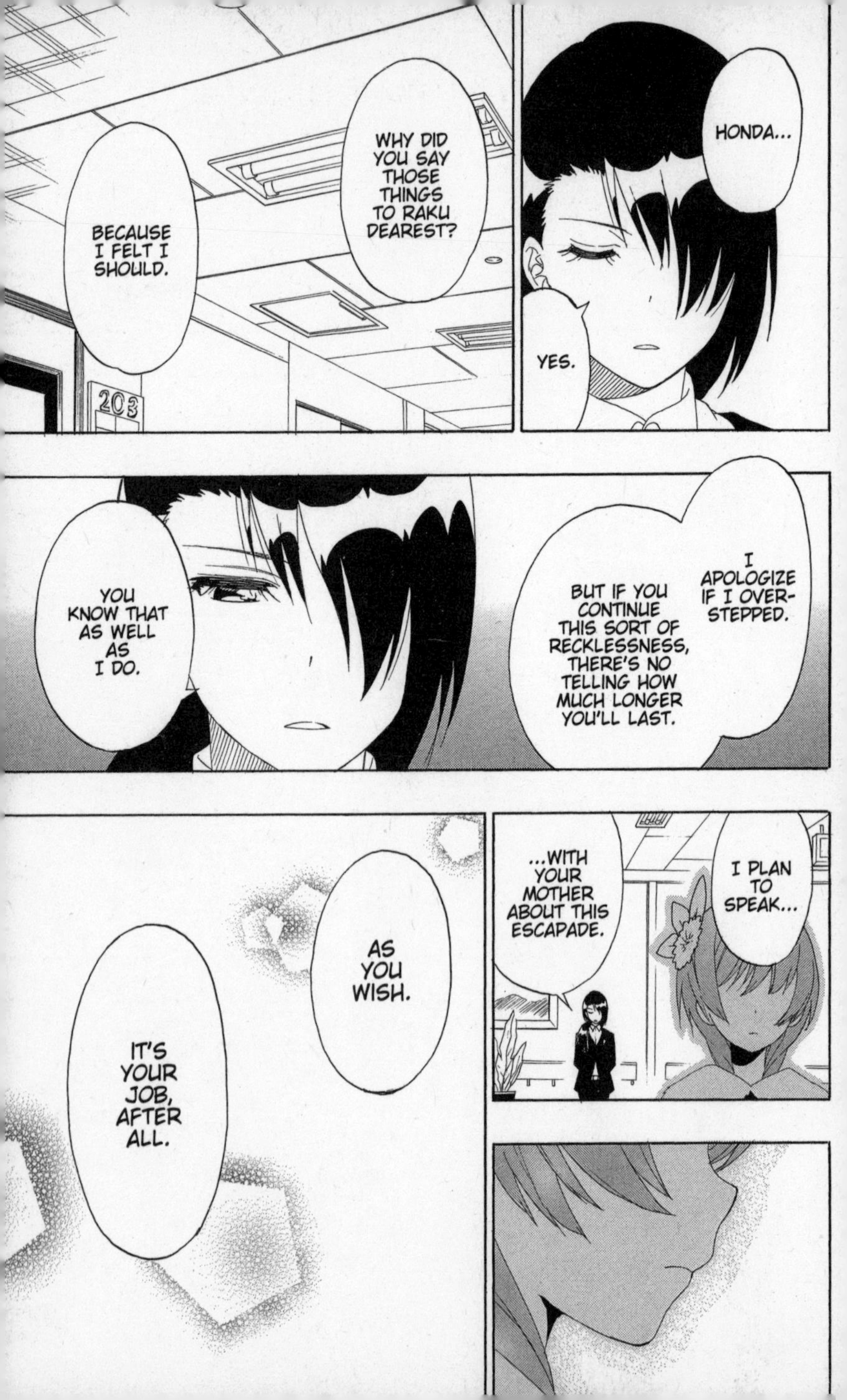
HONDA...
YES.
WHY DID YOU SAY THOSE THINGS TO RAKU DEAREST?
BECAUSE I FELT I SHOULD.
203
I APOLOGIZE IF I OVER-STEPPED.
BUT IF YOU CONTINUE THIS SORT OF RECKLESSNESS, THERE'S NO TELLING HOW MUCH LONGER YOU'LL LAST.
YOU KNOW THAT AS WELL AS I DO.
I PLAN TO SPEAK...
...WITH YOUR MOTHER ABOUT THIS ESCAPADE.
AS YOU WISH.
IT'S YOUR JOB, AFTER ALL.

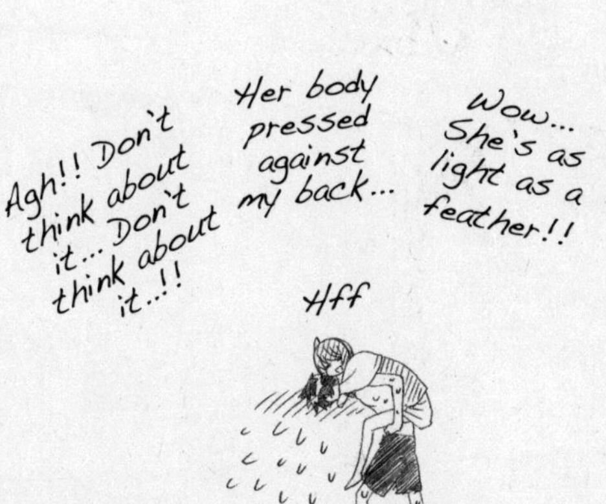
Wow... She's as light as a feather!!
Her body pressed against my back...
Agh!! Don't think about it... Don't think about it..!!
Hff

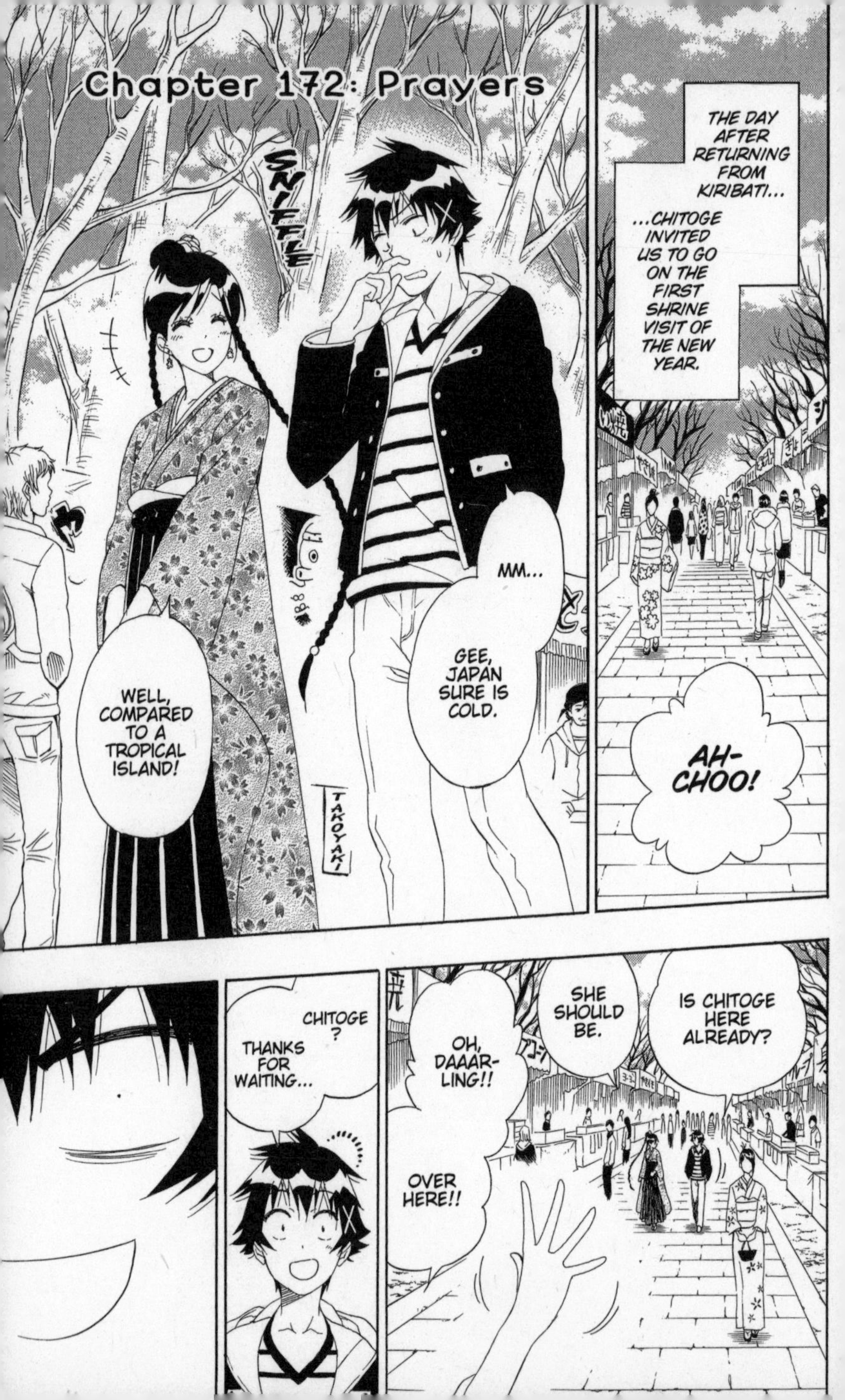
THE DAY AFTER RETURNING FROM KIRIBATI...
...CHITOGE INVITED US TO GO ON THE FIRST SHRINE VISIT OF THE NEW YEAR.
AH-CHOO!
Chapter 172: Prayers
SNIFFLE
MM...
GEE, JAPAN SURE IS COLD.
WELL, COMPARED TO A TROPICAL ISLAND!
TAKOYAKI
IS CHITOGE HERE ALREADY?
SHE SHOULD BE.
OH, DAAAR-LING!!
OVER HERE!!
CHITOGE?
THANKS FOR WAITING...

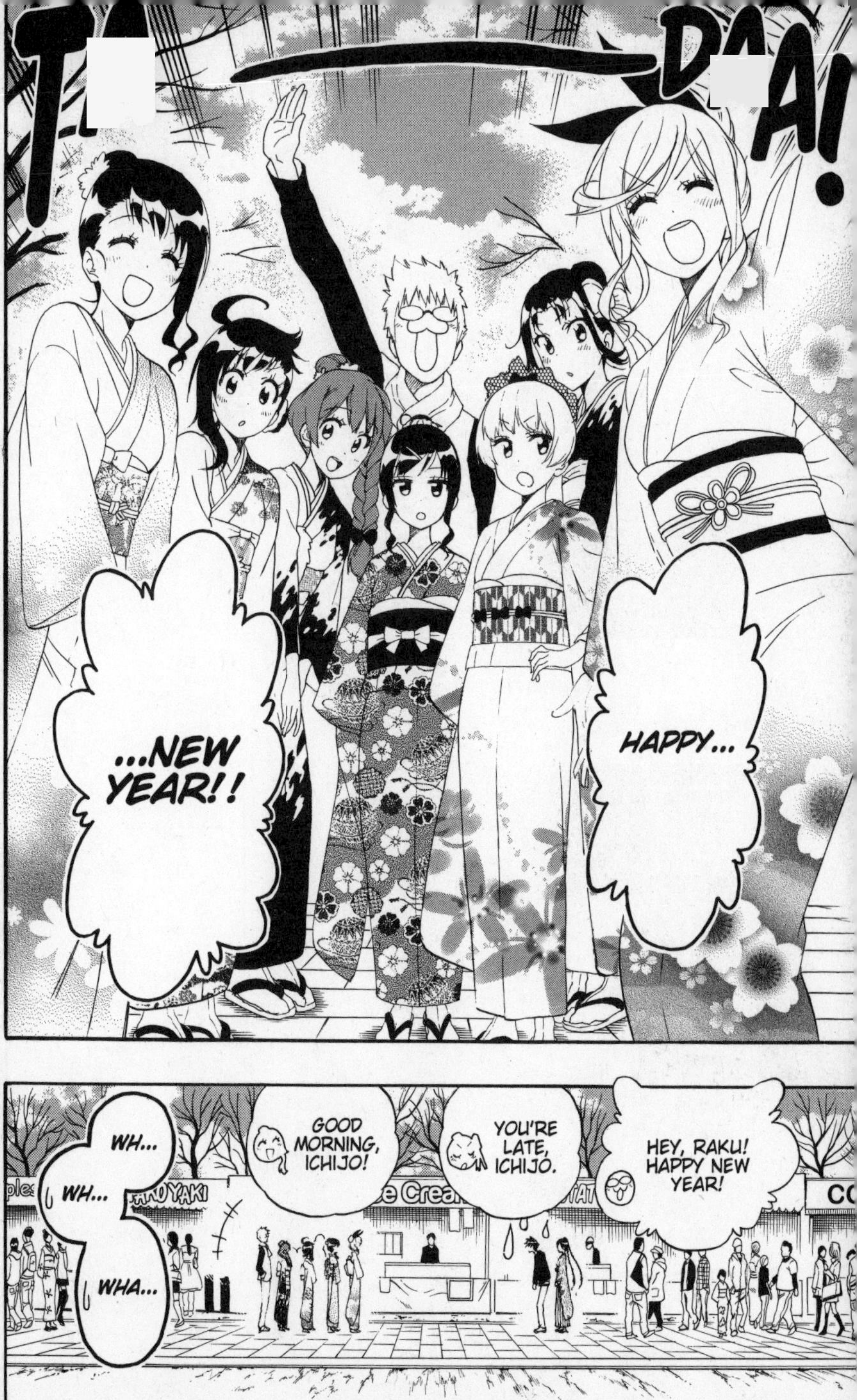
TA—DA!
HAPPY...
...NEW YEAR!!
HEY, RAKU! HAPPY NEW YEAR!
YOU'RE LATE, ICHIJO.
GOOD MORNING, ICHIJO!
WH...
WH...
WHA...

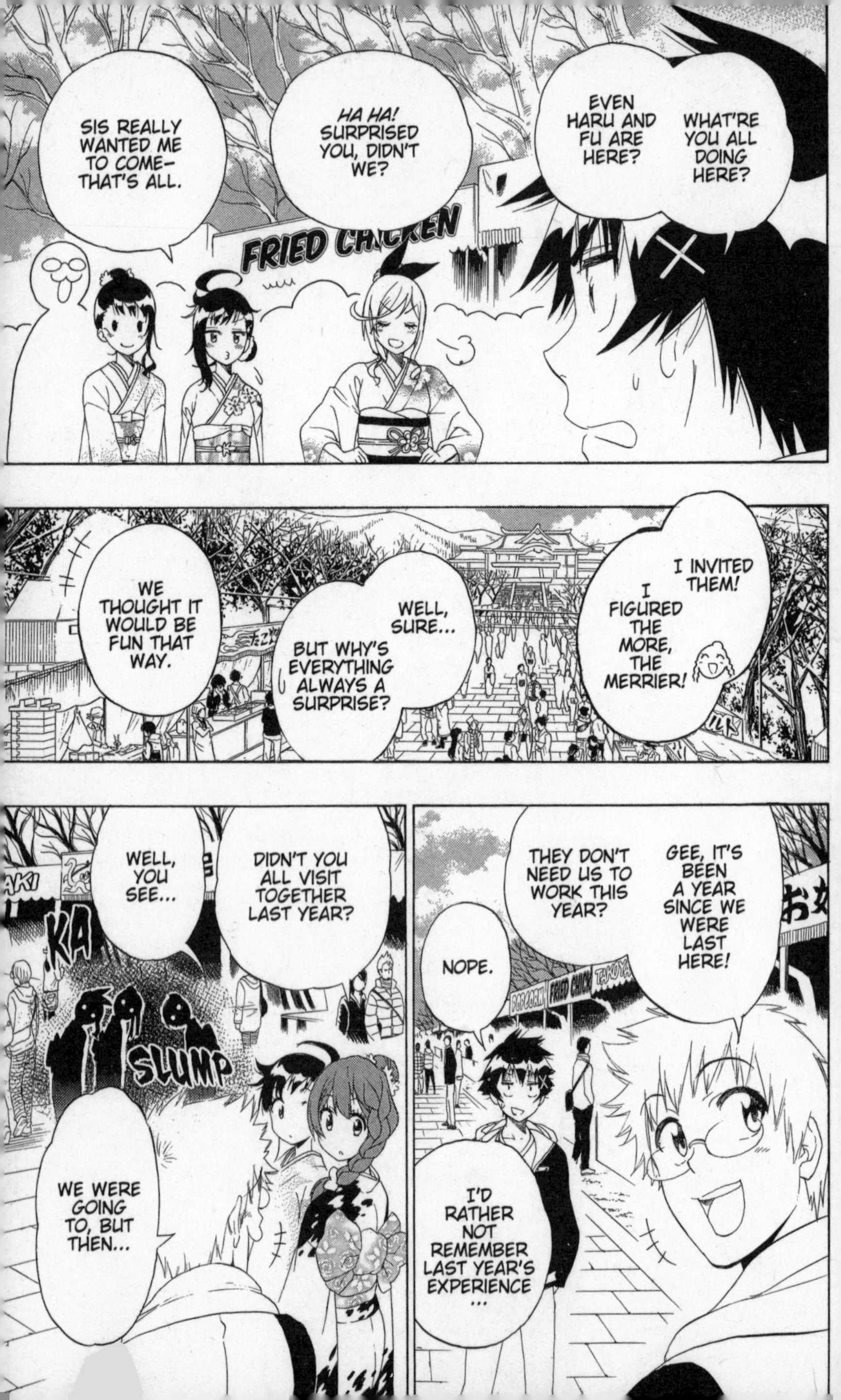
WHAT'RE YOU ALL DOING HERE?
EVEN HARU AND FU ARE HERE?
HA HA! SURPRISED YOU, DIDN'T WE?
FRIED CHICKEN
SIS REALLY WANTED ME TO COME— THAT'S ALL.
I INVITED THEM!
I FIGURED THE MORE, THE MERRIER!
WELL, SURE...
BUT WHY'S EVERYTHING ALWAYS A SURPRISE?
WE THOUGHT IT WOULD BE FUN THAT WAY.
GEE, IT'S BEEN A YEAR SINCE WE WERE LAST HERE!
THEY DON'T NEED US TO WORK THIS YEAR?
NOPE.
POPCORN
FRIED CHICK
TAKOYA
I'D RATHER NOT REMEMBER LAST YEAR'S EXPERIENCE ...
DIDN'T YOU ALL VISIT TOGETHER LAST YEAR?
WELL, YOU SEE...
KA
SLUMP
WE WERE GOING TO, BUT THEN...

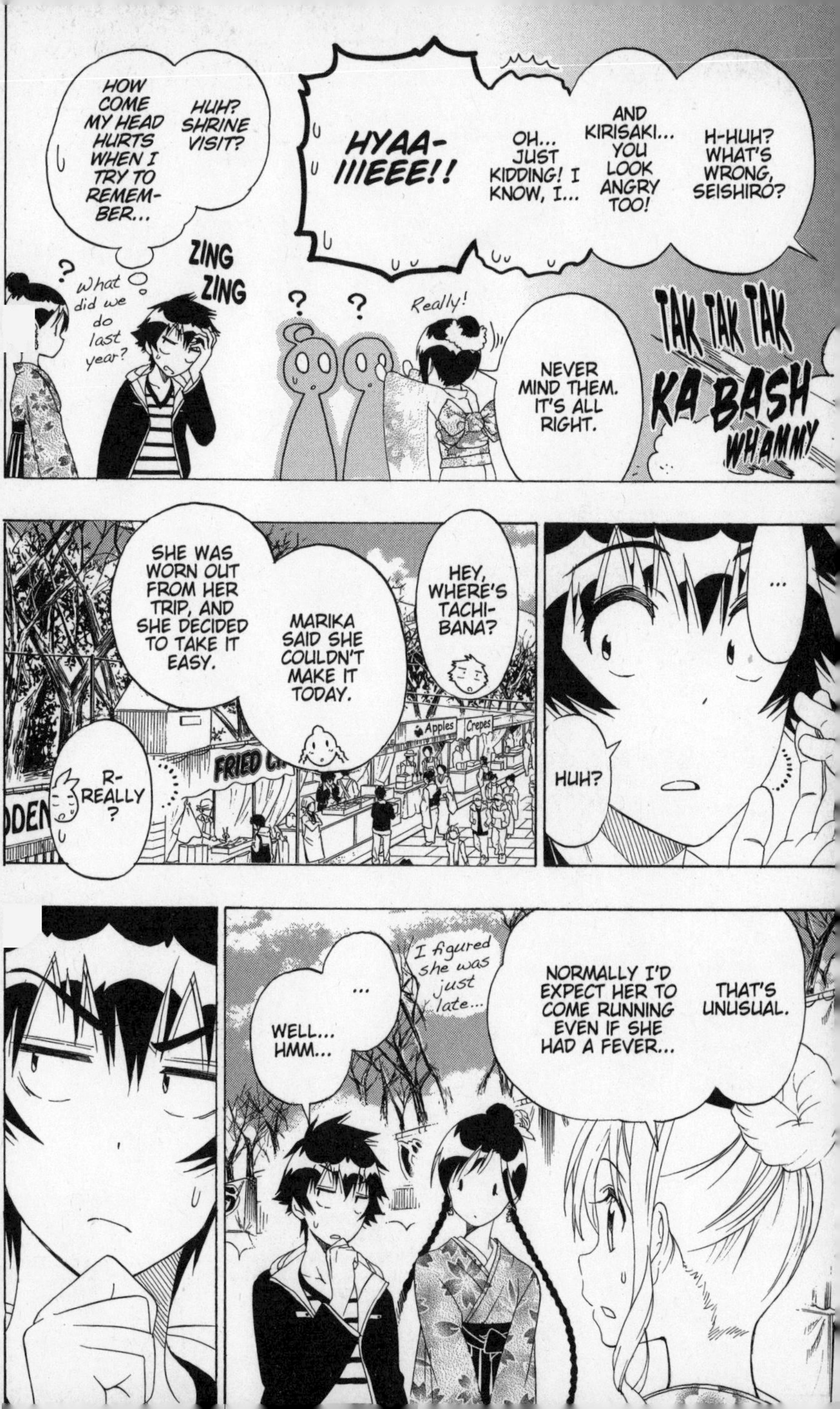
H-HUH? WHAT'S WRONG, SEISHIRO?
AND KIRISAKI... YOU LOOK ANGRY TOO!
OH... JUST KIDDING! I KNOW, I...
HYAA-IIIEEE!!
HUH? SHRINE VISIT?
HOW COME MY HEAD HURTS WHEN I TRY TO REMEMBER...
TAK TAK TAK
KA BASH
WHAMMY
NEVER MIND THEM. IT'S ALL RIGHT.
Really!
ZING ZING
What did we do last year?
...
HUH?
HEY, WHERE'S TACHIBANA?
MARIKA SAID SHE COULDN'T MAKE IT TODAY.
SHE WAS WORN OUT FROM HER TRIP, AND SHE DECIDED TO TAKE IT EASY.
Apples
Crepes
R-REALLY?
THAT'S UNUSUAL.
NORMALLY I'D EXPECT HER TO COME RUNNING EVEN IF SHE HAD A FEVER...
I figured she was just late...
...
WELL... HMM...

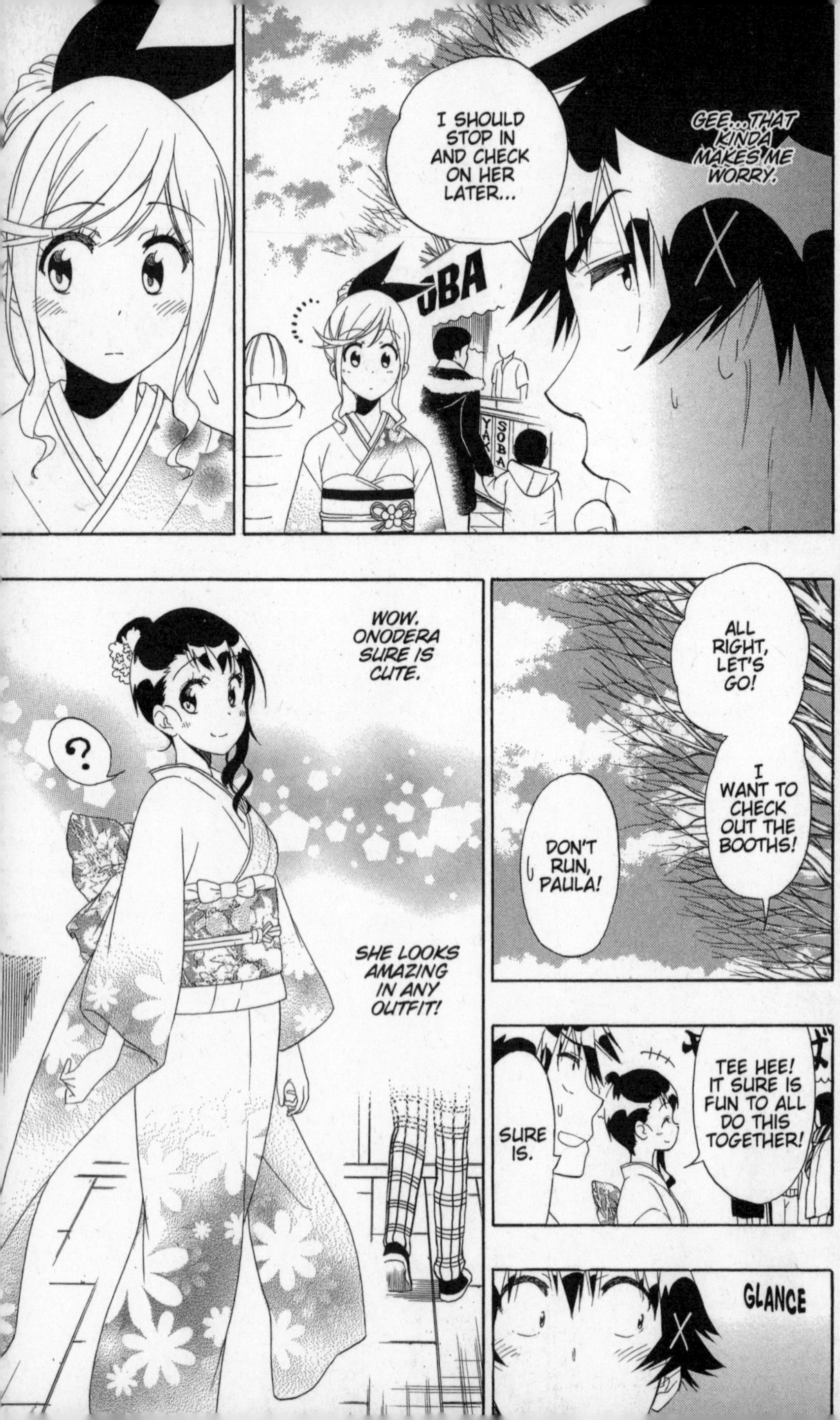
GEE...THAT KINDA MAKES ME WORRY.
I SHOULD STOP IN AND CHECK ON HER LATER...
SOBA
ALL RIGHT, LET'S GO!
I WANT TO CHECK OUT THE BOOTHS!
DON'T RUN, PAULA!
TEE HEE! IT SURE IS FUN TO ALL DO THIS TOGETHER!
SURE IS.
GLANCE
WOW. ONODERA SURE IS CUTE.
?
SHE LOOKS AMAZING IN ANY OUTFIT!

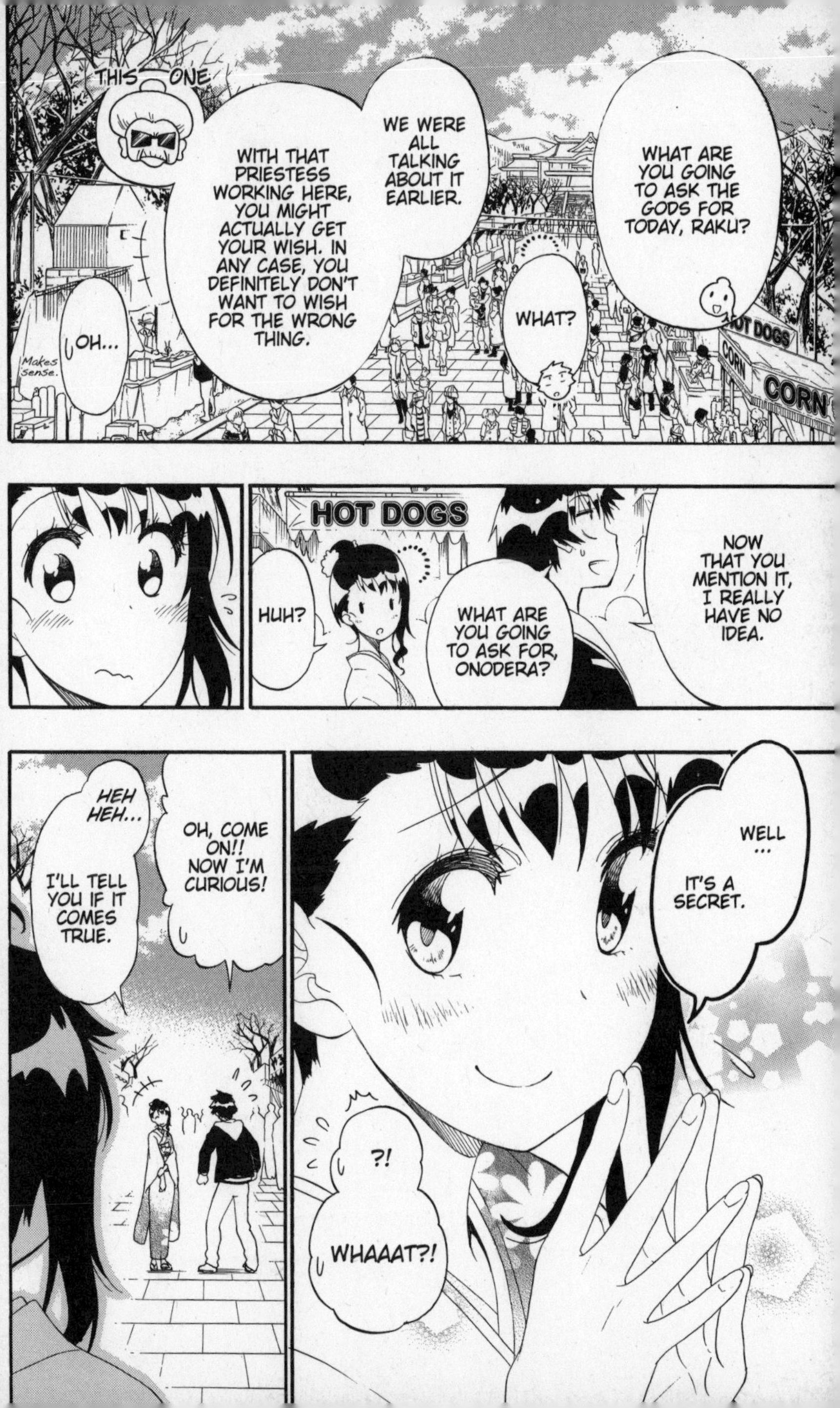
WHAT ARE YOU GOING TO ASK THE GODS FOR TODAY, RAKU?
HOT DOGS
CORN
CORN
WHAT?
WE WERE ALL TALKING ABOUT IT EARLIER.
WITH THAT PRIESTESS WORKING HERE, YOU MIGHT ACTUALLY GET YOUR WISH. IN ANY CASE, YOU DEFINITELY DON'T WANT TO WISH FOR THE WRONG THING.
THIS ONE
OH...
Makes sense.
NOW THAT YOU MENTION IT, I REALLY HAVE NO IDEA.
WHAT ARE YOU GOING TO ASK FOR, ONODERA?
HOT DOGS
HUH?
WELL ...
IT'S A SECRET.
?!
WHAAAT?!
HEH HEH...
I'LL TELL YOU IF IT COMES TRUE.
OH, COME ON!! NOW I'M CURIOUS!

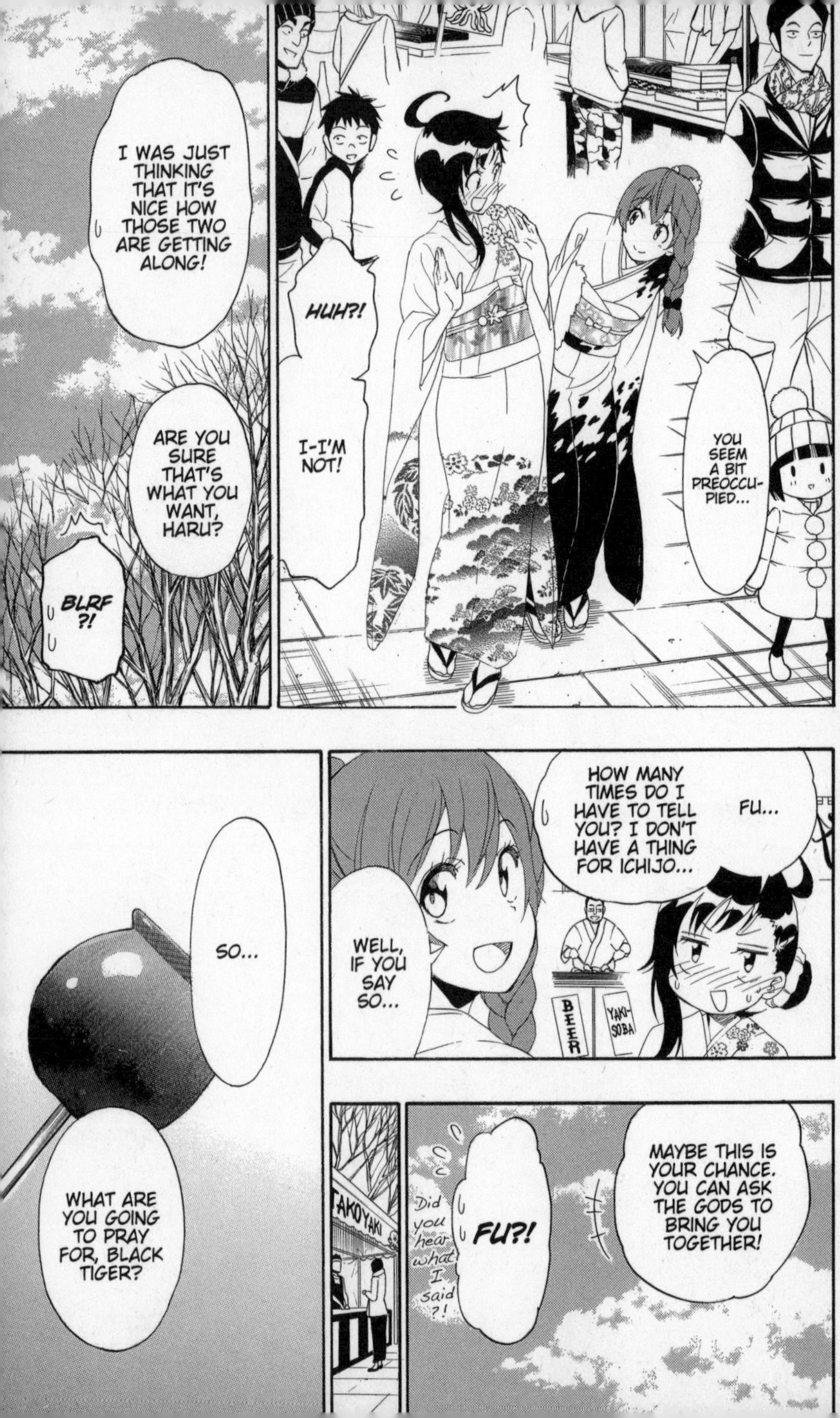
YOU SEEM A BIT PREOCCUPIED...
HUH?!
I-I'M NOT!
I WAS JUST THINKING THAT IT'S NICE HOW THOSE TWO ARE GETTING ALONG!
ARE YOU SURE THAT'S WHAT YOU WANT, HARU?
BLRF ?!
FU...
HOW MANY TIMES DO I HAVE TO TELL YOU? I DON'T HAVE A THING FOR ICHIJO...
WELL, IF YOU SAY SO...
BEER
YAKISOBA
MAYBE THIS IS YOUR CHANCE. YOU CAN ASK THE GODS TO BRING YOU TOGETHER!
FU?!
Did you hear what I said ?!
TAKOYAKI
SO...
WHAT ARE YOU GOING TO PRAY FOR, BLACK TIGER?

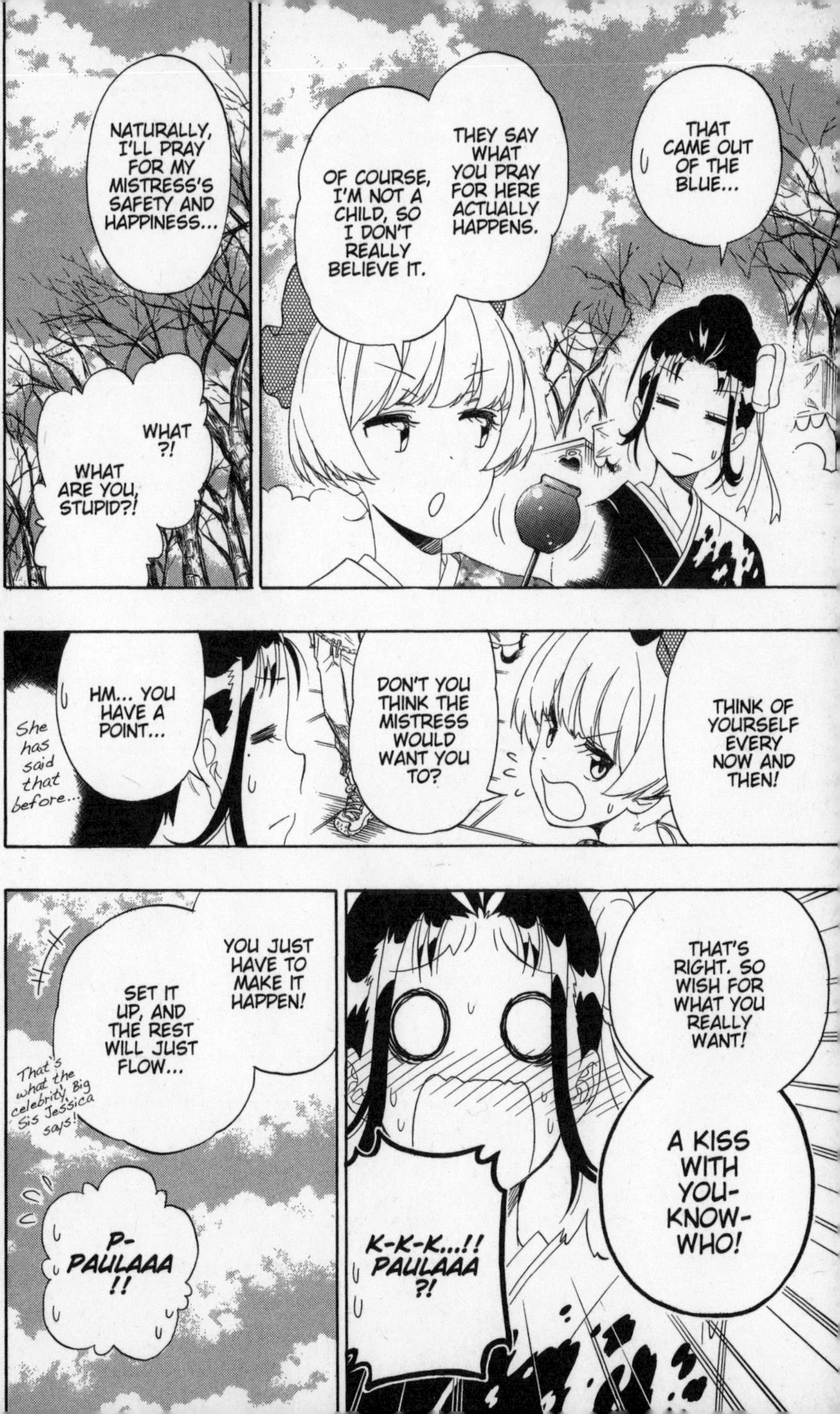
THAT CAME OUT OF THE BLUE...
THEY SAY WHAT YOU PRAY FOR HERE ACTUALLY HAPPENS.
OF COURSE, I'M NOT A CHILD, SO I DON'T REALLY BELIEVE IT.
NATURALLY, I'LL PRAY FOR MY MISTRESS'S SAFETY AND HAPPINESS...
WHAT?!
WHAT ARE YOU, STUPID?!
THINK OF YOURSELF EVERY NOW AND THEN!
DON'T YOU THINK THE MISTRESS WOULD WANT YOU TO?
HM... YOU HAVE A POINT...
She has said that before...
THAT'S RIGHT. SO WISH FOR WHAT YOU REALLY WANT!
A KISS WITH YOU-KNOW-WHO!
K-K-K...!! PAULAAA?!
YOU JUST HAVE TO MAKE IT HAPPEN!
SET IT UP, AND THE REST WILL JUST FLOW...
That's what the celebrity, Big Sis Jessica says!
P-PAULAAA!!

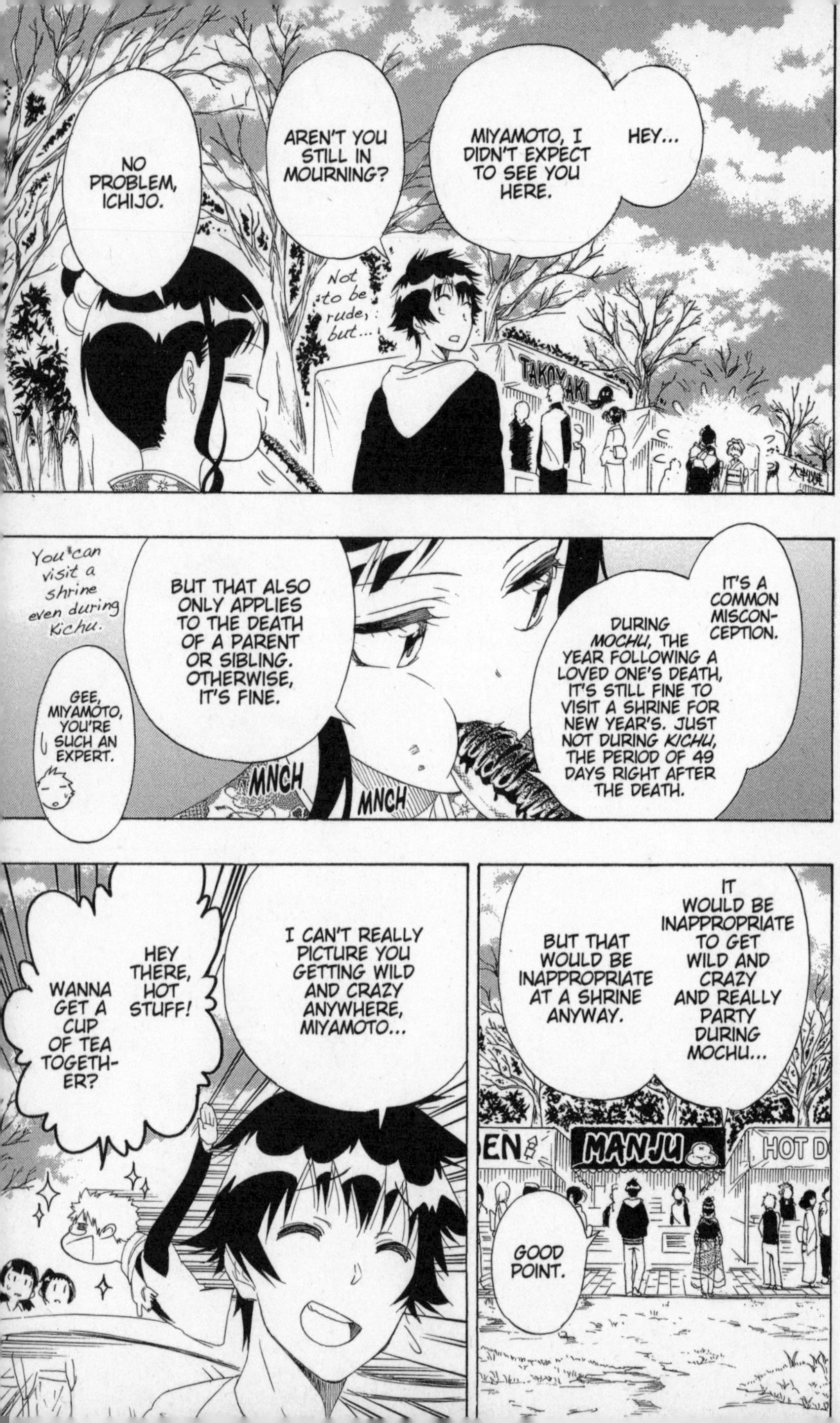
HEY...
MIYAMOTO, I DIDN'T EXPECT TO SEE YOU HERE.
Not to be rude, but...
AREN'T YOU STILL IN MOURNING?
NO PROBLEM, ICHIJO.
TAKOYAKI
IT'S A COMMON MISCONCEPTION.
DURING *MOCHU*, THE YEAR FOLLOWING A LOVED ONE'S DEATH, IT'S STILL FINE TO VISIT A SHRINE FOR NEW YEAR'S. JUST NOT DURING *KICHU*, THE PERIOD OF 49 DAYS RIGHT AFTER THE DEATH.
BUT THAT ALSO ONLY APPLIES TO THE DEATH OF A PARENT OR SIBLING. OTHERWISE, IT'S FINE.
MNCH
MNCH
You can visit a shrine even during Kichu.
GEE, MIYAMOTO, YOU'RE SUCH AN EXPERT.
IT WOULD BE INAPPROPRIATE TO GET WILD AND CRAZY AND REALLY PARTY DURING MOCHU...
BUT THAT WOULD BE INAPPROPRIATE AT A SHRINE ANYWAY.
MANJU
GOOD POINT.
I CAN'T REALLY PICTURE YOU GETTING WILD AND CRAZY ANYWHERE, MIYAMOTO...
HEY THERE, HOT STUFF!
WANNA GET A CUP OF TEA TOGETH-ER?

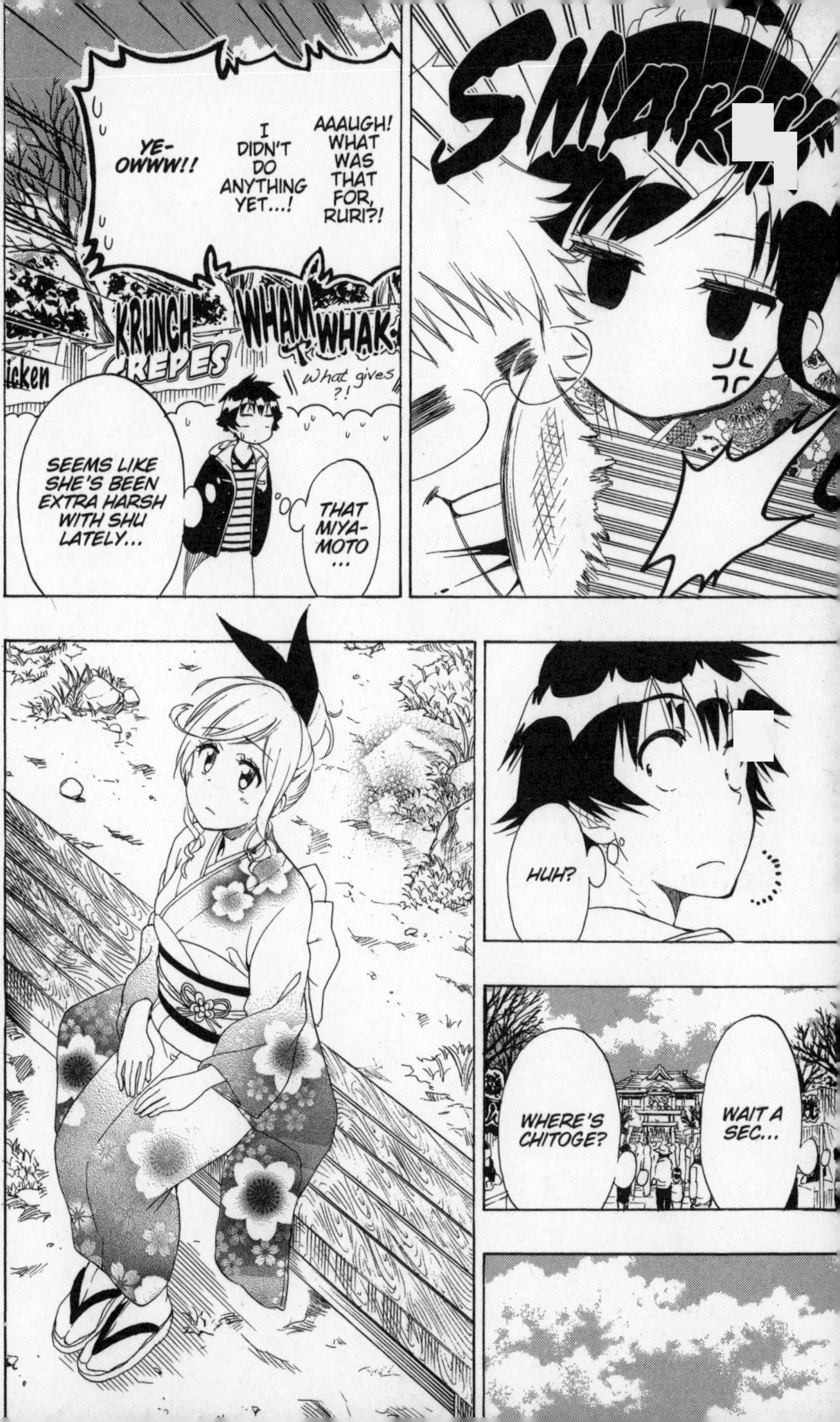
AAAUGH! WHAT WAS THAT FOR, RURI?!
I DIDN'T DO ANYTHING YET...!
YE-OWWW!!
KRUNCH
WHAM
WHAK
CREPES
What gives?!
THAT MIYA-MOTO...
SEEMS LIKE SHE'S BEEN EXTRA HARSH WITH SHU LATELY...
HUH?
WAIT A SEC...
WHERE'S CHITOGE?

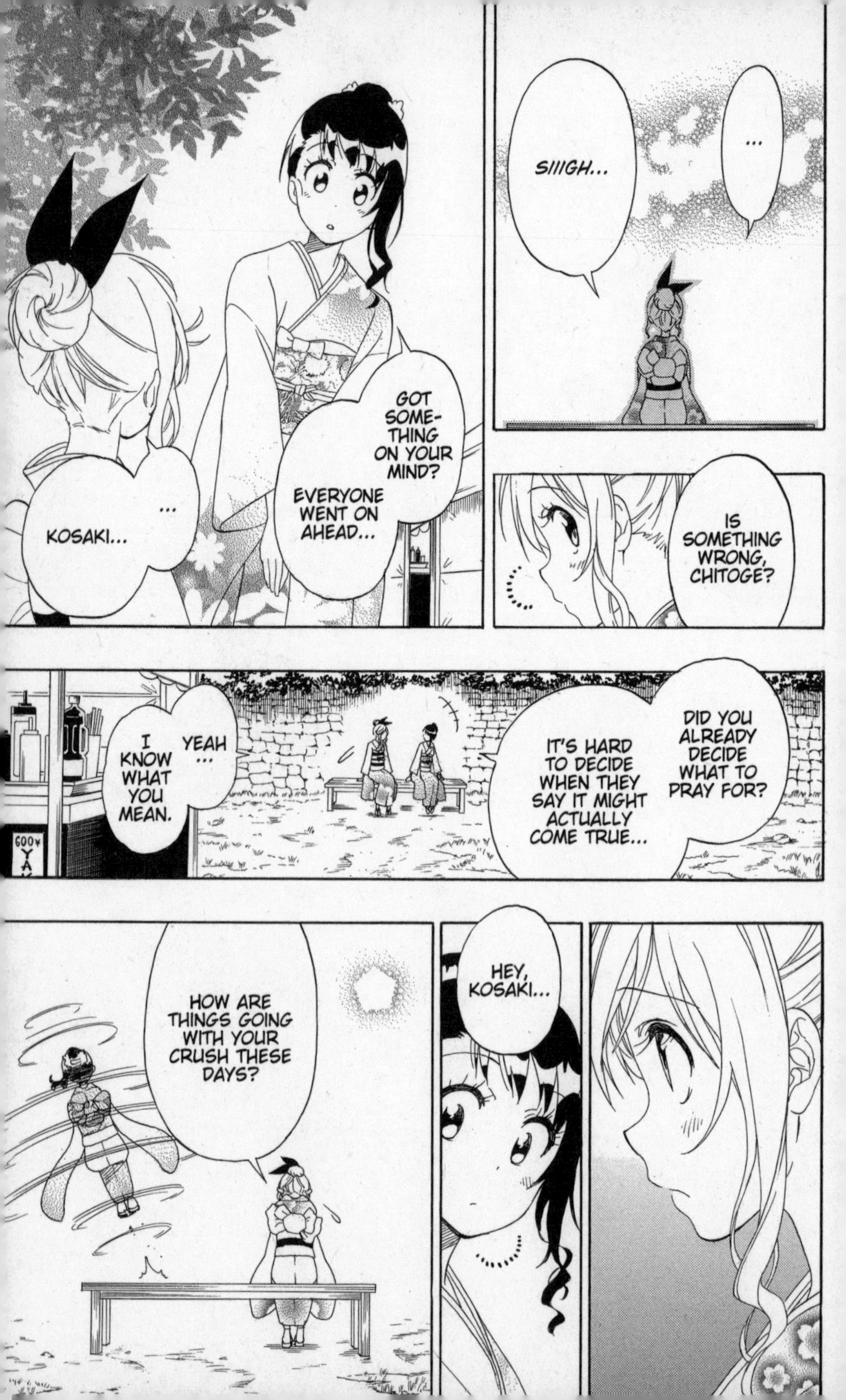
...
SIIIGH...
IS SOMETHING WRONG, CHITOGE?
GOT SOMETHING ON YOUR MIND?
EVERYONE WENT ON AHEAD...
...
KOSAKI...
DID YOU ALREADY DECIDE WHAT TO PRAY FOR?
IT'S HARD TO DECIDE WHEN THEY SAY IT MIGHT ACTUALLY COME TRUE...
YEAH... I KNOW WHAT YOU MEAN.
600¥
HEY, KOSAKI...
HOW ARE THINGS GOING WITH YOUR CRUSH THESE DAYS?

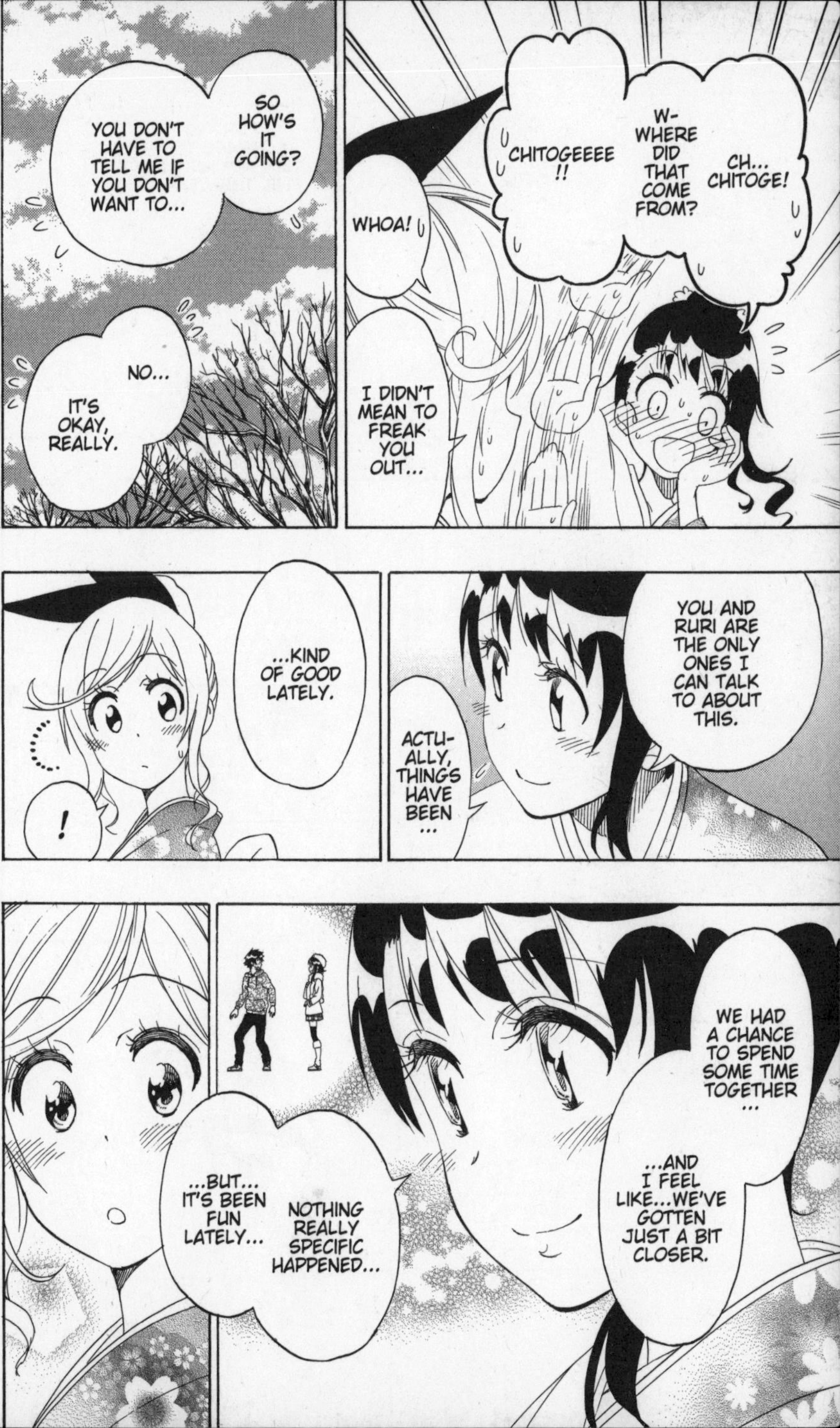
CH... CHITOGE!
W-WHERE DID THAT COME FROM?
CHITOGEEEE !!
WHOA!
I DIDN'T MEAN TO FREAK YOU OUT...
SO HOW'S IT GOING?
YOU DON'T HAVE TO TELL ME IF YOU DON'T WANT TO...
NO...
IT'S OKAY, REALLY.
YOU AND RURI ARE THE ONLY ONES I CAN TALK TO ABOUT THIS.
ACTU-ALLY, THINGS HAVE BEEN ...
...KIND OF GOOD LATELY.
!
WE HAD A CHANCE TO SPEND SOME TIME TOGETHER ...
...AND I FEEL LIKE...WE'VE GOTTEN JUST A BIT CLOSER.
NOTHING REALLY SPECIFIC HAPPENED...
...BUT... IT'S BEEN FUN LATELY...

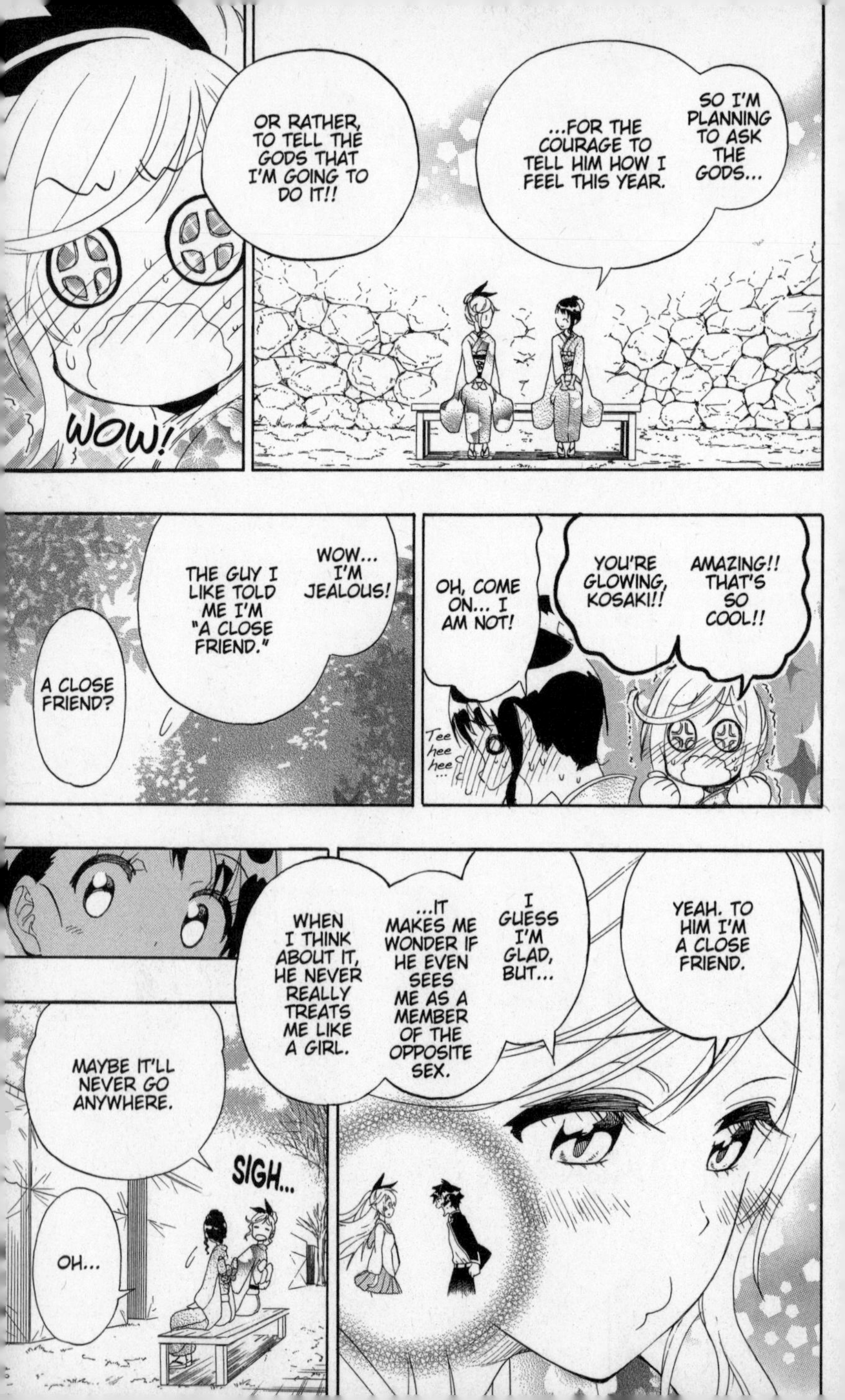
SO I'M PLANNING TO ASK THE GODS...
...FOR THE COURAGE TO TELL HIM HOW I FEEL THIS YEAR.
OR RATHER, TO TELL THE GODS THAT I'M GOING TO DO IT!!
WOW!
AMAZING!! THAT'S SO COOL!!
YOU'RE GLOWING, KOSAKI!!
OH, COME ON... I AM NOT!
Tee hee hee...
WOW... I'M JEALOUS!
THE GUY I LIKE TOLD ME I'M "A CLOSE FRIEND."
A CLOSE FRIEND?
YEAH. TO HIM I'M A CLOSE FRIEND.
I GUESS I'M GLAD, BUT...
...IT MAKES ME WONDER IF HE EVEN SEES ME AS A MEMBER OF THE OPPOSITE SEX.
WHEN I THINK ABOUT IT, HE NEVER REALLY TREATS ME LIKE A GIRL.
MAYBE IT'LL NEVER GO ANYWHERE.
SIGH...
OH...

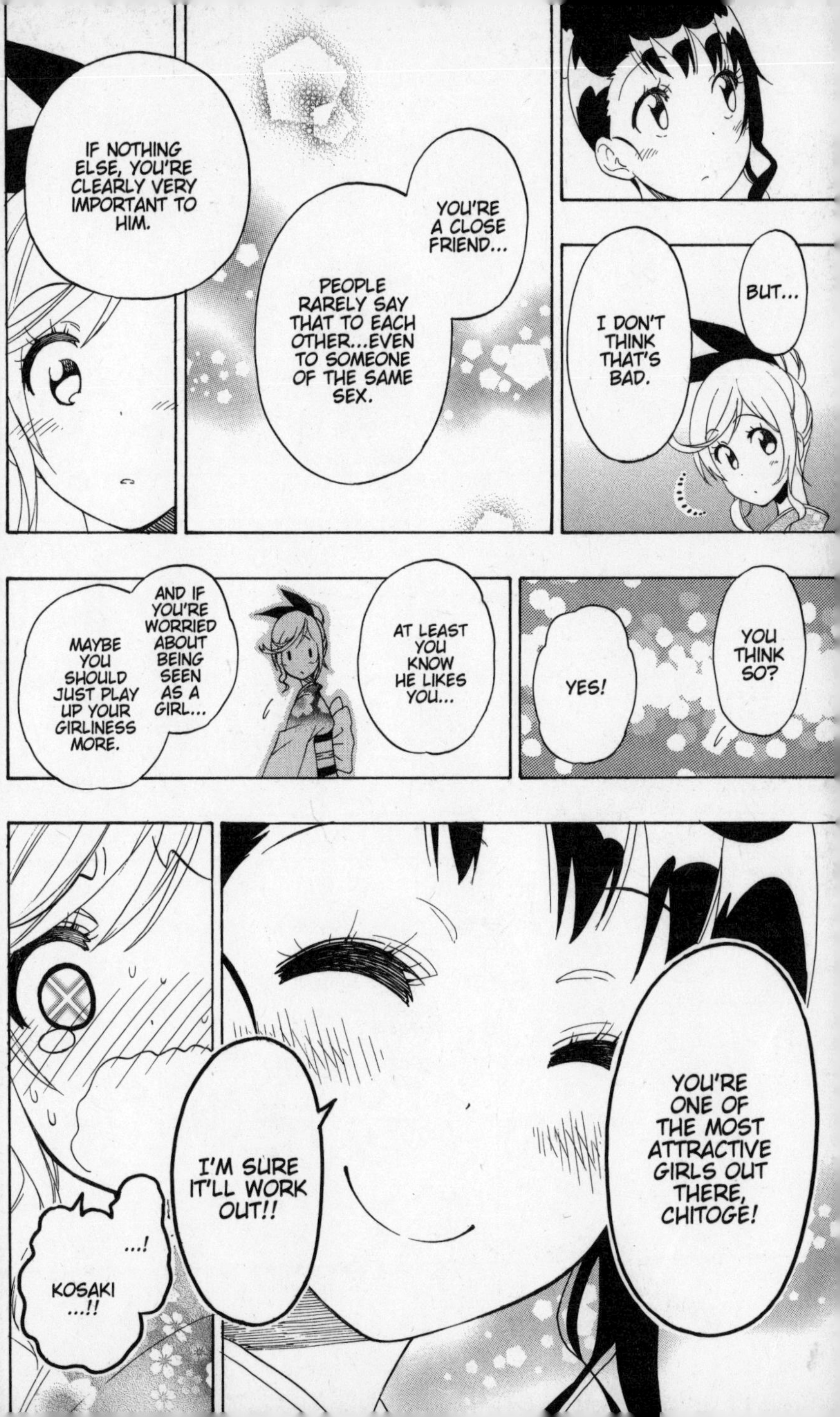
BUT...
I DON'T THINK THAT'S BAD.
YOU'RE A CLOSE FRIEND...
PEOPLE RARELY SAY THAT TO EACH OTHER...EVEN TO SOMEONE OF THE SAME SEX.
IF NOTHING ELSE, YOU'RE CLEARLY VERY IMPORTANT TO HIM.
YOU THINK SO?
YES!
AT LEAST YOU KNOW HE LIKES YOU...
AND IF YOU'RE WORRIED ABOUT BEING SEEN AS A GIRL...
MAYBE YOU SHOULD JUST PLAY UP YOUR GIRLINESS MORE.
YOU'RE ONE OF THE MOST ATTRACTIVE GIRLS OUT THERE, CHITOGE!
I'M SURE IT'LL WORK OUT!!
...!
KOSAKI ...!!

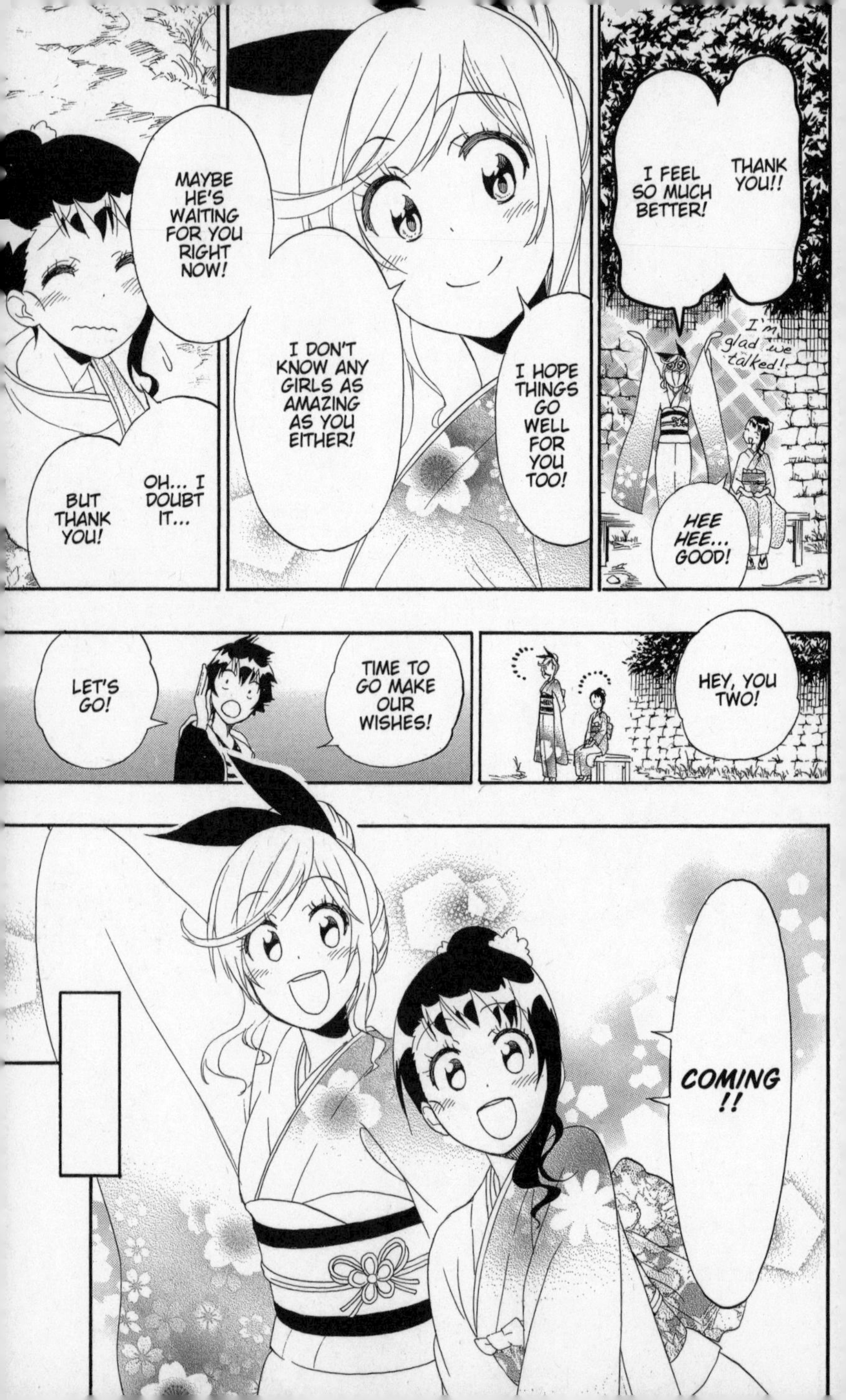
THANK YOU!! I FEEL SO MUCH BETTER!
I'm glad we talked!
HEE HEE... GOOD!
I HOPE THINGS GO WELL FOR YOU TOO!
I DON'T KNOW ANY GIRLS AS AMAZING AS YOU EITHER!
MAYBE HE'S WAITING FOR YOU RIGHT NOW!
OH... I DOUBT IT... BUT THANK YOU!
HEY, YOU TWO!
TIME TO GO MAKE OUR WISHES!
LET'S GO!
COMING!!

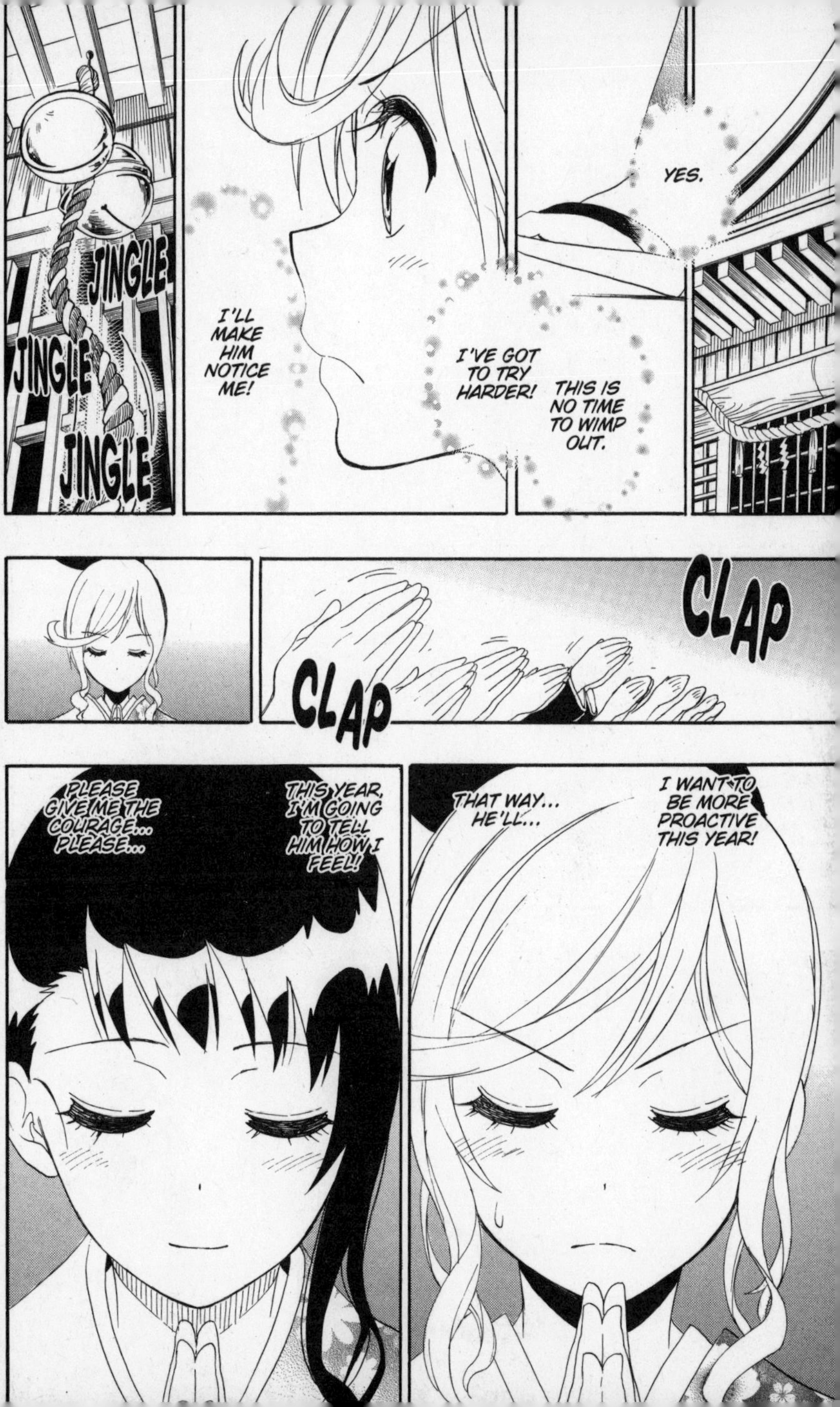
YES.
THIS IS NO TIME TO WIMP OUT.
I'VE GOT TO TRY HARDER!
I'LL MAKE HIM NOTICE ME!
JINGLE
JINGLE
JINGLE
CLAP
CLAP
I WANT TO BE MORE PROACTIVE THIS YEAR!
THAT WAY... HE'LL...
THIS YEAR, I'M GOING TO TELL HIM HOW I FEEL!
PLEASE GIVE ME THE COURAGE... PLEASE...

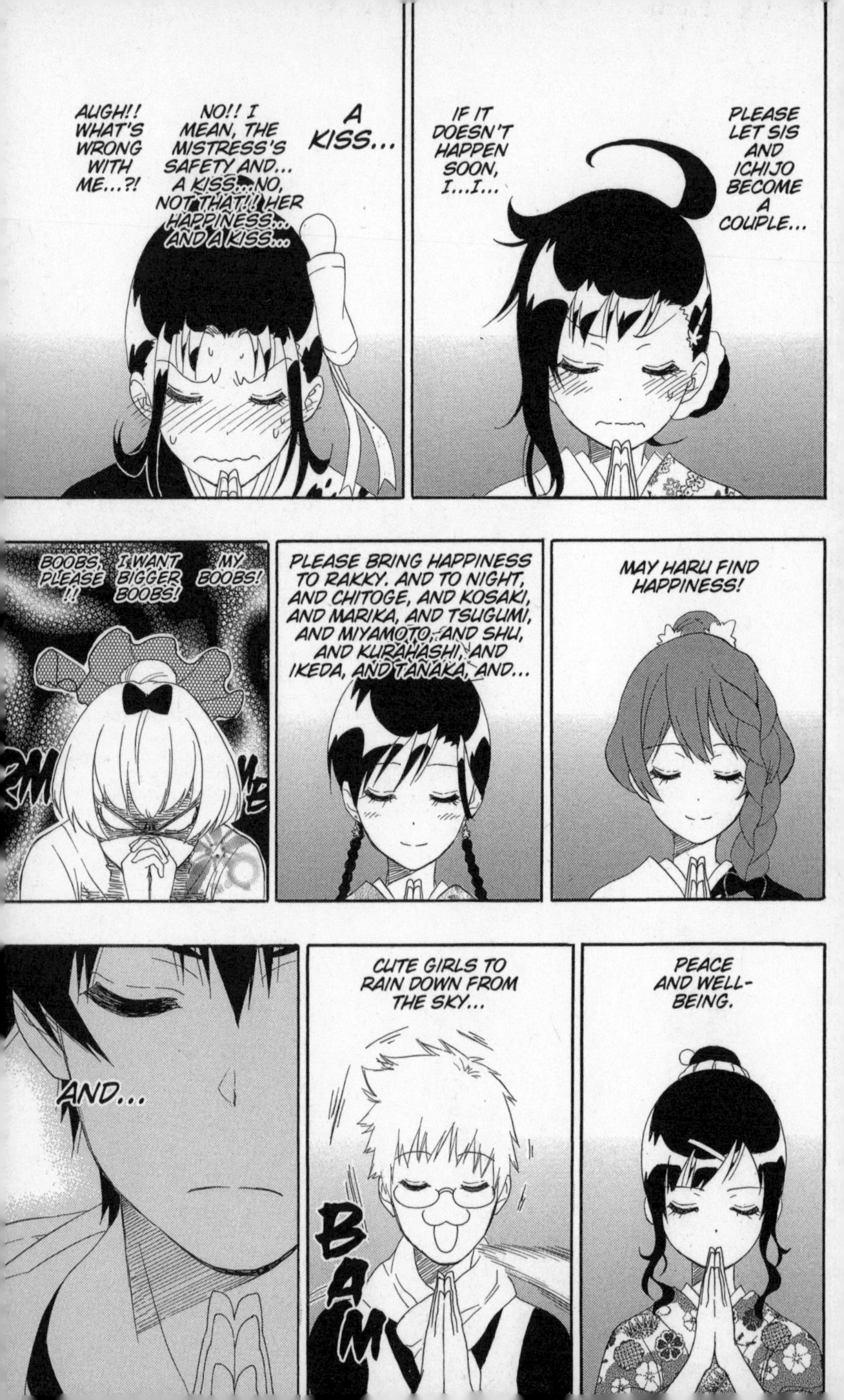
PLEASE LET SIS AND ICHIJO BECOME A COUPLE...
IF IT DOESN'T HAPPEN SOON, I...I...
A KISS...
NO!! I MEAN, THE MISTRESS'S SAFETY AND... A KISS...NO, NOT THAT!! HER HAPPINESS... AND A KISS...
AUGH!! WHAT'S WRONG WITH ME...?!
MAY HARU FIND HAPPINESS!
PLEASE BRING HAPPINESS TO RAKKY. AND TO NIGHT, AND CHITOGE, AND KOSAKI, AND MARIKA, AND TSUGUMI, AND MIYAMOTO, AND SHU, AND KURAHASHI, AND IKEDA, AND TANAKA, AND...
MY BOOBS!
I WANT BIGGER BOOBS!
BOOBS, PLEASE!!
PEACE AND WELL-BEING.
CUTE GIRLS TO RAIN DOWN FROM THE SKY...
BAM
AND...

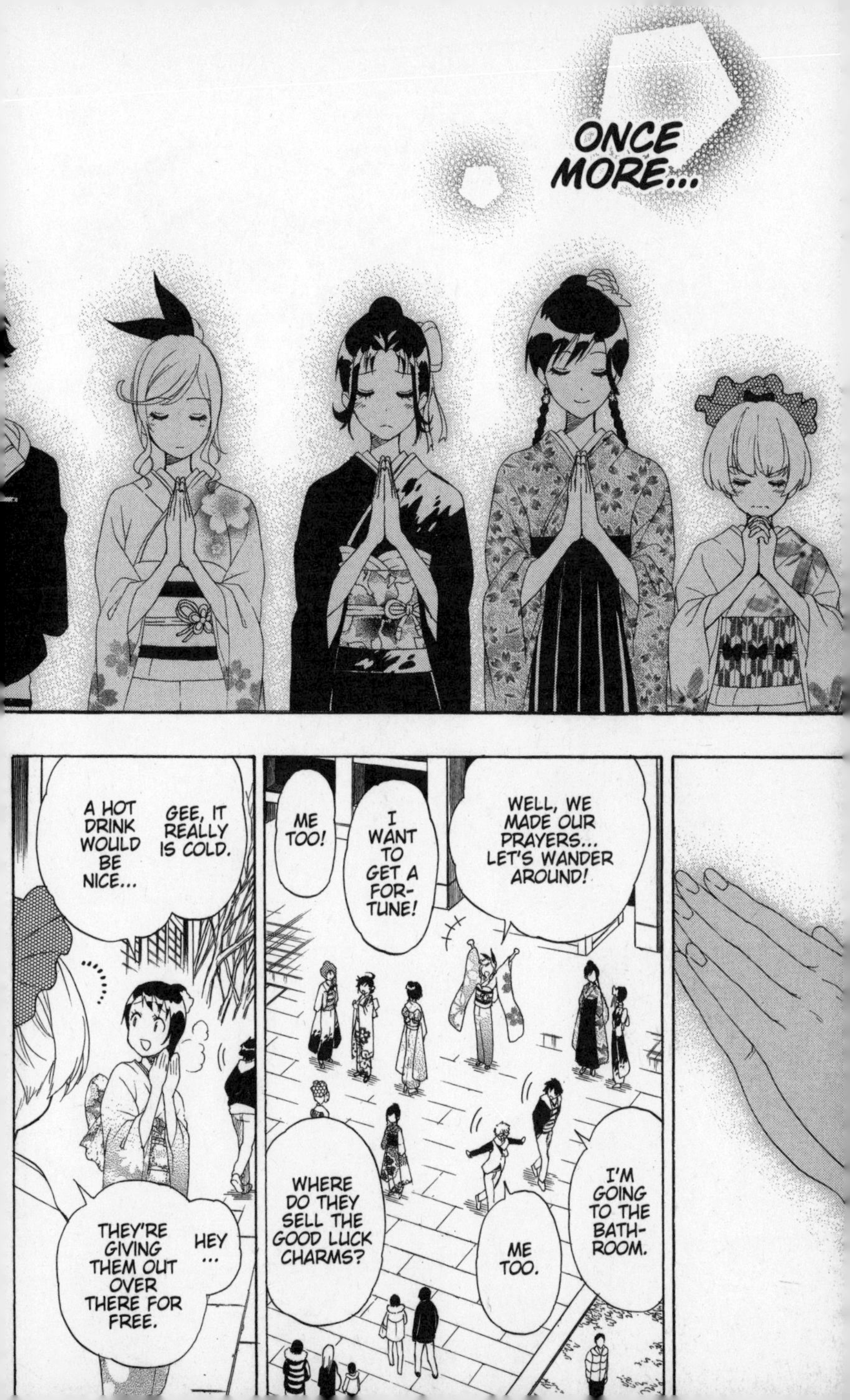
ONCE MORE...
WELL, WE MADE OUR PRAYERS... LET'S WANDER AROUND!
I WANT TO GET A FOR-TUNE!
ME TOO!
I'M GOING TO THE BATH-ROOM.
ME TOO.
WHERE DO THEY SELL THE GOOD LUCK CHARMS?
GEE, IT REALLY IS COLD.
A HOT DRINK WOULD BE NICE...
...
HEY ...
THEY'RE GIVING THEM OUT OVER THERE FOR FREE.

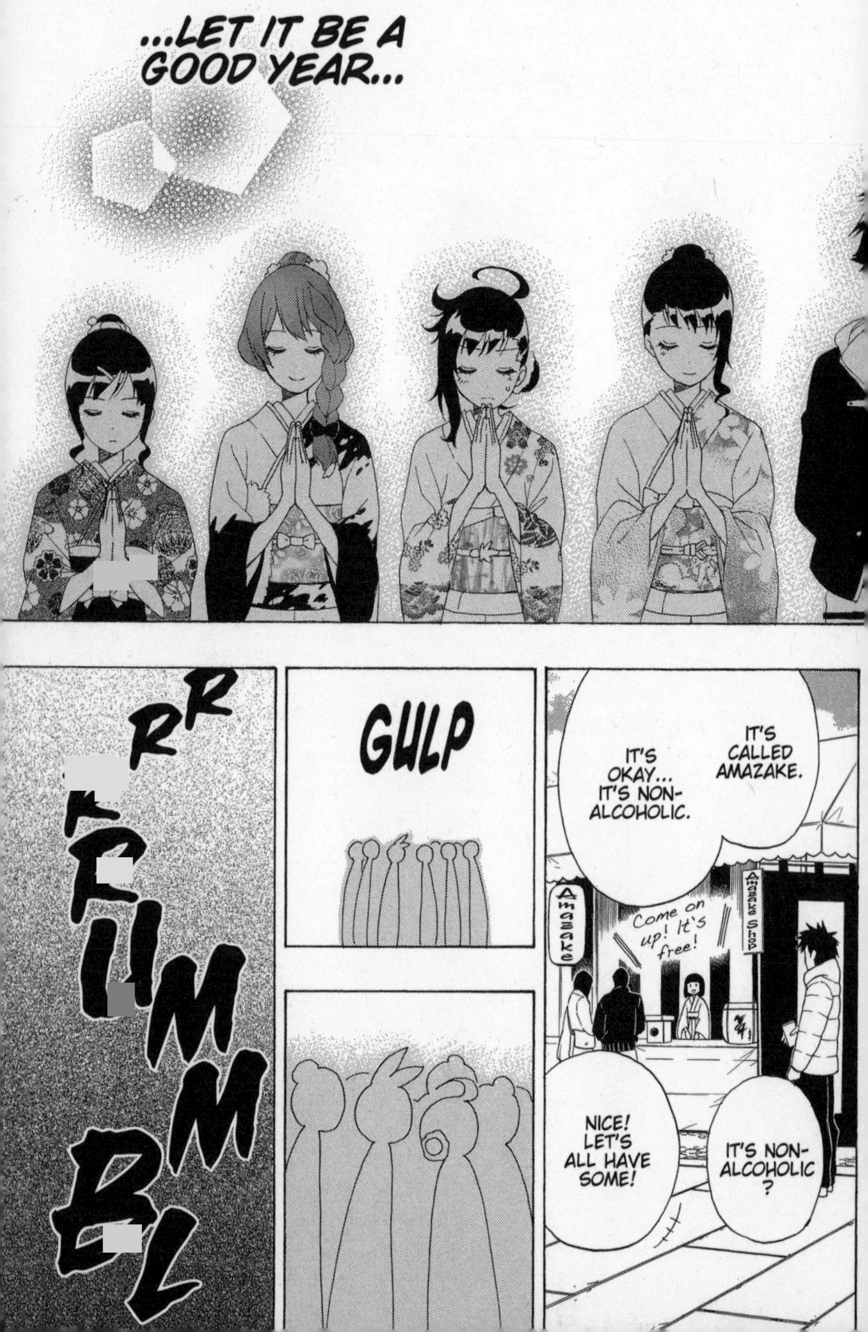
...LET IT BE A GOOD YEAR...
IT'S CALLED AMAZAKE.
IT'S OKAY... IT'S NON-ALCOHOLIC.
Amazake Shop
Amazake
Come on up! It's free!
IT'S NON-ALCOHOLIC?
NICE! LET'S ALL HAVE SOME!
GULP
RRRRUMMBL

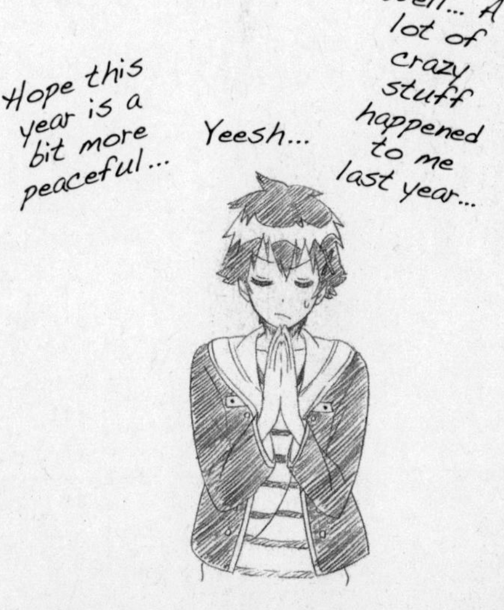
Well... A lot of crazy stuff happened to me last year...
Yeesh...
Hope this year is a bit more peaceful...

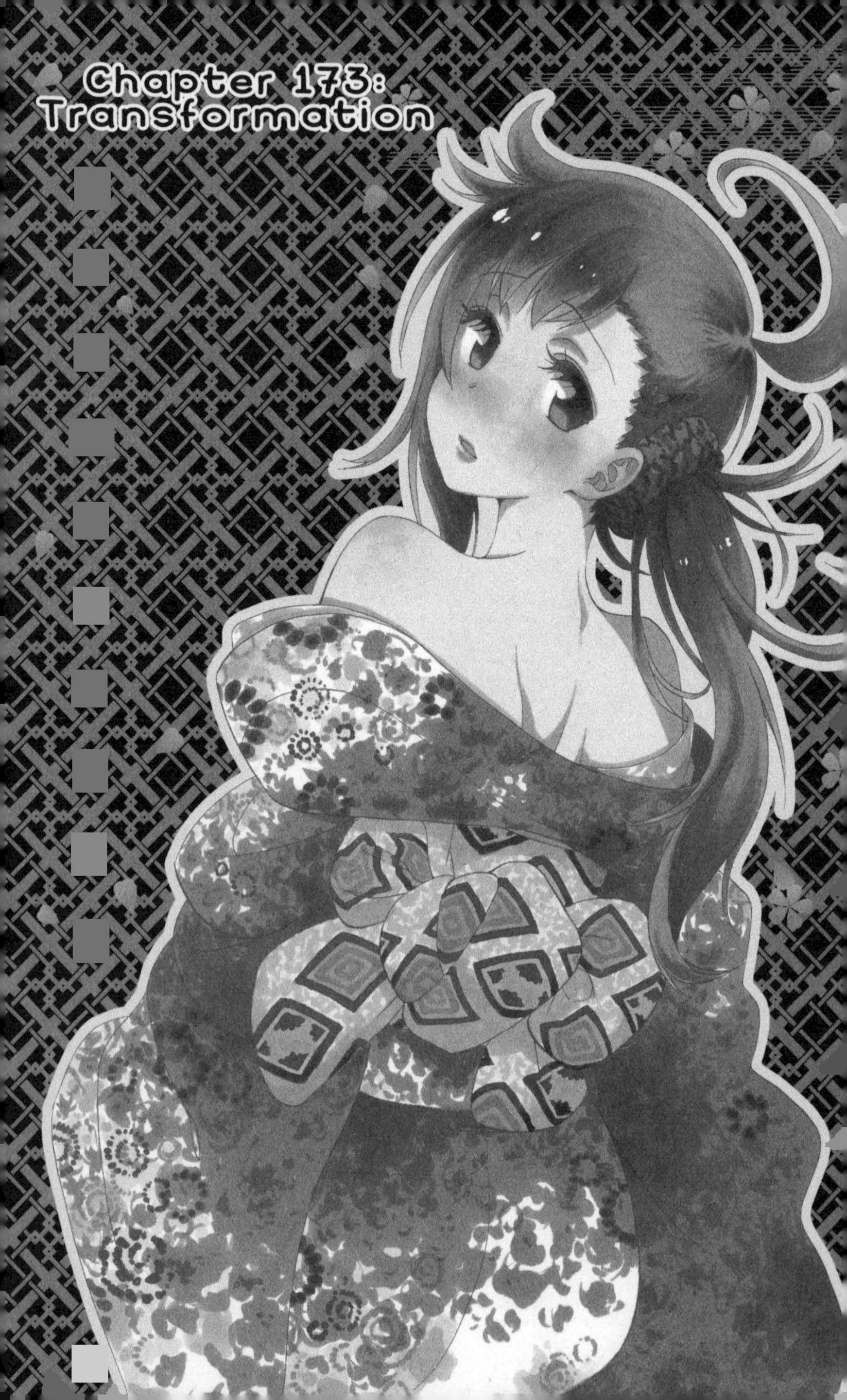
Chapter 173:
Transformation

Way to Go!

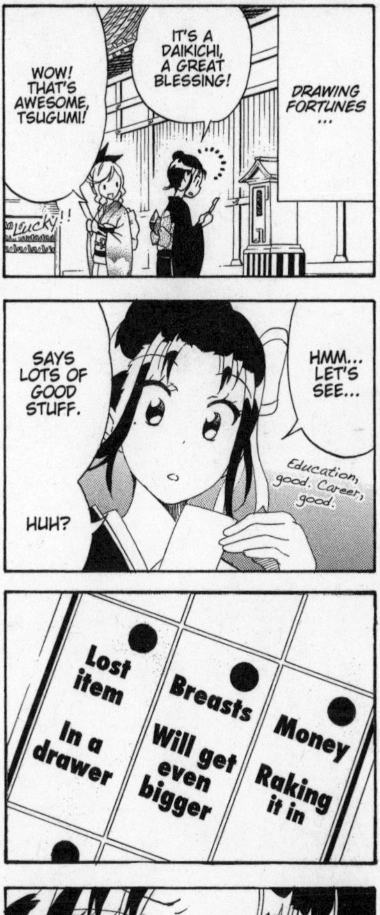
DRAWING FORTUNES...
IT'S A DAIKICHI, A GREAT BLESSING!
WOW! THAT'S AWESOME, TSUGUMI!
LUCKY!!
HMM... LET'S SEE...
Education, good. Career, good.
SAYS LOTS OF GOOD STUFF.
HUH?
Money
Raking it in
Breasts
Will get even bigger
Lost item
In a drawer

You're Kidding!

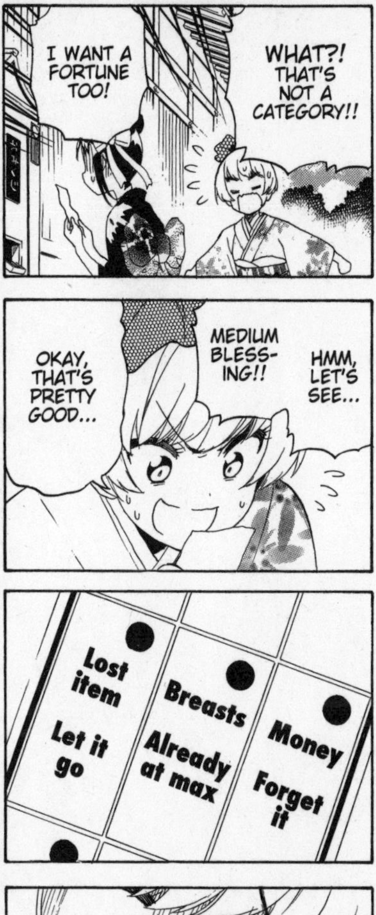
WHAT?! THAT'S NOT A CATEGORY!!
I WANT A FORTUNE TOO!
HMM, LET'S SEE...
MEDIUM BLESSING!!
OKAY, THAT'S PRETTY GOOD...
Money
Forget it
Breasts
Already at max
Lost item
Let it go

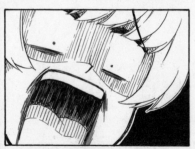

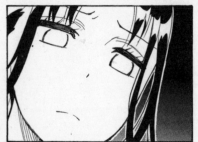

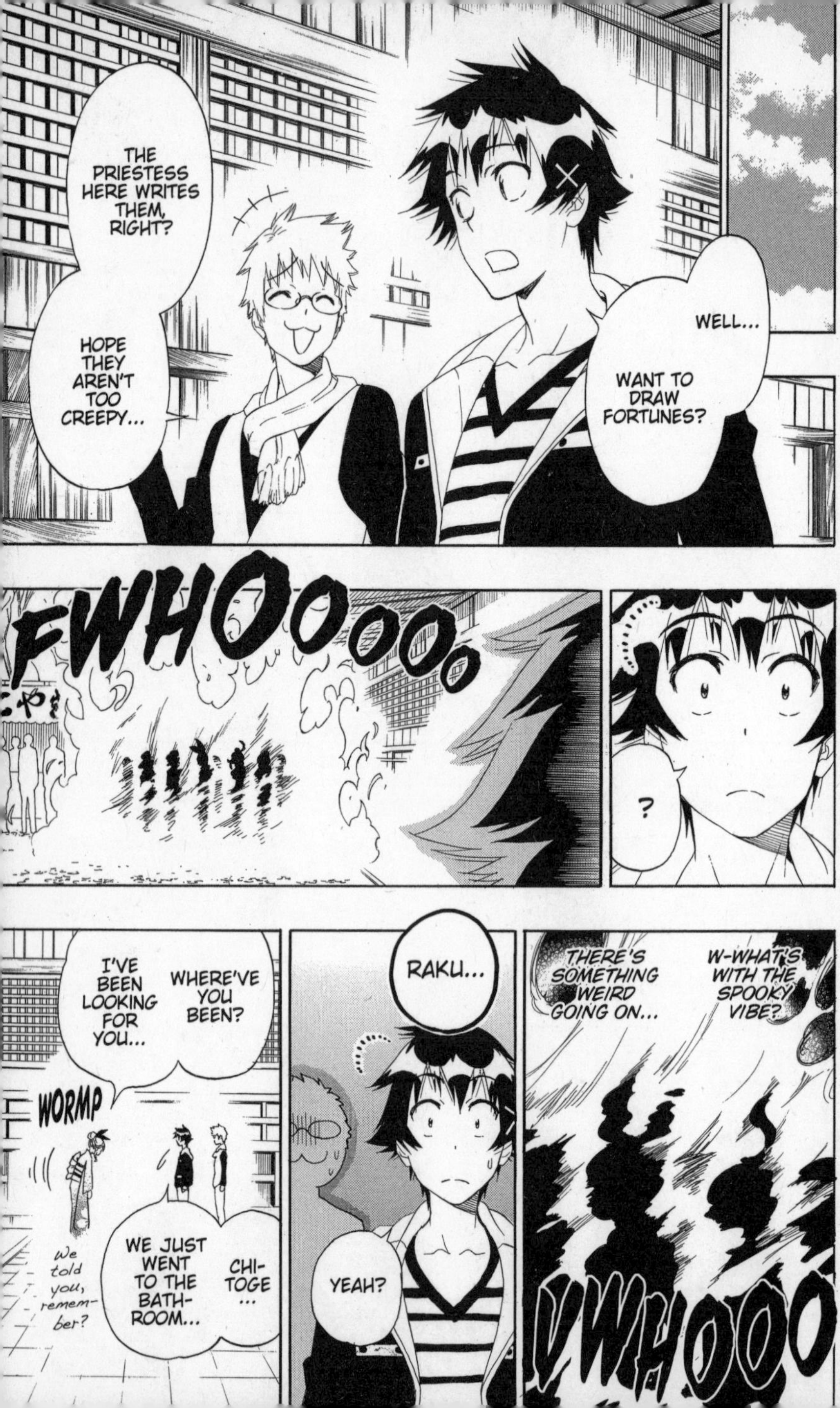
WELL...
WANT TO DRAW FORTUNES?
THE PRIESTESS HERE WRITES THEM, RIGHT?
HOPE THEY AREN'T TOO CREEPY...
?
FWHOOOOO
W-WHAT'S WITH THE SPOOKY VIBE?
THERE'S SOMETHING WEIRD GOING ON...
WHOOO
RAKU...
YEAH?
WHERE'VE YOU BEEN?
I'VE BEEN LOOKING FOR YOU...
WORMP
CHI-TOGE...
WE JUST WENT TO THE BATH-ROOM...
We told you, remem-ber?

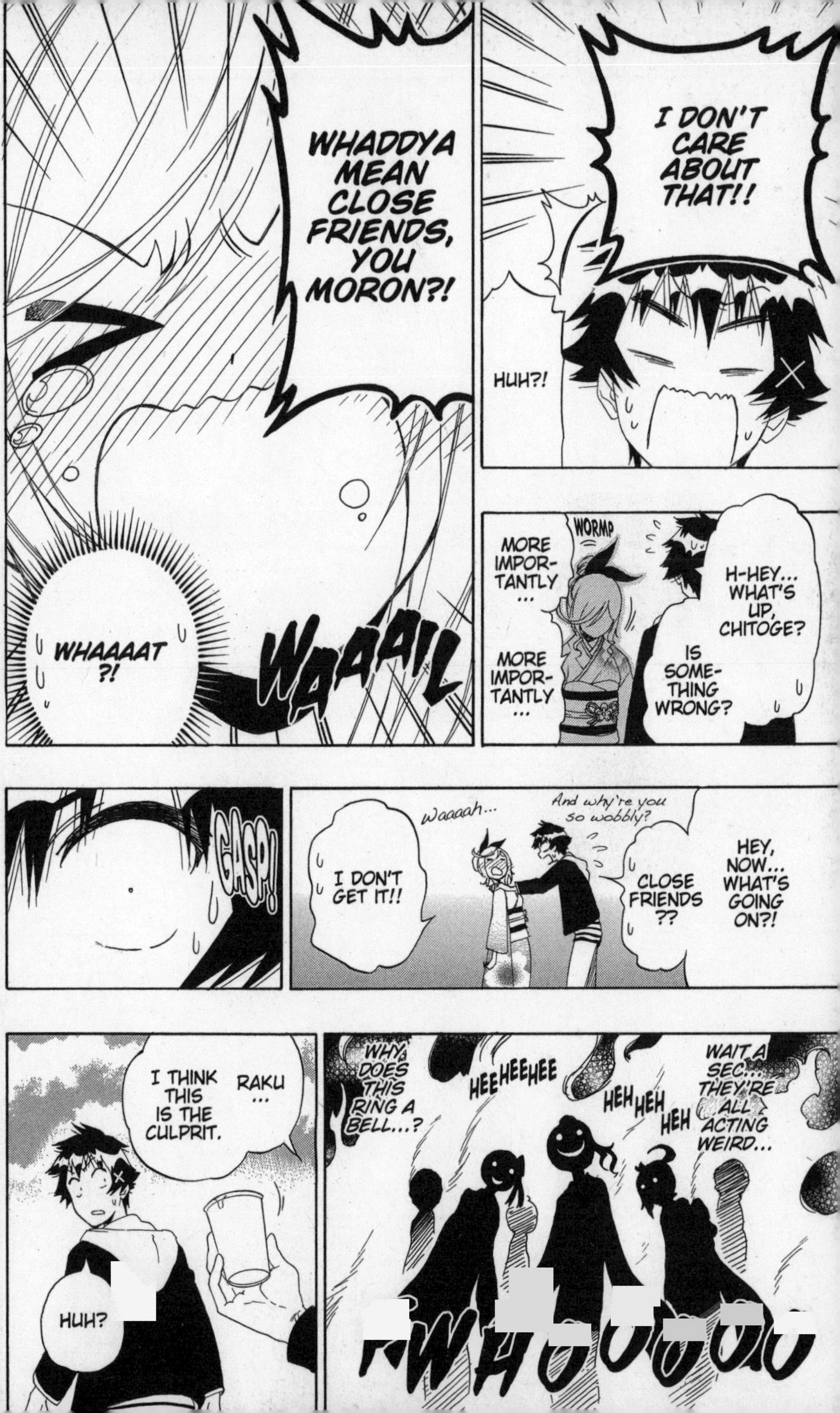
I DON'T CARE ABOUT THAT!!
HUH?!
H-HEY... WHAT'S UP, CHITOGE?
IS SOMETHING WRONG?
WORMP
MORE IMPORTANTLY...
MORE IMPORTANTLY...
WHADDYA MEAN CLOSE FRIENDS, YOU MORON?!
WAAAIL
WHAAAAT?!
HEY, NOW... WHAT'S GOING ON?!
CLOSE FRIENDS??
And why're you so wobbly?
Waaaah...
I DON'T GET IT!!
GASP!
WAIT A SEC... THEY'RE ALL ACTING WEIRD...
HEH HEH HEH
HEEHEEHEE
WHY DOES THIS RING A BELL...?
RAKU...
I THINK THIS IS THE CULPRIT.
HUH?

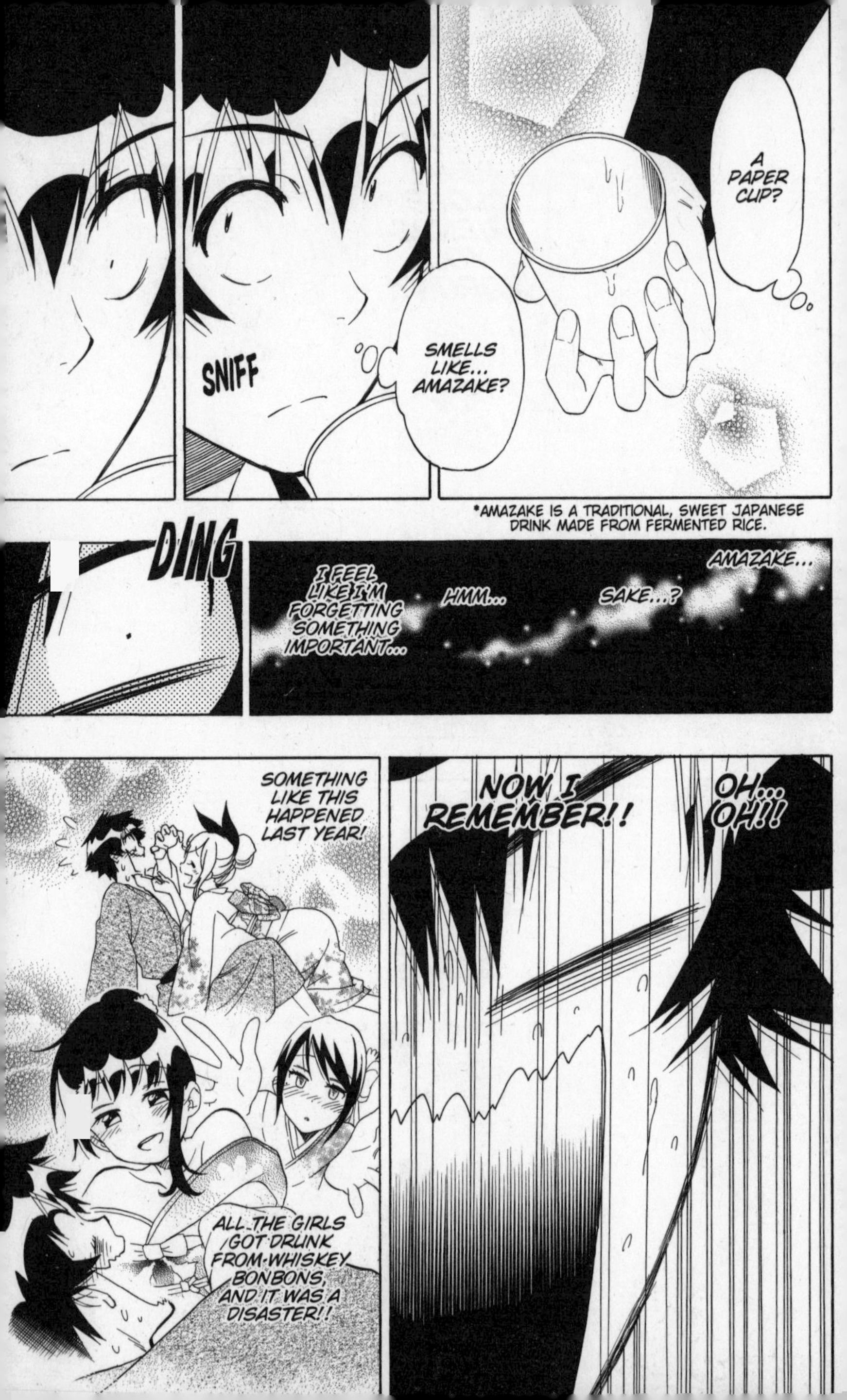
A PAPER CUP?
SMELLS LIKE... AMAZAKE?
SNIFF
*AMAZAKE IS A TRADITIONAL, SWEET JAPANESE DRINK MADE FROM FERMENTED RICE.
AMAZAKE...
SAKE...?
HMM...
I FEEL LIKE I'M FORGETTING SOMETHING IMPORTANT...
DING
OH... OH!!
NOW I REMEMBER!!
SOMETHING LIKE THIS HAPPENED LAST YEAR!
ALL THE GIRLS GOT DRUNK FROM WHISKEY BONBONS, AND IT WAS A DISASTER!!

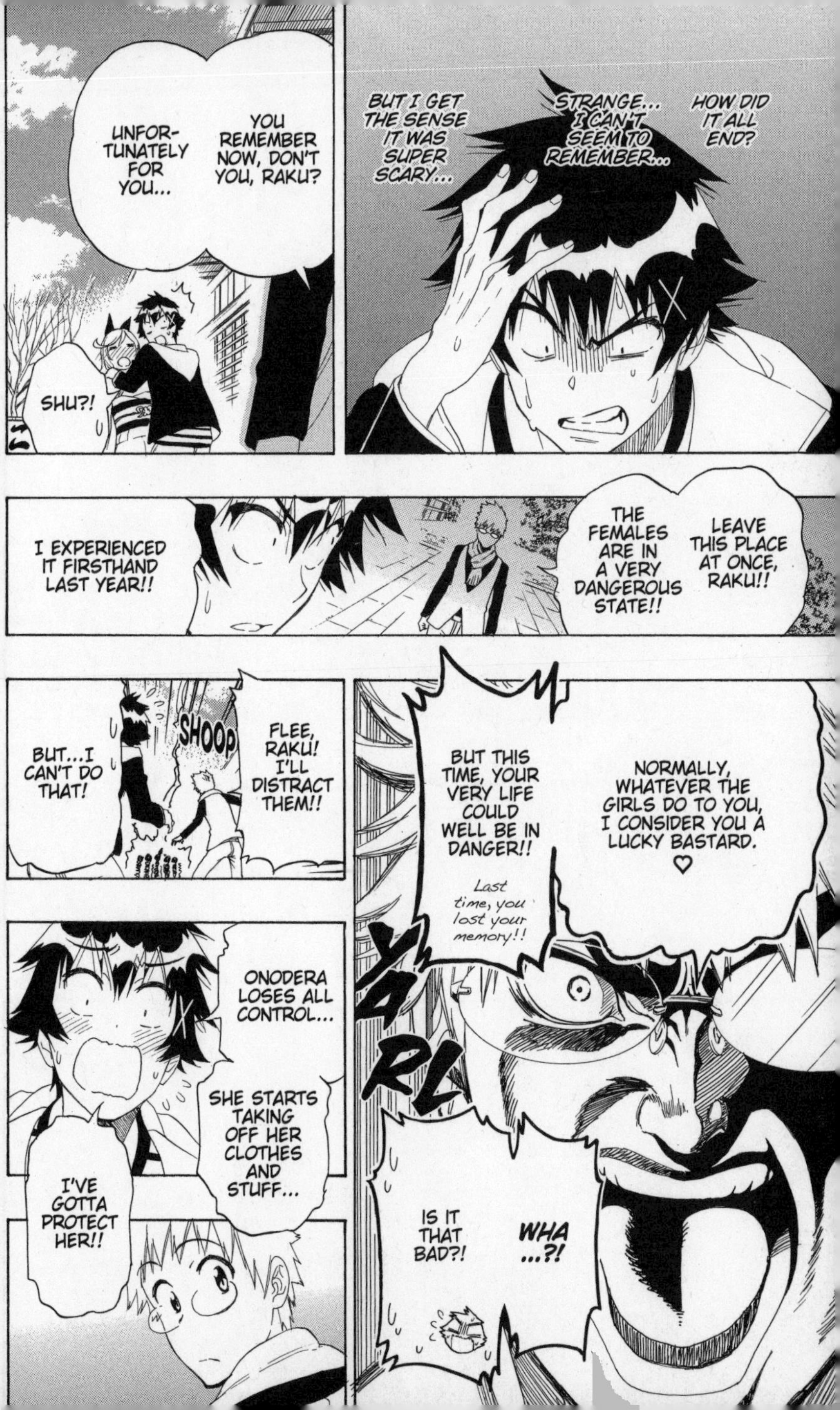
HOW DID IT ALL END?
STRANGE... I CAN'T SEEM TO REMEMBER...
BUT I GET THE SENSE IT WAS SUPER SCARY...
YOU REMEMBER NOW, DON'T YOU, RAKU?
UNFORTUNATELY FOR YOU...
SHU?!
LEAVE THIS PLACE AT ONCE, RAKU!!
THE FEMALES ARE IN A VERY DANGEROUS STATE!!
I EXPERIENCED IT FIRSTHAND LAST YEAR!!
NORMALLY, WHATEVER THE GIRLS DO TO YOU, I CONSIDER YOU A LUCKY BASTARD. ♡
BUT THIS TIME, YOUR VERY LIFE COULD WELL BE IN DANGER!!
Last time, you lost your memory!!
YARL
WHA ...?!
IS IT THAT BAD?!
FLEE, RAKU! I'LL DISTRACT THEM!!
SHOOP
BUT...I CAN'T DO THAT!
ONODERA LOSES ALL CONTROL...
SHE STARTS TAKING OFF HER CLOTHES AND STUFF...
I'VE GOTTA PROTECT HER!!

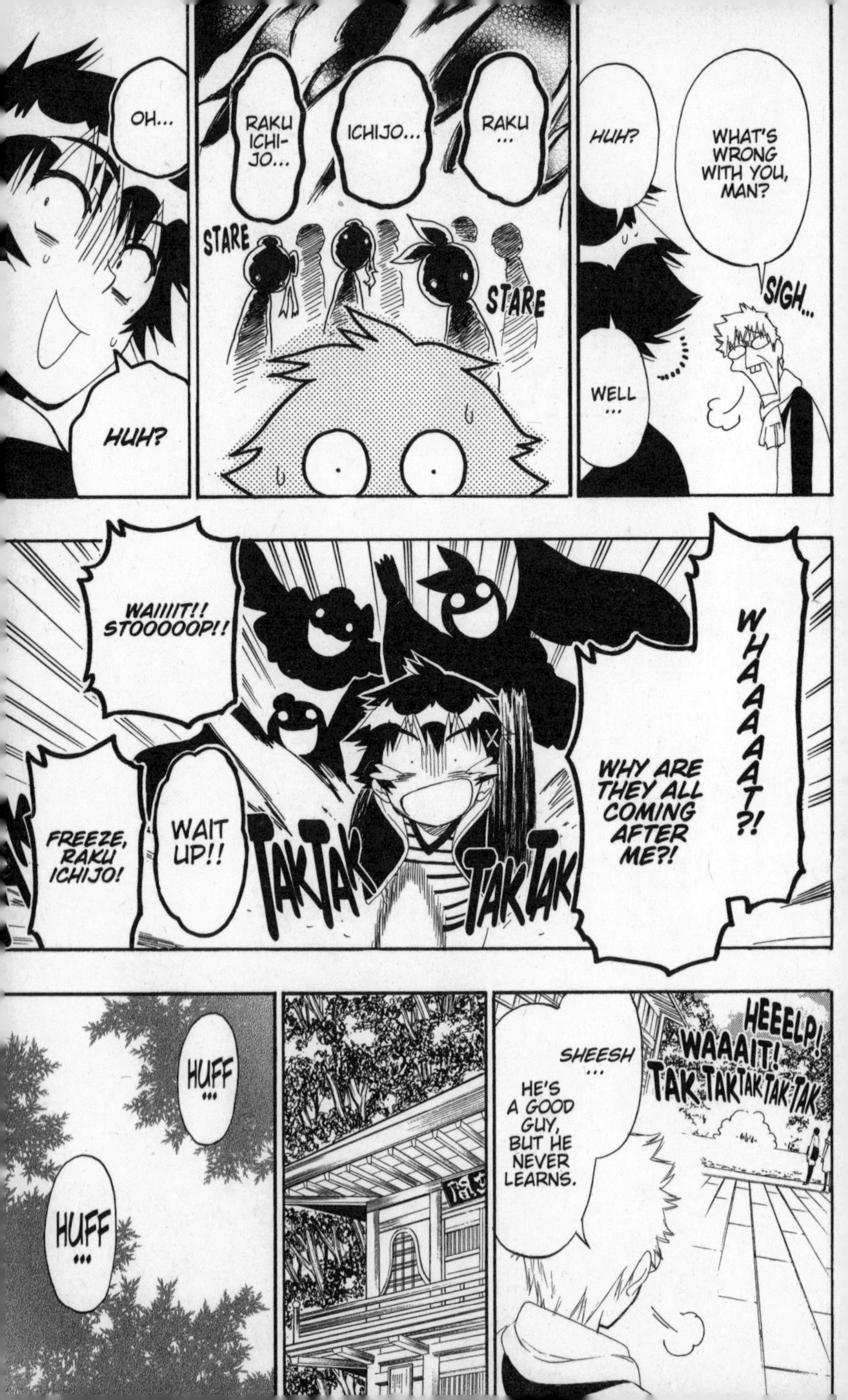
WHAT'S WRONG WITH YOU, MAN?
HUH?
SIGH...
...
WELL ...
RAKU ...
ICHIJO...
RAKU ICHIJO...
STARE
STARE
OH...
HUH?
WHAAAAAAAT?!
WHY ARE THEY ALL COMING AFTER ME?!
WAIIIIT!! STOOOOOP!!
TAK TAK
WAIT UP!!
TAK TAK
FREEZE, RAKU ICHIJO!
HEEELP!
WAAAIT!
TAK TAK TAK TAK TAK
SHEESH ...
HE'S A GOOD GUY, BUT HE NEVER LEARNS.
HUFF ...
HUFF ...

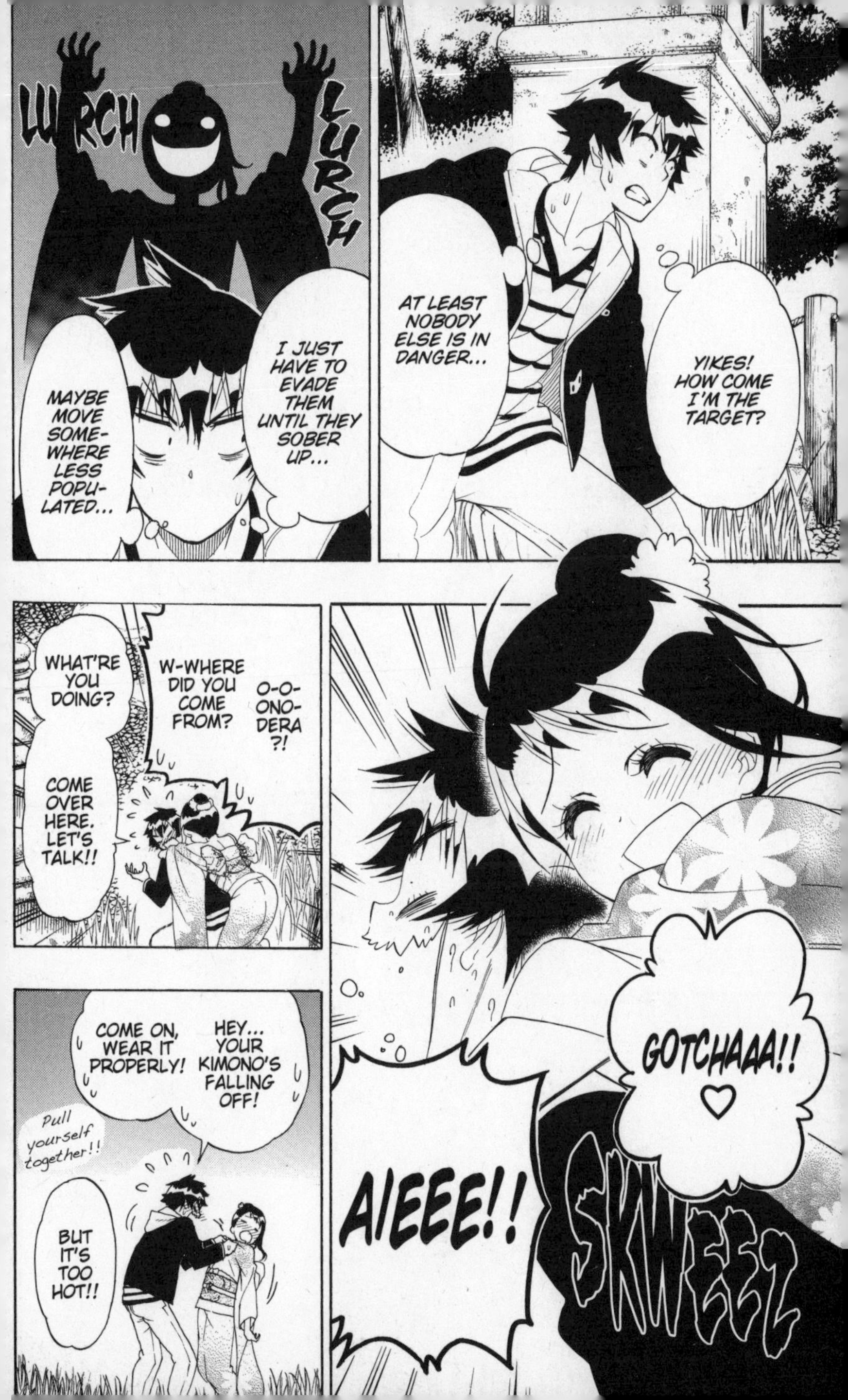
YIKES! HOW COME I'M THE TARGET?
AT LEAST NOBODY ELSE IS IN DANGER...
LURCH
LURCH
I JUST HAVE TO EVADE THEM UNTIL THEY SOBER UP...
MAYBE MOVE SOME-WHERE LESS POPU-LATED...
GOTCHAAA!! ♡
SKWEEZ
AIEEE!!
O-O-ONO-DERA?!
W-WHERE DID YOU COME FROM?
WHAT'RE YOU DOING?
COME OVER HERE. LET'S TALK!!
HEY... YOUR KIMONO'S FALLING OFF!
COME ON, WEAR IT PROPERLY!
Pull yourself together!!
BUT IT'S TOO HOT!!

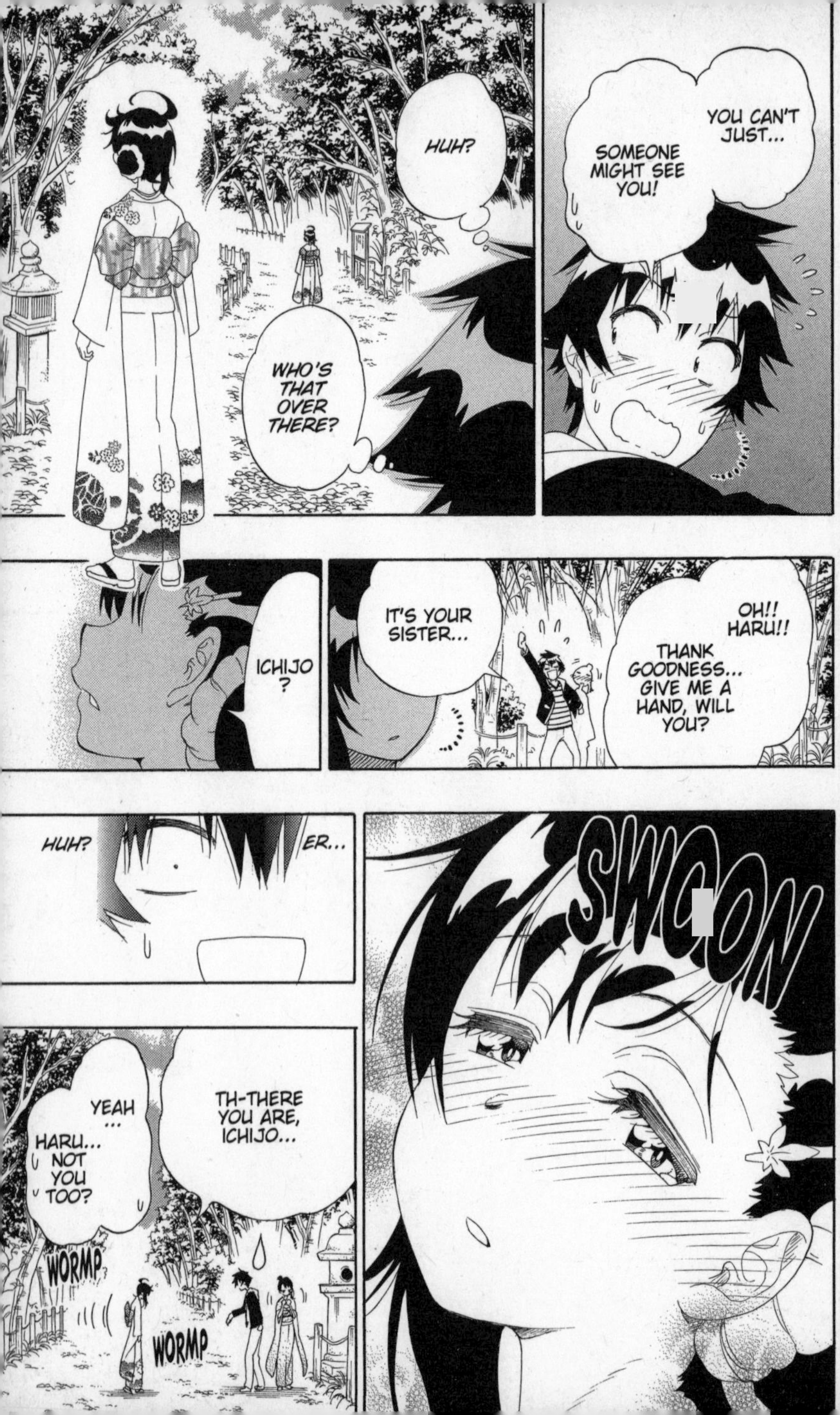
YOU CAN'T JUST...
SOMEONE MIGHT SEE YOU!
HUH?
WHO'S THAT OVER THERE?
OH!! HARU!!
THANK GOODNESS... GIVE ME A HAND, WILL YOU?
IT'S YOUR SISTER...
ICHIJO?
SWOON
ER...
HUH?
TH-THERE YOU ARE, ICHIJO...
YEAH...
HARU... NOT YOU TOO?
WORMP
WORMP

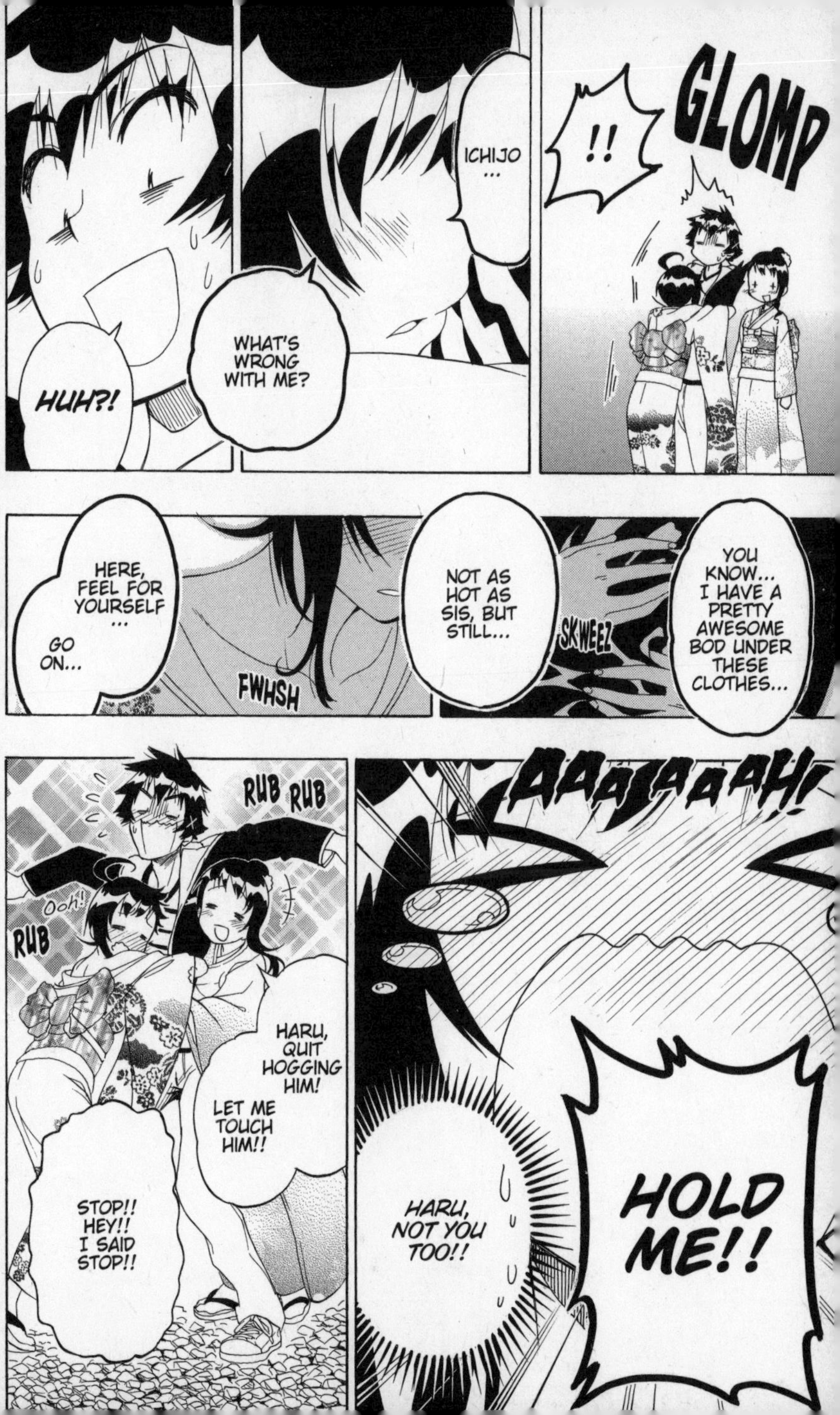
GLOMP
!!
ICHIJO ...
WHAT'S WRONG WITH ME?
HUH?!
YOU KNOW... I HAVE A PRETTY AWESOME BOD UNDER THESE CLOTHES...
SKWEEZ
NOT AS HOT AS SIS, BUT STILL...
FWHSH
HERE, FEEL FOR YOURSELF ...
GO ON...
AAAAAAAH!
HOLD ME!!
HARU, NOT YOU TOO!!
RUB RUB
HARU, QUIT HOGGING HIM!
LET ME TOUCH HIM!!
Ooh!
RUB
STOP!! HEY!! I SAID STOP!!

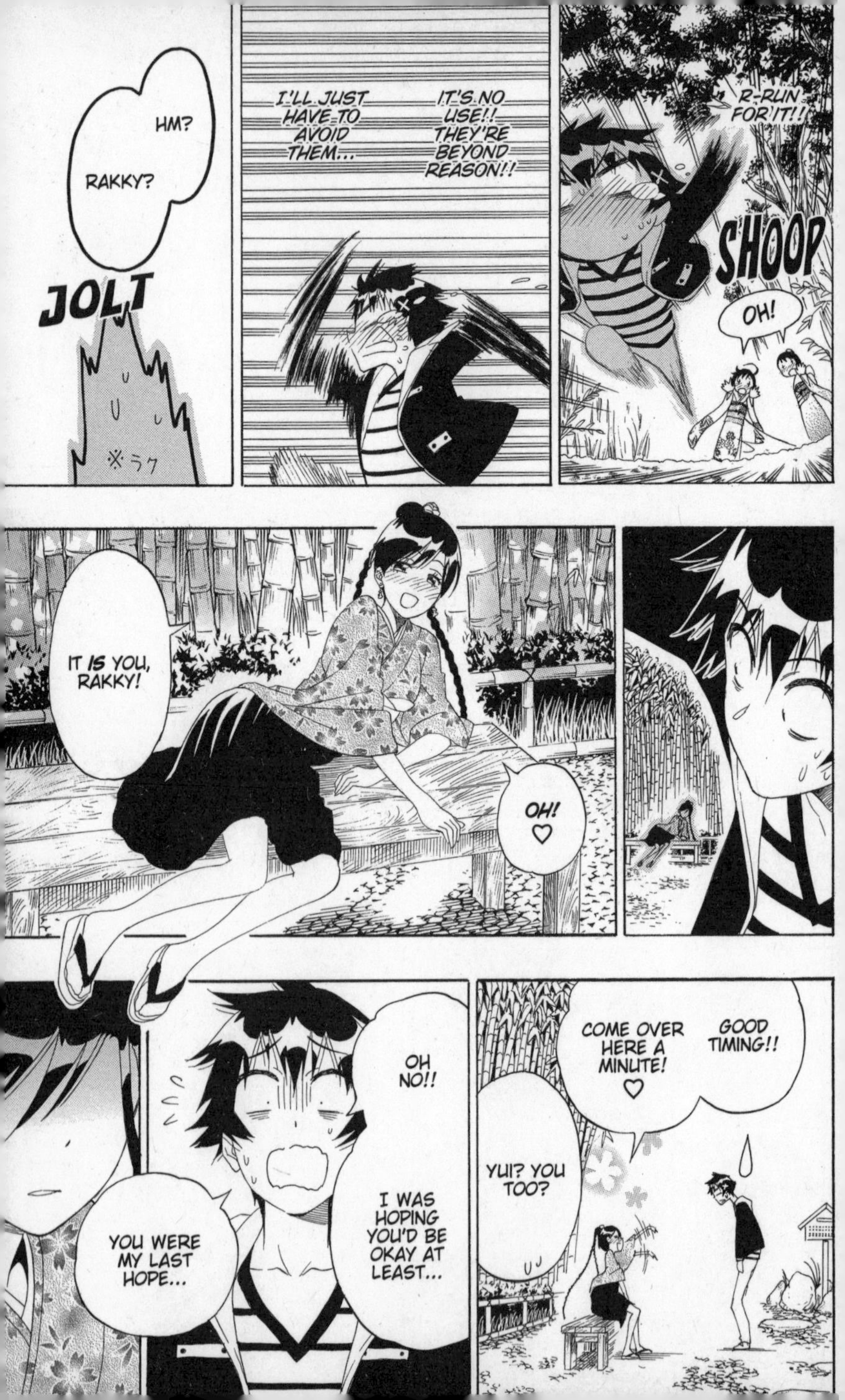
R-RUN FOR IT!!
SHOOP
OH!
IT'S NO USE!! THEY'RE BEYOND REASON!!
I'LL JUST HAVE TO AVOID THEM...
HM?
RAKKY?
JOLT
※ラク
OH! ♡
IT IS YOU, RAKKY!
GOOD TIMING!!
COME OVER HERE A MINUTE! ♡
YUI? YOU TOO?
OH NO!!
I WAS HOPING YOU'D BE OKAY AT LEAST...
YOU WERE MY LAST HOPE...

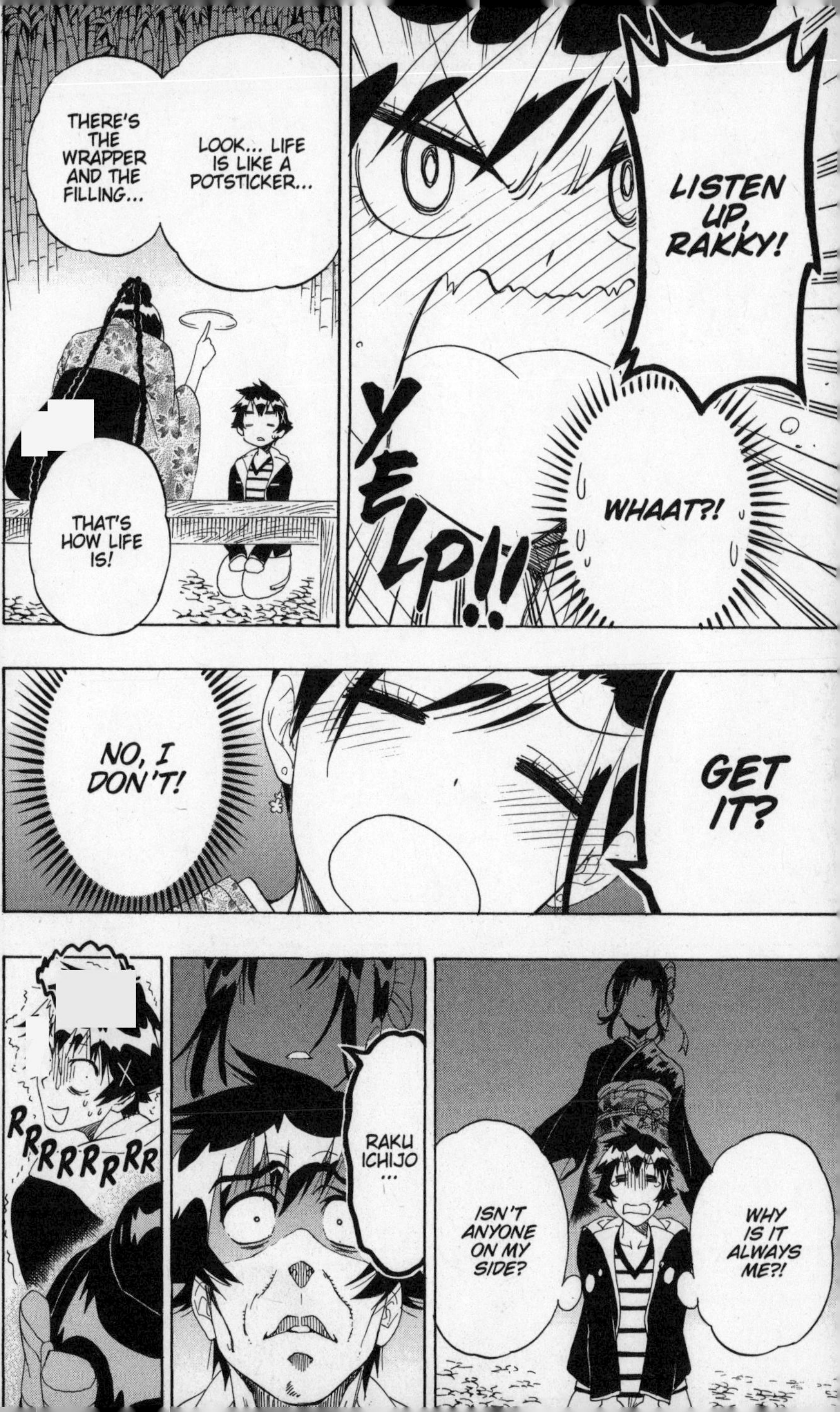
LISTEN UP, RAKKY!
WHAAT?!
YELP!!!
LOOK... LIFE IS LIKE A POTSTICKER...
THERE'S THE WRAPPER AND THE FILLING...
THAT'S HOW LIFE IS!
GET IT?
NO, I DON'T!
WHY IS IT ALWAYS ME?!
ISN'T ANYONE ON MY SIDE?
RAKU ICHIJO...
RRRRRRRRR

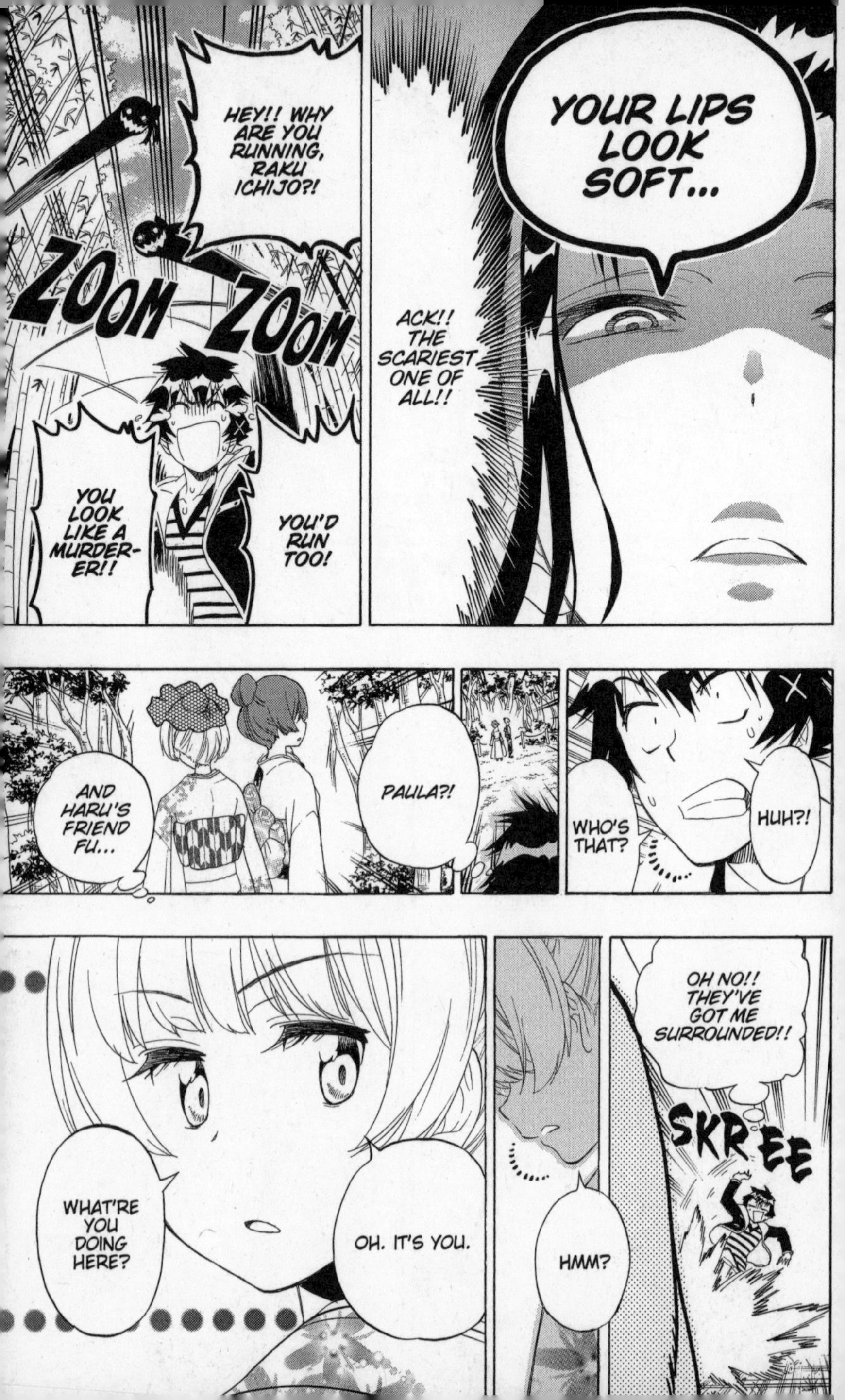
YOUR LIPS LOOK SOFT...
ACK!! THE SCARIEST ONE OF ALL!!
HEY!! WHY ARE YOU RUNNING, RAKU ICHIJO?!
ZOOM ZOOM
YOU'D RUN TOO!
YOU LOOK LIKE A MURDERER!!
HUH?!
WHO'S THAT?
PAULA?!
AND HARU'S FRIEND FU...
OH NO!! THEY'VE GOT ME SURROUNDED!!
SKREE
HMM?
OH. IT'S YOU.
WHAT'RE YOU DOING HERE?

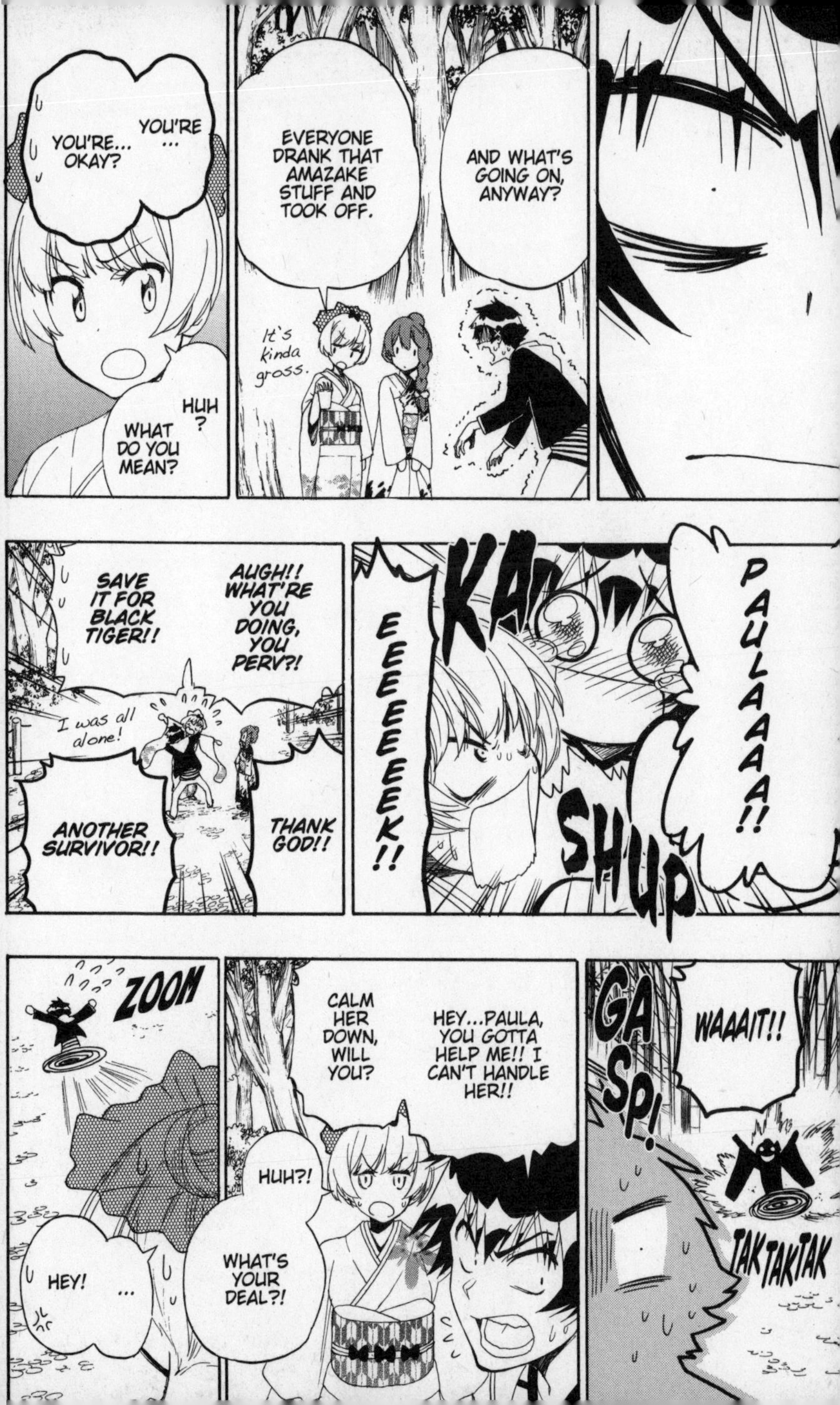
AND WHAT'S GOING ON, ANYWAY?
EVERYONE DRANK THAT AMAZAKE STUFF AND TOOK OFF.
It's kinda gross.
YOU'RE ...
YOU'RE... OKAY?
HUH?
WHAT DO YOU MEAN?
PAULAAAAA!!
KA
EEEEEEEEK!!
SHUP
AUGH!! WHAT'RE YOU DOING, YOU PERV?!
SAVE IT FOR BLACK TIGER!!
THANK GOD!!
I was all alone!
ANOTHER SURVIVOR!!
WAAAIT!!
GASP!
TAKTAKTAK
HEY...PAULA, YOU GOTTA HELP ME!! I CAN'T HANDLE HER!!
CALM HER DOWN, WILL YOU?
HUH?!
WHAT'S YOUR DEAL?!
ZOOM
...
HEY!

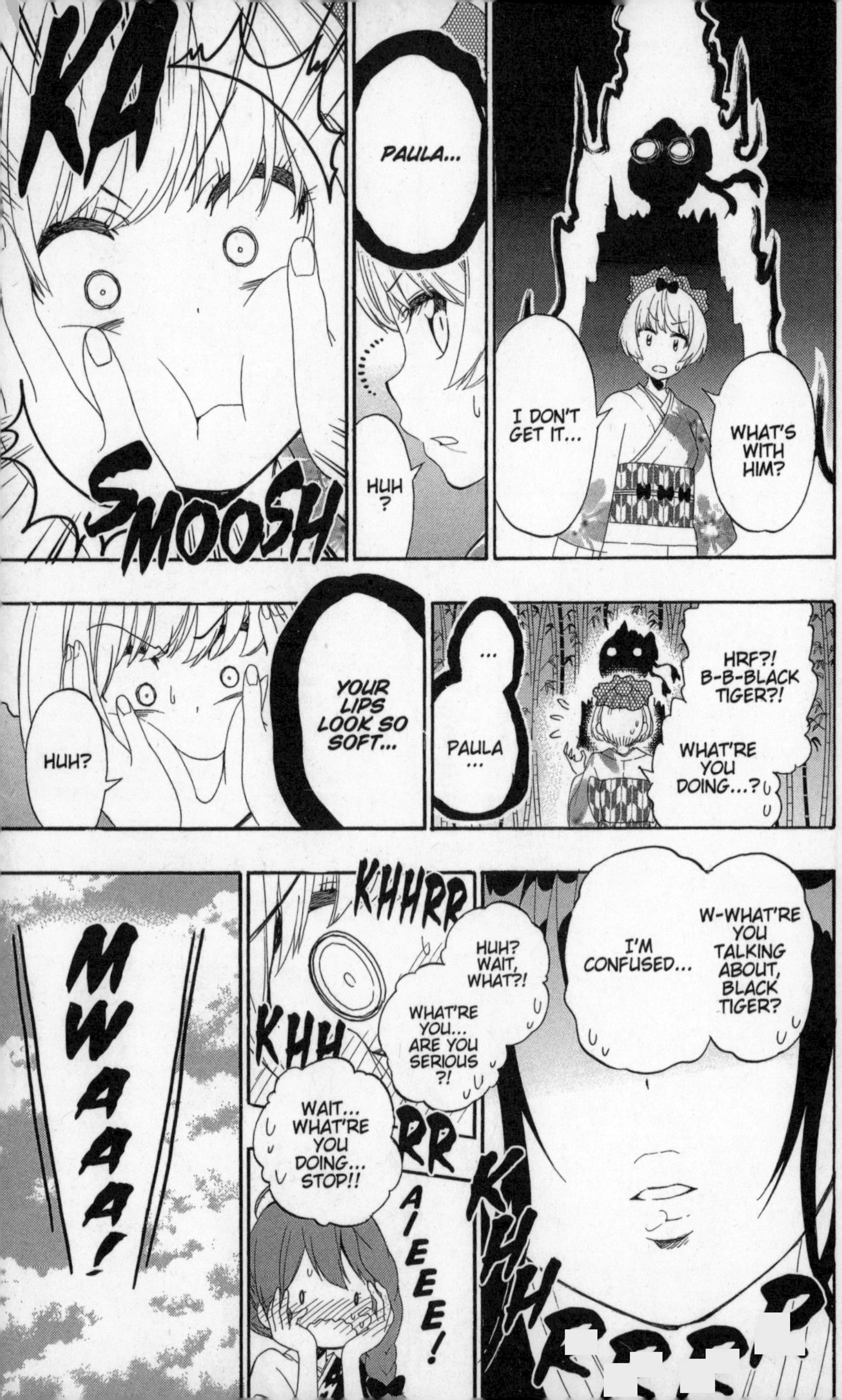
WHAT'S WITH HIM?
I DON'T GET IT...
PAULA...
HUH?
KA
SMOOSH
HRF?! B-B-BLACK TIGER?!
WHAT'RE YOU DOING...?
...
PAULA...
YOUR LIPS LOOK SO SOFT...
HUH?
W-WHAT'RE YOU TALKING ABOUT, BLACK TIGER?
I'M CONFUSED...
KHHRR
HUH? WAIT, WHAT?!
WHAT'RE YOU... ARE YOU SERIOUS?!
KHH
RR
WAIT... WHAT'RE YOU DOING... STOP!!
AIEEEE!
MWAAA!

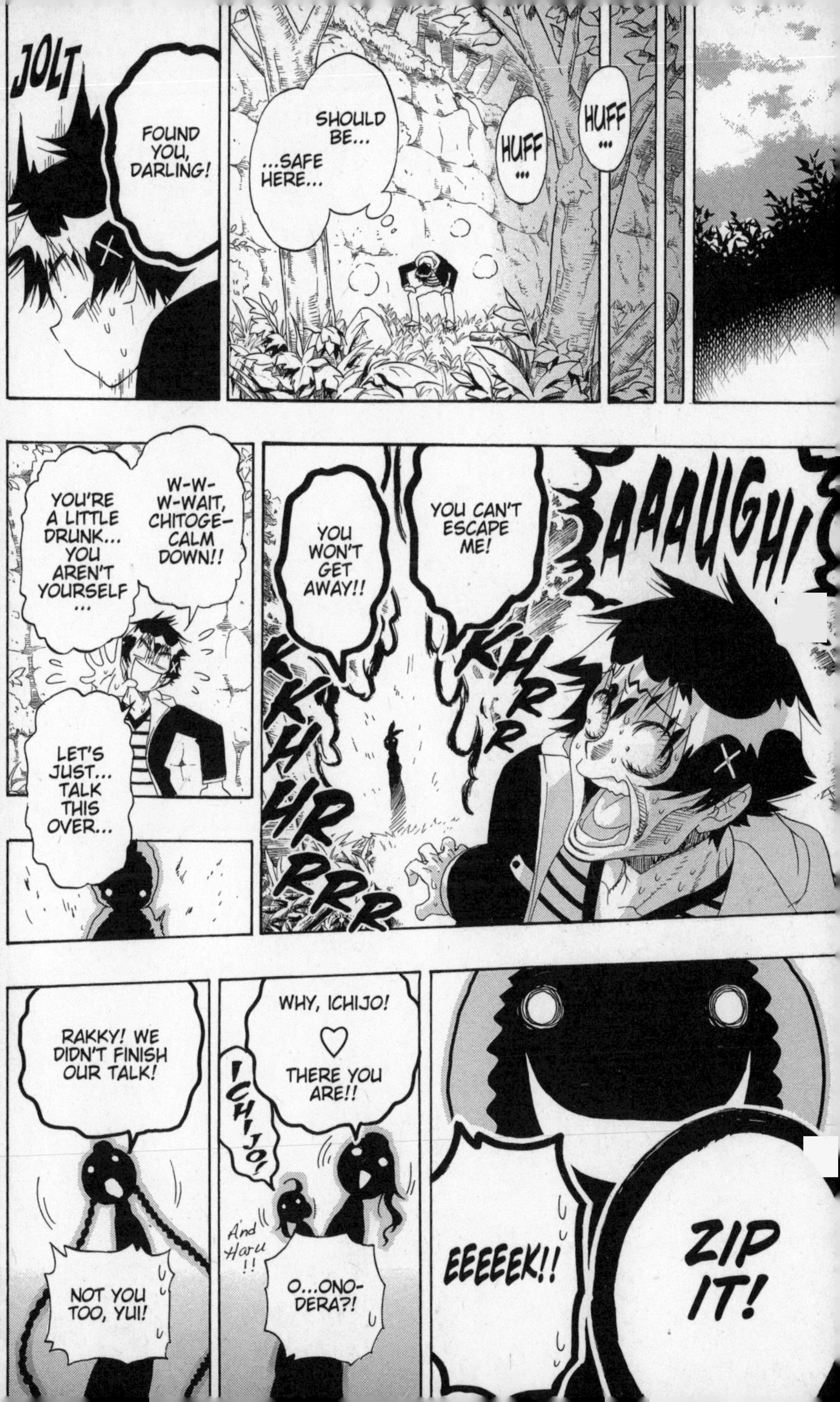
HUFF...
HUFF...
SHOULD BE... ...SAFE HERE...
JOLT
FOUND YOU, DARLING!
AAAUGH!
YOU CAN'T ESCAPE ME!
KHRRR
YOU WON'T GET AWAY!!
KKHHRRRR
W-W-W-WAIT, CHITOGE—CALM DOWN!!
YOU'RE A LITTLE DRUNK... YOU AREN'T YOURSELF...
LET'S JUST... TALK THIS OVER...
ZIP IT!
EEEEEK!!
WHY, ICHIJO! ♡ THERE YOU ARE!!
ICHIJO!
And Haru!!
O...ONODERA?!
RAKKY! WE DIDN'T FINISH OUR TALK!
NOT YOU TOO, YUI!

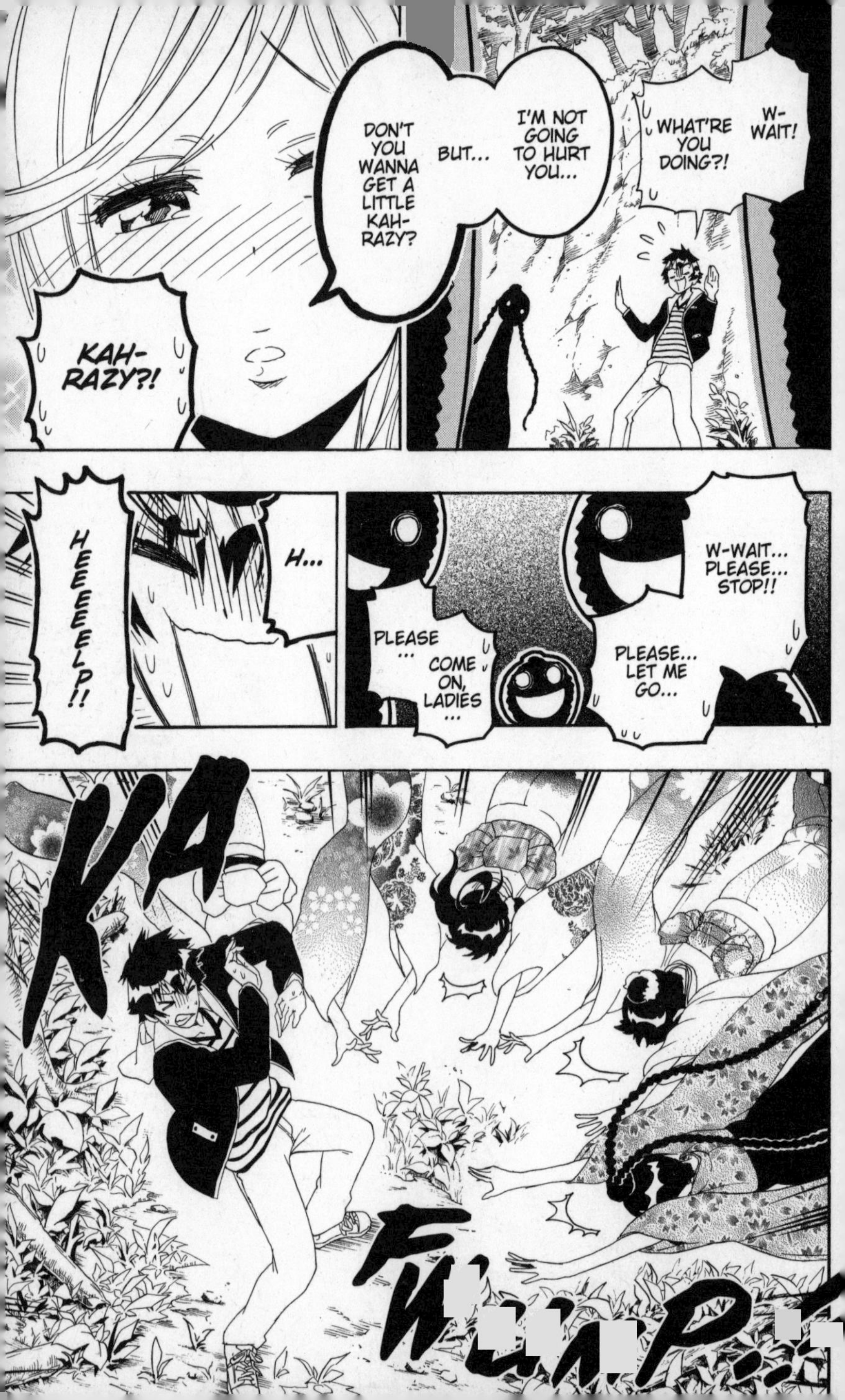
W-WAIT!
WHAT'RE YOU DOING?!
I'M NOT GOING TO HURT YOU...
BUT...
DON'T YOU WANNA GET A LITTLE KAH-RAZY?
KAH-RAZY?!
W-WAIT... PLEASE... STOP!!
PLEASE... LET ME GO...
COME ON, LADIES...
PLEASE...
H...
HEEEEEELP!!
KA

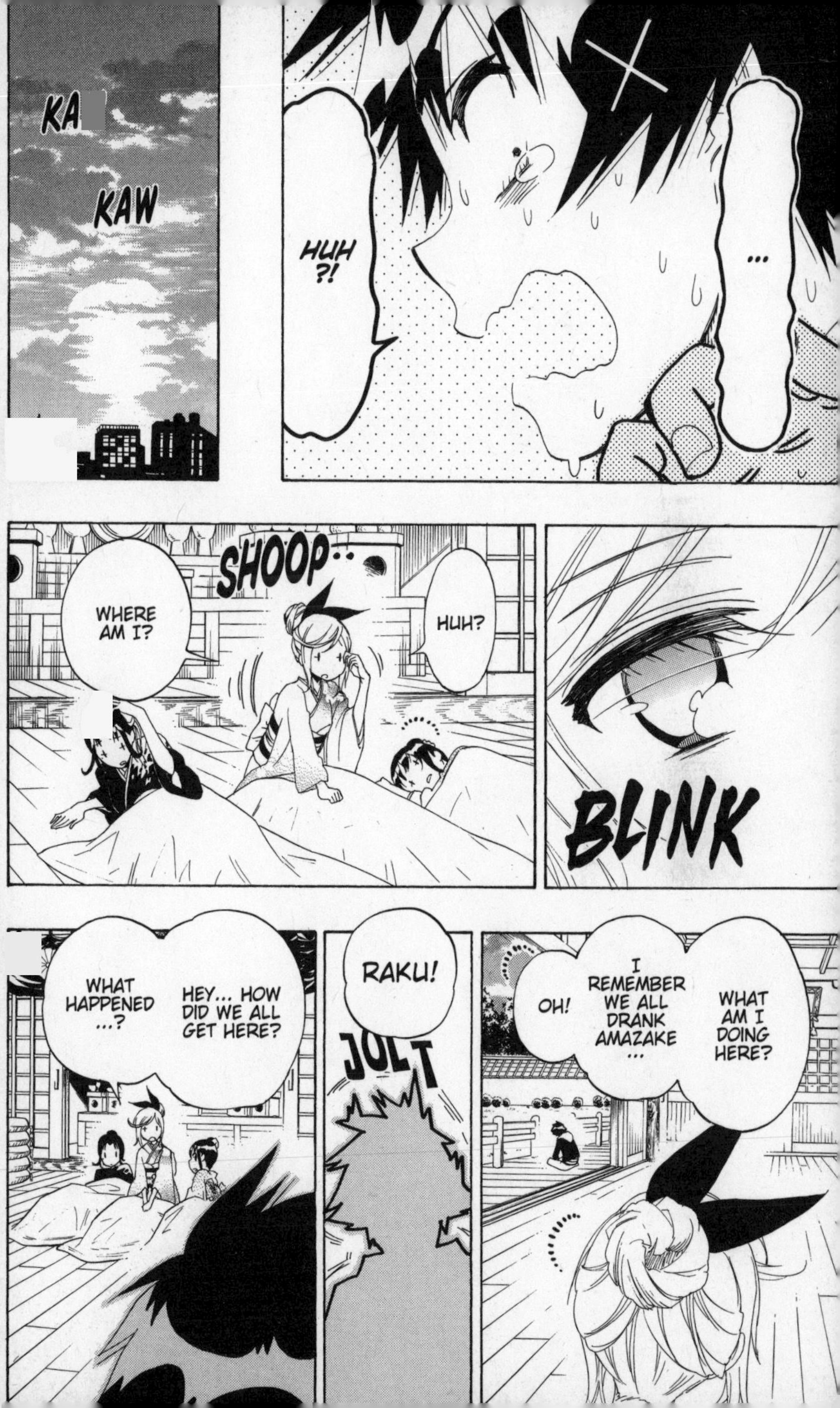
...
HUH ?!
KA
KAW
BLINK
HUH?
SHOOP
WHERE AM I?
WHAT AM I DOING HERE?
I REMEMBER WE ALL DRANK AMAZAKE ...
OH!
RAKU!
JOLT
HEY... HOW DID WE ALL GET HERE?
WHAT HAPPENED ...?

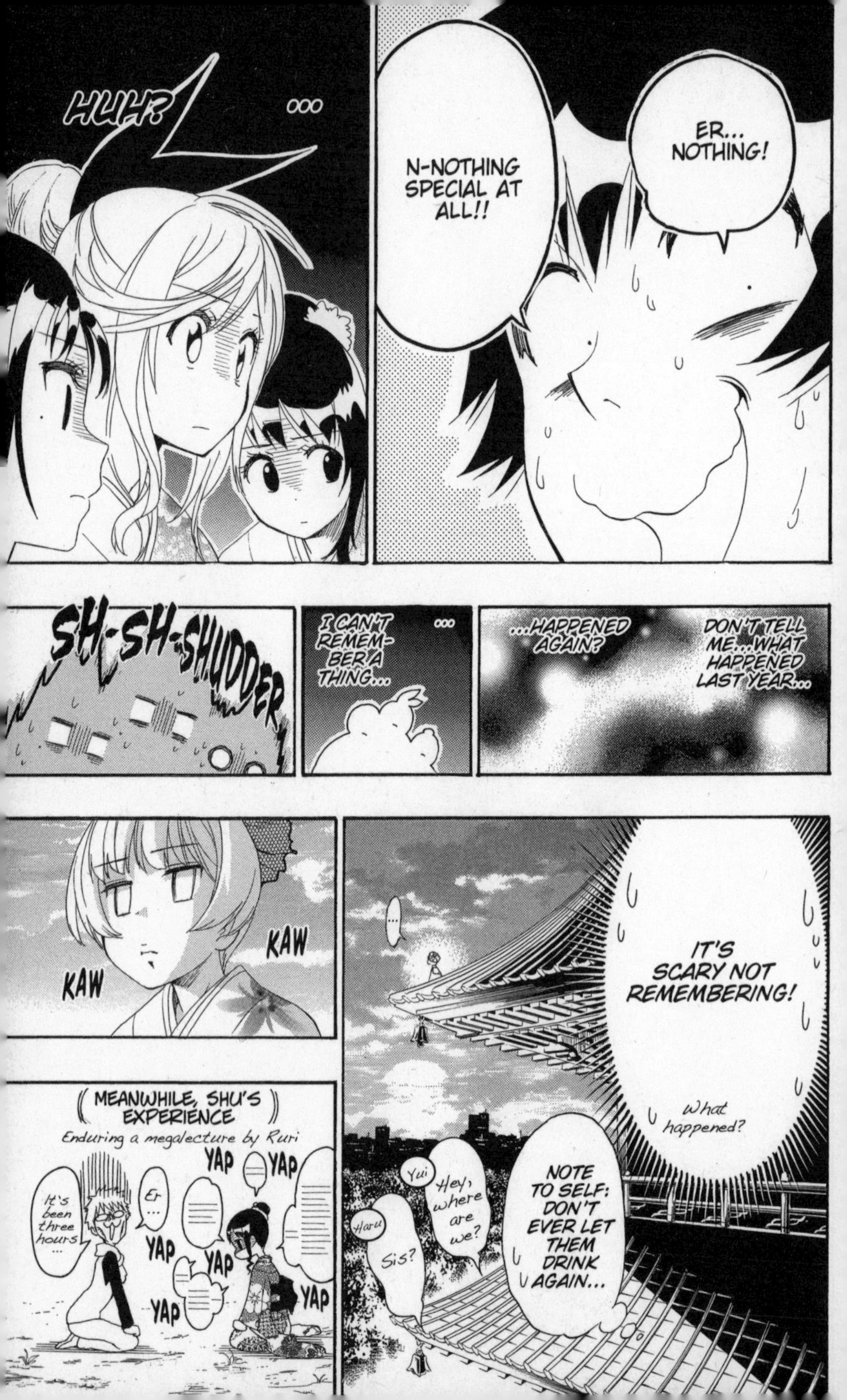
ER... NOTHING!
N-NOTHING SPECIAL AT ALL!!
...
HUH?
DON'T TELL ME... WHAT HAPPENED LAST YEAR...
...HAPPENED AGAIN?
...
I CAN'T REMEM-BER A THING...
SH-SH-SHUDDER
IT'S SCARY NOT REMEMBERING!
...
What happened?
NOTE TO SELF: DON'T EVER LET THEM DRINK AGAIN...
Yui
Hey, where are we?
Haru
Sis?
KAW
KAW
MEANWHILE, SHU'S EXPERIENCE
Enduring a megalecture by Ruri
YAP
YAP
Er ...
It's been three hours ...
YAP
YAP
YAP
YAP

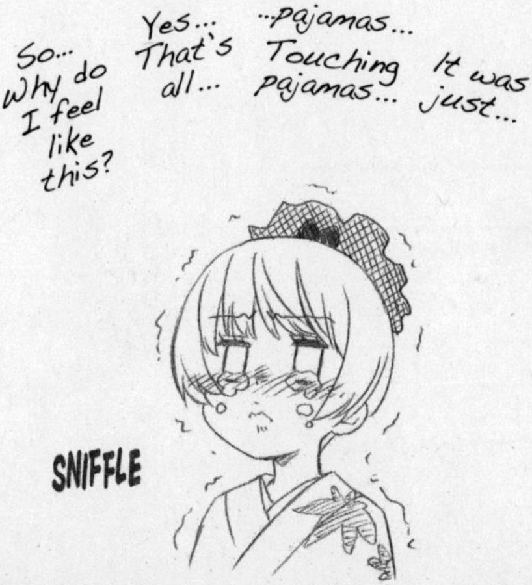
It was just...
...pajamas... Touching pajamas...
Yes... That's all...
So... Why do I feel like this?
SNIFFLE

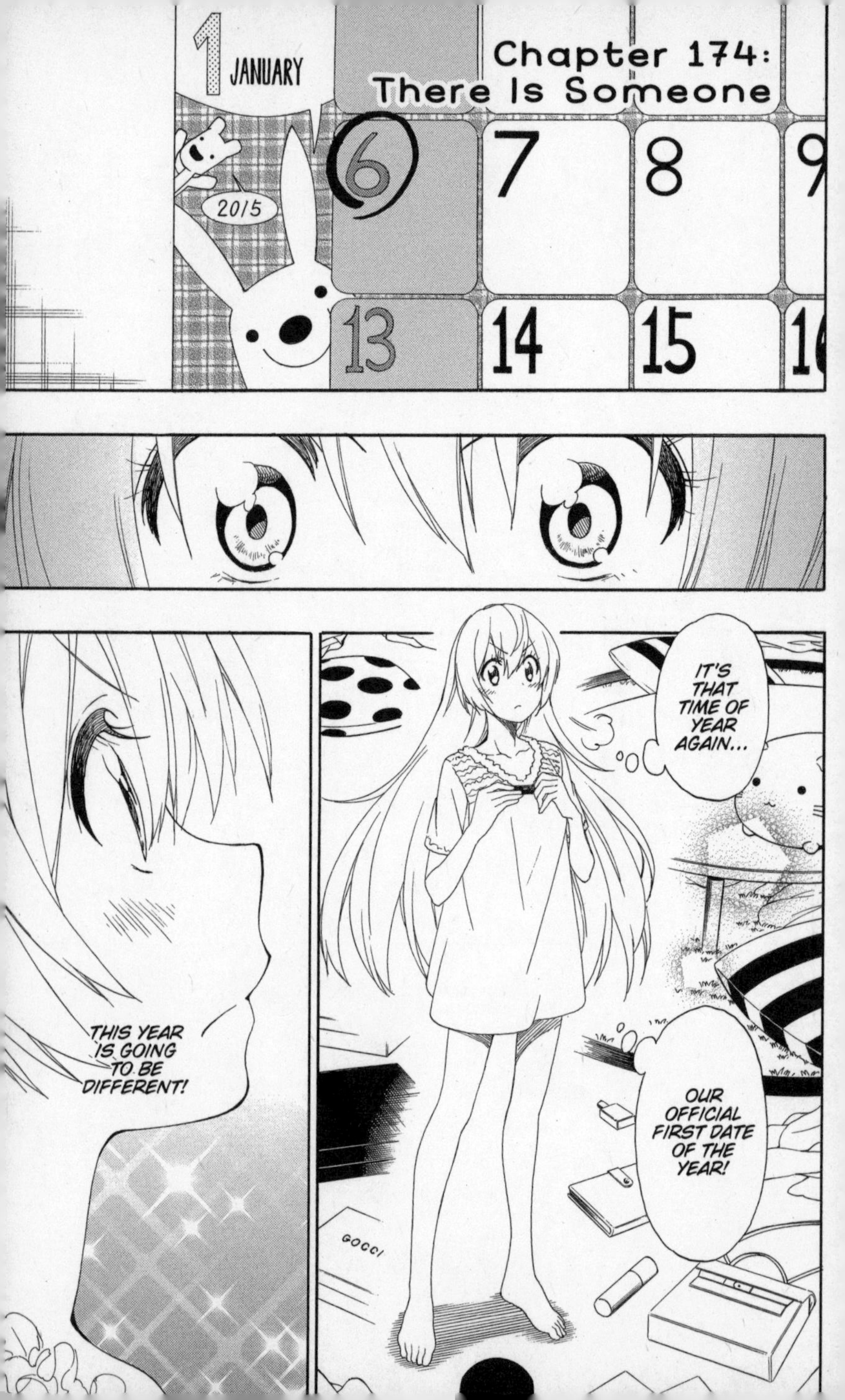
Chapter 174: There Is Someone
1 JANUARY
2015
6
7
8
9
13
14
15
IT'S THAT TIME OF YEAR AGAIN...
OUR OFFICIAL FIRST DATE OF THE YEAR!
GOCCI
THIS YEAR IS GOING TO BE DIFFERENT!

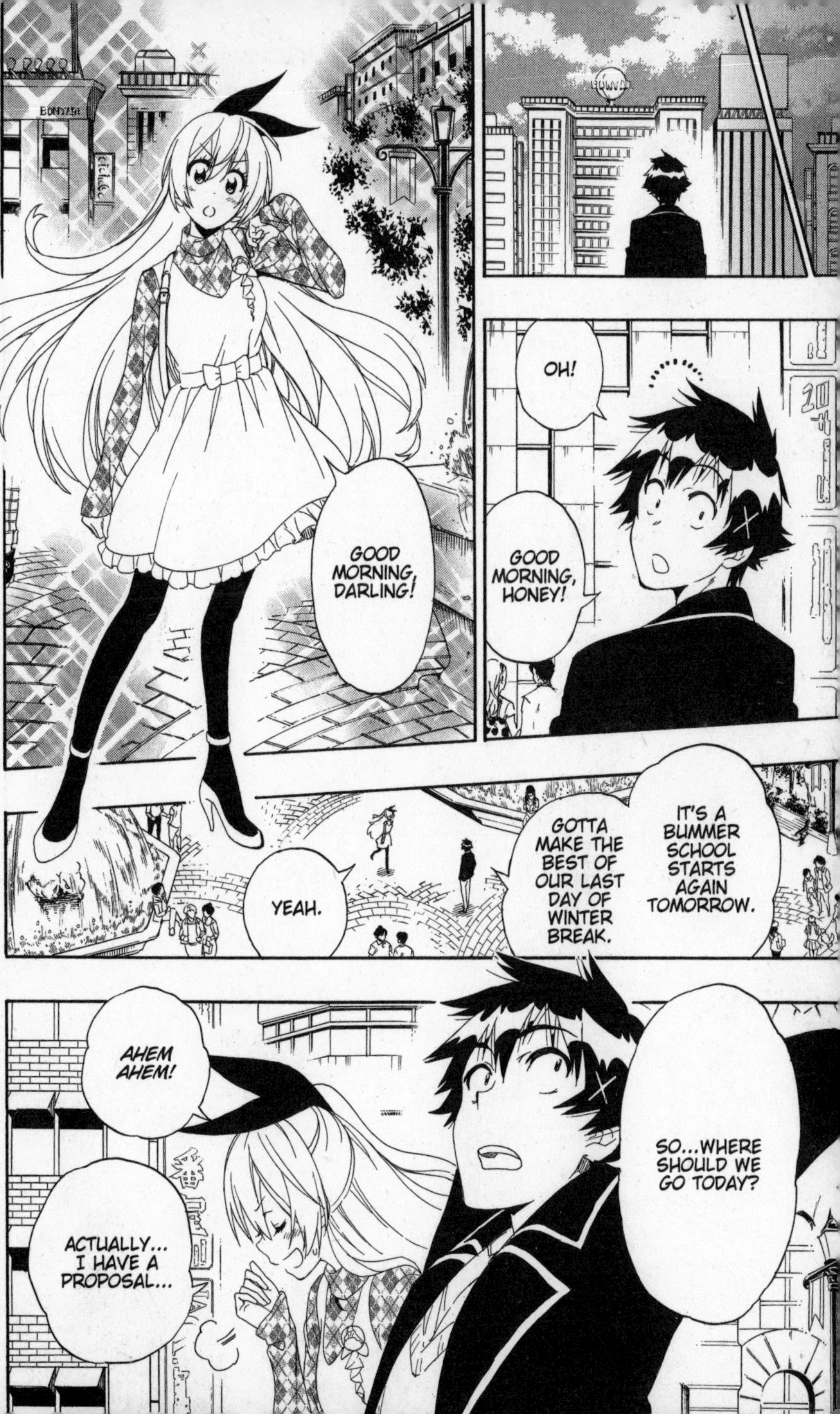
OH!
GOOD MORNING, HONEY!
GOOD MORNING, DARLING!
IT'S A BUMMER SCHOOL STARTS AGAIN TOMORROW.
GOTTA MAKE THE BEST OF OUR LAST DAY OF WINTER BREAK.
YEAH.
SO...WHERE SHOULD WE GO TODAY?
AHEM AHEM!
ACTUALLY... I HAVE A PROPOSAL...

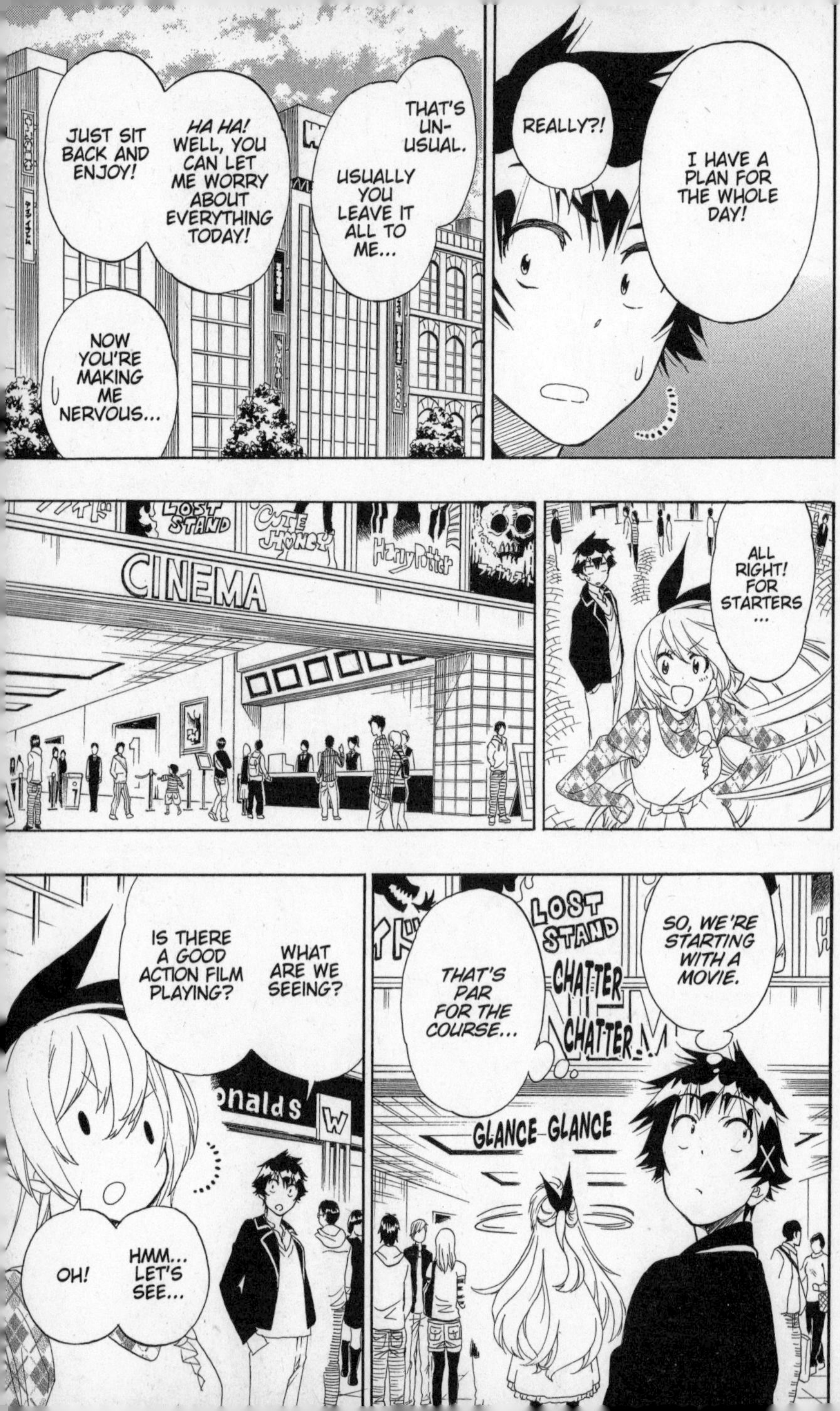
I HAVE A PLAN FOR THE WHOLE DAY!
REALLY?!
THAT'S UN-USUAL.
USUALLY YOU LEAVE IT ALL TO ME...
HA HA! WELL, YOU CAN LET ME WORRY ABOUT EVERYTHING TODAY!
JUST SIT BACK AND ENJOY!
NOW YOU'RE MAKING ME NERVOUS...
ALL RIGHT! FOR STARTERS...
LOST STAND
CUTE HONEY
Henry Potter
CINEMA
SO, WE'RE STARTING WITH A MOVIE.
LOST STAND
CHATTER CHATTER
THAT'S PAR FOR THE COURSE...
GLANCE GLANCE
WHAT ARE WE SEEING?
IS THERE A GOOD ACTION FILM PLAYING?
...
HMM... LET'S SEE...
OH!

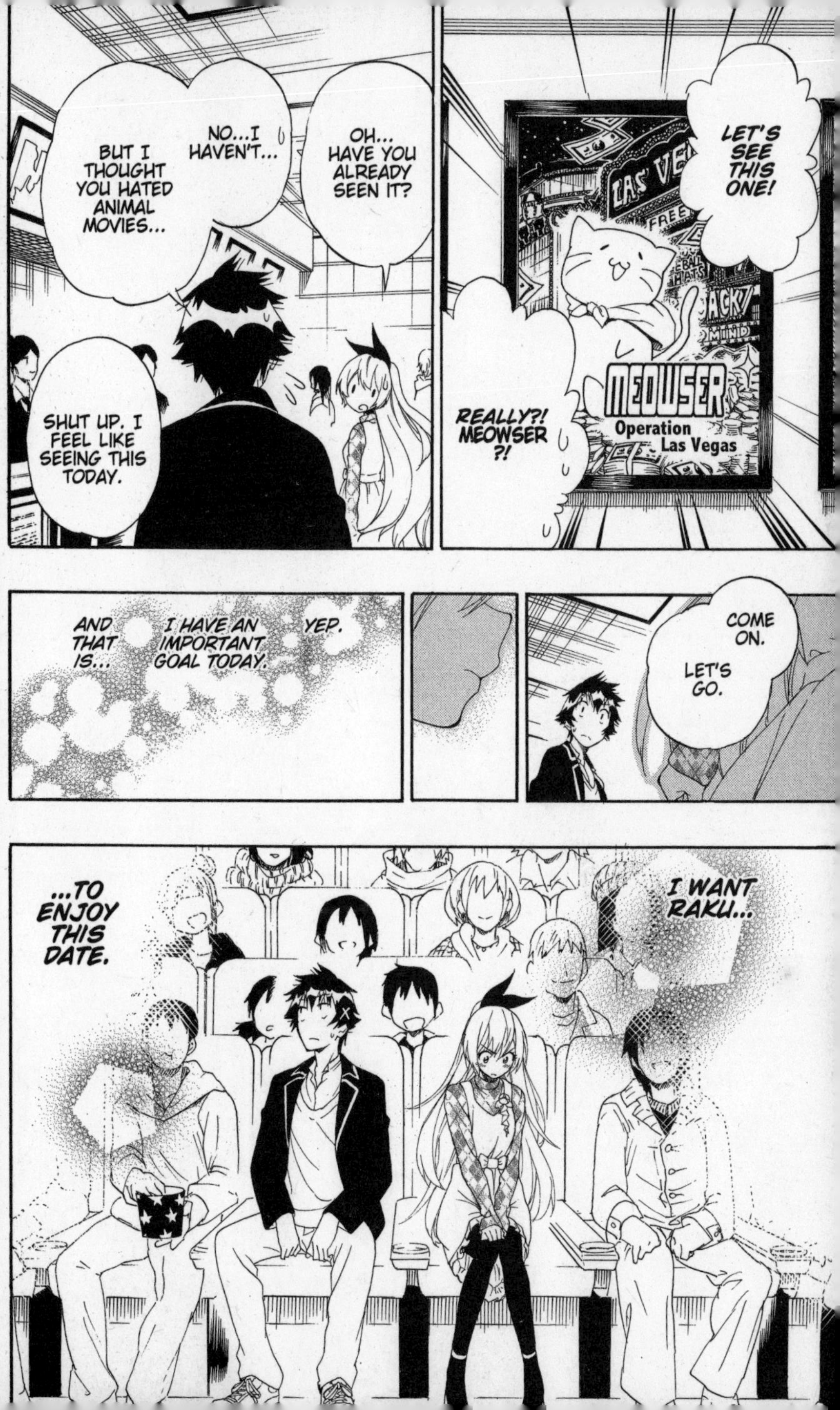
LET'S SEE THIS ONE!
REALLY?! MEOWSER ?!
MEOWSER
Operation Las Vegas
OH... HAVE YOU ALREADY SEEN IT?
NO...I HAVEN'T...
BUT I THOUGHT YOU HATED ANIMAL MOVIES...
SHUT UP. I FEEL LIKE SEEING THIS TODAY.
COME ON.
LET'S GO.
YEP.
I HAVE AN IMPORTANT GOAL TODAY.
AND THAT IS...
I WANT RAKU...
...TO ENJOY THIS DATE.

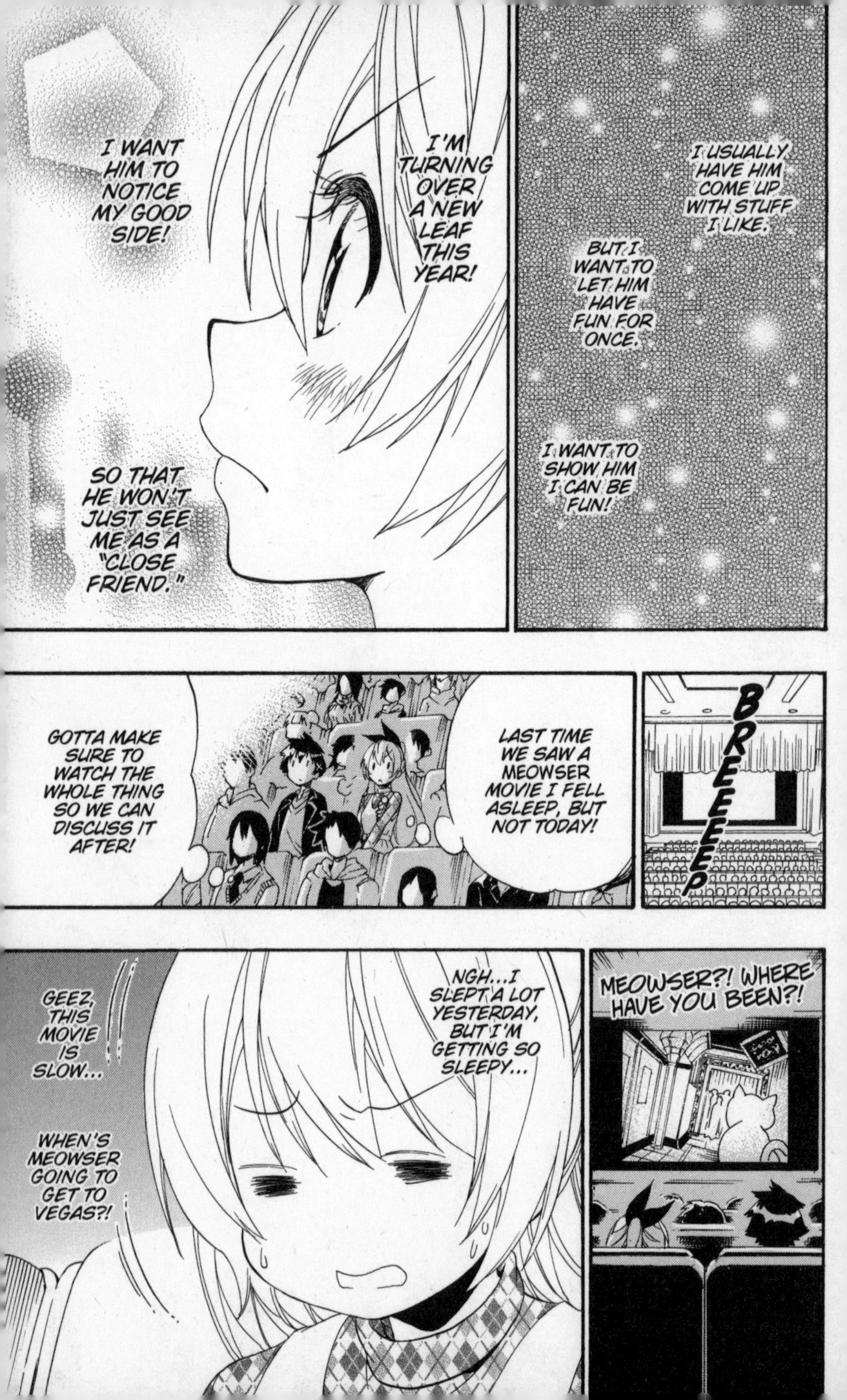
I USUALLY HAVE HIM COME UP WITH STUFF I LIKE.
BUT I WANT TO LET HIM HAVE FUN FOR ONCE.
I WANT TO SHOW HIM I CAN BE FUN!
I'M TURNING OVER A NEW LEAF THIS YEAR!
I WANT HIM TO NOTICE MY GOOD SIDE!
SO THAT HE WON'T JUST SEE ME AS A "CLOSE FRIEND."
BREEEEEP
LAST TIME WE SAW A MEOWSER MOVIE I FELL ASLEEP, BUT NOT TODAY!
GOTTA MAKE SURE TO WATCH THE WHOLE THING SO WE CAN DISCUSS IT AFTER!
MEOWSER?! WHERE HAVE YOU BEEN?!
NGH...I SLEPT A LOT YESTERDAY, BUT I'M GETTING SO SLEEPY...
GEEZ, THIS MOVIE IS SLOW...
WHEN'S MEOWSER GOING TO GET TO VEGAS?!

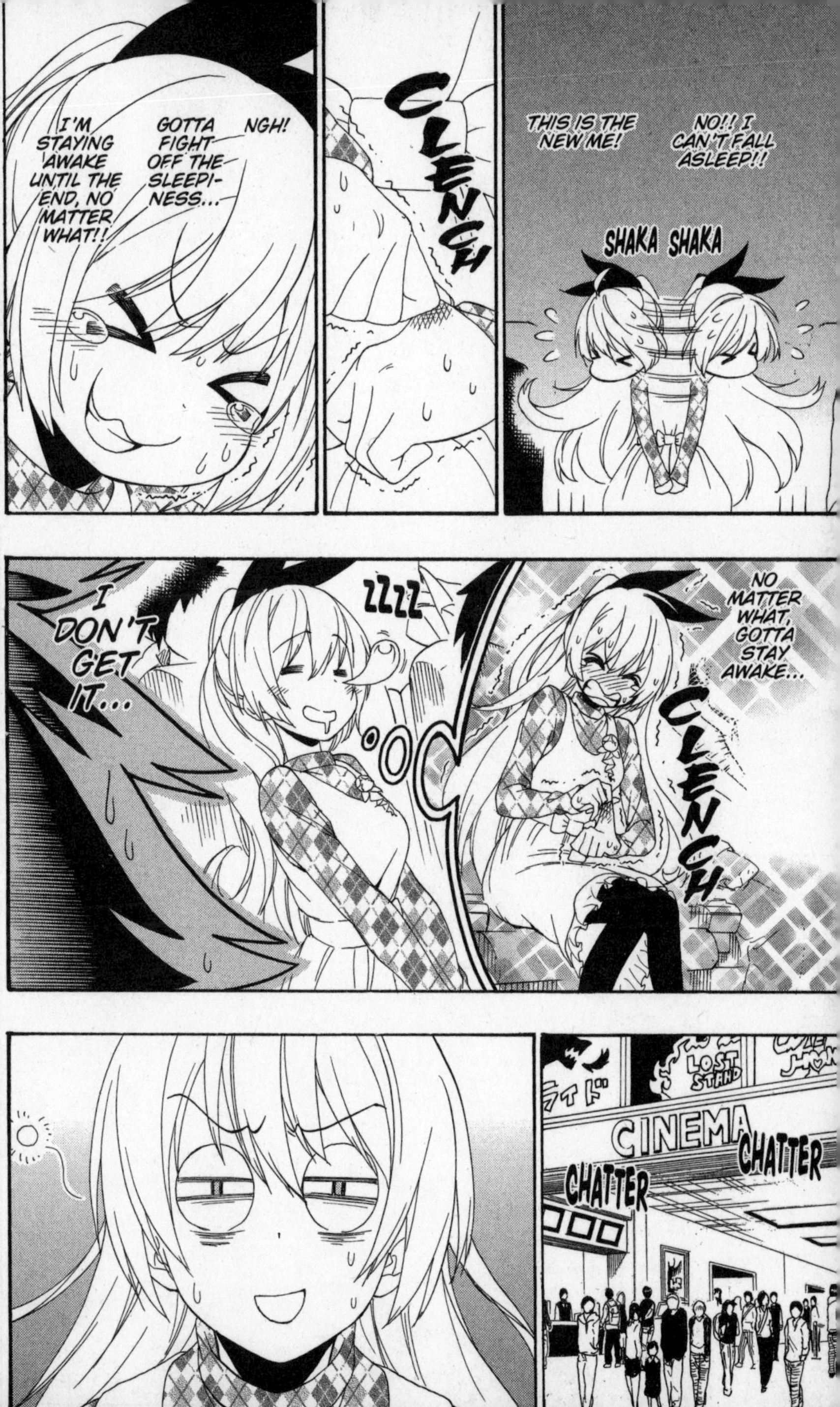
NO!! I CAN'T FALL ASLEEP!!
THIS IS THE NEW ME!
SHAKA SHAKA
CLENCH
NGH!
GOTTA FIGHT OFF THE SLEEPI-NESS...
I'M STAYING AWAKE UNTIL THE END, NO MATTER WHAT!!
NO MATTER WHAT, GOTTA STAY AWAKE...
CLENCH
ZZZZ
I DON'T GET IT...
LOST STAND
CINEMA
CHATTER
CHATTER

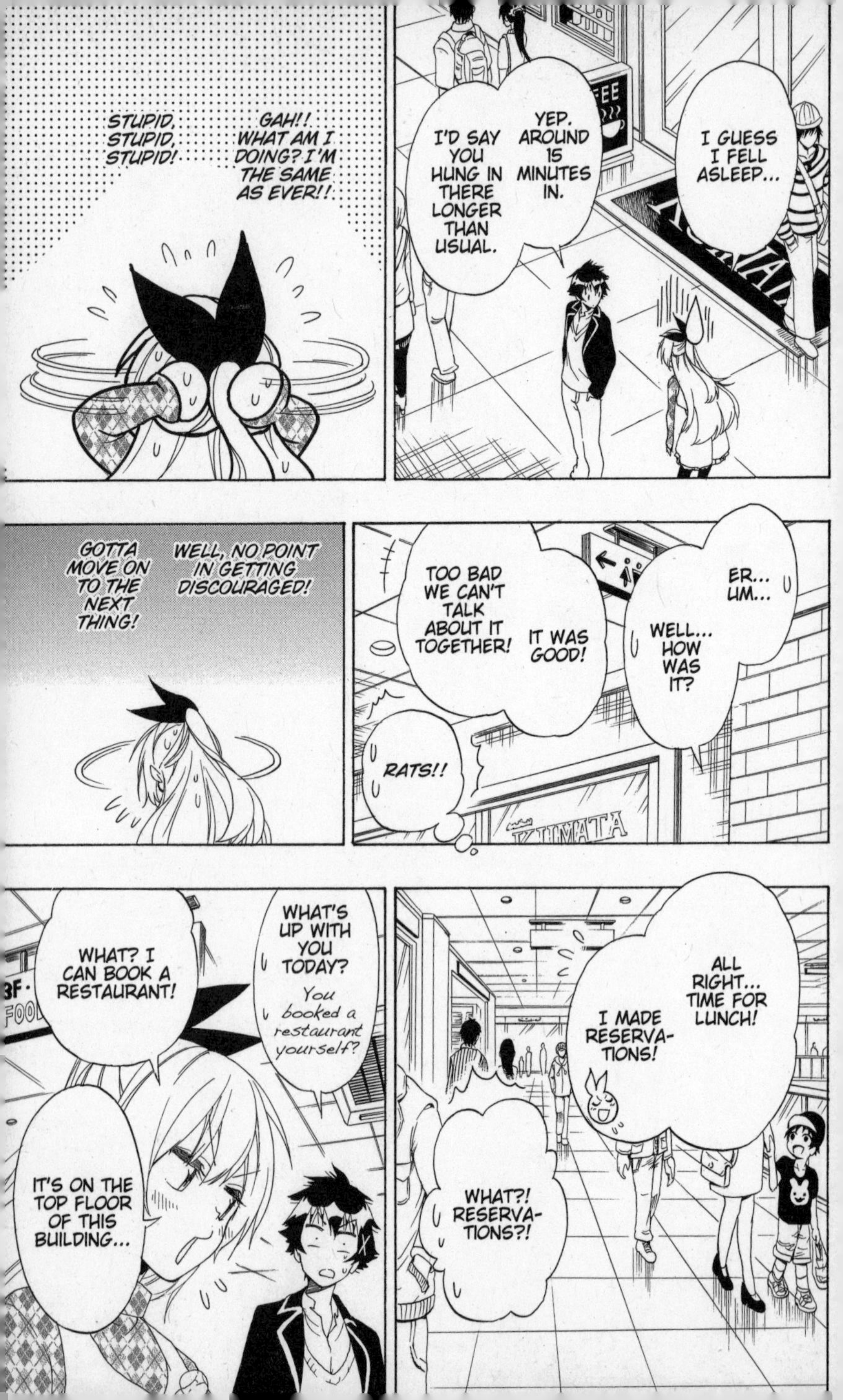
I GUESS I FELL ASLEEP...
YEP. AROUND 15 MINUTES IN.
I'D SAY YOU HUNG IN THERE LONGER THAN USUAL.
GAH!! WHAT AM I DOING? I'M THE SAME AS EVER!!
STUPID, STUPID, STUPID!
ER... UM...
WELL... HOW WAS IT?
IT WAS GOOD!
TOO BAD WE CAN'T TALK ABOUT IT TOGETHER!
RATS!!
KUMATA
WELL, NO POINT IN GETTING DISCOURAGED!
GOTTA MOVE ON TO THE NEXT THING!
ALL RIGHT... TIME FOR LUNCH!
I MADE RESERVATIONS!
WHAT?! RESERVATIONS?!
WHAT'S UP WITH YOU TODAY? You booked a restaurant yourself?
WHAT? I CAN BOOK A RESTAURANT!
IT'S ON THE TOP FLOOR OF THIS BUILDING...

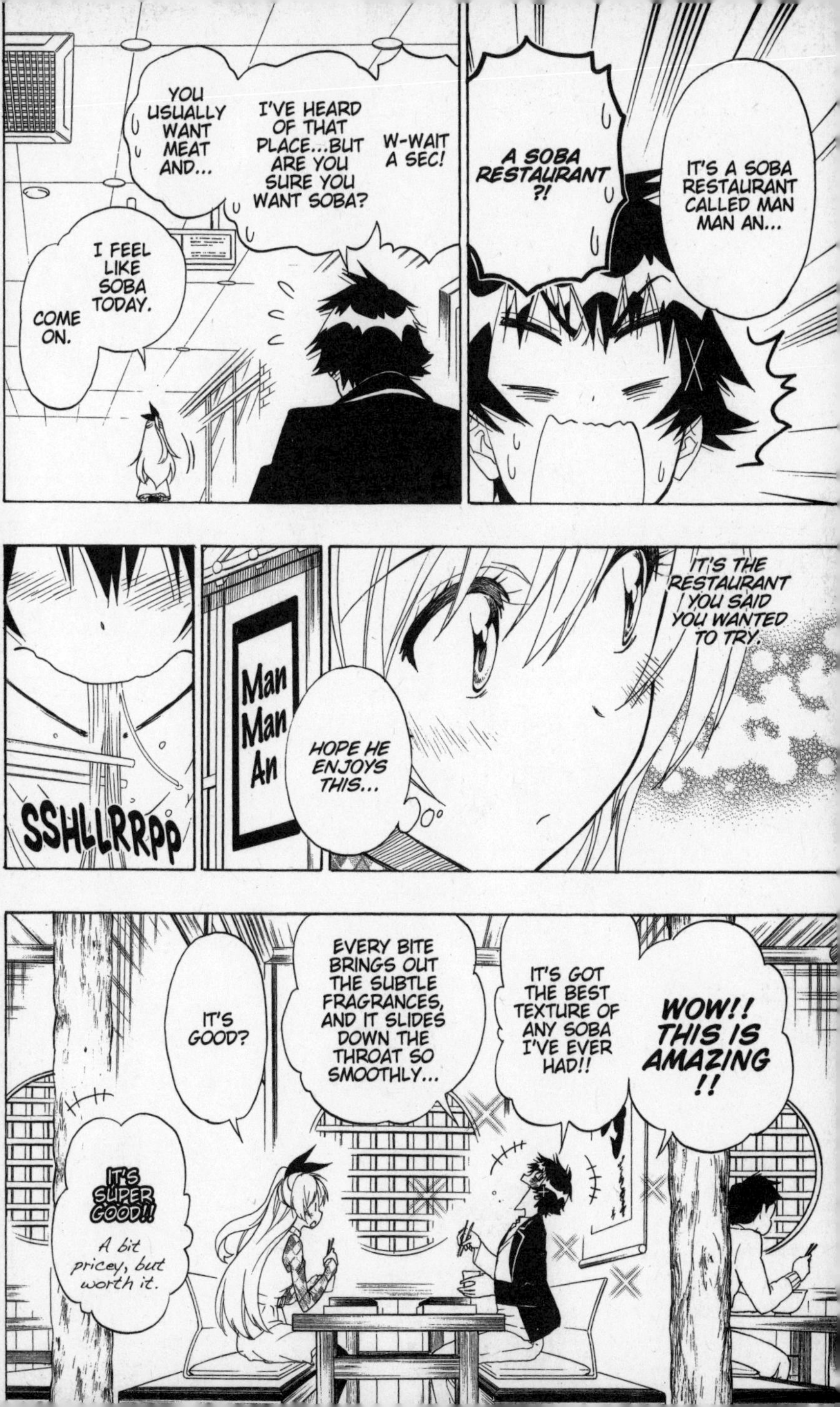
IT'S A SOBA RESTAURANT CALLED MAN MAN AN...
A SOBA RESTAURANT?!
W-WAIT A SEC!
I'VE HEARD OF THAT PLACE...BUT ARE YOU SURE YOU WANT SOBA?
YOU USUALLY WANT MEAT AND...
I FEEL LIKE SOBA TODAY.
COME ON.
IT'S THE RESTAURANT YOU SAID YOU WANTED TO TRY.
HOPE HE ENJOYS THIS...
Man Man An
SSHLLRRPP
WOW!! THIS IS AMAZING!!
IT'S GOT THE BEST TEXTURE OF ANY SOBA I'VE EVER HAD!!
EVERY BITE BRINGS OUT THE SUBTLE FRAGRANCES, AND IT SLIDES DOWN THE THROAT SO SMOOTHLY...
IT'S GOOD?
IT'S SUPER GOOD!!
A bit pricey, but worth it.

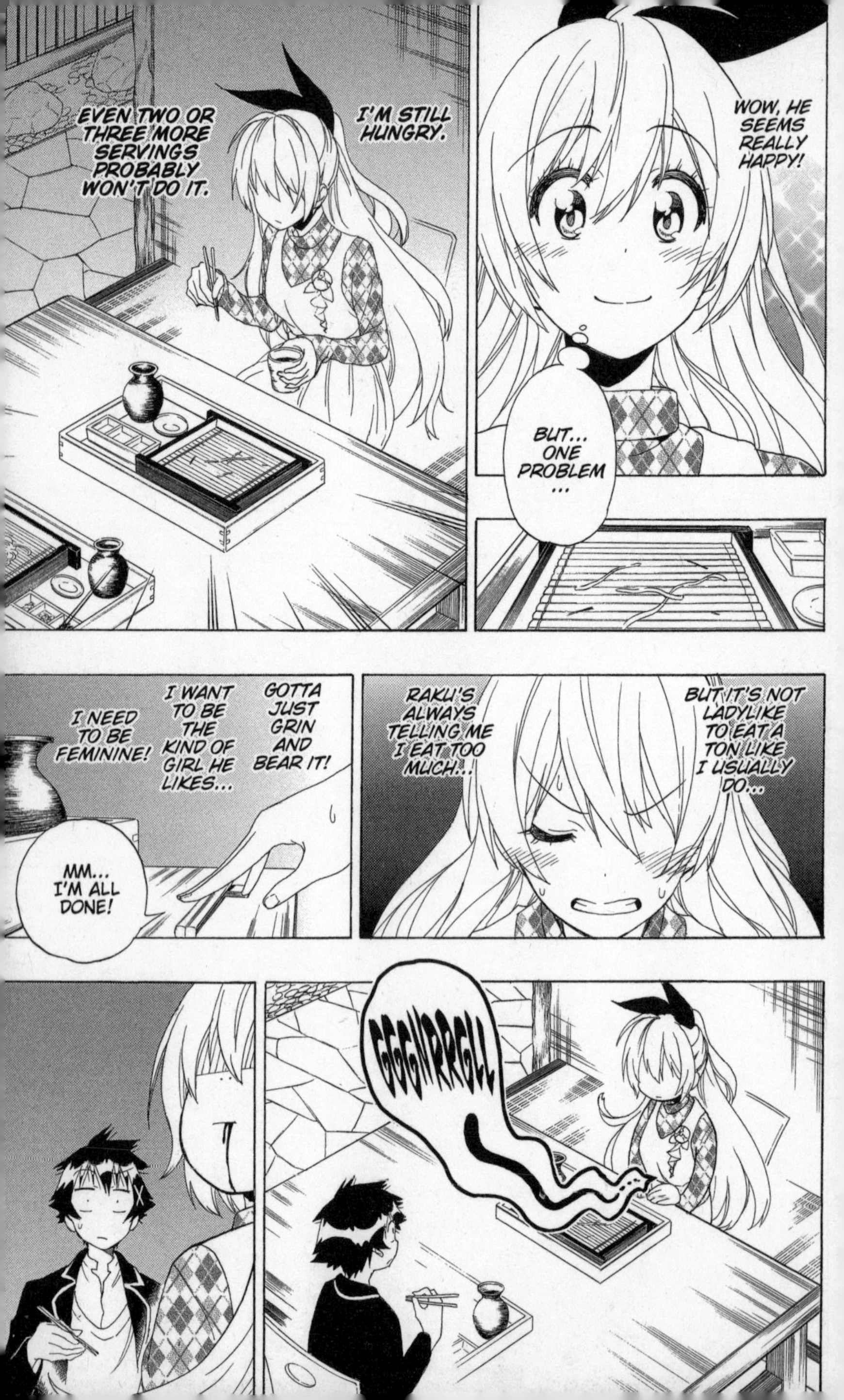
WOW, HE SEEMS REALLY HAPPY!
BUT... ONE PROBLEM...
I'M STILL HUNGRY.
EVEN TWO OR THREE MORE SERVINGS PROBABLY WON'T DO IT.
BUT IT'S NOT LADYLIKE TO EAT A TON LIKE I USUALLY DO...
RAKU'S ALWAYS TELLING ME I EAT TOO MUCH...
GOTTA JUST GRIN AND BEAR IT!
I WANT TO BE THE KIND OF GIRL HE LIKES...
I NEED TO BE FEMININE!
MM... I'M ALL DONE!
GGGNRRGLL

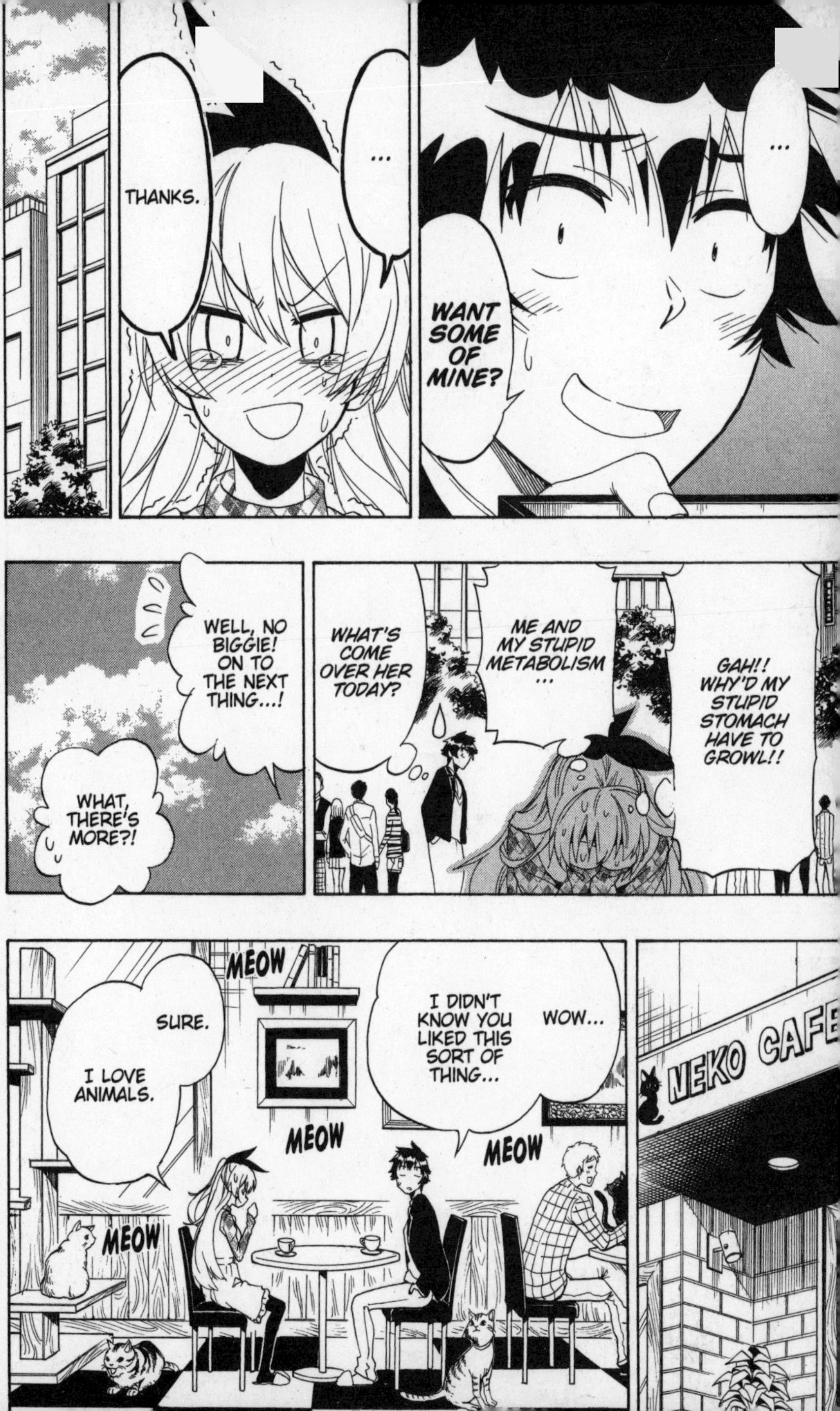
...
WANT SOME OF MINE?
...
THANKS.
GAH!! WHY'D MY STUPID STOMACH HAVE TO GROWL!!
ME AND MY STUPID METABOLISM ...
WHAT'S COME OVER HER TODAY?
WELL, NO BIGGIE! ON TO THE NEXT THING...!
WHAT, THERE'S MORE?!
NEKO CAFE
MEOW
WOW... I DIDN'T KNOW YOU LIKED THIS SORT OF THING...
SURE. I LOVE ANIMALS.
MEOW
MEOW
MEOW

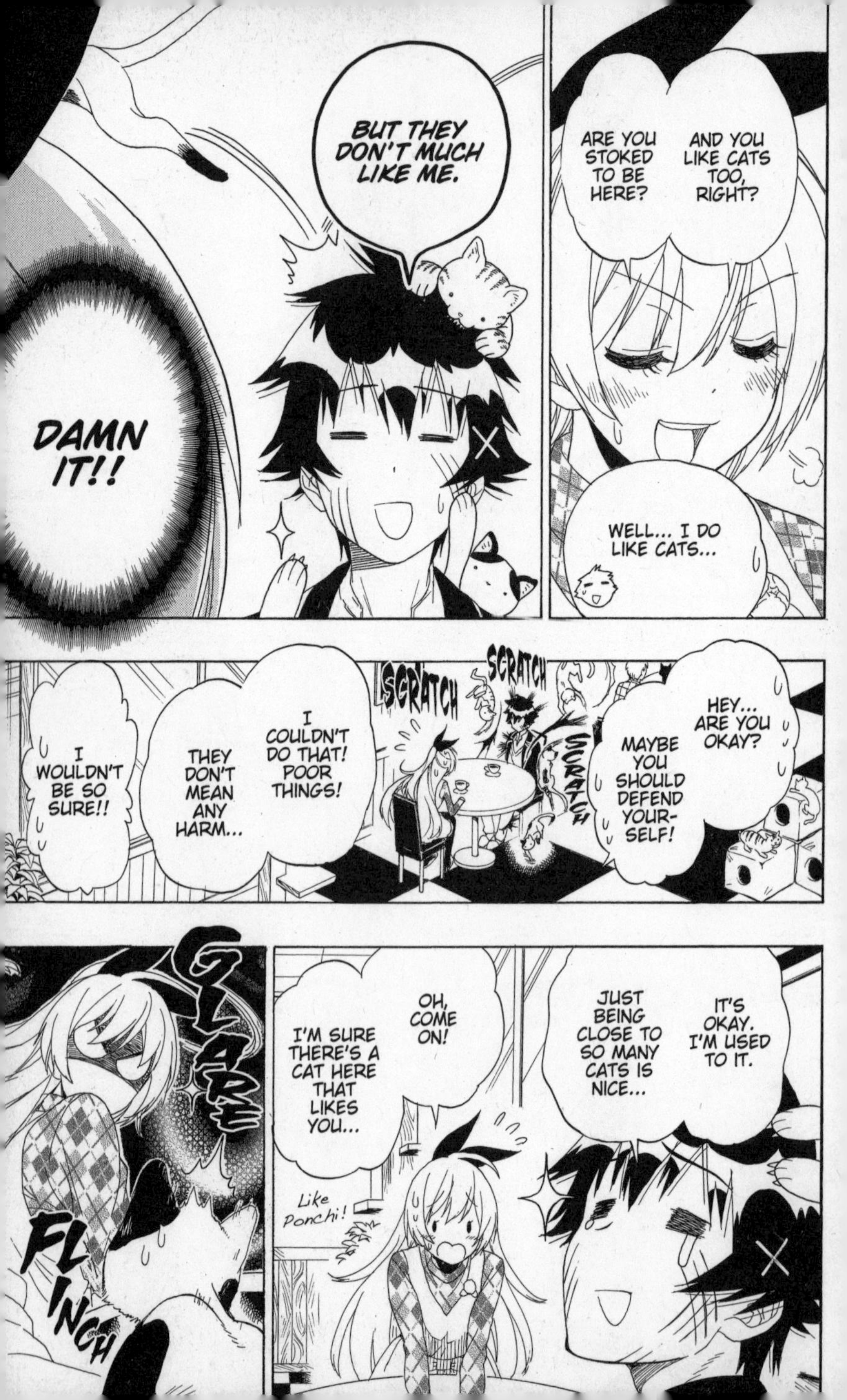
ARE YOU STOKED TO BE HERE?
AND YOU LIKE CATS TOO, RIGHT?
WELL... I DO LIKE CATS...
BUT THEY DON'T MUCH LIKE ME.
DAMN IT!!
HEY... ARE YOU OKAY?
MAYBE YOU SHOULD DEFEND YOUR-SELF!
SCRATCH
SCRATCH
SCRATCH
I COULDN'T DO THAT! POOR THINGS!
THEY DON'T MEAN ANY HARM...
I WOULDN'T BE SO SURE!!
IT'S OKAY. I'M USED TO IT.
JUST BEING CLOSE TO SO MANY CATS IS NICE...
OH, COME ON!
I'M SURE THERE'S A CAT HERE THAT LIKES YOU...
Like Ponchi!
GLARE
FLINCH

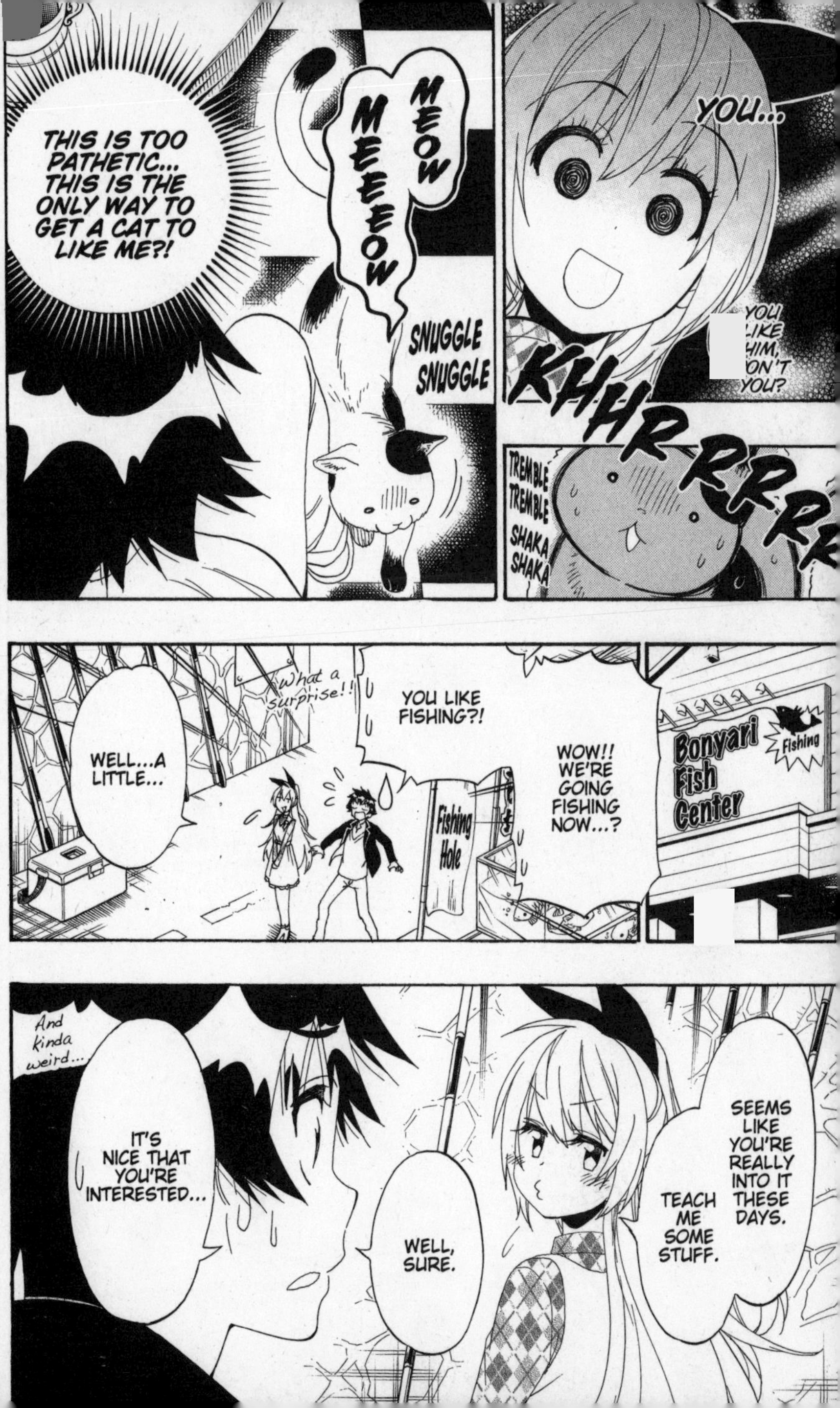
YOU...
YOU LIKE HIM, ON'T YOU?
KHHRRRRK
TREMBLE TREMBLE
SHAKA SHAKA
MEOW
MEEEEOW
SNUGGLE SNUGGLE
THIS IS TOO PATHETIC... THIS IS THE ONLY WAY TO GET A CAT TO LIKE ME?!
Bonyari Fish Center
Fishing
WOW!! WE'RE GOING FISHING NOW...?
Fishing Hole
YOU LIKE FISHING?!
What a surprise!!
WELL...A LITTLE...
SEEMS LIKE YOU'RE REALLY INTO IT THESE DAYS.
TEACH ME SOME STUFF.
WELL, SURE.
IT'S NICE THAT YOU'RE INTERESTED...
And kinda weird...

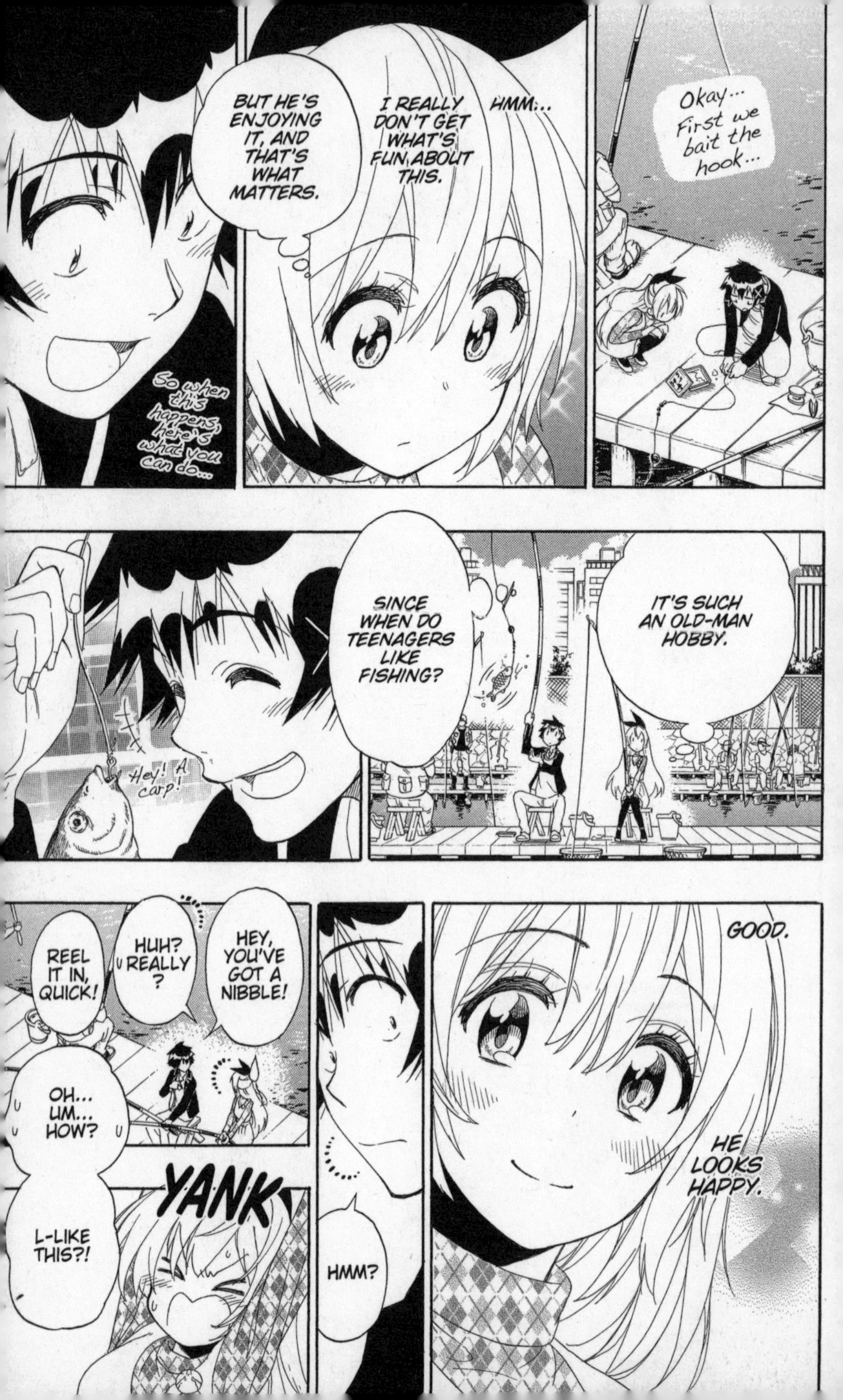
Okay... First we bait the hook...
HMM...
I REALLY DON'T GET WHAT'S FUN ABOUT THIS.
BUT HE'S ENJOYING IT, AND THAT'S WHAT MATTERS.
So when this happens, here's what you can do...
IT'S SUCH AN OLD-MAN HOBBY.
SINCE WHEN DO TEENAGERS LIKE FISHING?
Hey! A carp!
GOOD.
HE LOOKS HAPPY.
HMM?
HEY, YOU'VE GOT A NIBBLE!
HUH? REALLY?
REEL IT IN, QUICK!
OH... UM... HOW?
YANK
L-LIKE THIS?!

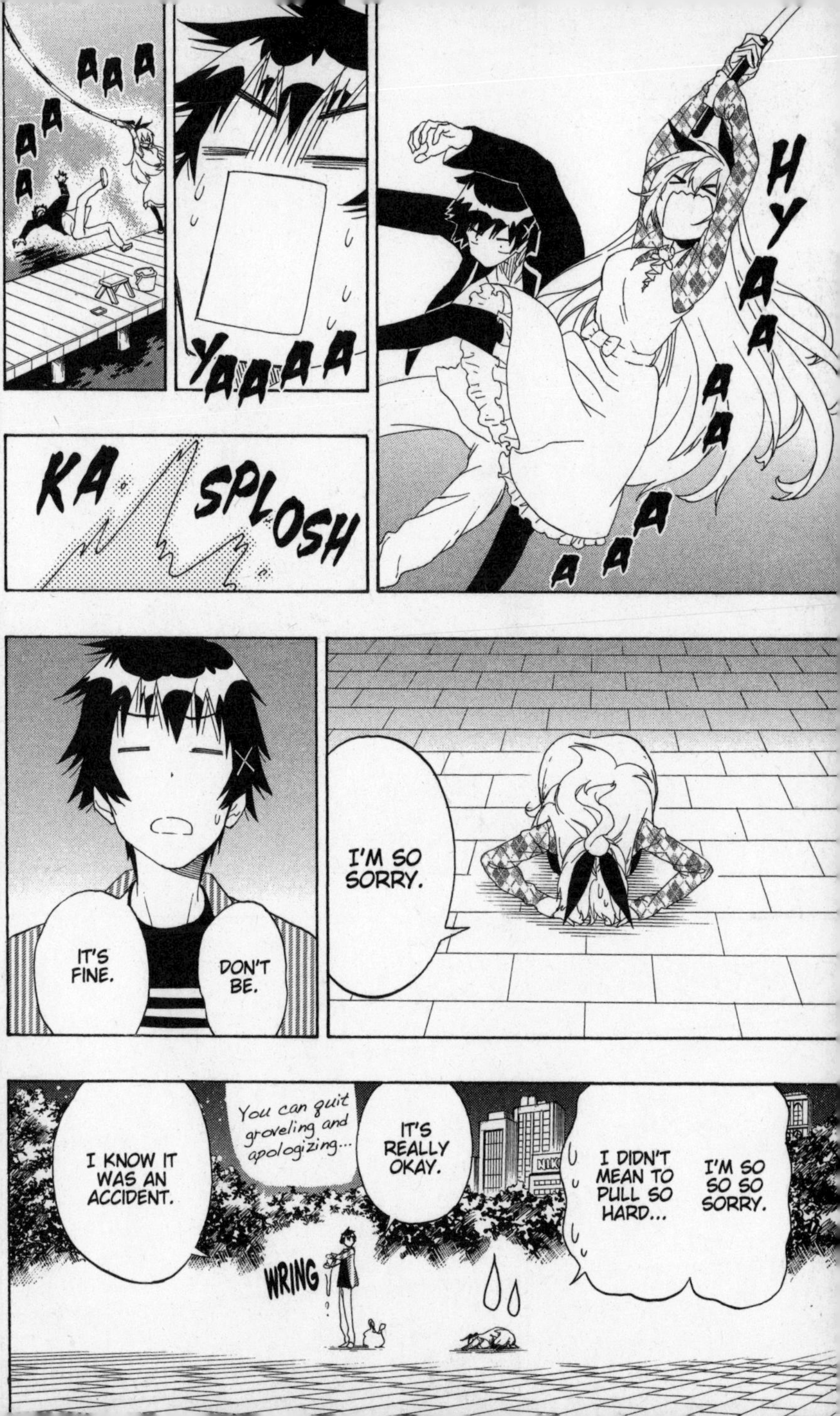

HYAAAAAAAAA
YAAAAA
AAAAAAA
KA SPLOSH
I'M SO SORRY.
DON'T BE.
IT'S FINE.
I'M SO SO SO SORRY.
I DIDN'T MEAN TO PULL SO HARD...
IT'S REALLY OKAY.
You can quit groveling and apologizing...
I KNOW IT WAS AN ACCIDENT.
WRING

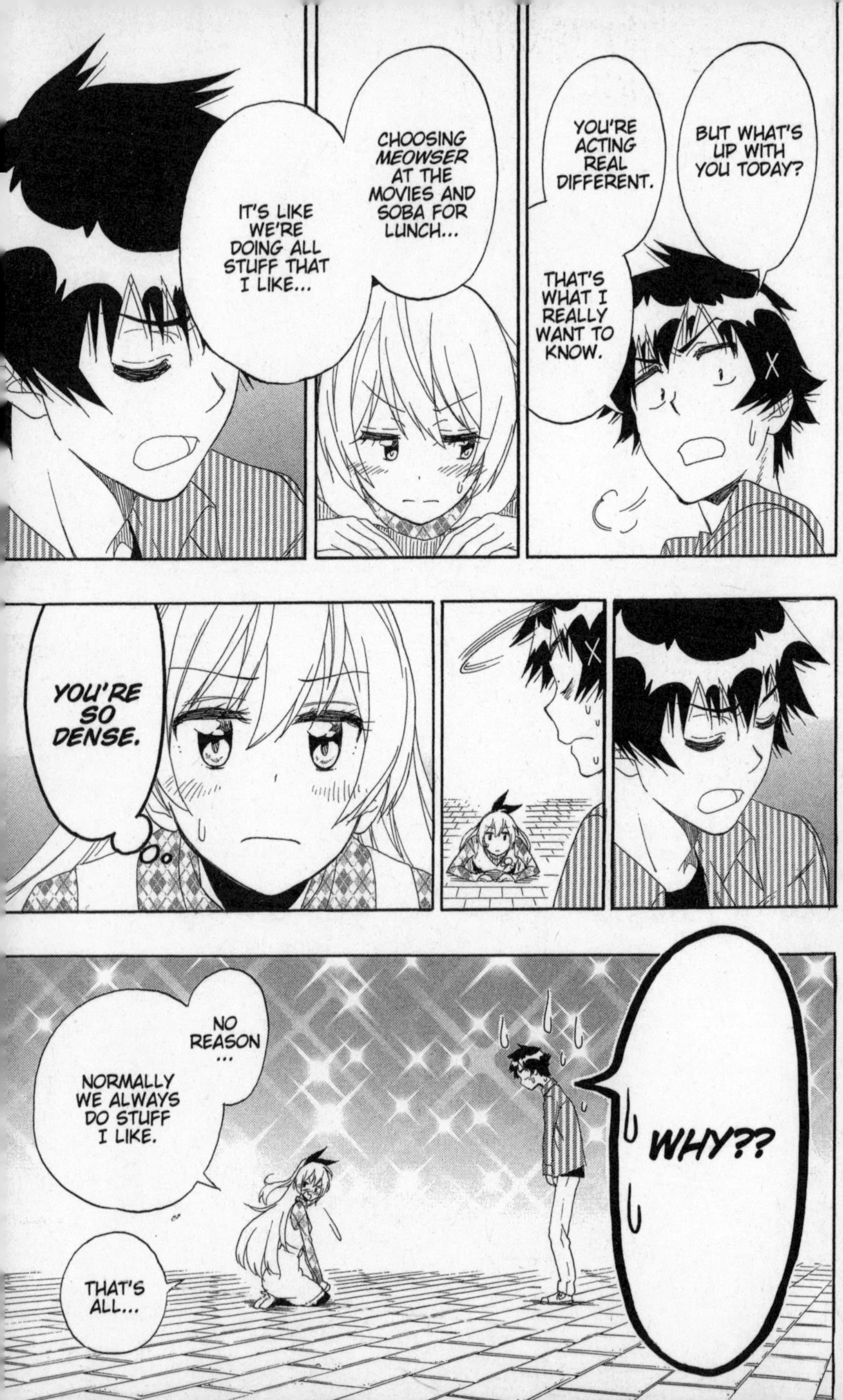
BUT WHAT'S UP WITH YOU TODAY?
YOU'RE ACTING REAL DIFFERENT.
THAT'S WHAT I REALLY WANT TO KNOW.
CHOOSING MEOWSER AT THE MOVIES AND SOBA FOR LUNCH...
IT'S LIKE WE'RE DOING ALL STUFF THAT I LIKE...
YOU'RE SO DENSE.
WHY??
NO REASON...
NORMALLY WE ALWAYS DO STUFF I LIKE.
THAT'S ALL...

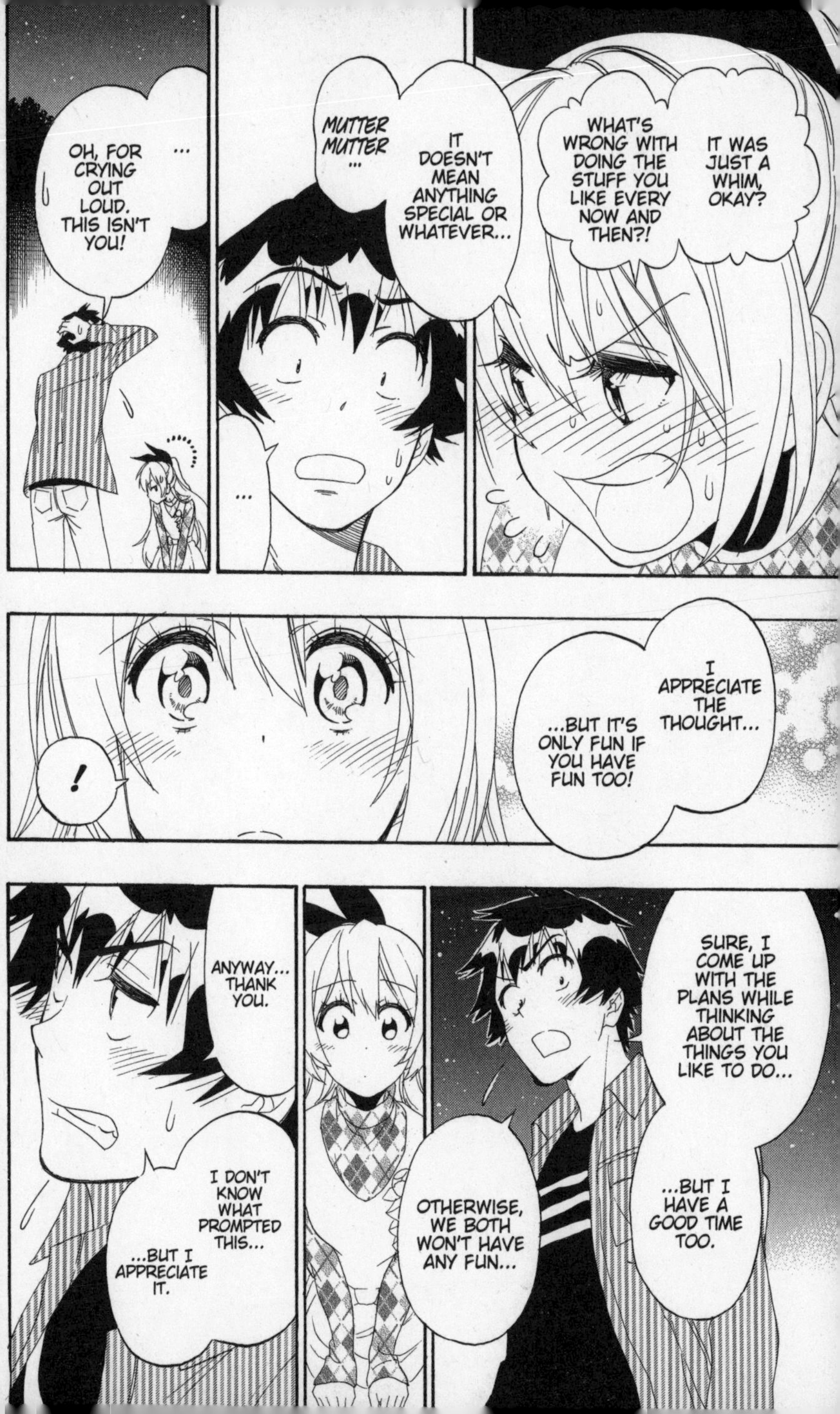
IT WAS JUST A WHIM, OKAY?
WHAT'S WRONG WITH DOING THE STUFF YOU LIKE EVERY NOW AND THEN?!
IT DOESN'T MEAN ANYTHING SPECIAL OR WHATEVER...
MUTTER MUTTER ...
...
...
OH, FOR CRYING OUT LOUD. THIS ISN'T YOU!
I APPRECIATE THE THOUGHT...
...BUT IT'S ONLY FUN IF YOU HAVE FUN TOO!
!
SURE, I COME UP WITH THE PLANS WHILE THINKING ABOUT THE THINGS YOU LIKE TO DO...
...BUT I HAVE A GOOD TIME TOO.
OTHERWISE, WE BOTH WON'T HAVE ANY FUN...
ANYWAY... THANK YOU.
I DON'T KNOW WHAT PROMPTED THIS...
...BUT I APPRECIATE IT.

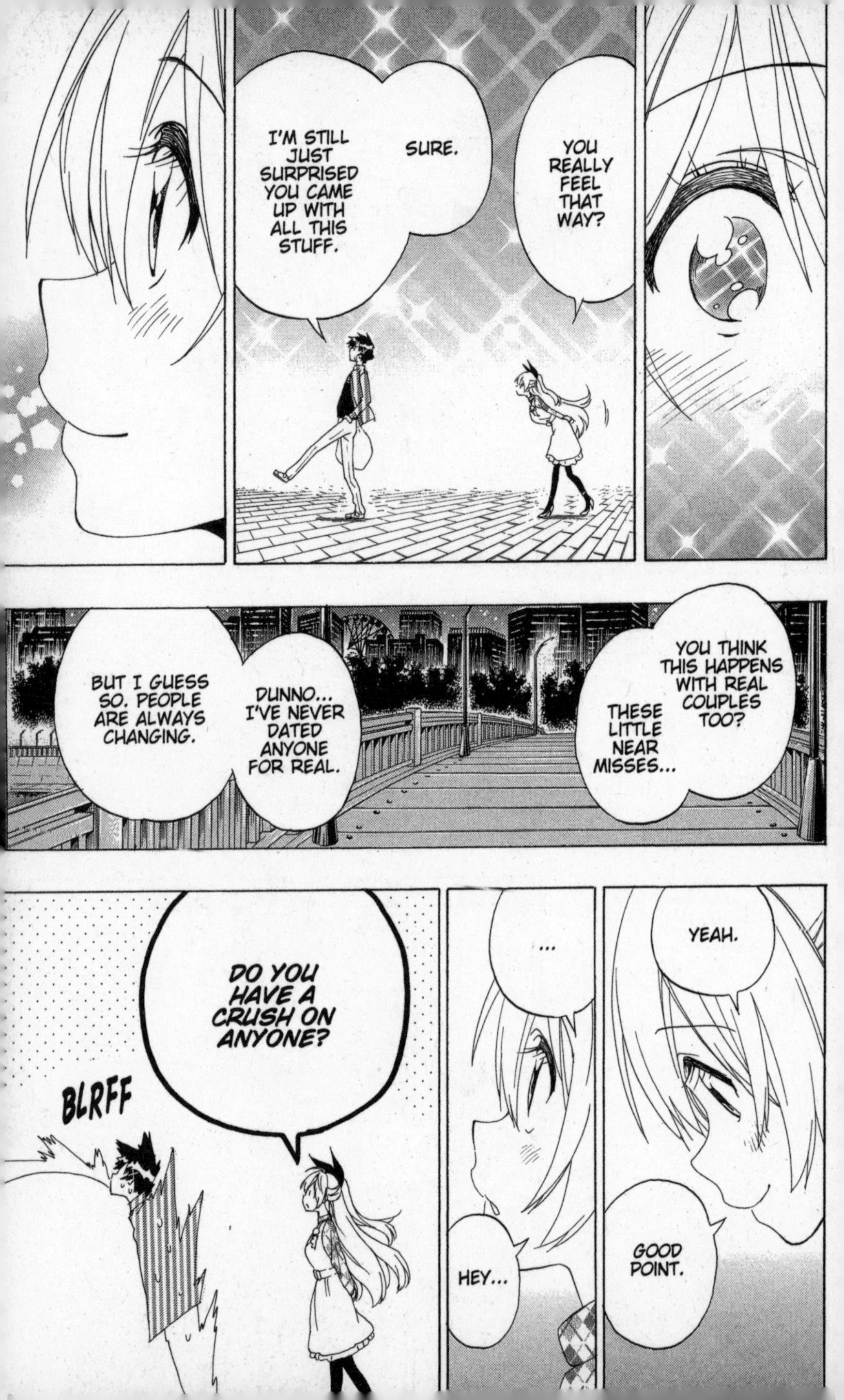
YOU REALLY FEEL THAT WAY?
SURE.
I'M STILL JUST SURPRISED YOU CAME UP WITH ALL THIS STUFF.
YOU THINK THIS HAPPENS WITH REAL COUPLES TOO?
THESE LITTLE NEAR MISSES...
DUNNO... I'VE NEVER DATED ANYONE FOR REAL.
BUT I GUESS SO. PEOPLE ARE ALWAYS CHANGING.
YEAH.
GOOD POINT.
...
HEY...
DO YOU HAVE A CRUSH ON ANYONE?
BLRFF

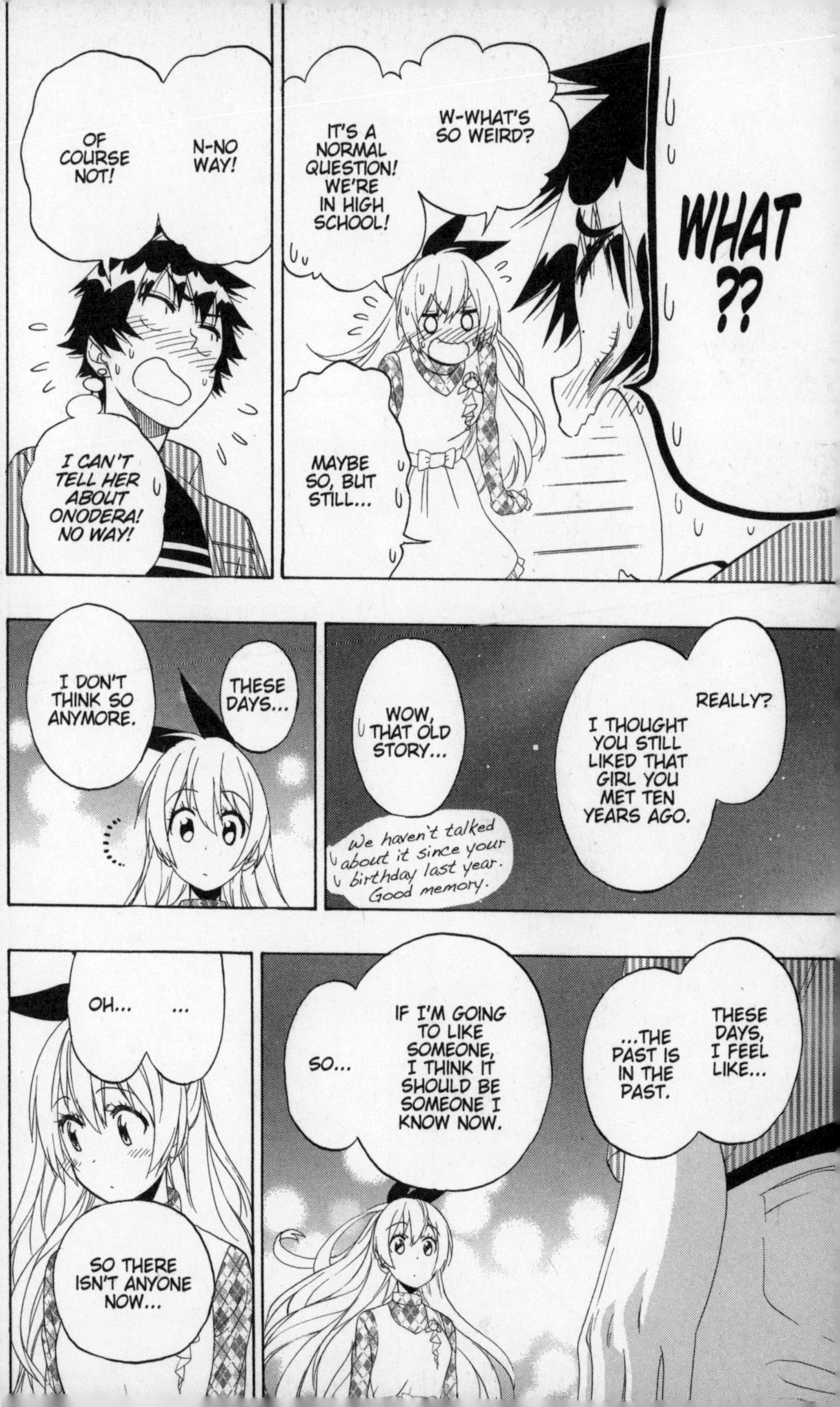
WHAT ??
W-WHAT'S SO WEIRD?
IT'S A NORMAL QUESTION! WE'RE IN HIGH SCHOOL!
MAYBE SO, BUT STILL...
N-NO WAY!
OF COURSE NOT!
I CAN'T TELL HER ABOUT ONODERA! NO WAY!
REALLY?
I THOUGHT YOU STILL LIKED THAT GIRL YOU MET TEN YEARS AGO.
WOW, THAT OLD STORY...
We haven't talked about it since your birthday last year. Good memory.
THESE DAYS...
I DON'T THINK SO ANYMORE.
THESE DAYS, I FEEL LIKE...
...THE PAST IS IN THE PAST.
IF I'M GOING TO LIKE SOMEONE, I THINK IT SHOULD BE SOMEONE I KNOW NOW.
SO...
OH... ...
SO THERE ISN'T ANYONE NOW...

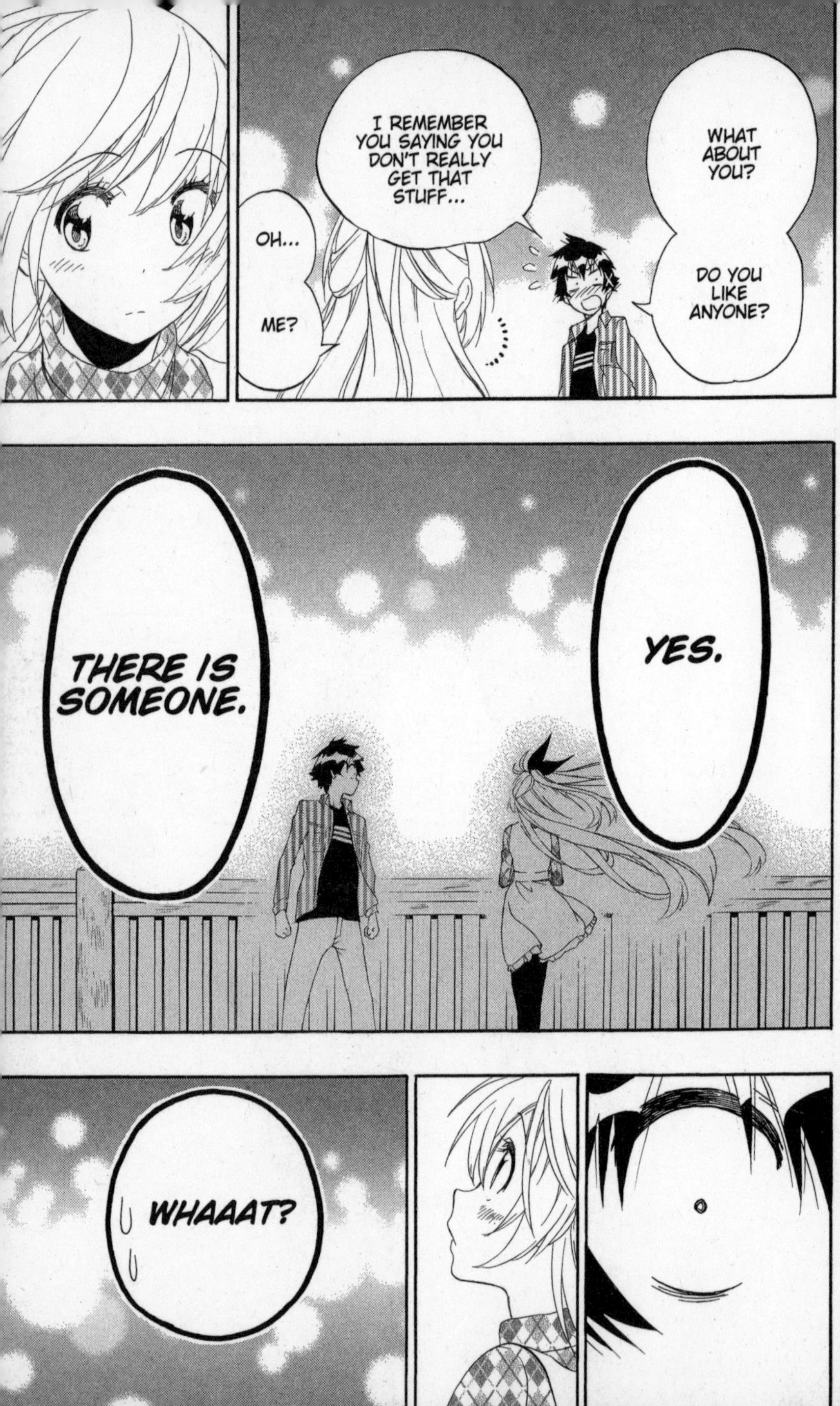
WHAT ABOUT YOU?
DO YOU LIKE ANYONE?
I REMEMBER YOU SAYING YOU DON'T REALLY GET THAT STUFF...
OH...
ME?
YES.
THERE IS SOMEONE.
WHAAAT?

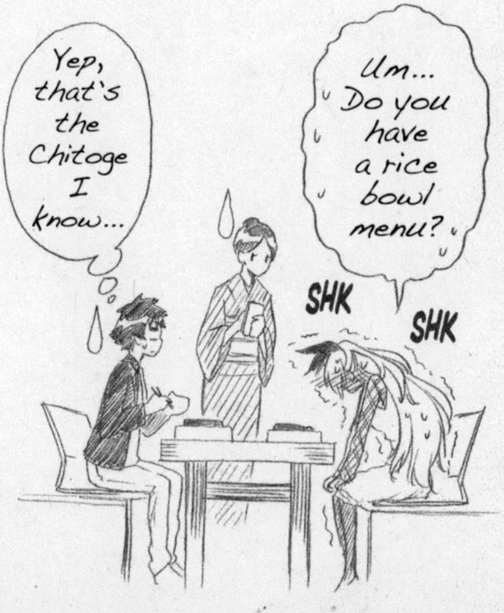
Um... Do you have a rice bowl menu?
SHK
SHK
Yep, that's the Chitoge I know...

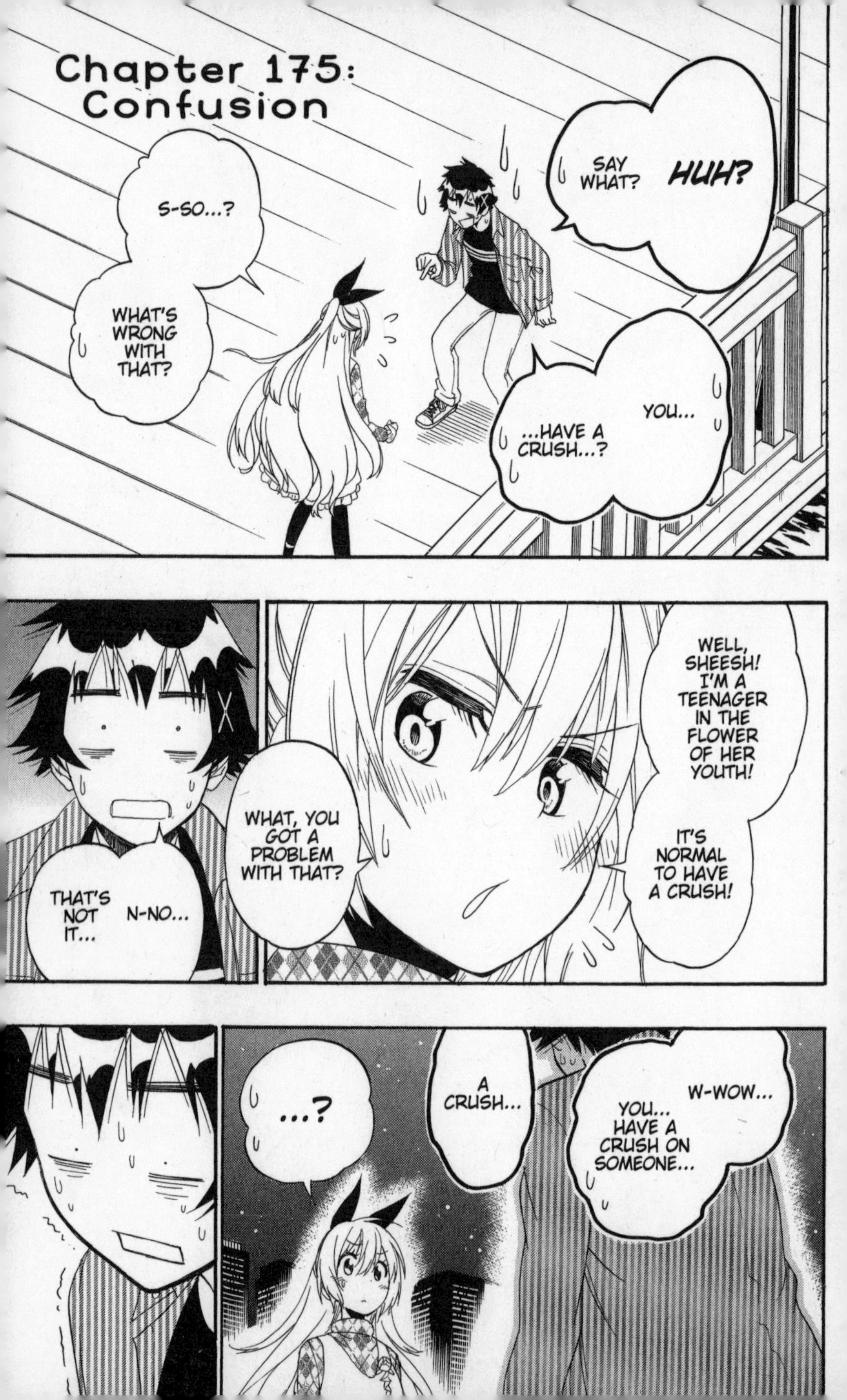
Chapter 175: Confusion
SAY WHAT? HUH?
YOU... ...HAVE A CRUSH...?
S-SO...?
WHAT'S WRONG WITH THAT?
WELL, SHEESH! I'M A TEENAGER IN THE FLOWER OF HER YOUTH!
IT'S NORMAL TO HAVE A CRUSH!
WHAT, YOU GOT A PROBLEM WITH THAT?
N-NO... THAT'S NOT IT...
W-WOW... YOU... HAVE A CRUSH ON SOMEONE...
A CRUSH...
...?

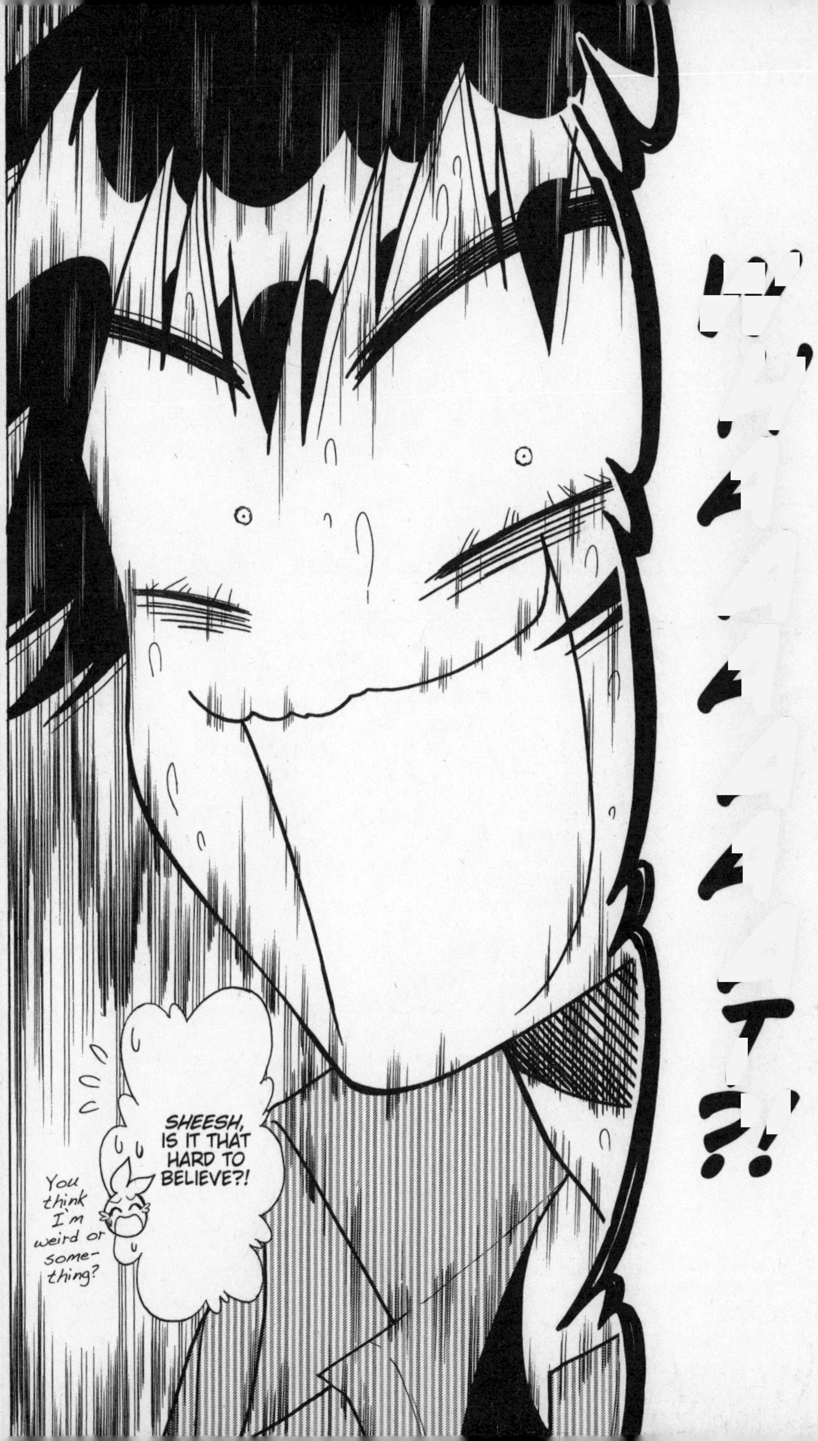
SHEESH, IS IT THAT HARD TO BELIEVE?!
You think I'm weird or some-thing?

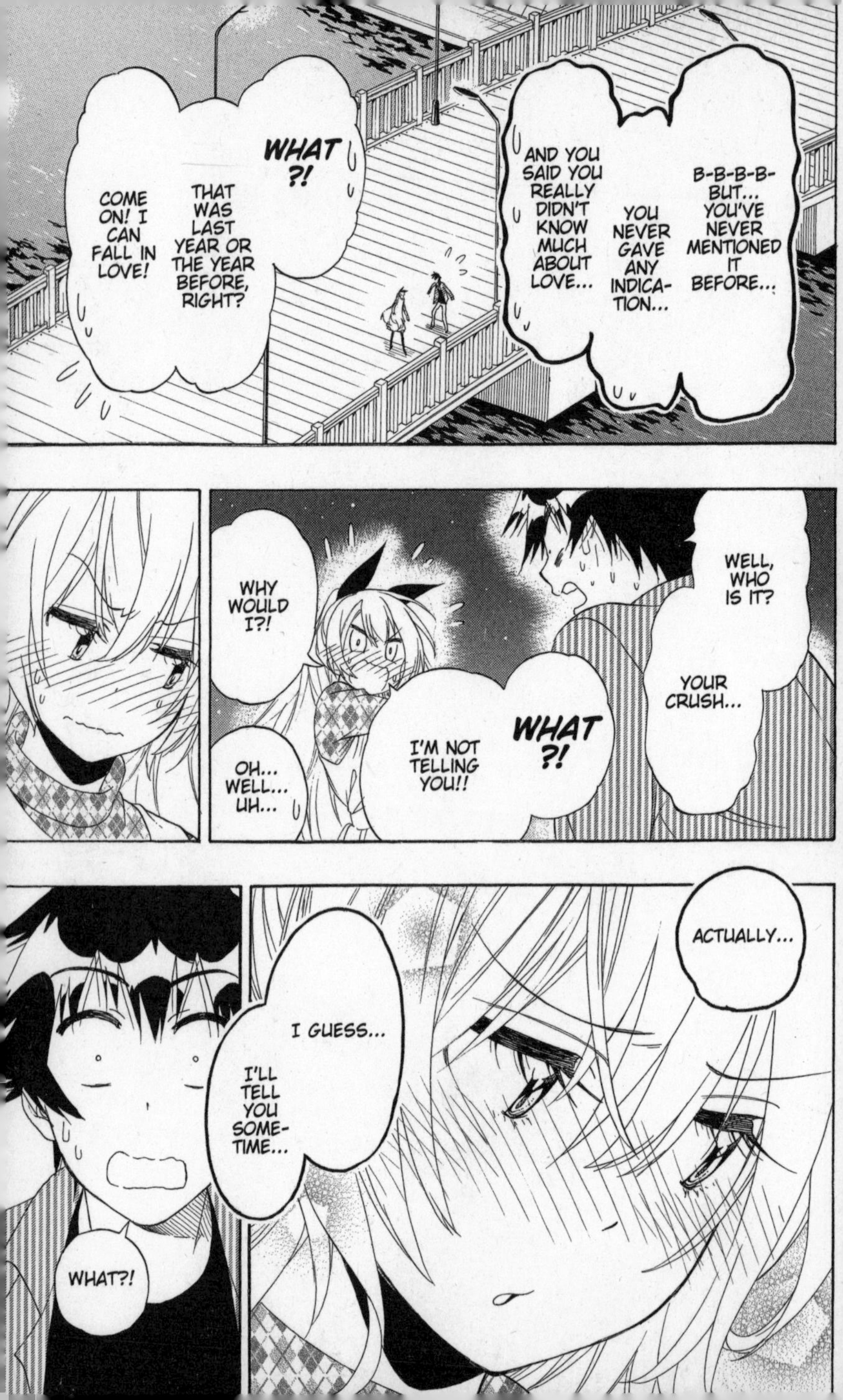
B-B-B-B-BUT... YOU'VE NEVER MENTIONED IT BEFORE...
YOU NEVER GAVE ANY INDICATION...
AND YOU SAID YOU REALLY DIDN'T KNOW MUCH ABOUT LOVE...
WHAT?!
THAT WAS LAST YEAR OR THE YEAR BEFORE, RIGHT?
COME ON! I CAN FALL IN LOVE!
WELL, WHO IS IT?
YOUR CRUSH...
WHAT?!
I'M NOT TELLING YOU!!
WHY WOULD I?!
OH... WELL... UH...
ACTUALLY...
I GUESS...
I'LL TELL YOU SOMETIME...
WHAT?!

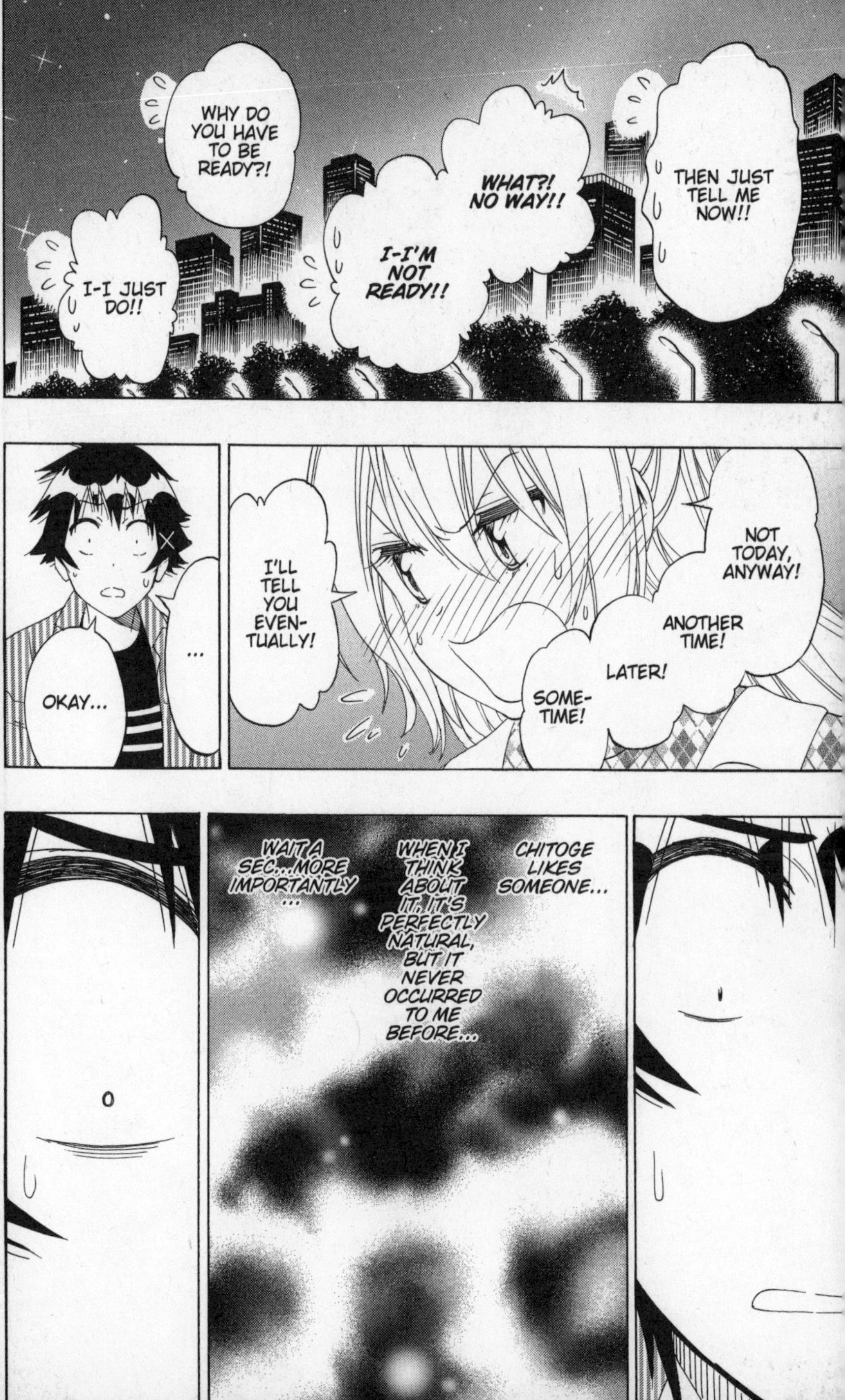

THEN JUST TELL ME NOW!!
WHAT?! NO WAY!!
I-I'M NOT READY!!
WHY DO YOU HAVE TO BE READY?!
I-I JUST DO!!
NOT TODAY, ANYWAY!
ANOTHER TIME!
LATER!
SOME-TIME!
I'LL TELL YOU EVEN-TUALLY!
...
OKAY...
CHITOGE LIKES SOMEONE...
WHEN I THINK ABOUT IT, IT'S PERFECTLY NATURAL, BUT IT NEVER OCCURRED TO ME BEFORE...
WAIT A SEC...MORE IMPORTANTLY...

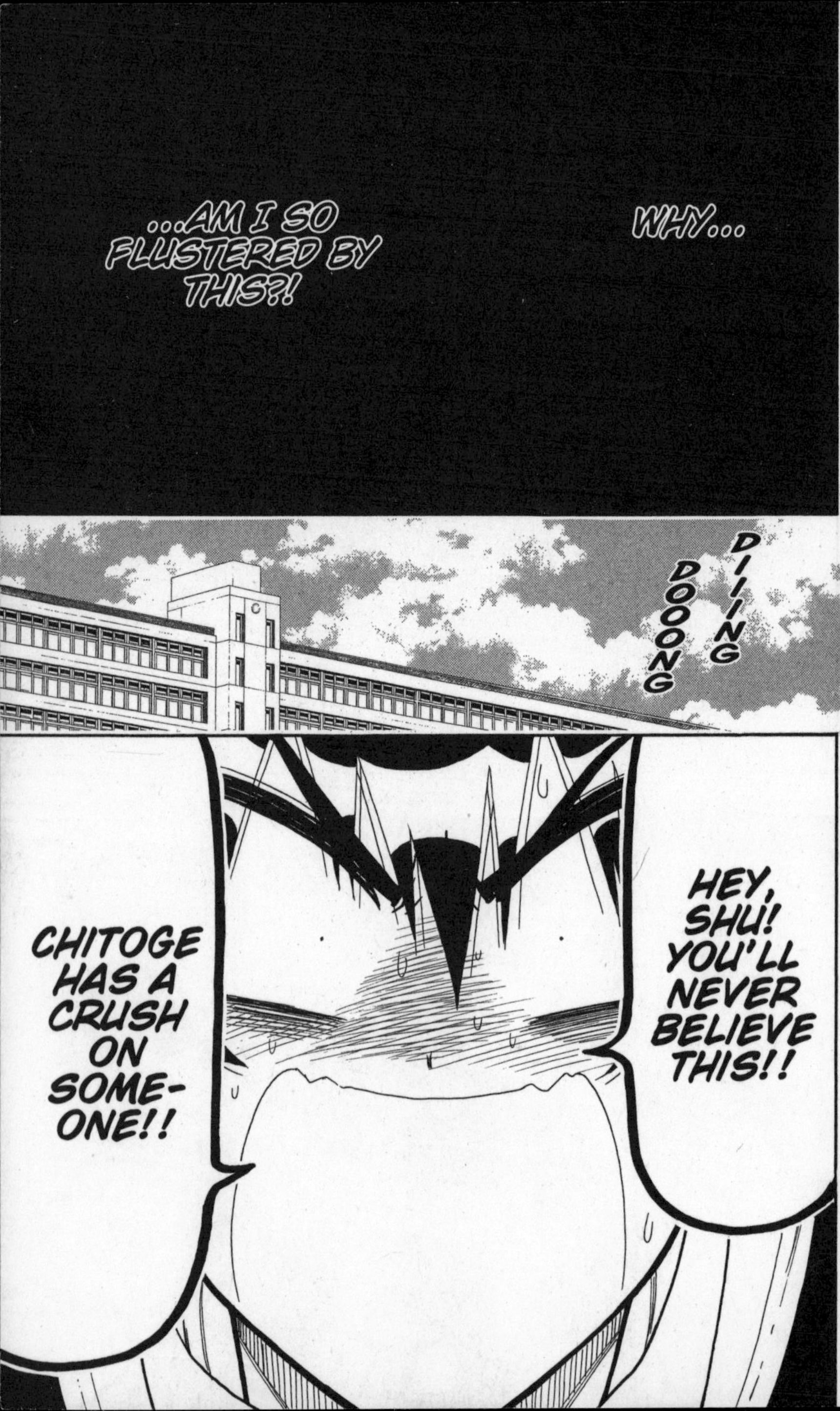
WHY...
...AM I SO FLUSTERED BY THIS?!
DIIING
DOOONG
HEY, SHU! YOU'LL NEVER BELIEVE THIS!!
CHITOGE HAS A CRUSH ON SOME-ONE!!

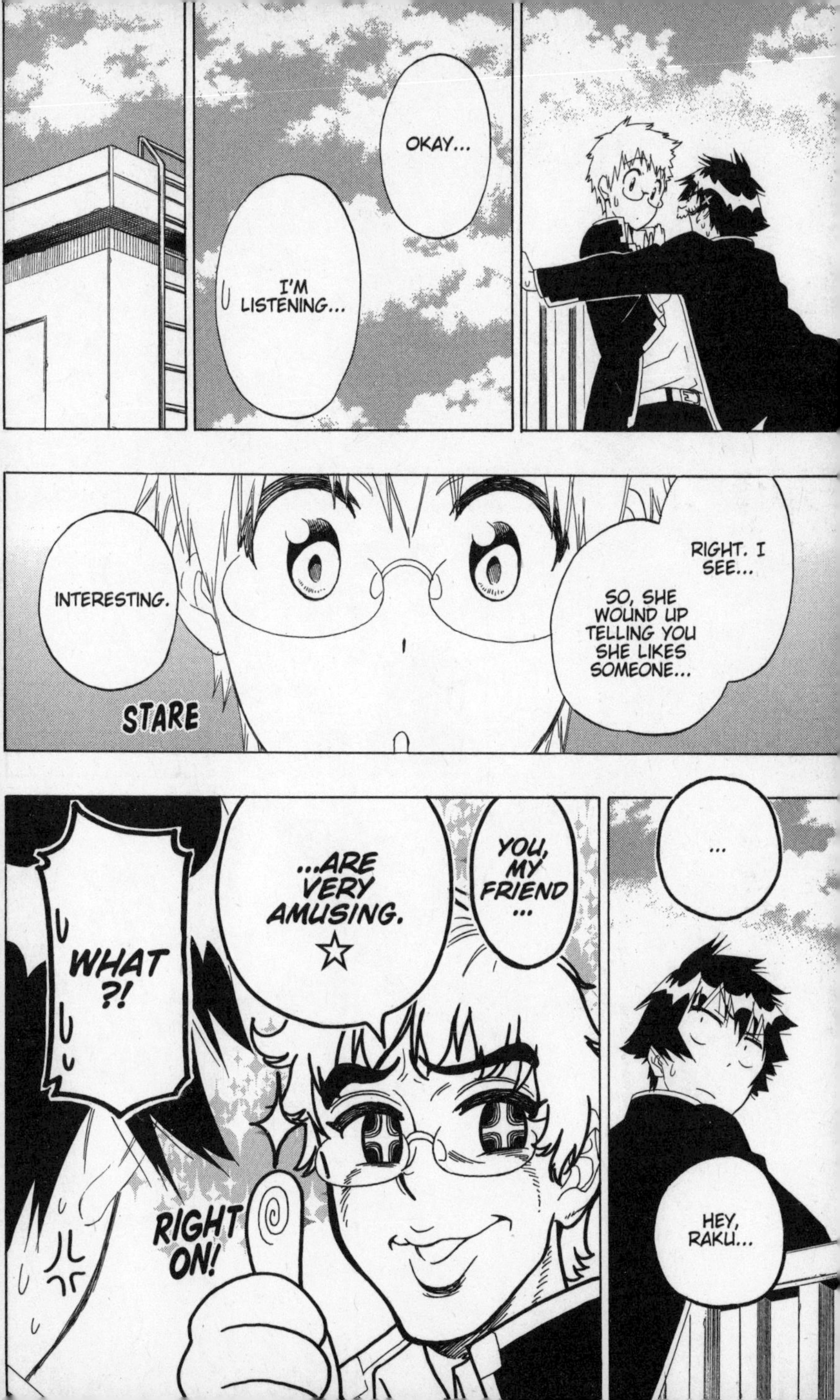
OKAY...
I'M LISTENING...
RIGHT. I SEE...
SO, SHE WOUND UP TELLING YOU SHE LIKES SOMEONE...
INTERESTING.
STARE
...
HEY, RAKU...
YOU, MY FRIEND...
...ARE VERY AMUSING. ☆
WHAT?!
RIGHT ON!

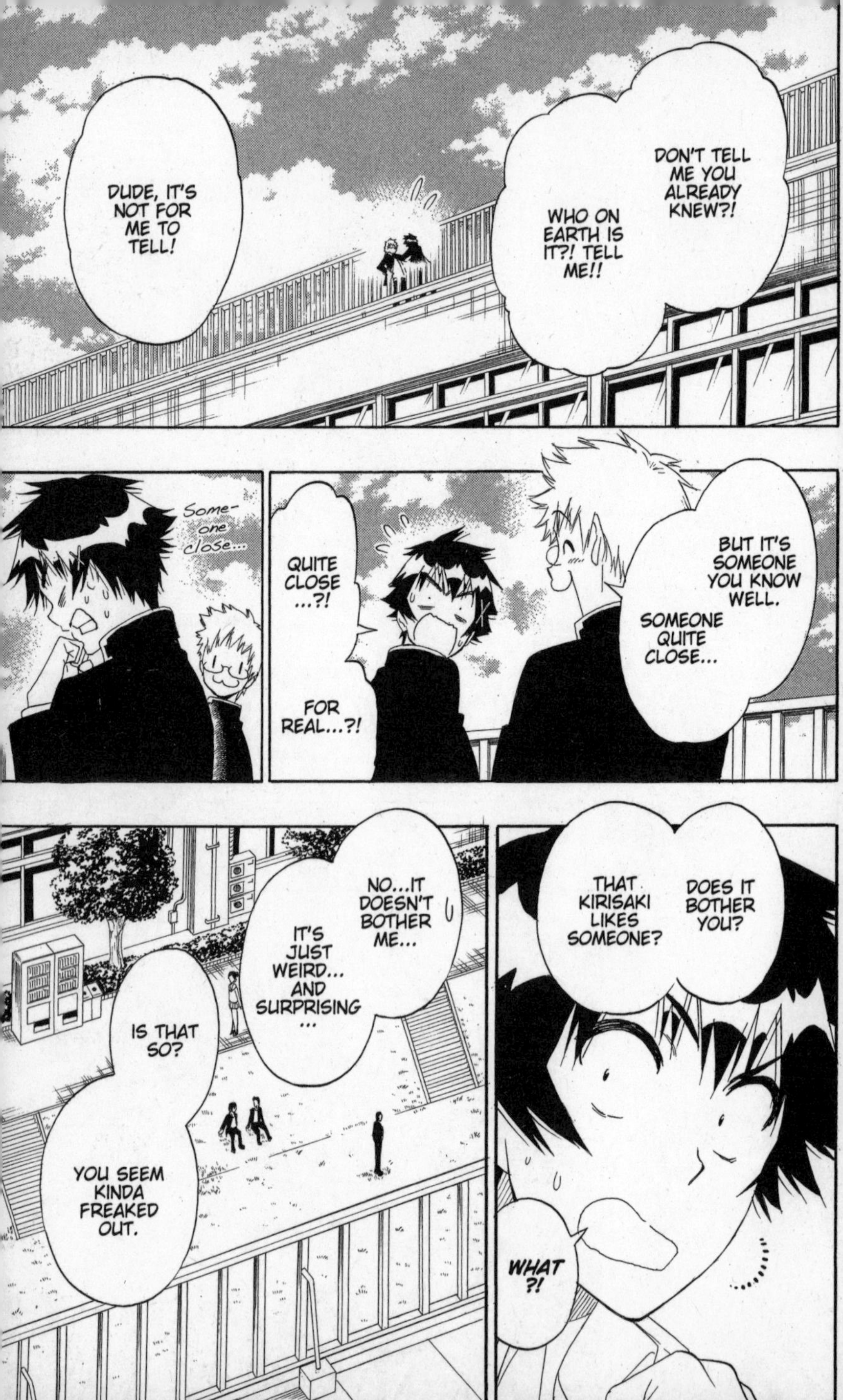
DON'T TELL ME YOU ALREADY KNEW?! WHO ON EARTH IS IT?! TELL ME!!
DUDE, IT'S NOT FOR ME TO TELL!
BUT IT'S SOMEONE YOU KNOW WELL. SOMEONE QUITE CLOSE...
QUITE CLOSE...?! FOR REAL...?!
Some-one close...
DOES IT BOTHER YOU? THAT KIRISAKI LIKES SOMEONE?
WHAT?!
NO...IT DOESN'T BOTHER ME... IT'S JUST WEIRD... AND SURPRISING...
IS THAT SO? YOU SEEM KINDA FREAKED OUT.

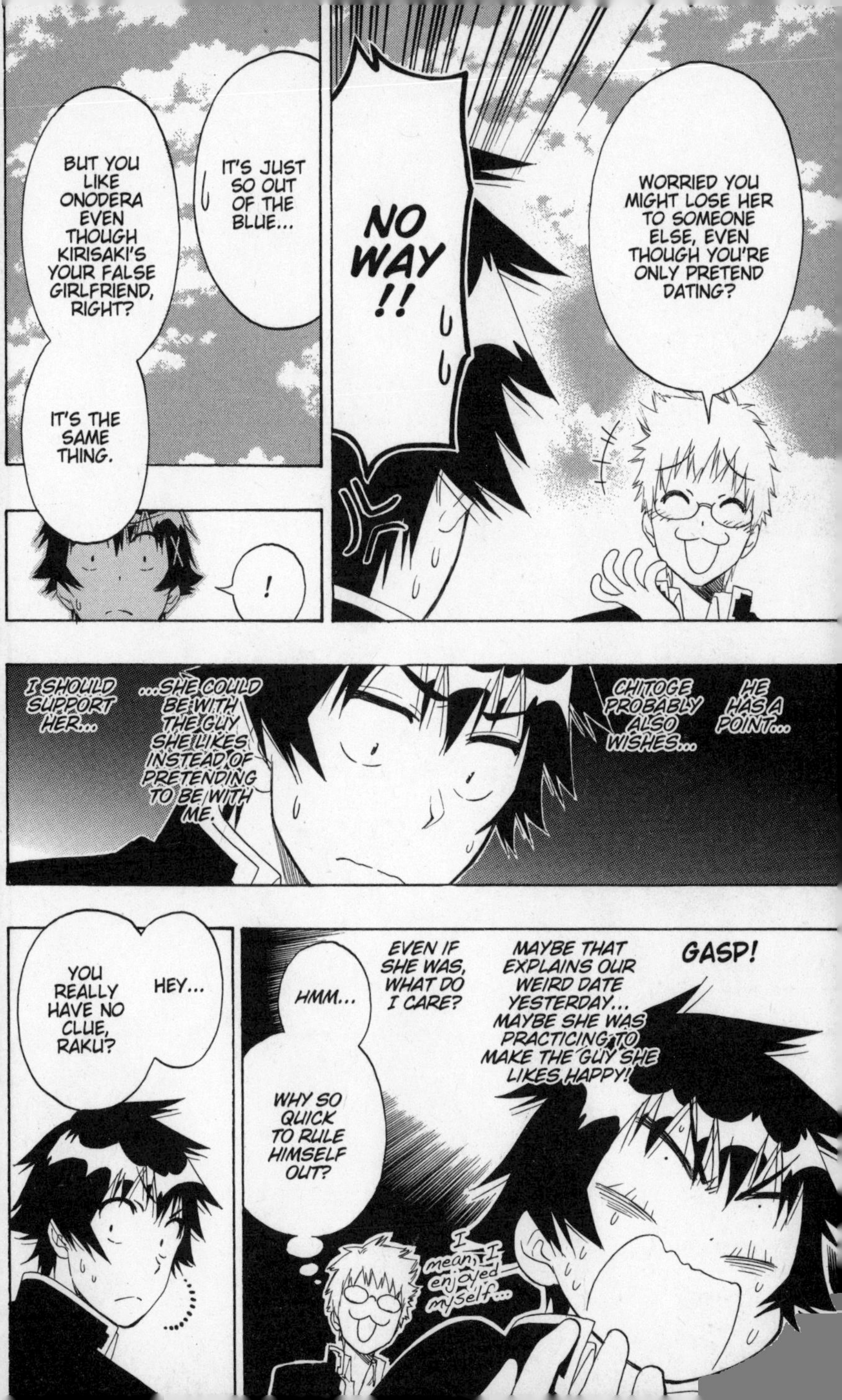

WORRIED YOU MIGHT LOSE HER TO SOMEONE ELSE, EVEN THOUGH YOU'RE ONLY PRETEND DATING?
NO WAY!!
IT'S JUST SO OUT OF THE BLUE...
BUT YOU LIKE ONODERA EVEN THOUGH KIRISAKI'S YOUR FALSE GIRLFRIEND, RIGHT?
IT'S THE SAME THING.
!
HE HAS A POINT...
CHITOGE PROBABLY ALSO WISHES...
...SHE COULD BE WITH THE GUY SHE LIKES INSTEAD OF PRETENDING TO BE WITH ME.
I SHOULD SUPPORT HER...
GASP!
MAYBE THAT EXPLAINS OUR WEIRD DATE YESTERDAY... MAYBE SHE WAS PRACTICING TO MAKE THE GUY SHE LIKES HAPPY!
EVEN IF SHE WAS, WHAT DO I CARE?
I mean, I enjoyed myself...
HMM...
WHY SO QUICK TO RULE HIMSELF OUT?
HEY...
YOU REALLY HAVE NO CLUE, RAKU?

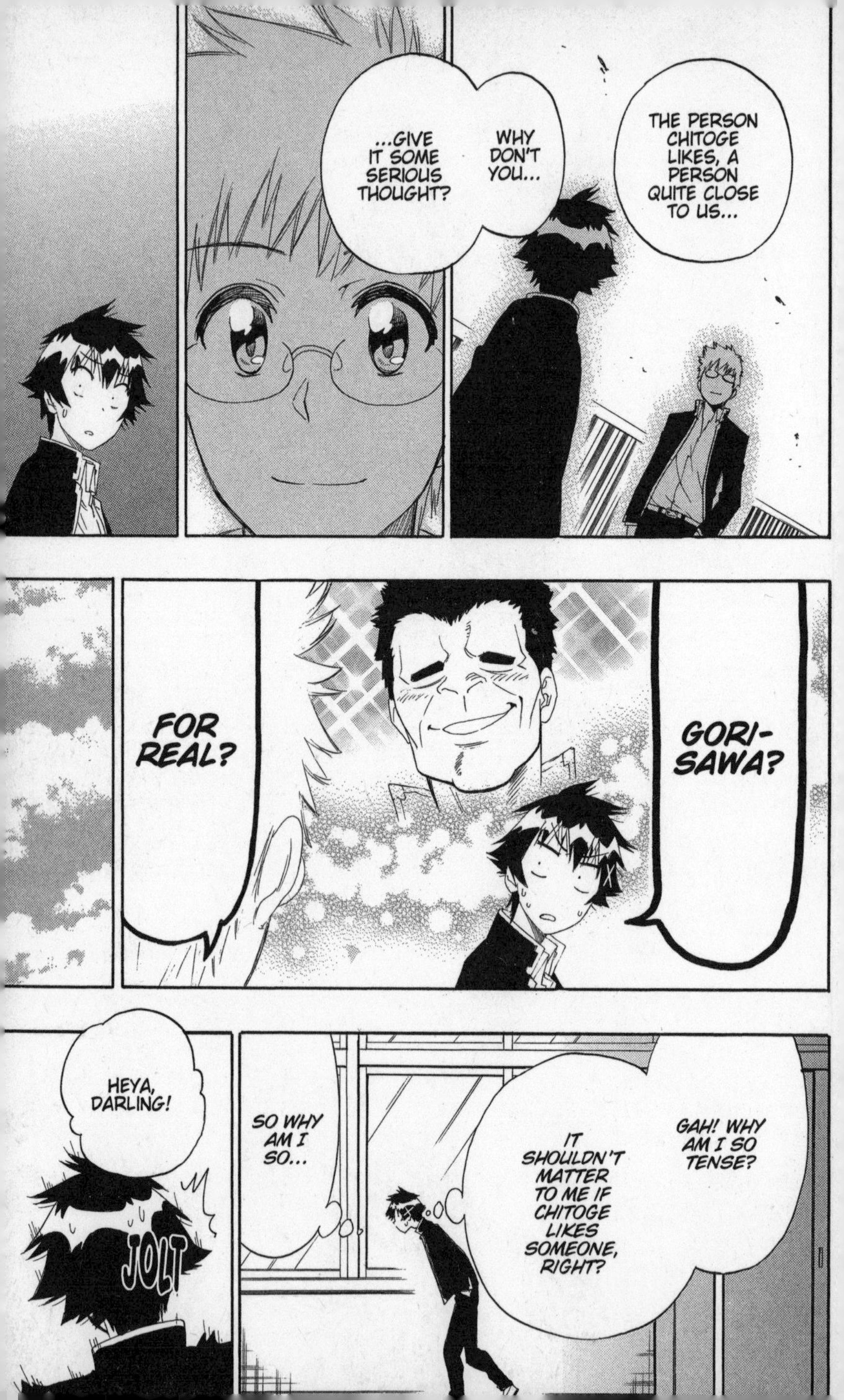
THE PERSON CHITOGE LIKES, A PERSON QUITE CLOSE TO US...
WHY DON'T YOU...
...GIVE IT SOME SERIOUS THOUGHT?
GORI-SAWA?
FOR REAL?
GAH! WHY AM I SO TENSE?
IT SHOULDN'T MATTER TO ME IF CHITOGE LIKES SOMEONE, RIGHT?
SO WHY AM I SO...
HEYA, DARLING!
JOLT

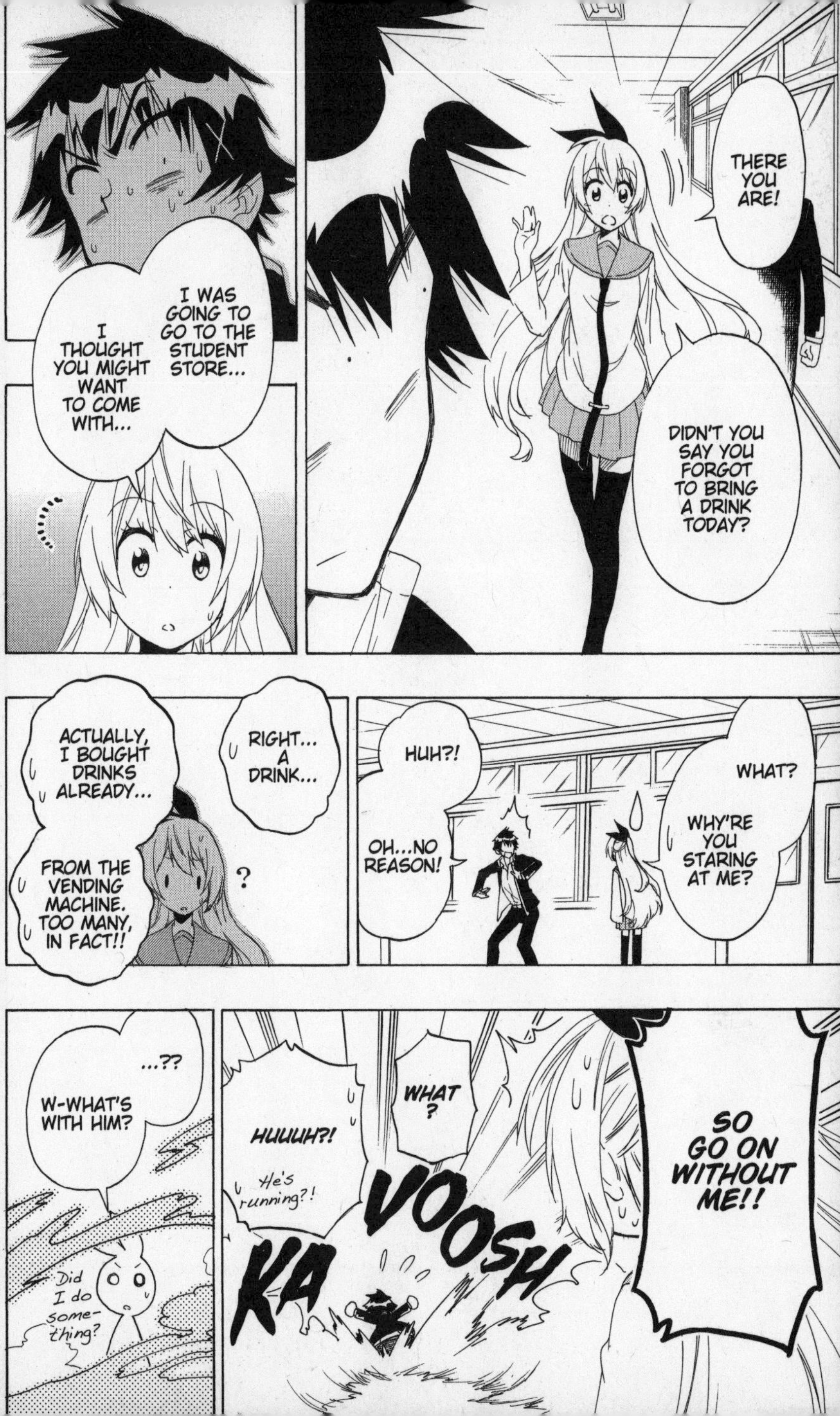
THERE YOU ARE!
DIDN'T YOU SAY YOU FORGOT TO BRING A DRINK TODAY?
I WAS GOING TO GO TO THE STUDENT STORE...
I THOUGHT YOU MIGHT WANT TO COME WITH...
WHAT?
WHY'RE YOU STARING AT ME?
HUH?!
OH...NO REASON!
RIGHT... A DRINK...
ACTUALLY, I BOUGHT DRINKS ALREADY...
FROM THE VENDING MACHINE. TOO MANY, IN FACT!!
?
SO GO ON WITHOUT ME!!
WHAT?
HUUUH?!
He's running?!
VOOSH
KA
...??
W-WHAT'S WITH HIM?
Did I do some-thing?

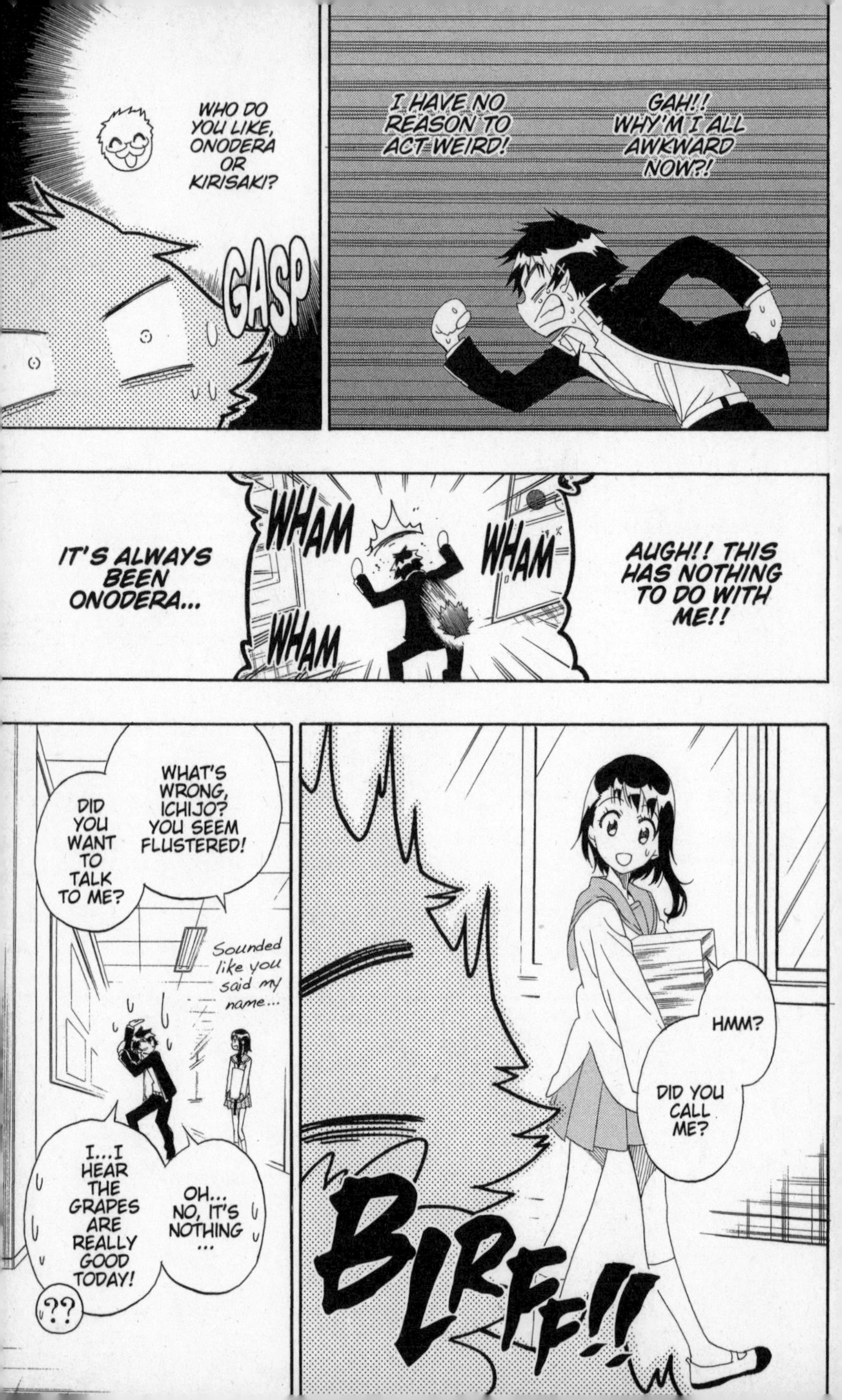
GAH!! WHY'M I ALL AWKWARD NOW?!
I HAVE NO REASON TO ACT WEIRD!
WHO DO YOU LIKE, ONODERA OR KIRISAKI?
GASP
AUGH!! THIS HAS NOTHING TO DO WITH ME!!
WHAM
WHAM
WHAM
IT'S ALWAYS BEEN ONODERA...
HMM?
DID YOU CALL ME?
BLRFF!!
WHAT'S WRONG, ICHIJO? YOU SEEM FLUSTERED!
DID YOU WANT TO TALK TO ME?
Sounded like you said my name...
OH... NO, IT'S NOTHING...
I...I HEAR THE GRAPES ARE REALLY GOOD TODAY!
??

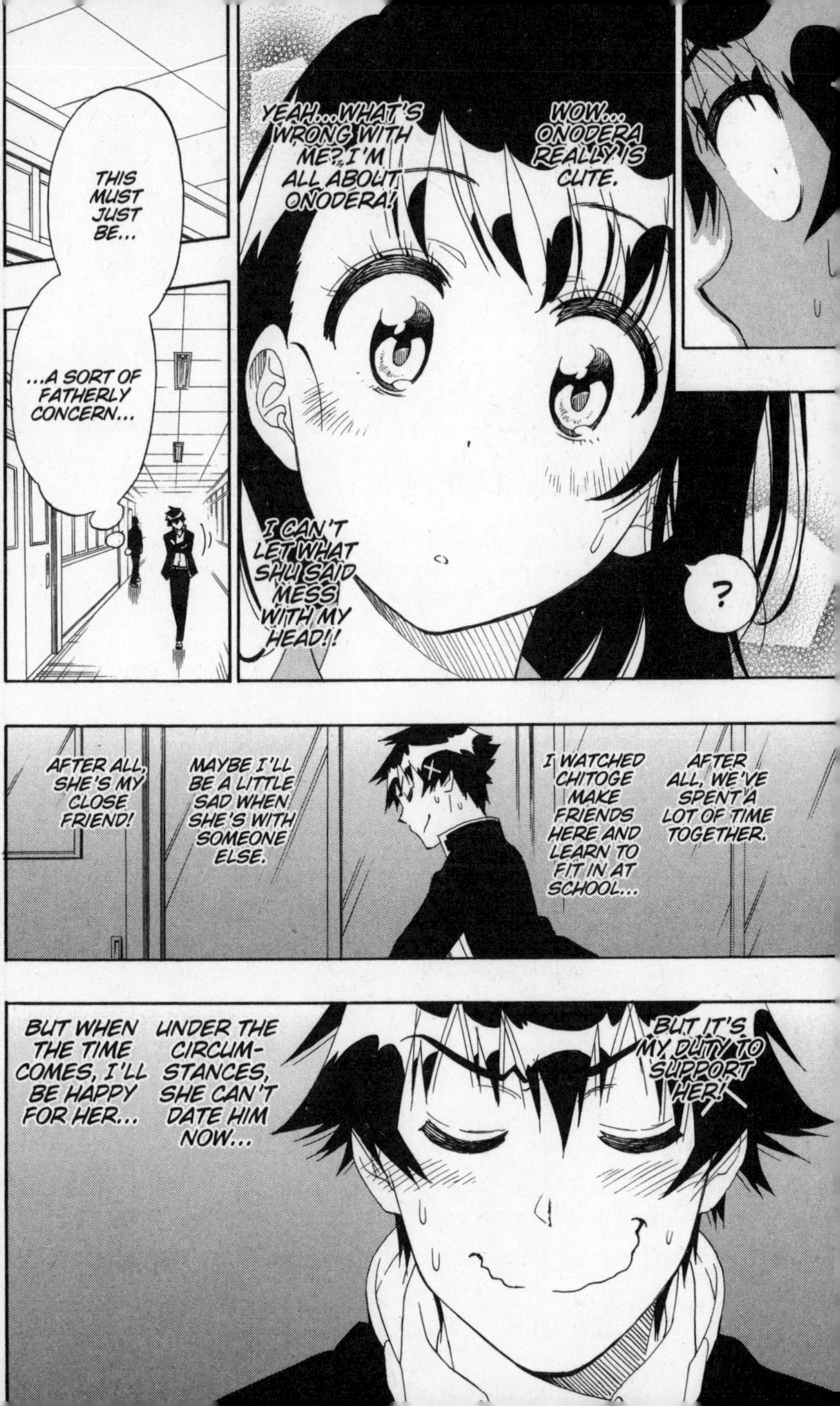
WOW... ONODERA REALLY IS CUTE.
YEAH...WHAT'S WRONG WITH ME? I'M ALL ABOUT ONODERA!
?
I CAN'T LET WHAT SHU SAID MESS WITH MY HEAD!!
THIS MUST JUST BE...
...A SORT OF FATHERLY CONCERN...
AFTER ALL, WE'VE SPENT A LOT OF TIME TOGETHER.
I WATCHED CHITOGE MAKE FRIENDS HERE AND LEARN TO FIT IN AT SCHOOL...
MAYBE I'LL BE A LITTLE SAD WHEN SHE'S WITH SOMEONE ELSE.
AFTER ALL, SHE'S MY CLOSE FRIEND!
BUT IT'S MY DUTY TO SUPPORT HER!
UNDER THE CIRCUM-STANCES, SHE CAN'T DATE HIM NOW...
BUT WHEN THE TIME COMES, I'LL BE HAPPY FOR HER...

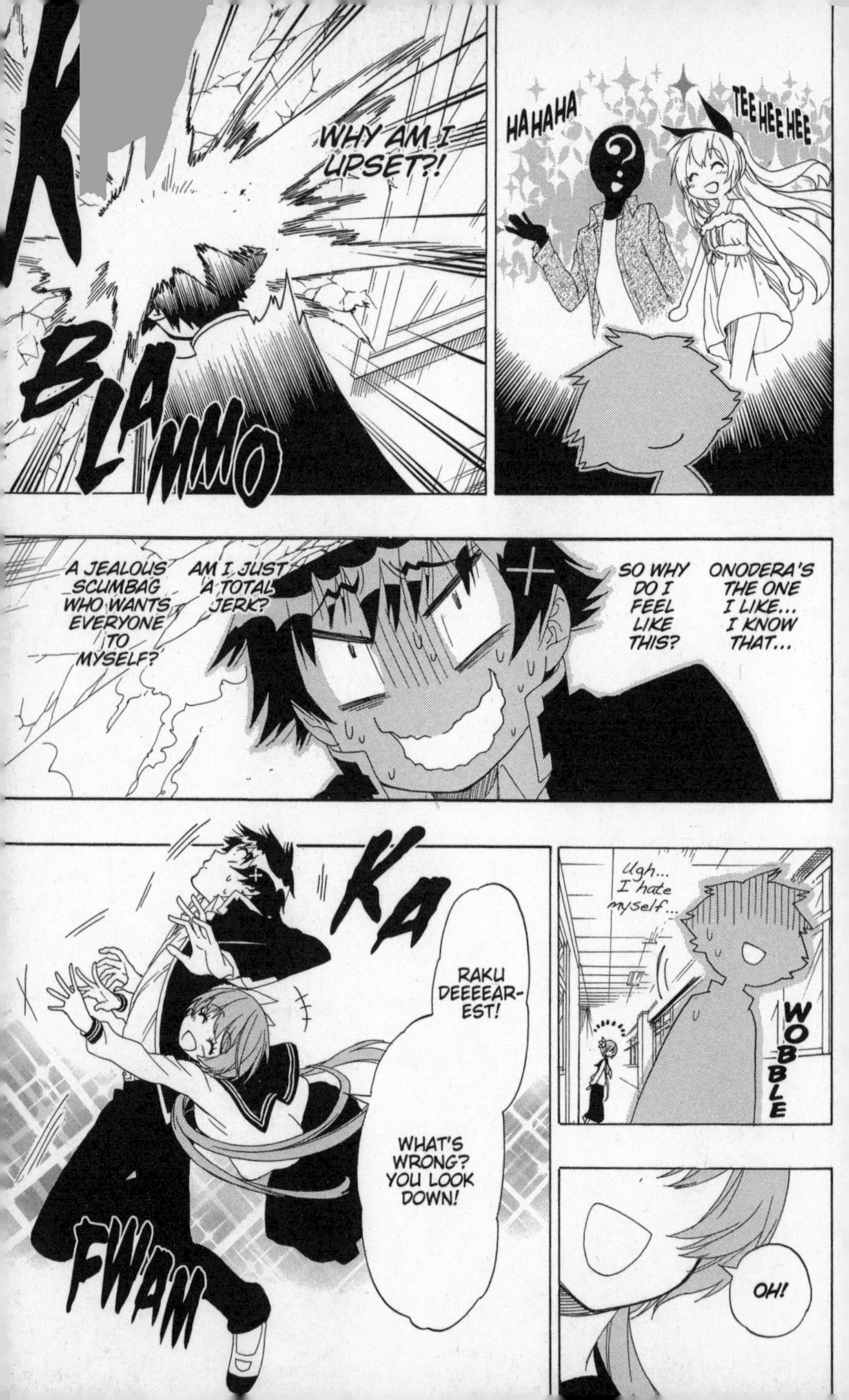
TEE HEE HEE
HAHAHA
WHY AM I UPSET?!
K
BLAMMO
ONODERA'S THE ONE I LIKE... I KNOW THAT...
SO WHY DO I FEEL LIKE THIS?
AM I JUST A TOTAL JERK?
A JEALOUS SCUMBAG WHO WANTS EVERYONE TO MYSELF?
Ugh... I hate myself...
WOBBLE
OH!
KA
RAKU DEEEEAR-EST!
WHAT'S WRONG? YOU LOOK DOWN!
FWAM

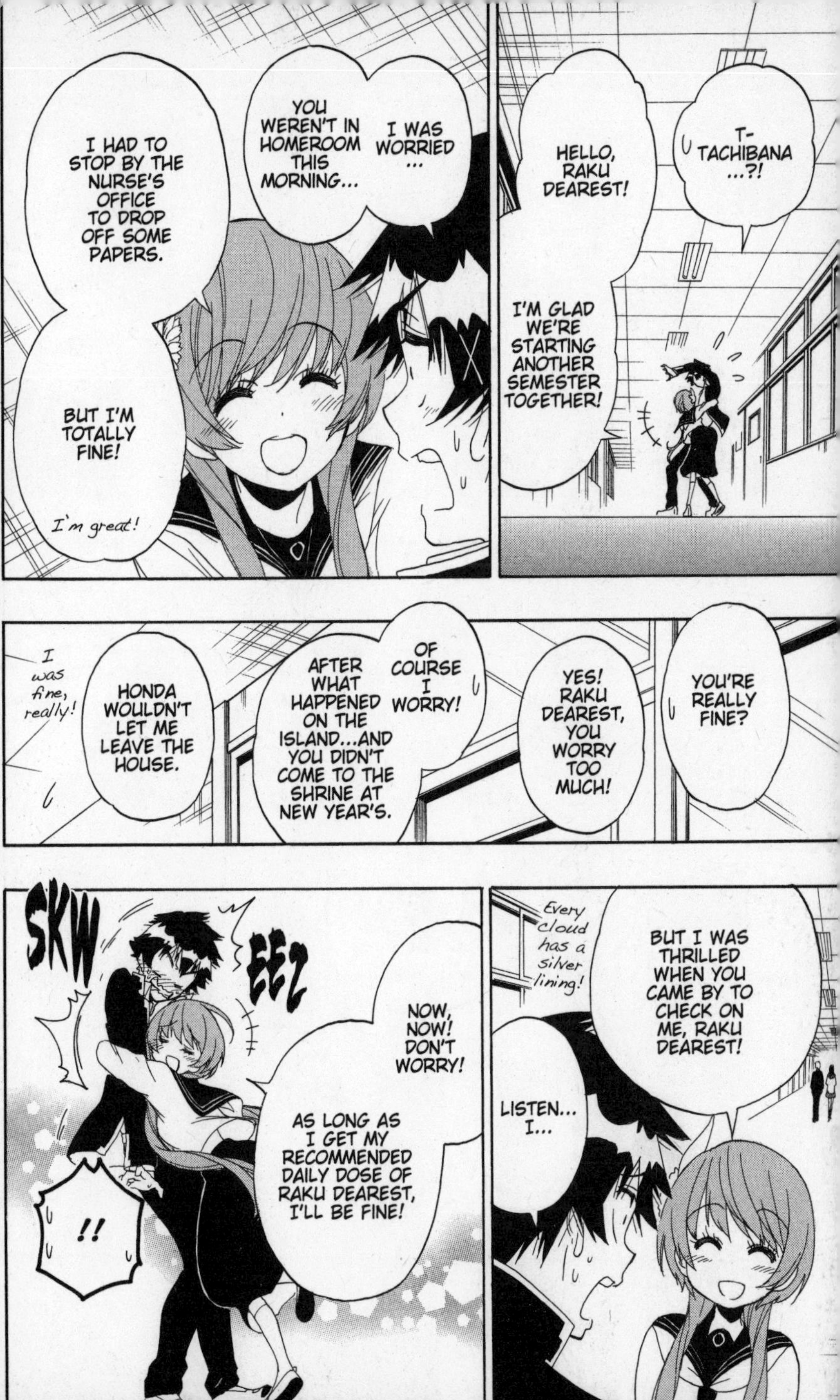
T-TACHIBANA...?!
HELLO, RAKU DEAREST!
I'M GLAD WE'RE STARTING ANOTHER SEMESTER TOGETHER!
I WAS WORRIED...
YOU WEREN'T IN HOMEROOM THIS MORNING...
I HAD TO STOP BY THE NURSE'S OFFICE TO DROP OFF SOME PAPERS.
BUT I'M TOTALLY FINE!
I'm great!
YOU'RE REALLY FINE?
YES! RAKU DEAREST, YOU WORRY TOO MUCH!
OF COURSE I WORRY!
AFTER WHAT HAPPENED ON THE ISLAND...AND YOU DIDN'T COME TO THE SHRINE AT NEW YEAR'S.
HONDA WOULDN'T LET ME LEAVE THE HOUSE.
I was fine, really!
BUT I WAS THRILLED WHEN YOU CAME BY TO CHECK ON ME, RAKU DEAREST!
Every cloud has a silver lining!
LISTEN... I...
NOW, NOW! DON'T WORRY!
AS LONG AS I GET MY RECOMMENDED DAILY DOSE OF RAKU DEAREST, I'LL BE FINE!
SKW EEZ
!!

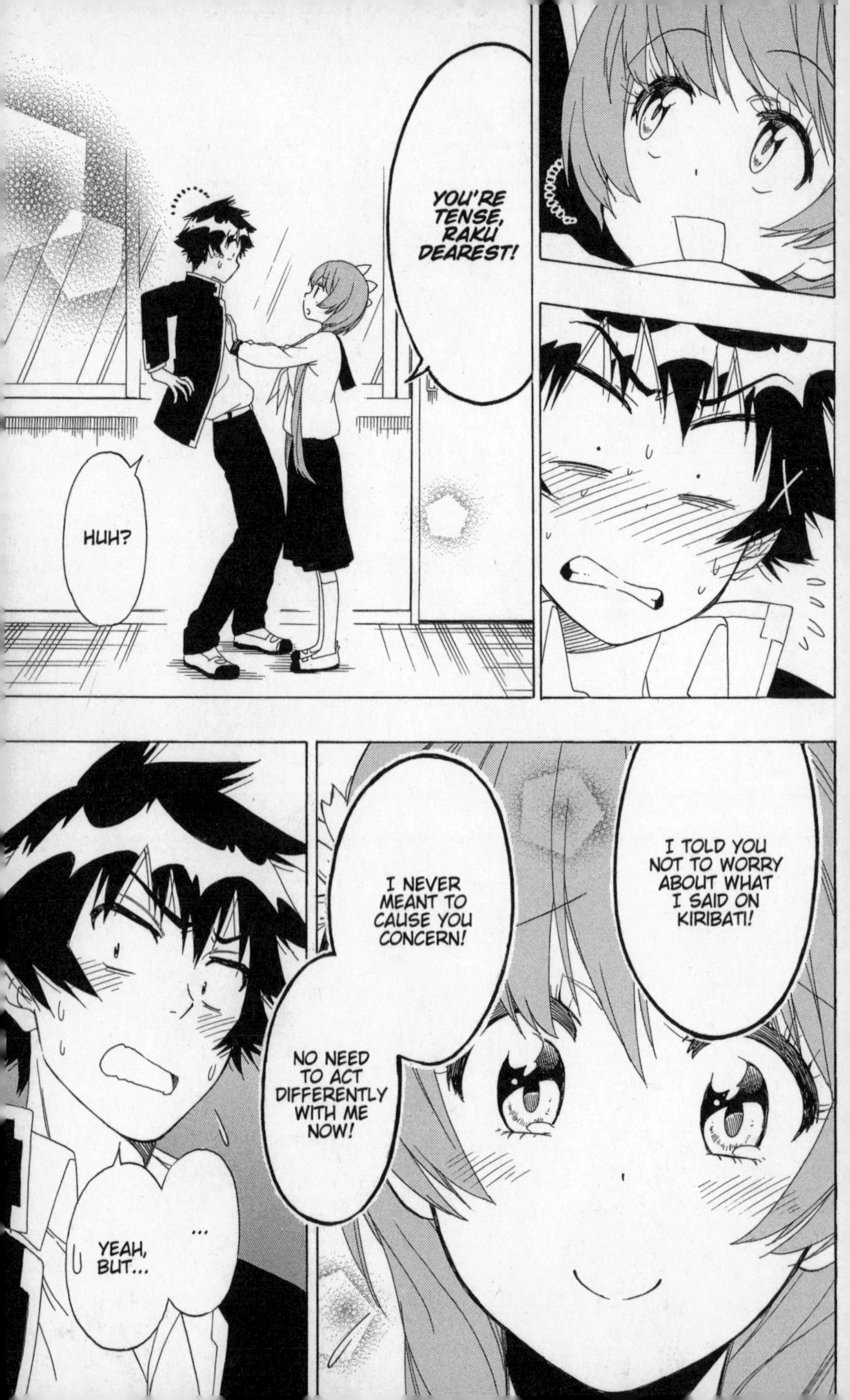
YOU'RE TENSE, RAKU DEAREST!
HUH?
I TOLD YOU NOT TO WORRY ABOUT WHAT I SAID ON KIRIBATI!
I NEVER MEANT TO CAUSE YOU CONCERN!
NO NEED TO ACT DIFFERENTLY WITH ME NOW!
...
YEAH, BUT...

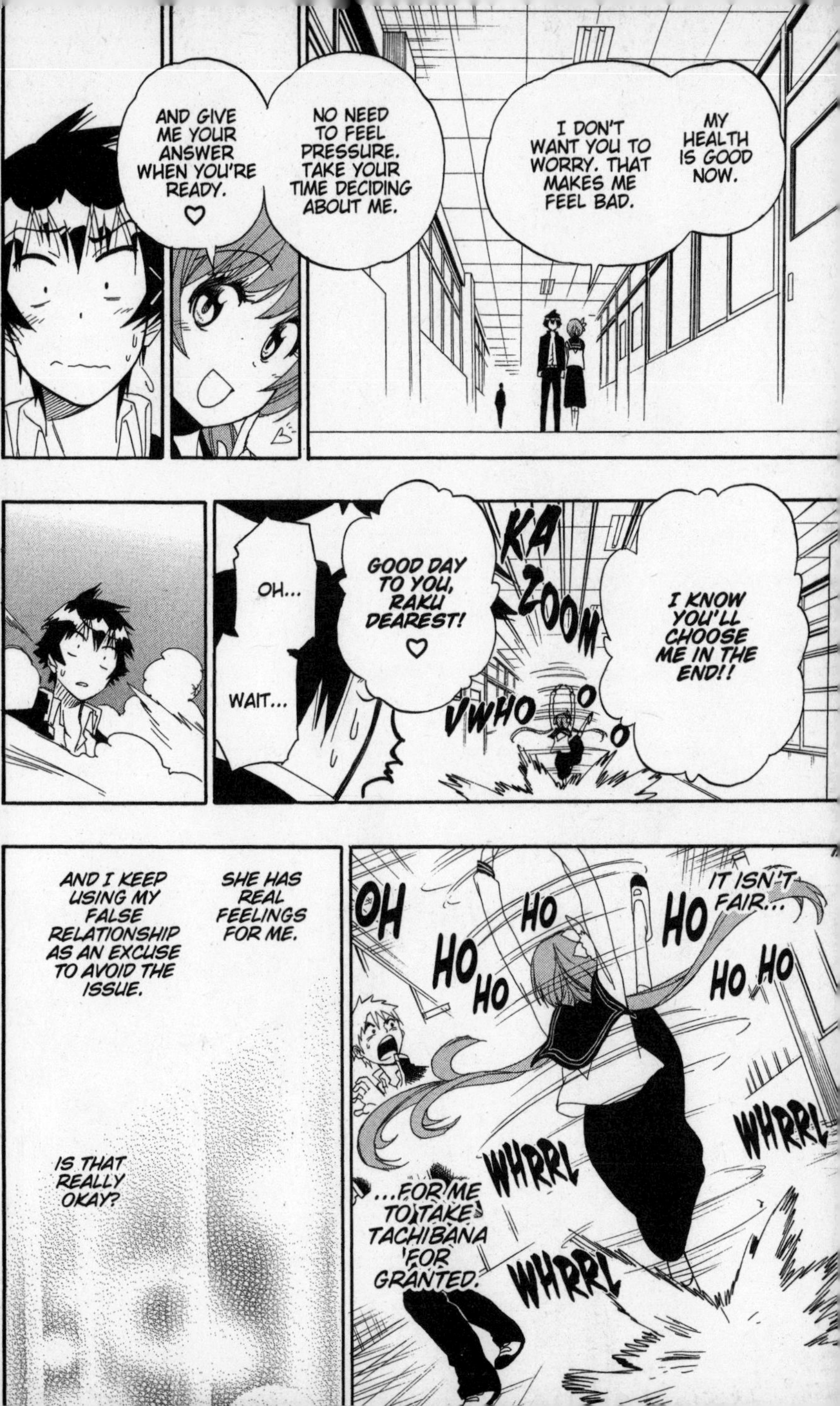
MY HEALTH IS GOOD NOW.
I DON'T WANT YOU TO WORRY. THAT MAKES ME FEEL BAD.
NO NEED TO FEEL PRESSURE. TAKE YOUR TIME DECIDING ABOUT ME.
AND GIVE ME YOUR ANSWER WHEN YOU'RE READY. ♡
I KNOW YOU'LL CHOOSE ME IN THE END!!
KA ZOOM
VWHOOOO
GOOD DAY TO YOU, RAKU DEAREST! ♡
OH...
WAIT...
IT ISN'T FAIR...
OH HO HO HO HO HO HO
...FOR ME TO TAKE TACHIBANA FOR GRANTED.
WHRRL WHRRL WHRRL
SHE HAS REAL FEELINGS FOR ME.
AND I KEEP USING MY FALSE RELATIONSHIP AS AN EXCUSE TO AVOID THE ISSUE.
IS THAT REALLY OKAY?

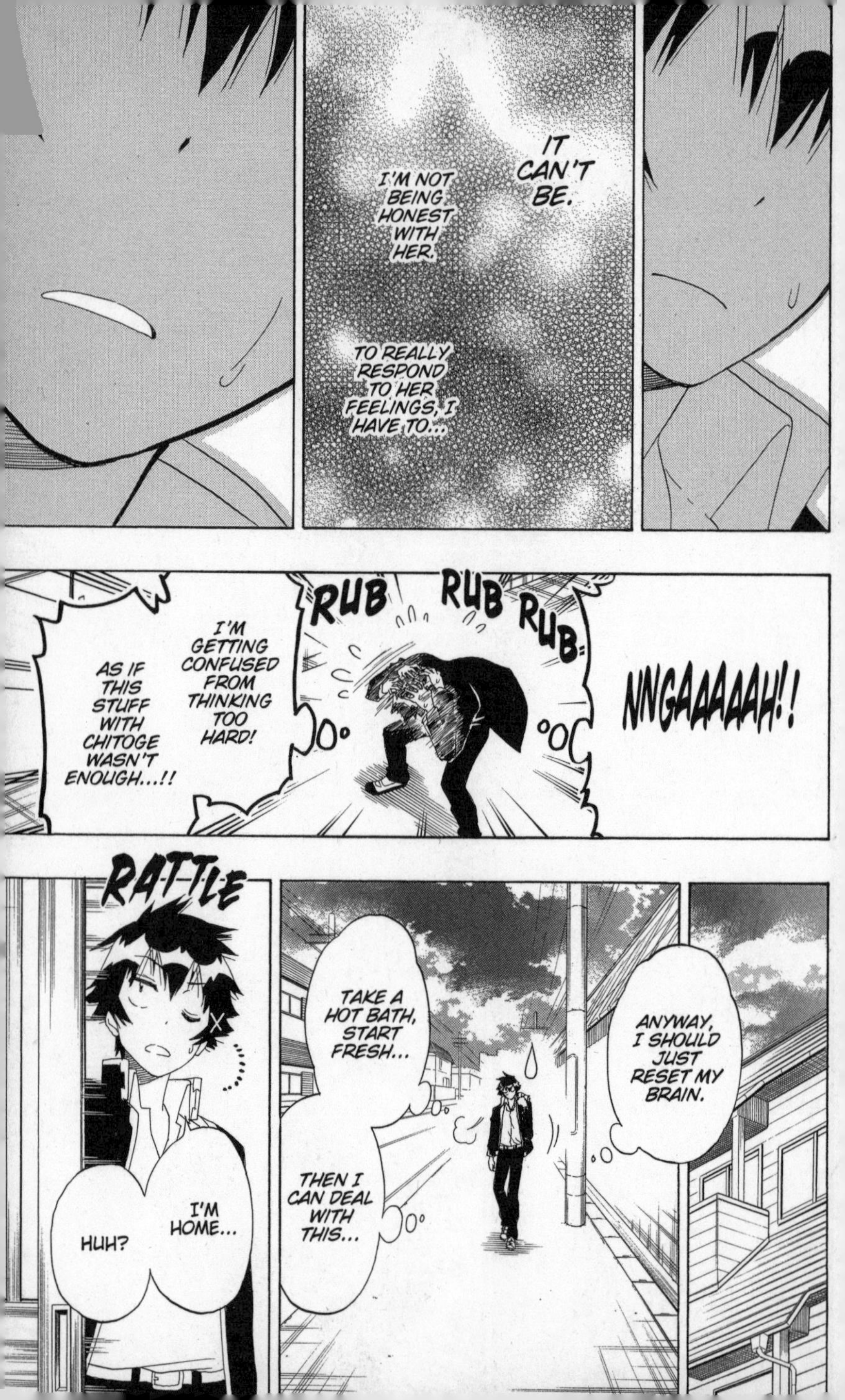
IT CAN'T BE.
I'M NOT BEING HONEST WITH HER.
TO REALLY RESPOND TO HER FEELINGS, I HAVE TO...
NNGAAAAAH!!
RUB RUB RUB
I'M GETTING CONFUSED FROM THINKING TOO HARD!
AS IF THIS STUFF WITH CHITOGE WASN'T ENOUGH...!!
ANYWAY, I SHOULD JUST RESET MY BRAIN.
TAKE A HOT BATH, START FRESH...
THEN I CAN DEAL WITH THIS...
RATTLE
I'M HOME...
HUH?

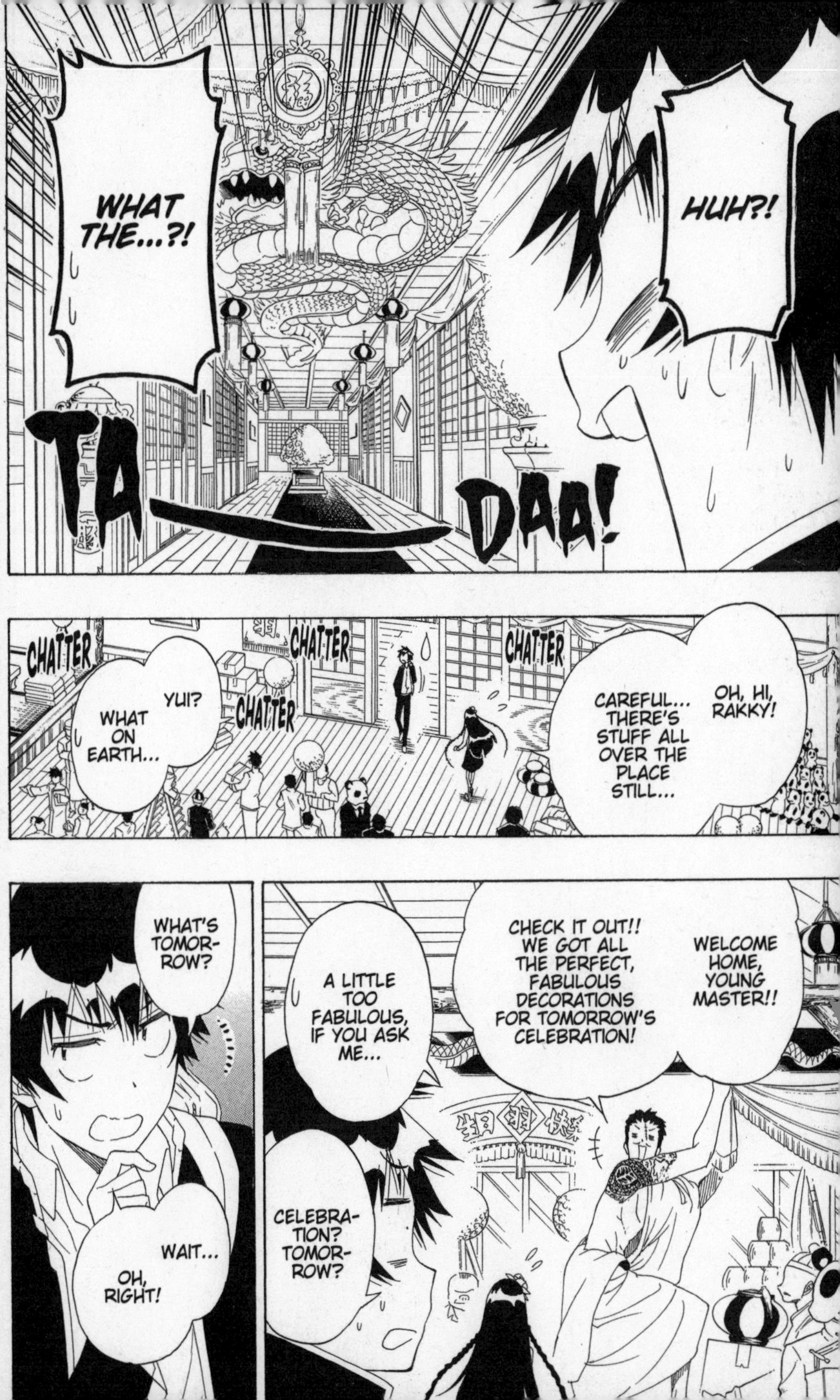
HUH?!
WHAT THE...?!
TA—DAA!
CHATTER
CHATTER
CHATTER
CHATTER
OH, HI, RAKKY!
CAREFUL... THERE'S STUFF ALL OVER THE PLACE STILL...
YUI? WHAT ON EARTH...
WELCOME HOME, YOUNG MASTER!!
CHECK IT OUT!! WE GOT ALL THE PERFECT, FABULOUS DECORATIONS FOR TOMORROW'S CELEBRATION!
A LITTLE TOO FABULOUS, IF YOU ASK ME...
CELEBRATION? TOMORROW?
WHAT'S TOMORROW?
WAIT...
OH, RIGHT!

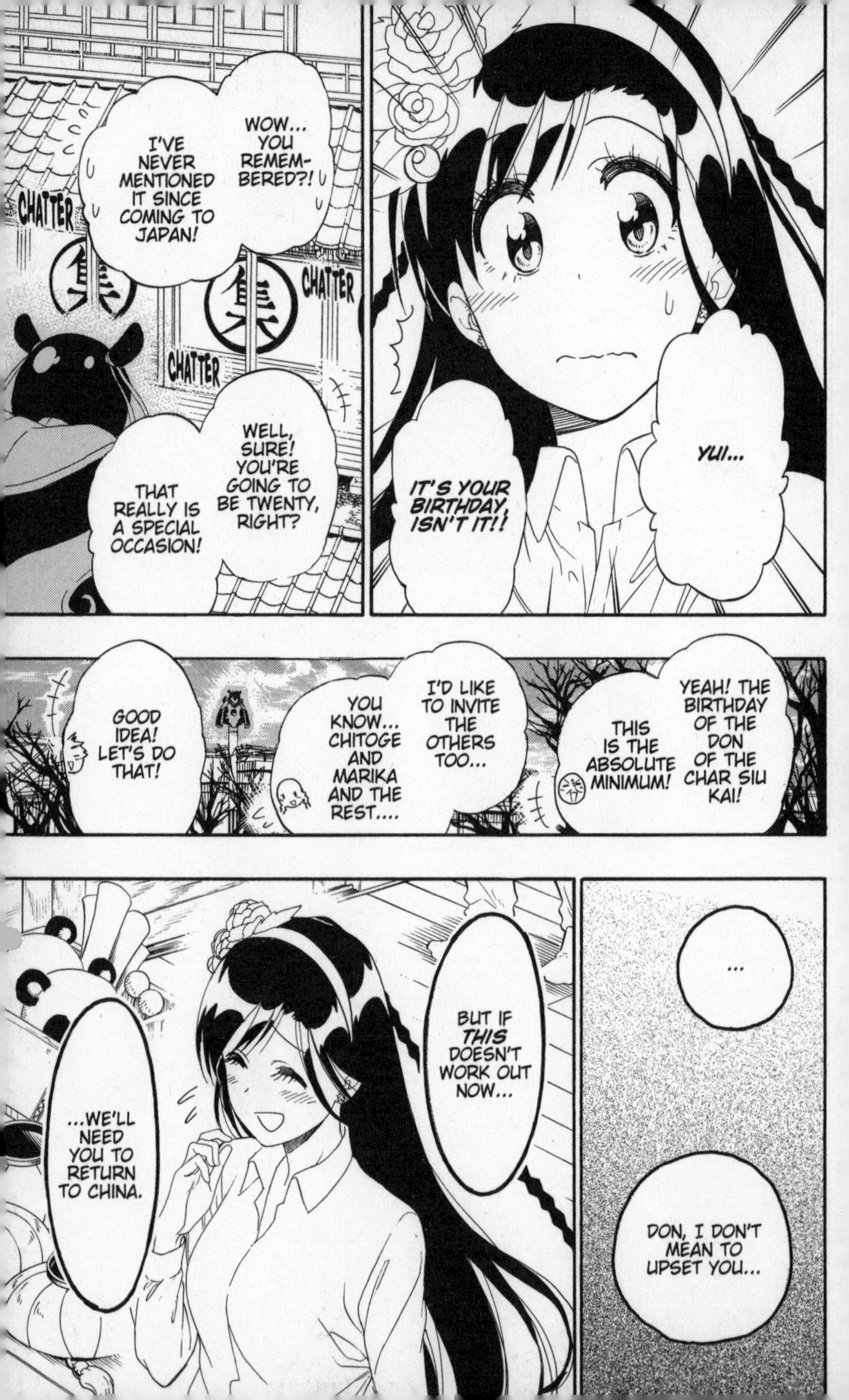
YUI...
IT'S YOUR BIRTHDAY, ISN'T IT!!
WOW... YOU REMEMBERED?!
I'VE NEVER MENTIONED IT SINCE COMING TO JAPAN!
CHATTER
CHATTER
CHATTER
WELL, SURE! YOU'RE GOING TO BE TWENTY, RIGHT?
THAT REALLY IS A SPECIAL OCCASION!
YEAH! THE BIRTHDAY OF THE DON OF THE CHAR SIU KAI!
THIS IS THE ABSOLUTE MINIMUM!
I'D LIKE TO INVITE THE OTHERS TOO...
YOU KNOW... CHITOGE AND MARIKA AND THE REST....
GOOD IDEA! LET'S DO THAT!
...
DON, I DON'T MEAN TO UPSET YOU...
BUT IF THIS DOESN'T WORK OUT NOW...
...WE'LL NEED YOU TO RETURN TO CHINA.

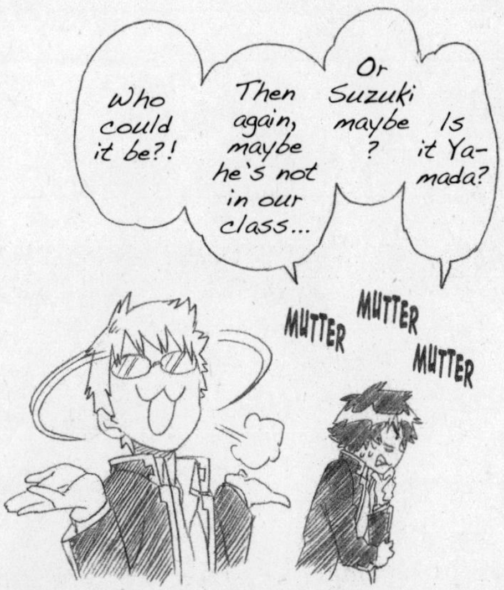
Is it Yamada?
Or Suzuki maybe?
Then again, maybe he's not in our class...
Who could it be?!
MUTTER
MUTTER
MUTTER

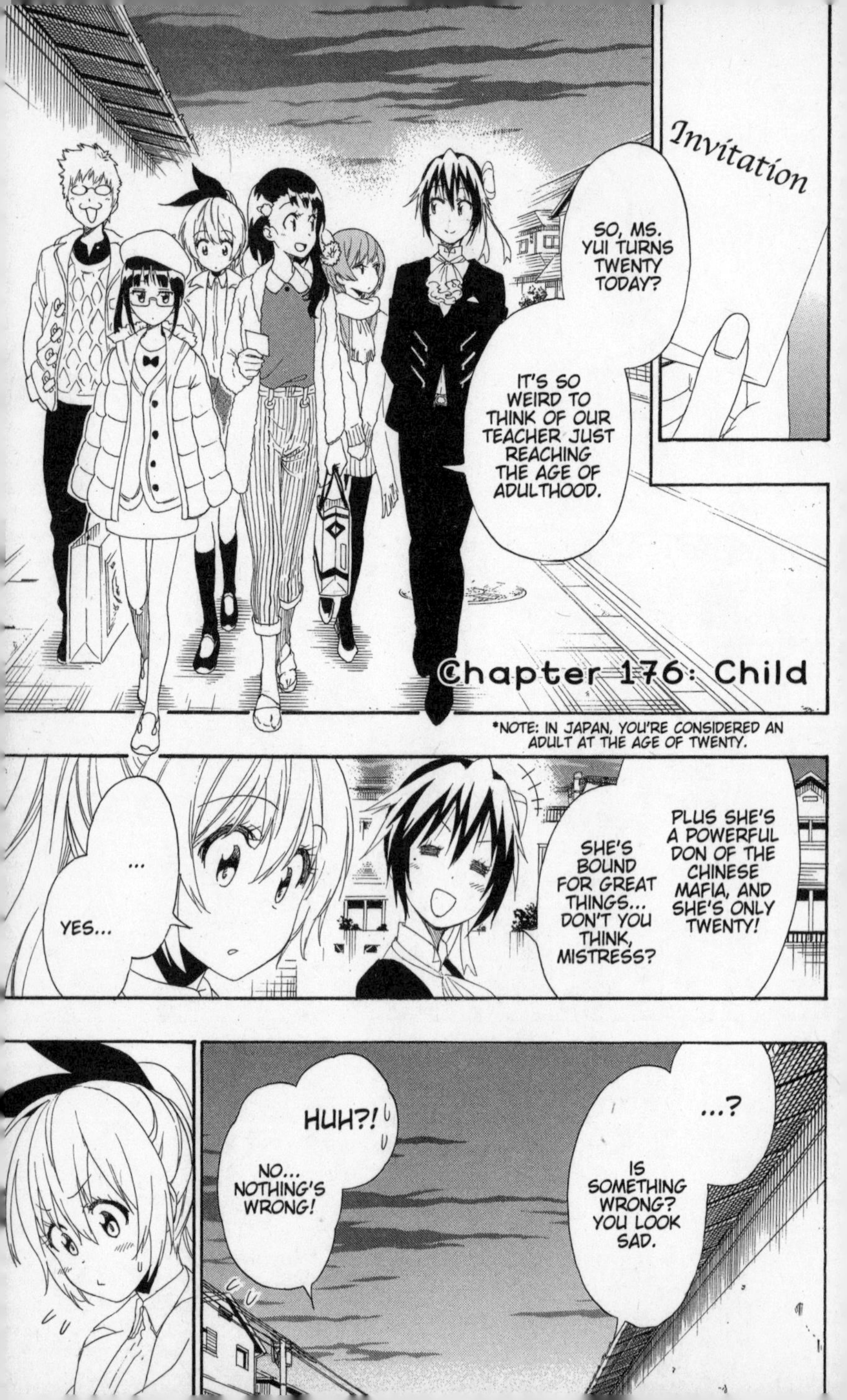
Invitation
SO, MS. YUI TURNS TWENTY TODAY?
IT'S SO WEIRD TO THINK OF OUR TEACHER JUST REACHING THE AGE OF ADULTHOOD.
Chapter 176: Child
*NOTE: IN JAPAN, YOU'RE CONSIDERED AN ADULT AT THE AGE OF TWENTY.
PLUS SHE'S A POWERFUL DON OF THE CHINESE MAFIA, AND SHE'S ONLY TWENTY!
SHE'S BOUND FOR GREAT THINGS... DON'T YOU THINK, MISTRESS?
...
YES...
...?
IS SOMETHING WRONG? YOU LOOK SAD.
HUH?!
NO... NOTHING'S WRONG!

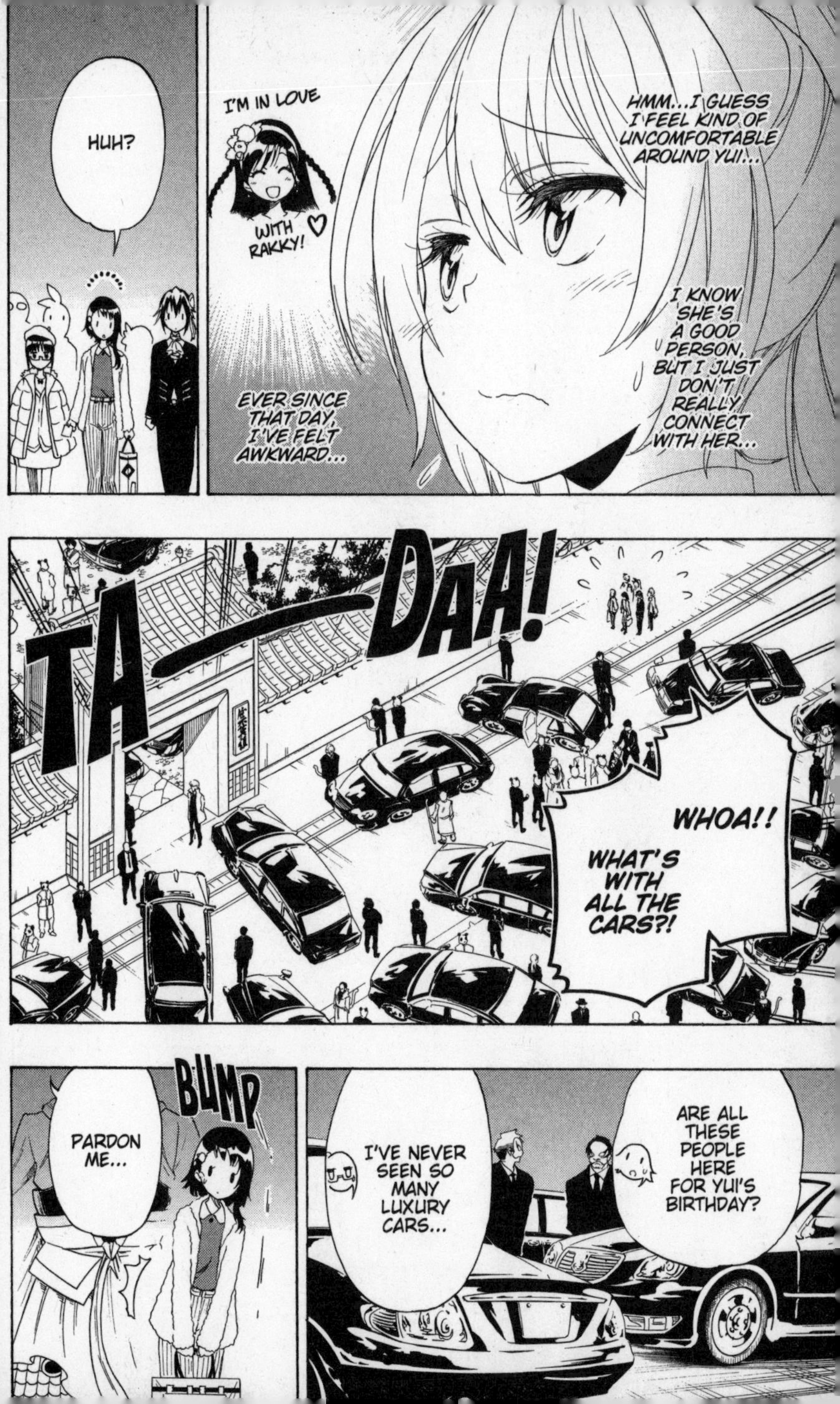
HMM...I GUESS I FEEL KIND OF UNCOMFORTABLE AROUND YUI...
I KNOW SHE'S A GOOD PERSON, BUT I JUST DON'T REALLY CONNECT WITH HER...
I'M IN LOVE
WITH RAKKY! ♡
EVER SINCE THAT DAY, I'VE FELT AWKWARD...
HUH?
TA—DAA!
WHOA!!
WHAT'S WITH ALL THE CARS?!
ARE ALL THESE PEOPLE HERE FOR YUI'S BIRTHDAY?
I'VE NEVER SEEN SO MANY LUXURY CARS...
BUMP
PARDON ME...

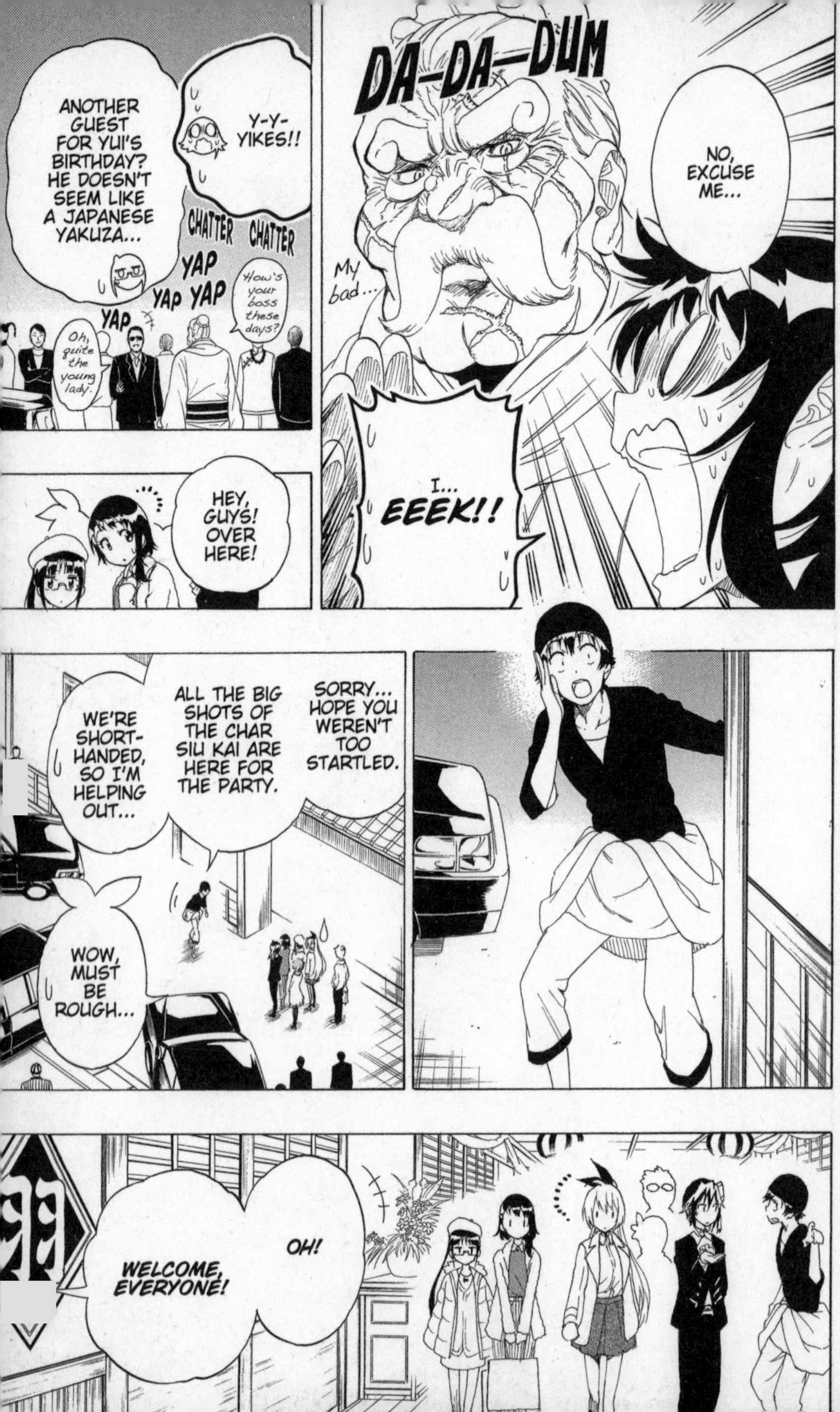
DA-DA-DUM
NO, EXCUSE ME...
My bad...
I... EEEK!!
Y-Y-YIKES!!
ANOTHER GUEST FOR YUI'S BIRTHDAY? HE DOESN'T SEEM LIKE A JAPANESE YAKUZA...
CHATTER CHATTER
YAP YAP YAP YAP
How's your boss these days?
Oh, quite the young lady.
HEY, GUYS! OVER HERE!
SORRY... HOPE YOU WEREN'T TOO STARTLED.
ALL THE BIG SHOTS OF THE CHAR SIU KAI ARE HERE FOR THE PARTY.
WE'RE SHORT-HANDED, SO I'M HELPING OUT...
WOW, MUST BE ROUGH...
OH!
WELCOME, EVERYONE!

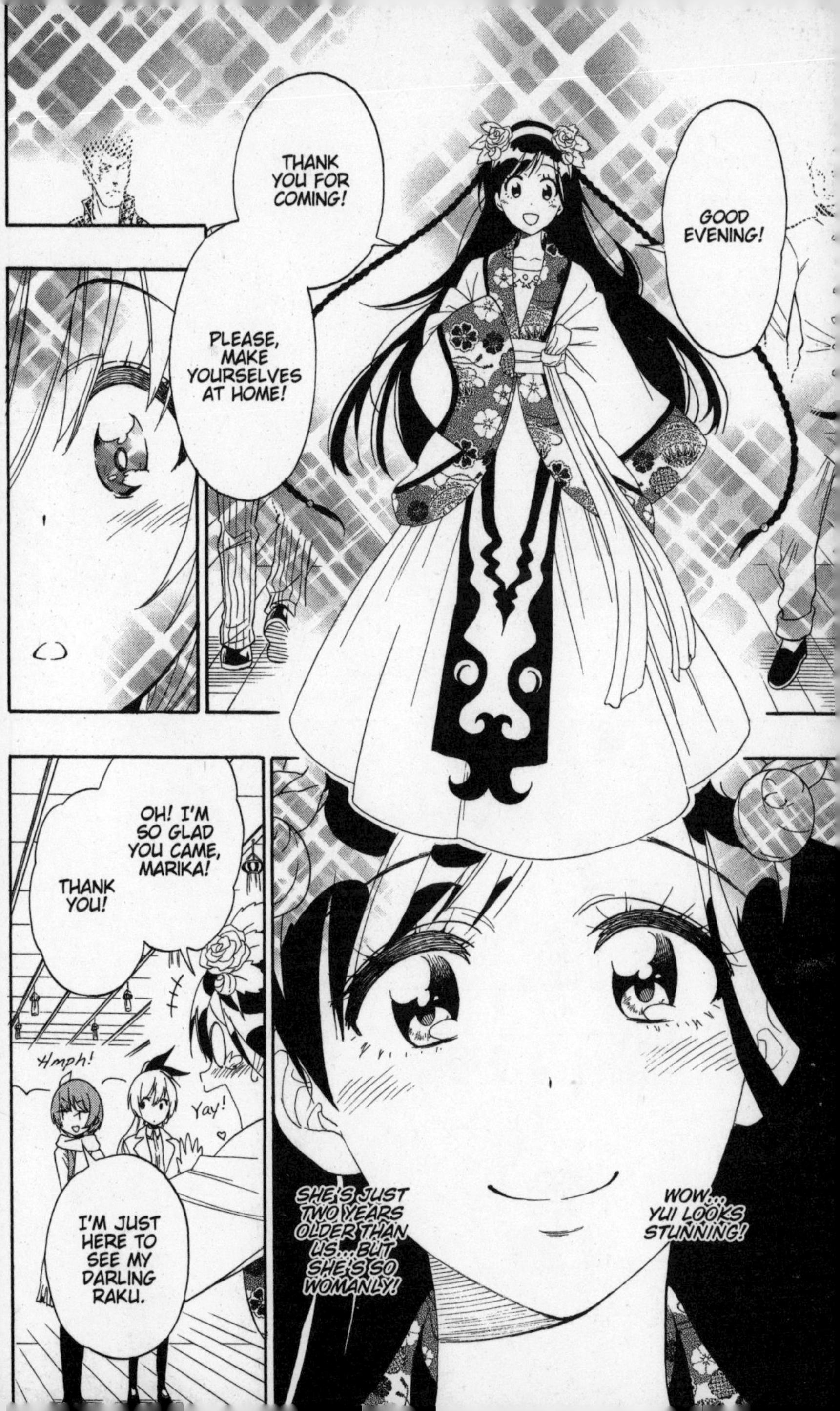
GOOD EVENING!
THANK YOU FOR COMING!
PLEASE, MAKE YOURSELVES AT HOME!
WOW... YUI LOOKS STUNNING!
SHE'S JUST TWO YEARS OLDER THAN US... BUT SHE'S SO WOMANLY!
OH! I'M SO GLAD YOU CAME, MARIKA!
THANK YOU!
Hmph!
Yay!
I'M JUST HERE TO SEE MY DARLING RAKU.

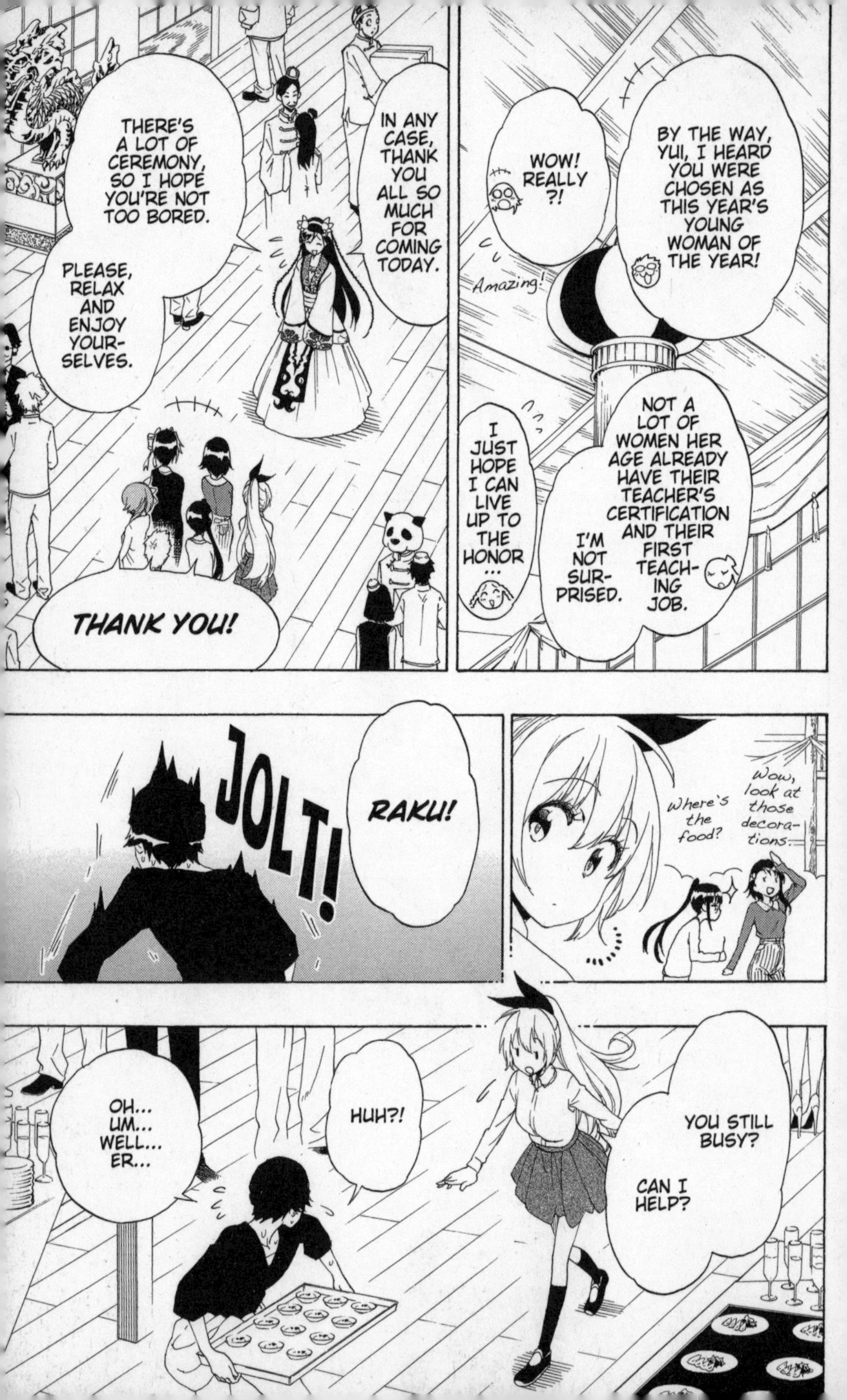
BY THE WAY, YUI, I HEARD YOU WERE CHOSEN AS THIS YEAR'S YOUNG WOMAN OF THE YEAR!
WOW! REALLY?!
Amazing!
NOT A LOT OF WOMEN HER AGE ALREADY HAVE THEIR TEACHER'S CERTIFICATION AND THEIR FIRST TEACHING JOB.
I'M NOT SURPRISED.
I JUST HOPE I CAN LIVE UP TO THE HONOR...
IN ANY CASE, THANK YOU ALL SO MUCH FOR COMING TODAY.
THERE'S A LOT OF CEREMONY, SO I HOPE YOU'RE NOT TOO BORED.
PLEASE, RELAX AND ENJOY YOURSELVES.
THANK YOU!
Wow, look at those decorations.
Where's the food?
RAKU!
JOLT!
YOU STILL BUSY?
CAN I HELP?
HUH?!
OH... UM... WELL... ER...

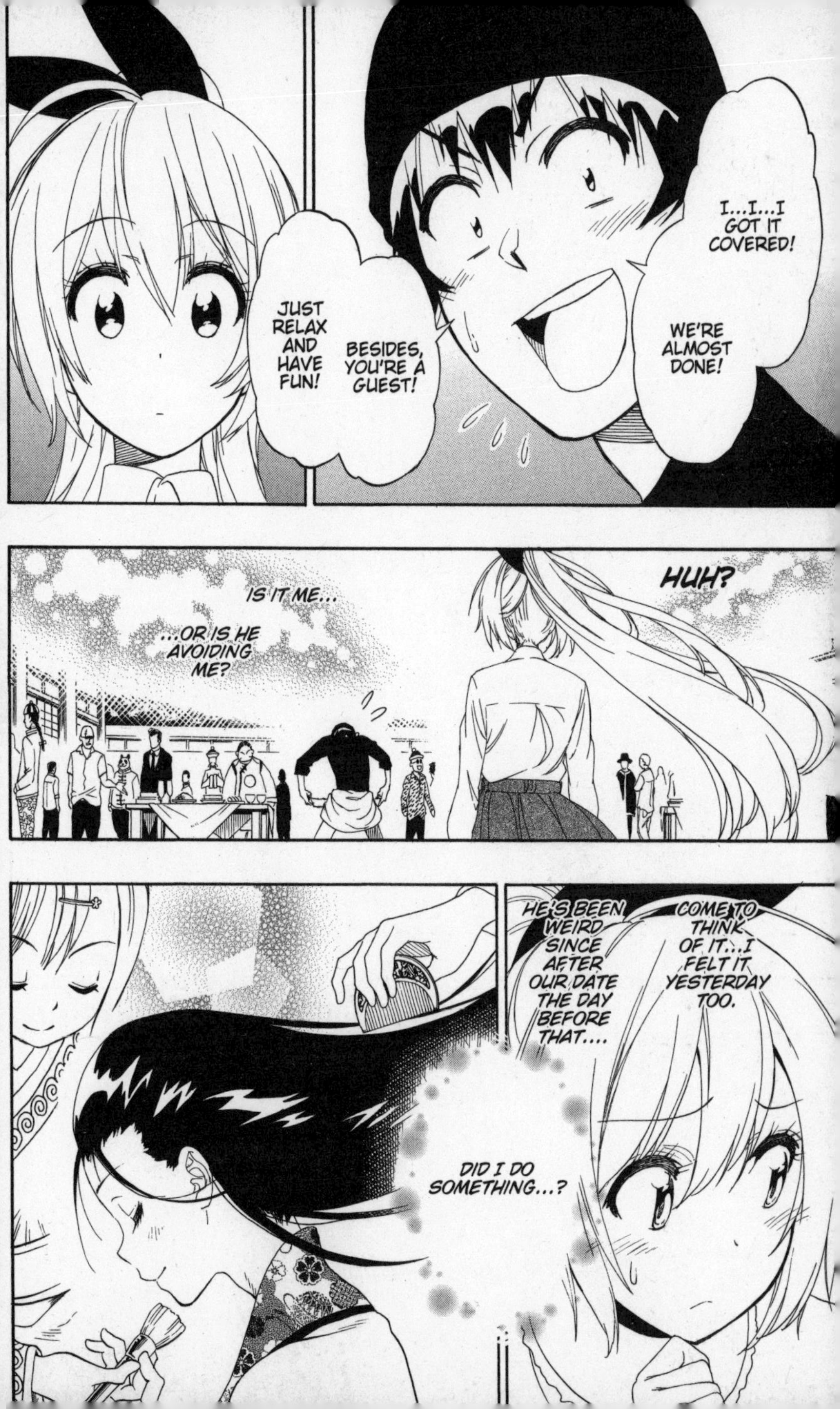
I...I...I GOT IT COVERED!
WE'RE ALMOST DONE!
BESIDES, YOU'RE A GUEST!
JUST RELAX AND HAVE FUN!
HUH?
IS IT ME...
...OR IS HE AVOIDING ME?
COME TO THINK OF IT...I FELT IT YESTERDAY TOO.
HE'S BEEN WEIRD SINCE AFTER OUR DATE THE DAY BEFORE THAT....
DID I DO SOMETHING...?

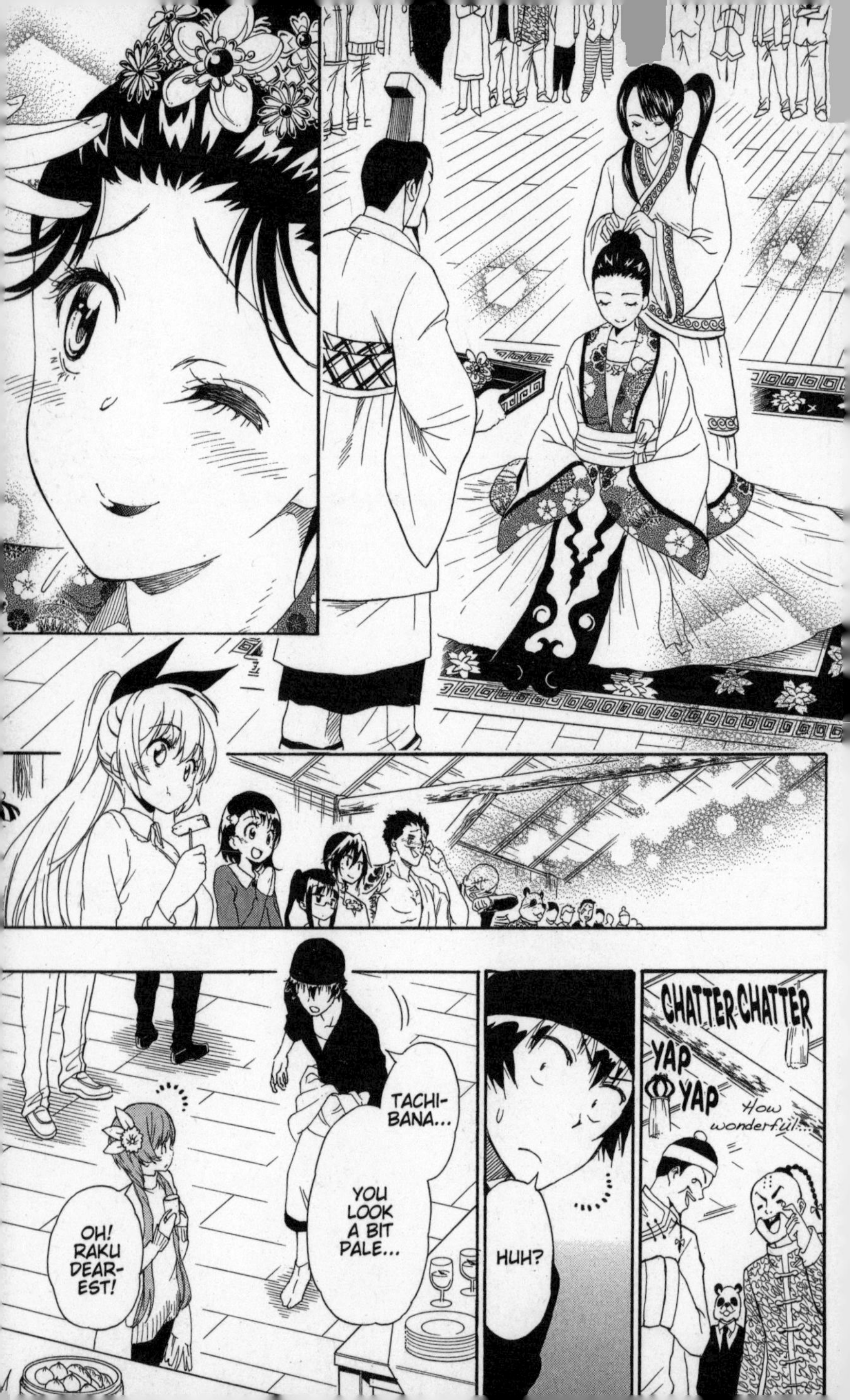

CHATTER CHATTER
YAP YAP
How wonderful...
.....
HUH?
TACHI-BANA...
YOU LOOK A BIT PALE...
OH! RAKU DEAR-EST!

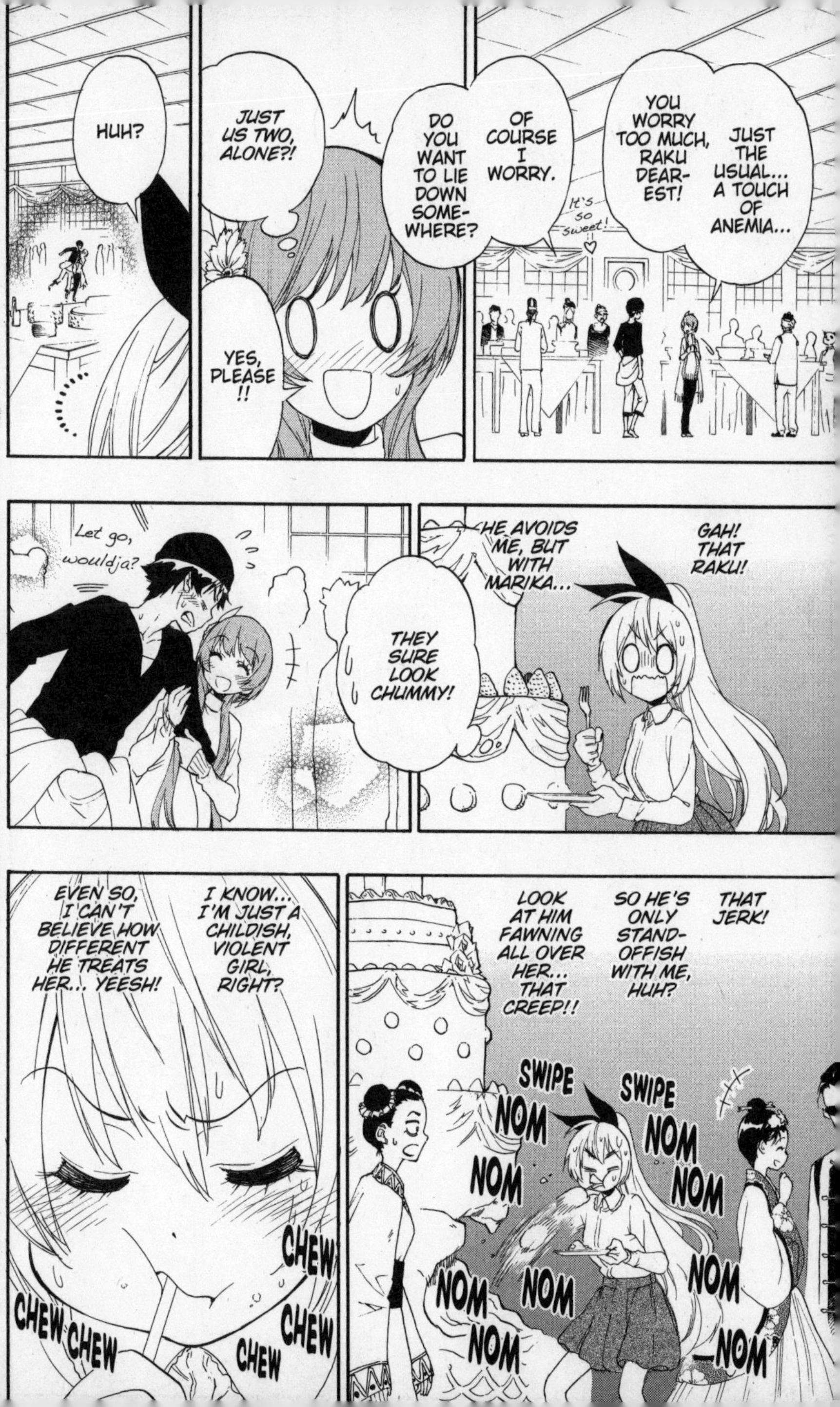
JUST THE USUAL... A TOUCH OF ANEMIA...
YOU WORRY TOO MUCH, RAKU DEAREST!
It's so sweet!
OF COURSE I WORRY.
DO YOU WANT TO LIE DOWN SOMEWHERE?
JUST US TWO, ALONE?!
YES, PLEASE!!
HUH?
GAH! THAT RAKU!
HE AVOIDS ME, BUT WITH MARIKA...
THEY SURE LOOK CHUMMY!
Let go, wouldja?
THAT JERK!
SO HE'S ONLY STANDOFFISH WITH ME, HUH?
LOOK AT HIM FAWNING ALL OVER HER... THAT CREEP!!
SWIPE
SWIPE
NOM NOM NOM
NOM NOM NOM
NOM NOM NOM
NOM
I KNOW... I'M JUST A CHILDISH, VIOLENT GIRL, RIGHT?
EVEN SO, I CAN'T BELIEVE HOW DIFFERENT HE TREATS HER... YEESH!
CHEW CHEW CHEW
CHEW CHEW CHEW

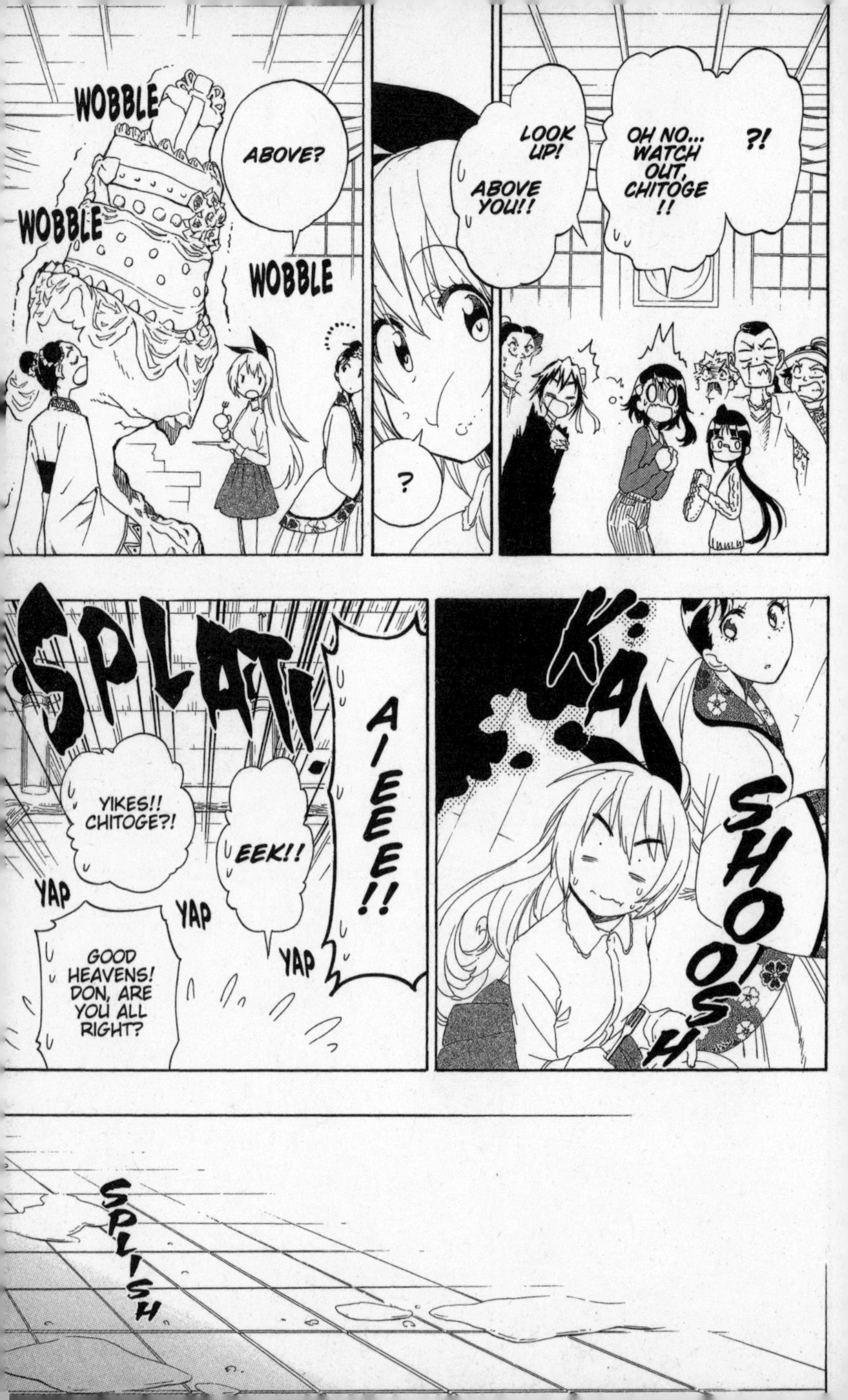
?!
OH NO... WATCH OUT, CHITOGE !!
LOOK UP! ABOVE YOU!!
?
ABOVE?
WOBBLE
WOBBLE
WOBBLE
KA
SHOOSH
AIEEE!!
EEK!!
YIKES!! CHITOGE?!
YAP
YAP
YAP
GOOD HEAVENS! DON, ARE YOU ALL RIGHT?
SPLISH

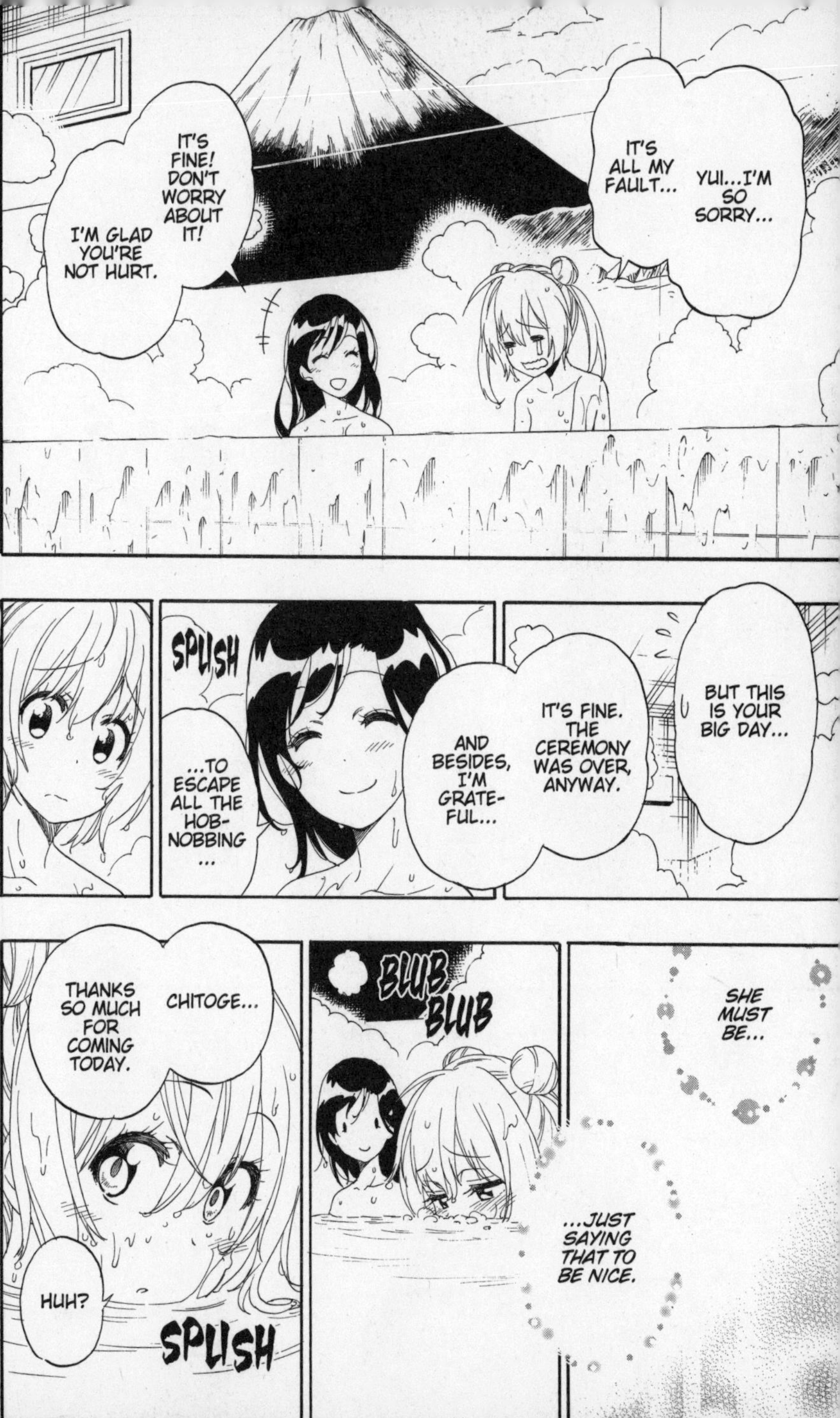
YUI...I'M SO SORRY...
IT'S ALL MY FAULT...
IT'S FINE! DON'T WORRY ABOUT IT!
I'M GLAD YOU'RE NOT HURT.
BUT THIS IS YOUR BIG DAY...
IT'S FINE. THE CEREMONY WAS OVER, ANYWAY.
AND BESIDES, I'M GRATE-FUL...
...TO ESCAPE ALL THE HOB-NOBBING...
SPLISH
SHE MUST BE...
...JUST SAYING THAT TO BE NICE.
BLUB BLUB
CHITOGE...
THANKS SO MUCH FOR COMING TODAY.
HUH?
SPLISH

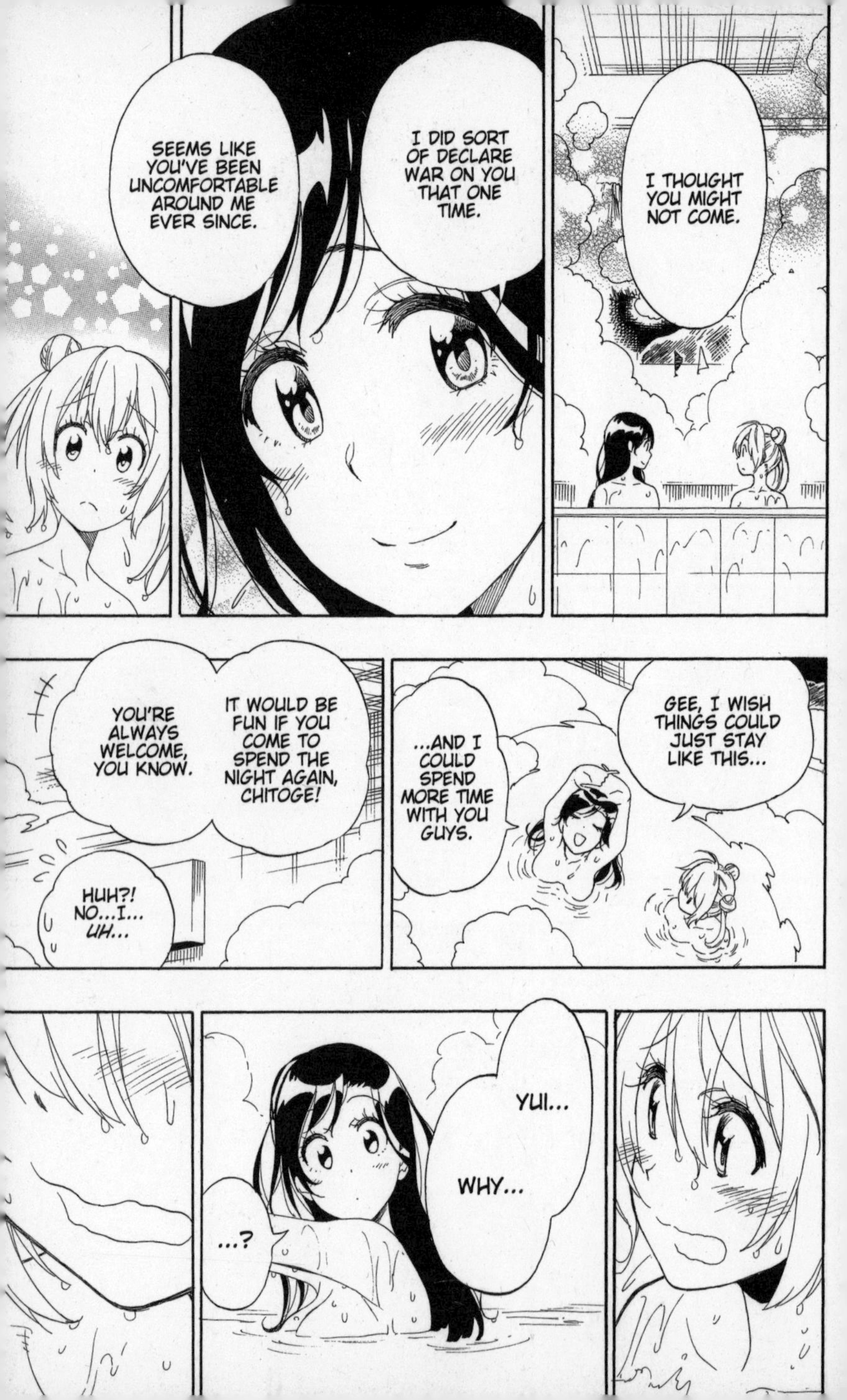
I THOUGHT YOU MIGHT NOT COME.
I DID SORT OF DECLARE WAR ON YOU THAT ONE TIME.
SEEMS LIKE YOU'VE BEEN UNCOMFORTABLE AROUND ME EVER SINCE.
GEE, I WISH THINGS COULD JUST STAY LIKE THIS...
...AND I COULD SPEND MORE TIME WITH YOU GUYS.
IT WOULD BE FUN IF YOU COME TO SPEND THE NIGHT AGAIN, CHITOGE!
YOU'RE ALWAYS WELCOME, YOU KNOW.
HUH?! NO...I... *UH...*
YUI...
WHY...
...?

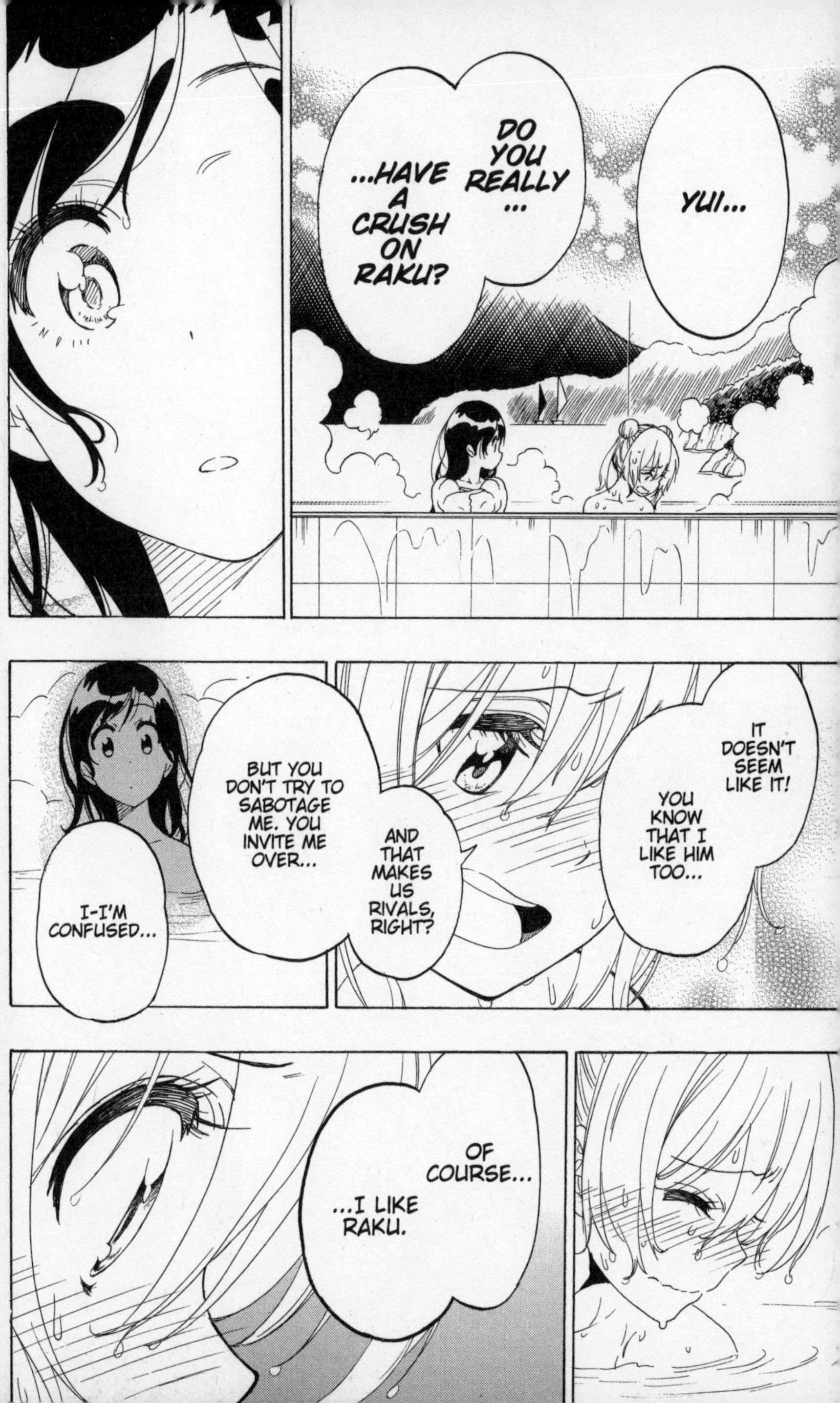
YUI...
DO YOU REALLY...
...HAVE A CRUSH ON RAKU?
IT DOESN'T SEEM LIKE IT!
YOU KNOW THAT I LIKE HIM TOO...
AND THAT MAKES US RIVALS, RIGHT?
BUT YOU DON'T TRY TO SABOTAGE ME. YOU INVITE ME OVER...
I-I'M CONFUSED...
OF COURSE...
...I LIKE RAKU.

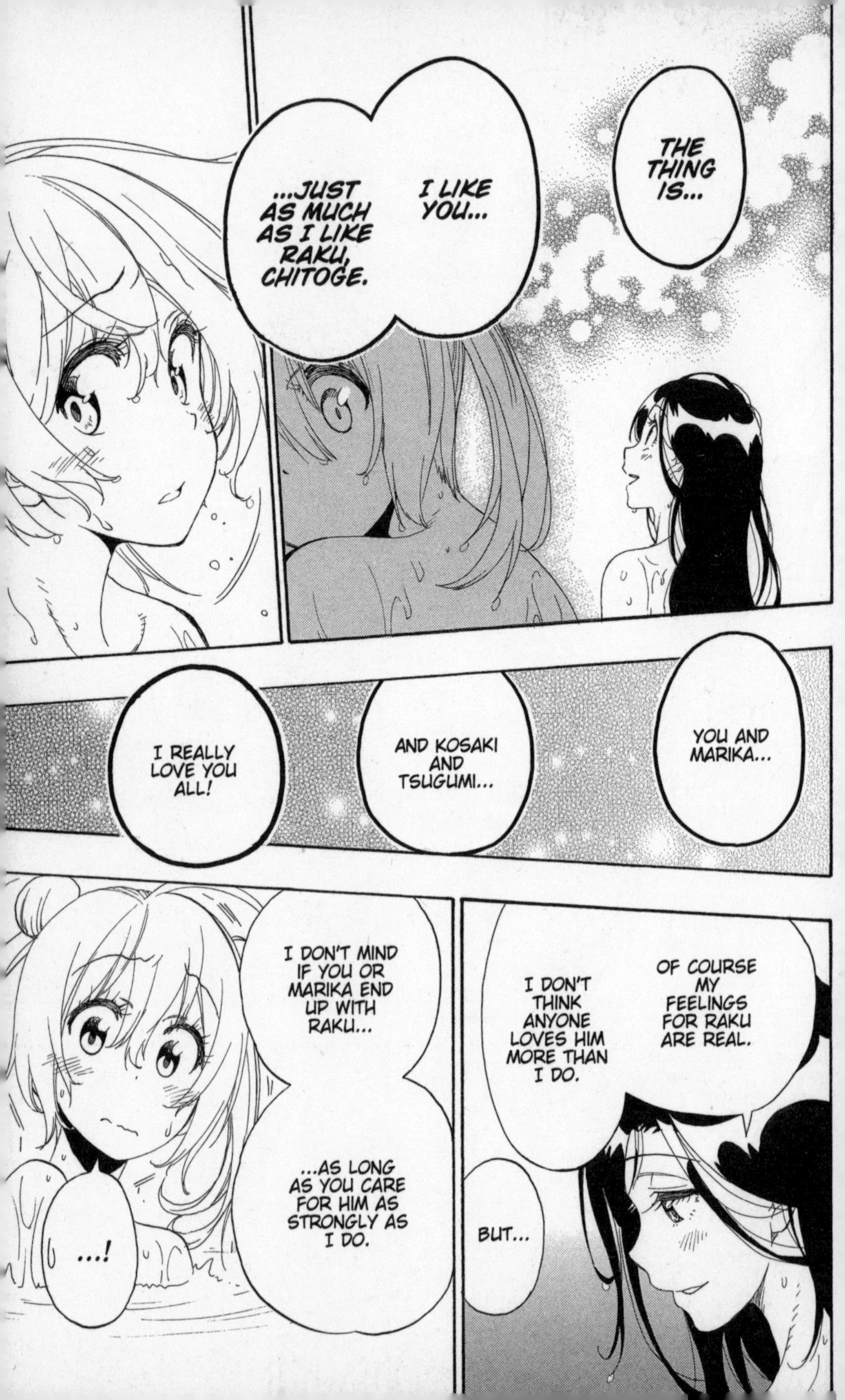
THE THING IS...
I LIKE YOU...
...JUST AS MUCH AS I LIKE RAKU, CHITOGE.
YOU AND MARIKA...
AND KOSAKI AND TSUGUMI...
I REALLY LOVE YOU ALL!
OF COURSE MY FEELINGS FOR RAKU ARE REAL.
I DON'T THINK ANYONE LOVES HIM MORE THAN I DO.
BUT...
I DON'T MIND IF YOU OR MARIKA END UP WITH RAKU...
...AS LONG AS YOU CARE FOR HIM AS STRONGLY AS I DO.
...!

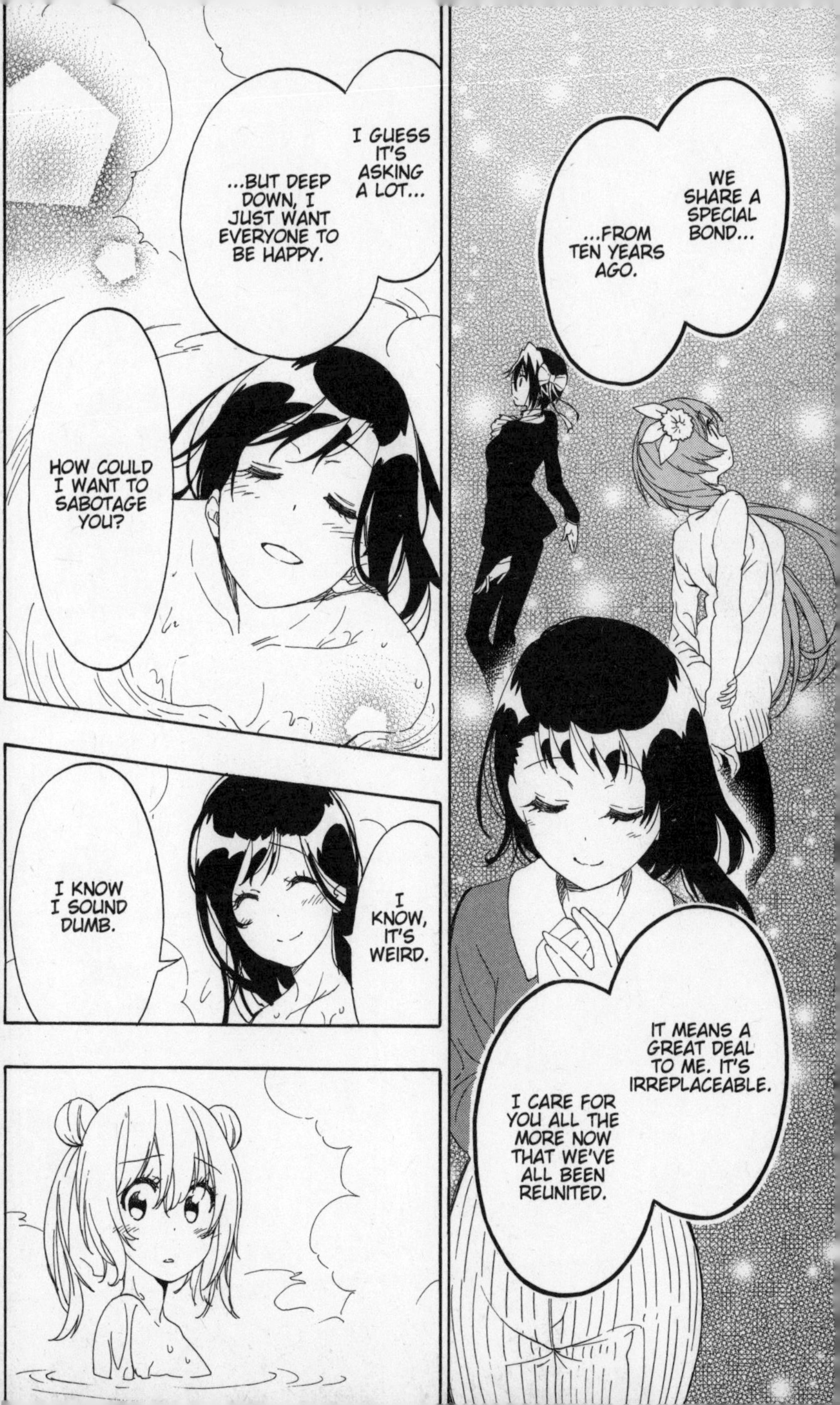
WE SHARE A SPECIAL BOND...
...FROM TEN YEARS AGO.
IT MEANS A GREAT DEAL TO ME. IT'S IRREPLACEABLE.
I CARE FOR YOU ALL THE MORE NOW THAT WE'VE ALL BEEN REUNITED.
I GUESS IT'S ASKING A LOT...
...BUT DEEP DOWN, I JUST WANT EVERYONE TO BE HAPPY.
HOW COULD I WANT TO SABOTAGE YOU?
I KNOW, IT'S WEIRD.
I KNOW I SOUND DUMB.

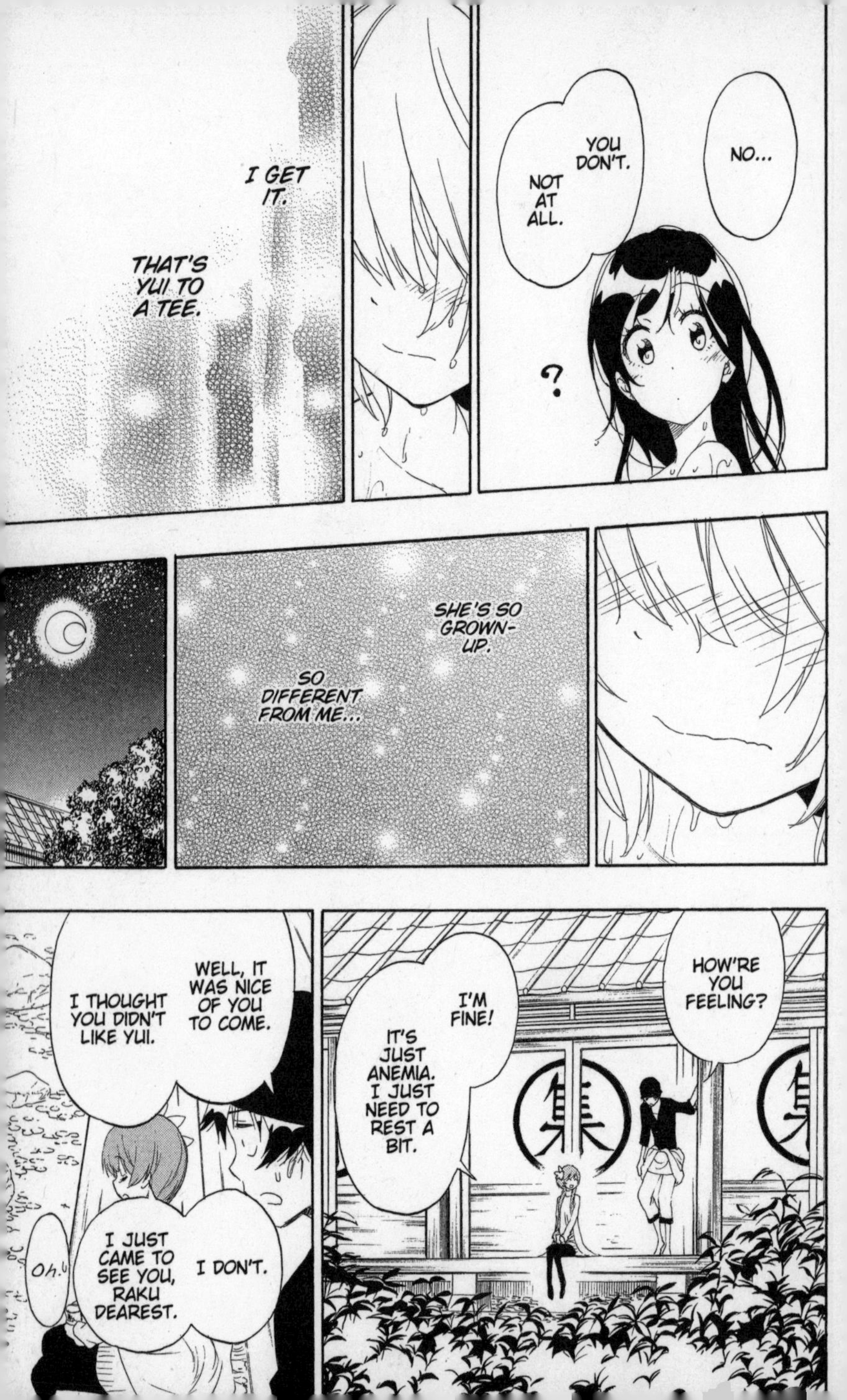
NO...
YOU DON'T.
NOT AT ALL.
?
I GET IT.
THAT'S YUI TO A TEE.
SHE'S SO GROWN-UP.
SO DIFFERENT FROM ME...
HOW'RE YOU FEELING?
I'M FINE!
IT'S JUST ANEMIA. I JUST NEED TO REST A BIT.
WELL, IT WAS NICE OF YOU TO COME.
I THOUGHT YOU DIDN'T LIKE YUI.
I DON'T.
I JUST CAME TO SEE YOU, RAKU DEAREST.
Oh.

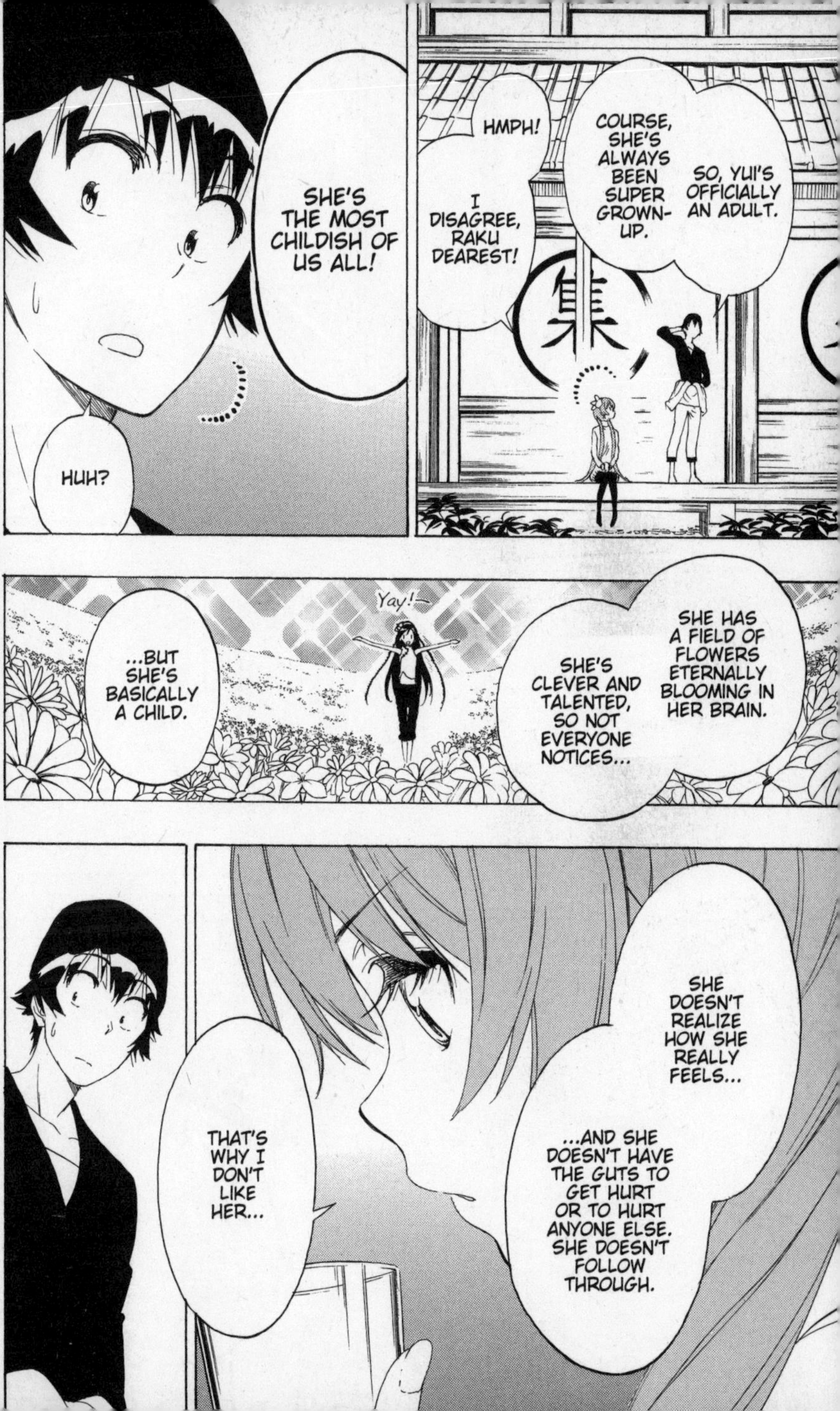
SO, YUI'S OFFICIALLY AN ADULT.
COURSE, SHE'S ALWAYS BEEN SUPER GROWN-UP.
HMPH!
I DISAGREE, RAKU DEAREST!
SHE'S THE MOST CHILDISH OF US ALL!
HUH?
SHE HAS A FIELD OF FLOWERS ETERNALLY BLOOMING IN HER BRAIN.
SHE'S CLEVER AND TALENTED, SO NOT EVERYONE NOTICES...
Yay!~
...BUT SHE'S BASICALLY A CHILD.
SHE DOESN'T REALIZE HOW SHE REALLY FEELS...
...AND SHE DOESN'T HAVE THE GUTS TO GET HURT OR TO HURT ANYONE ELSE. SHE DOESN'T FOLLOW THROUGH.
THAT'S WHY I DON'T LIKE HER...

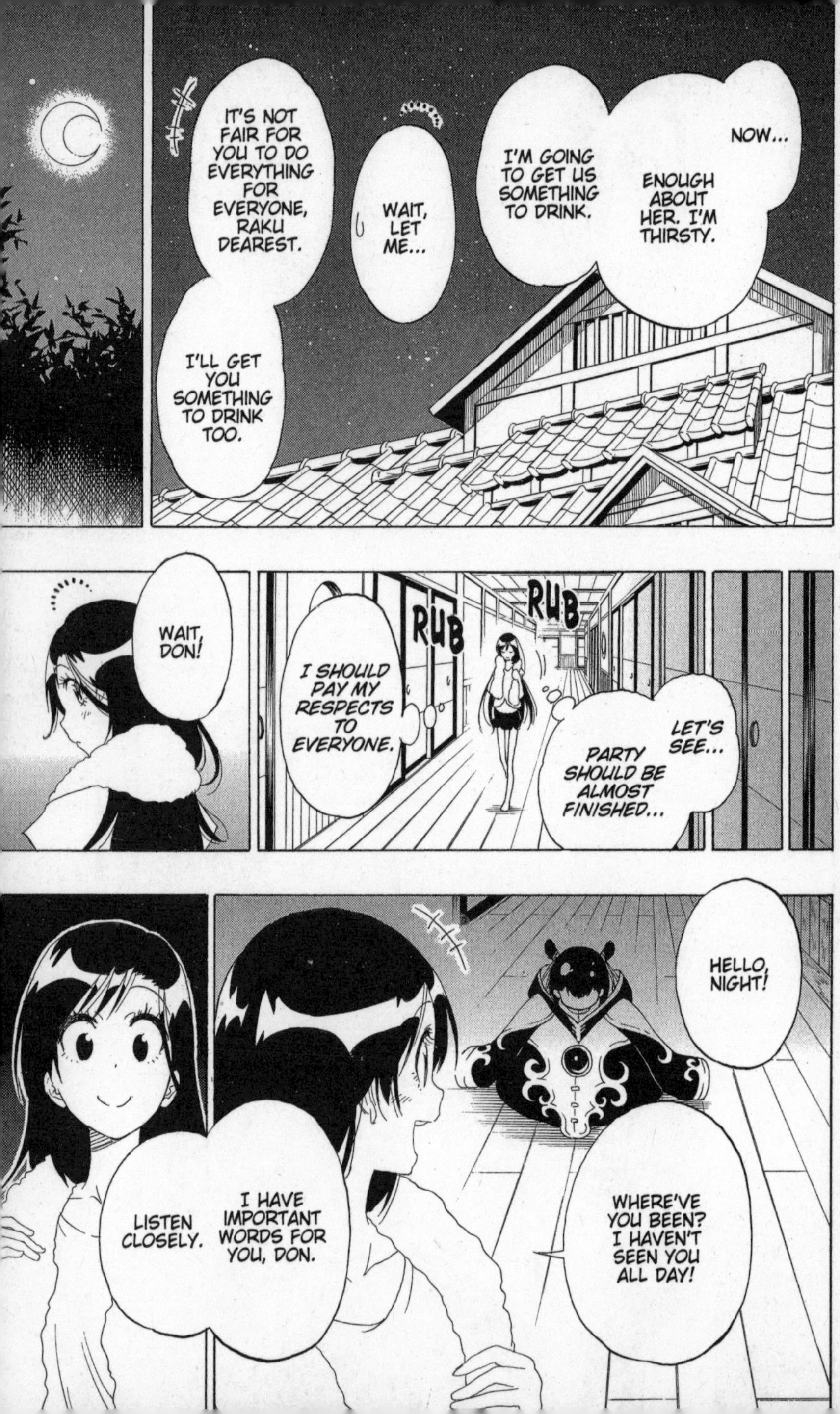
NOW...
ENOUGH ABOUT HER. I'M THIRSTY.
I'M GOING TO GET US SOMETHING TO DRINK.
WAIT, LET ME...
IT'S NOT FAIR FOR YOU TO DO EVERYTHING FOR EVERYONE, RAKU DEAREST.
I'LL GET YOU SOMETHING TO DRINK TOO.
LET'S SEE...
PARTY SHOULD BE ALMOST FINISHED...
RUB
RUB
I SHOULD PAY MY RESPECTS TO EVERYONE.
WAIT, DON!
HELLO, NIGHT!
WHERE'VE YOU BEEN? I HAVEN'T SEEN YOU ALL DAY!
I HAVE IMPORTANT WORDS FOR YOU, DON.
LISTEN CLOSELY.

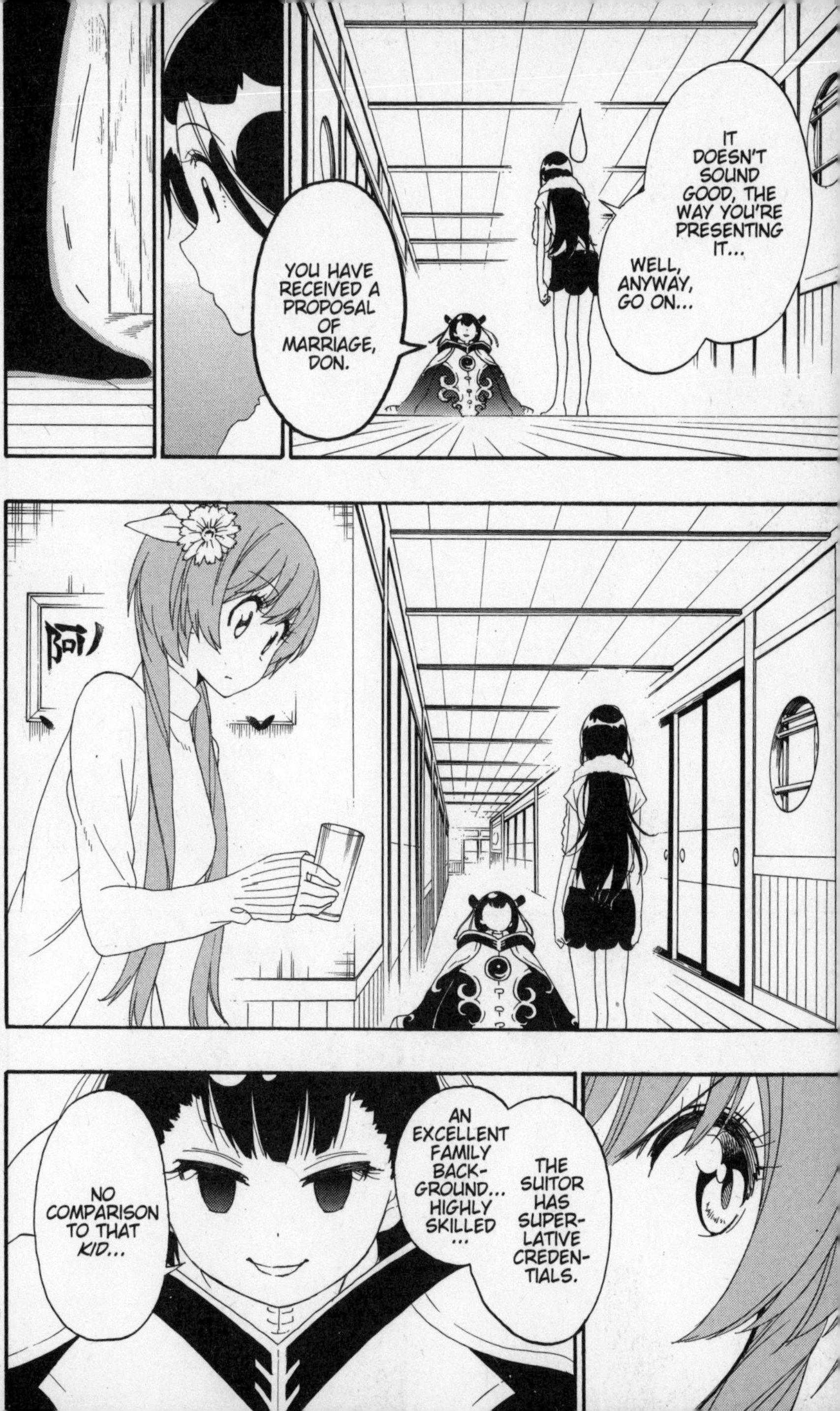

IT DOESN'T SOUND GOOD, THE WAY YOU'RE PRESENTING IT...
WELL, ANYWAY, GO ON...
YOU HAVE RECEIVED A PROPOSAL OF MARRIAGE, DON.
THE SUITOR HAS SUPERLATIVE CREDENTIALS.
AN EXCELLENT FAMILY BACKGROUND... HIGHLY SKILLED...
NO COMPARISON TO THAT KID...

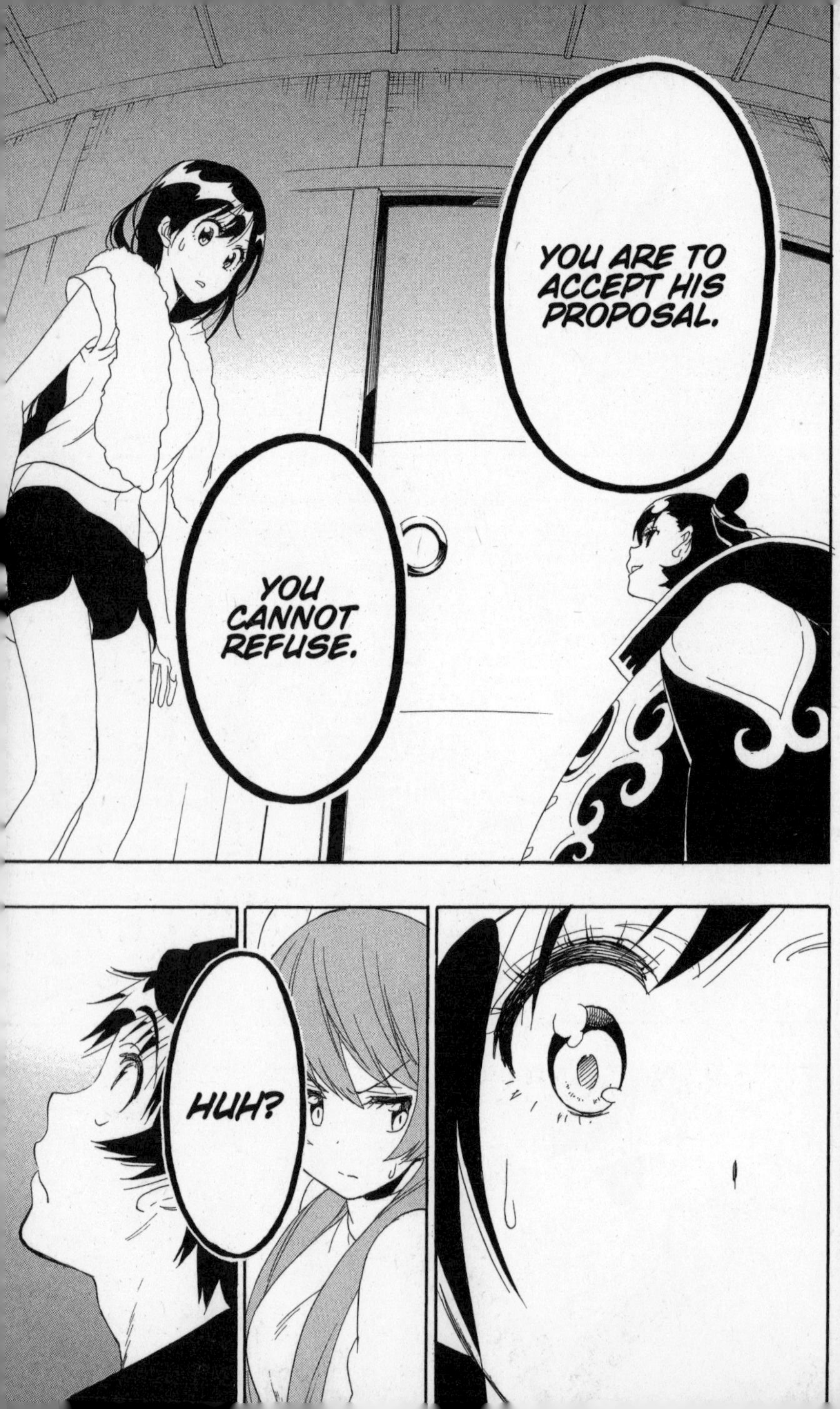
YOU ARE TO ACCEPT HIS PROPOSAL.
YOU CANNOT REFUSE.
HUH?

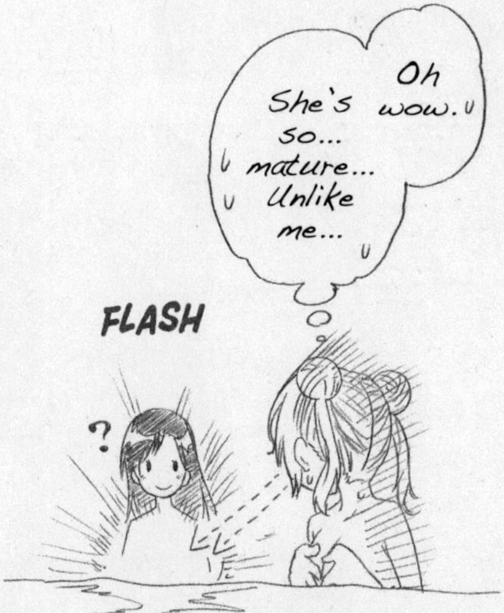
Oh wow.
She's so... mature... Unlike me...
FLASH
?

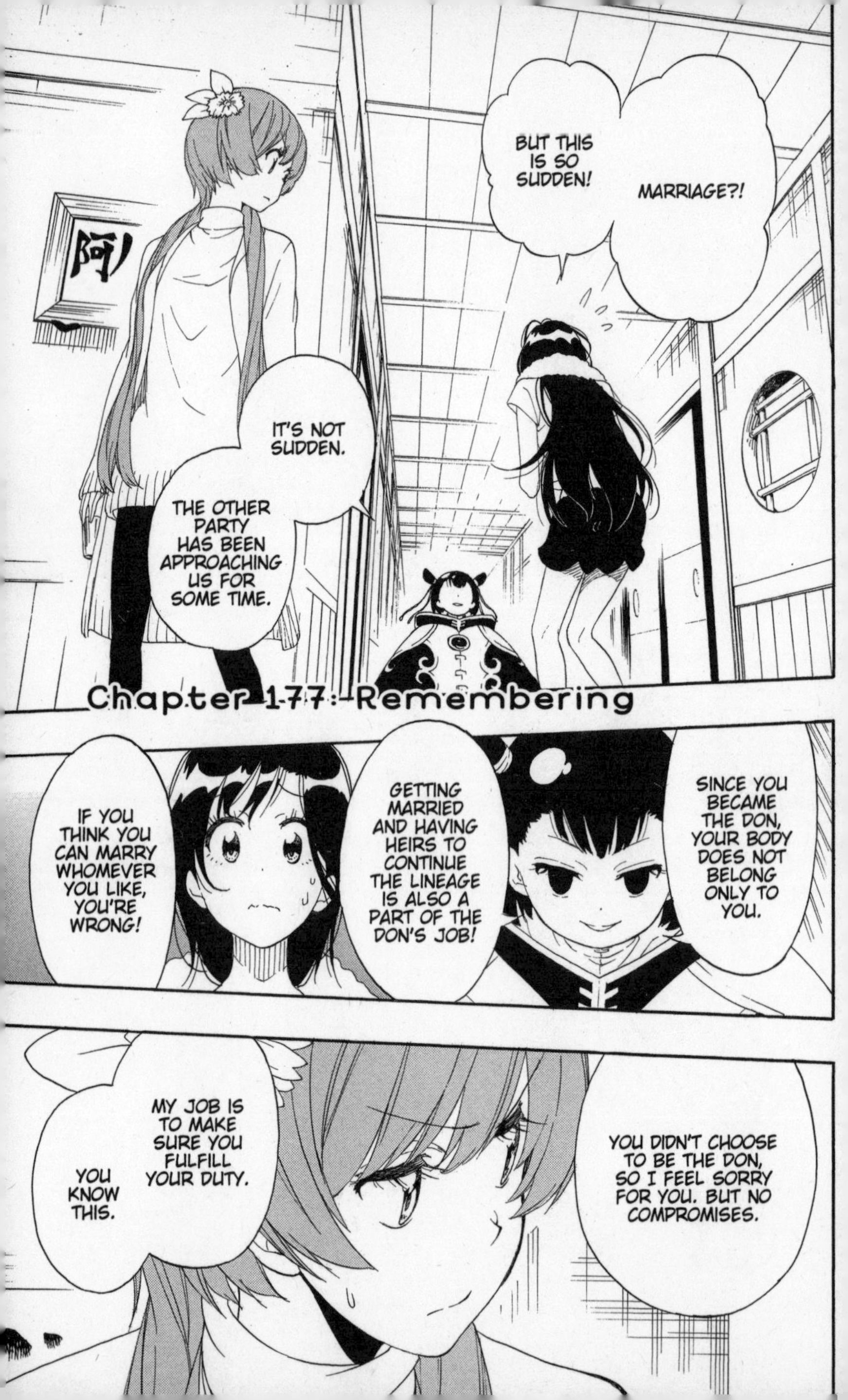
MARRIAGE?!
BUT THIS IS SO SUDDEN!
IT'S NOT SUDDEN.
THE OTHER PARTY HAS BEEN APPROACHING US FOR SOME TIME.
Chapter 177: Remembering
SINCE YOU BECAME THE DON, YOUR BODY DOES NOT BELONG ONLY TO YOU.
GETTING MARRIED AND HAVING HEIRS TO CONTINUE THE LINEAGE IS ALSO A PART OF THE DON'S JOB!
IF YOU THINK YOU CAN MARRY WHOMEVER YOU LIKE, YOU'RE WRONG!
YOU DIDN'T CHOOSE TO BE THE DON, SO I FEEL SORRY FOR YOU. BUT NO COMPROMISES.
MY JOB IS TO MAKE SURE YOU FULFILL YOUR DUTY.
YOU KNOW THIS.

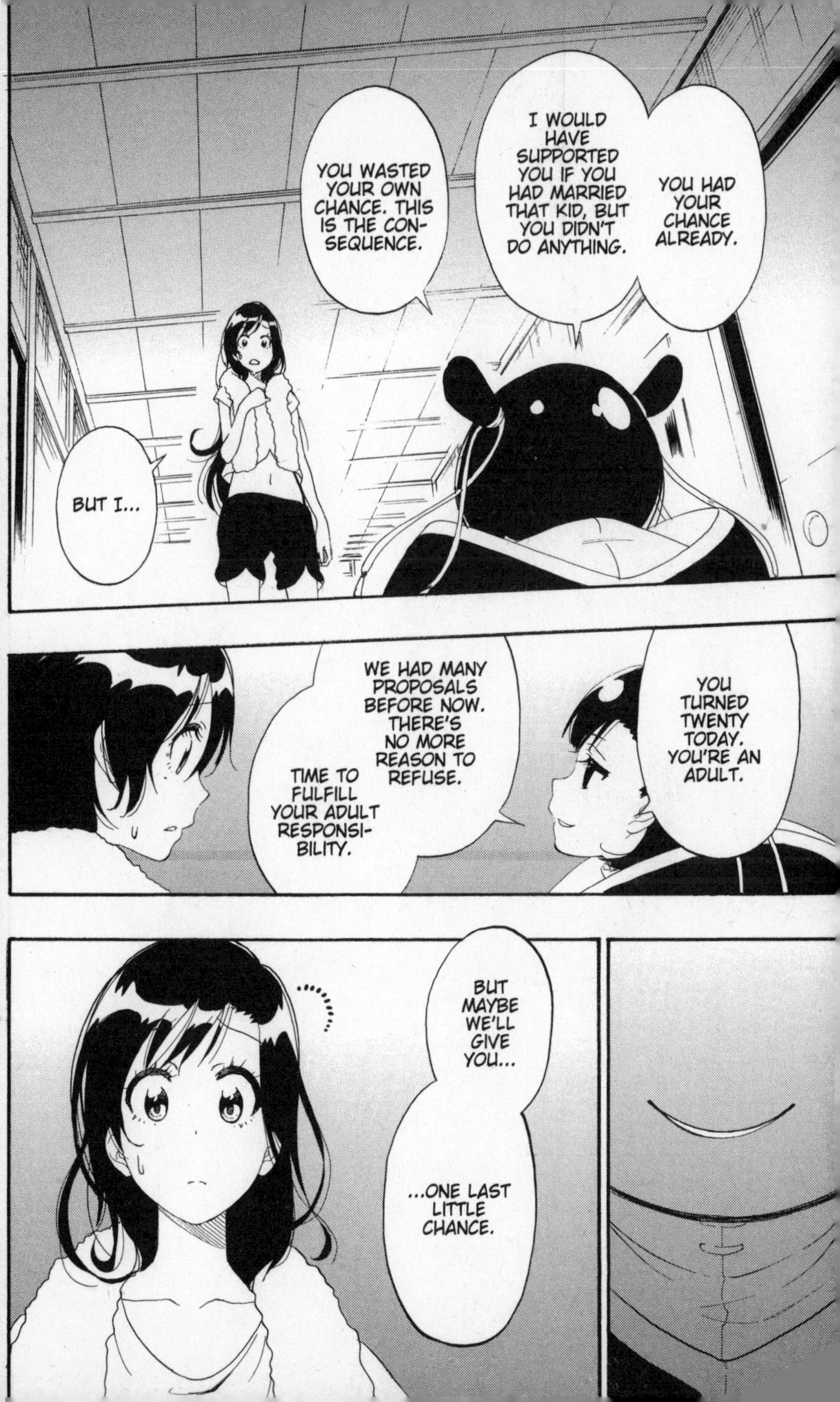

YOU HAD YOUR CHANCE ALREADY.
I WOULD HAVE SUPPORTED YOU IF YOU HAD MARRIED THAT KID, BUT YOU DIDN'T DO ANYTHING.
YOU WASTED YOUR OWN CHANCE. THIS IS THE CON-SEQUENCE.
BUT I...
YOU TURNED TWENTY TODAY. YOU'RE AN ADULT.
WE HAD MANY PROPOSALS BEFORE NOW. THERE'S NO MORE REASON TO REFUSE.
TIME TO FULFILL YOUR ADULT RESPONSI-BILITY.
BUT MAYBE WE'LL GIVE YOU...
...ONE LAST LITTLE CHANCE.

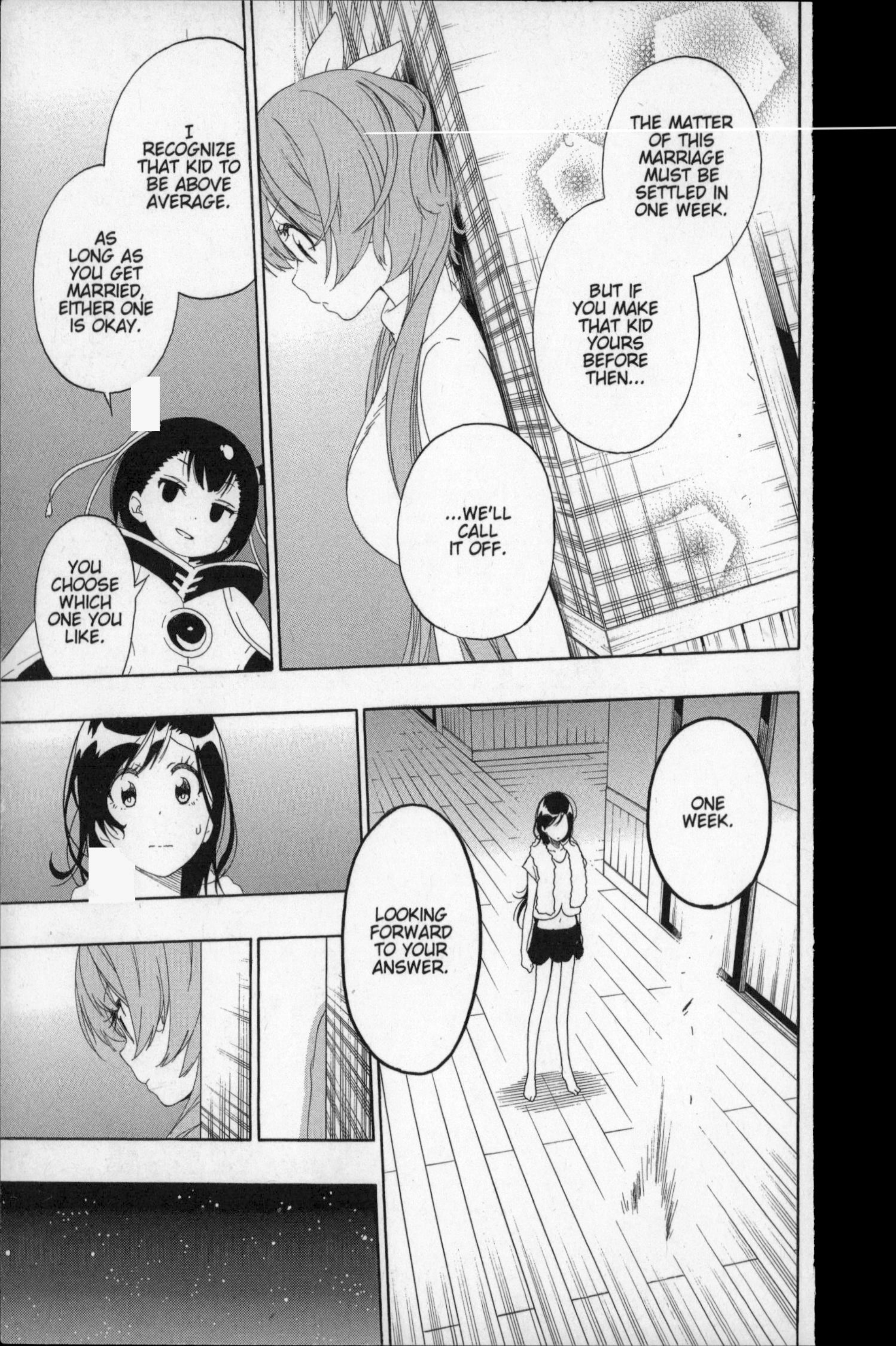
THE MATTER OF THIS MARRIAGE MUST BE SETTLED IN ONE WEEK.
BUT IF YOU MAKE THAT KID YOURS BEFORE THEN...
...WE'LL CALL IT OFF.
I RECOGNIZE THAT KID TO BE ABOVE AVERAGE.
AS LONG AS YOU GET MARRIED, EITHER ONE IS OKAY.
YOU CHOOSE WHICH ONE YOU LIKE.
ONE WEEK.
LOOKING FORWARD TO YOUR ANSWER.

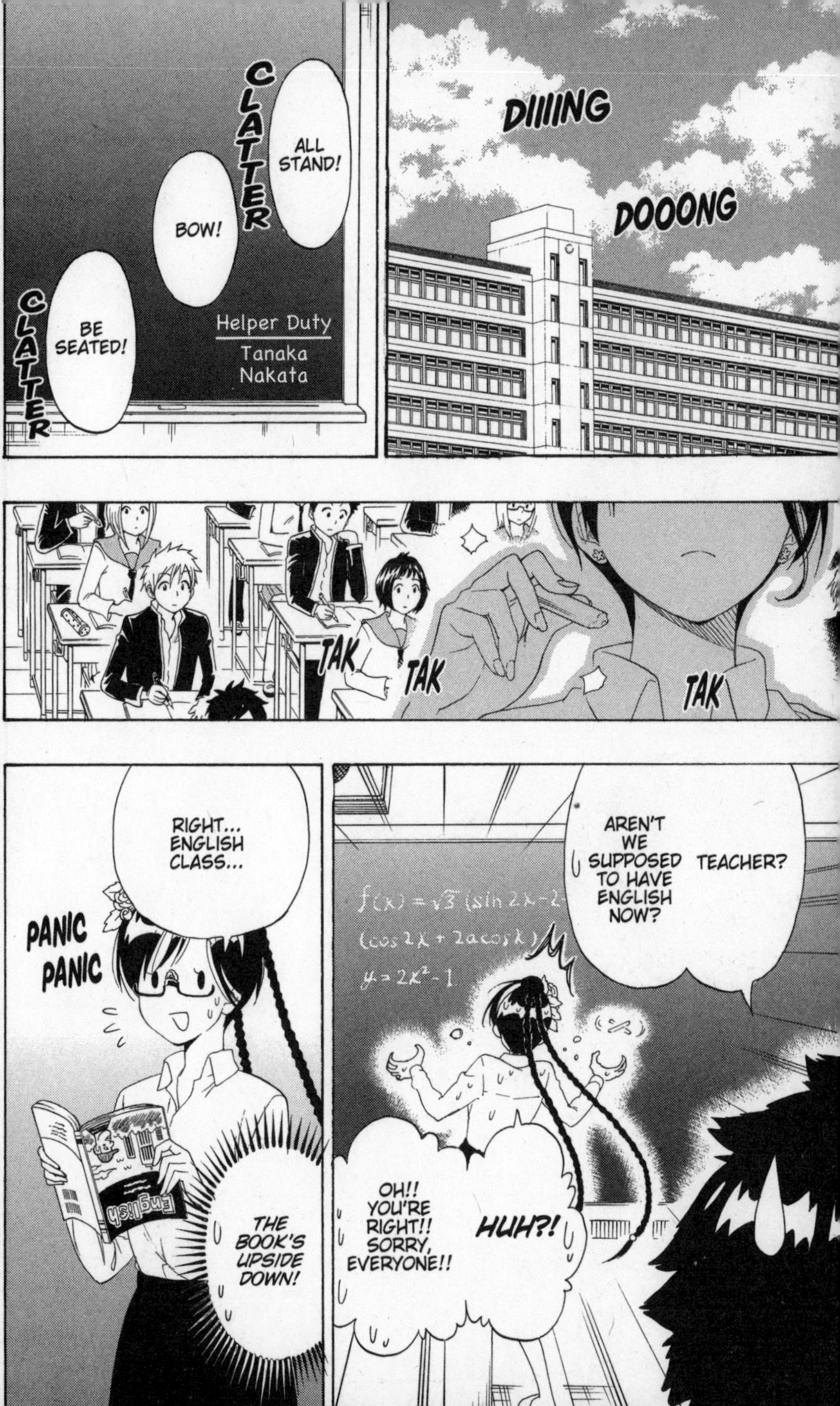
DIIIING
DOOONG
ALL STAND!
CLATTER
BOW!
BE SEATED!
CLATTER
Helper Duty
Tanaka
Nakata
TAK
TAK
TAK
TEACHER?
AREN'T WE SUPPOSED TO HAVE ENGLISH NOW?
HUH?!
OH!! YOU'RE RIGHT!! SORRY, EVERYONE!!
RIGHT... ENGLISH CLASS...
PANIC PANIC
THE BOOK'S UPSIDE DOWN!
English

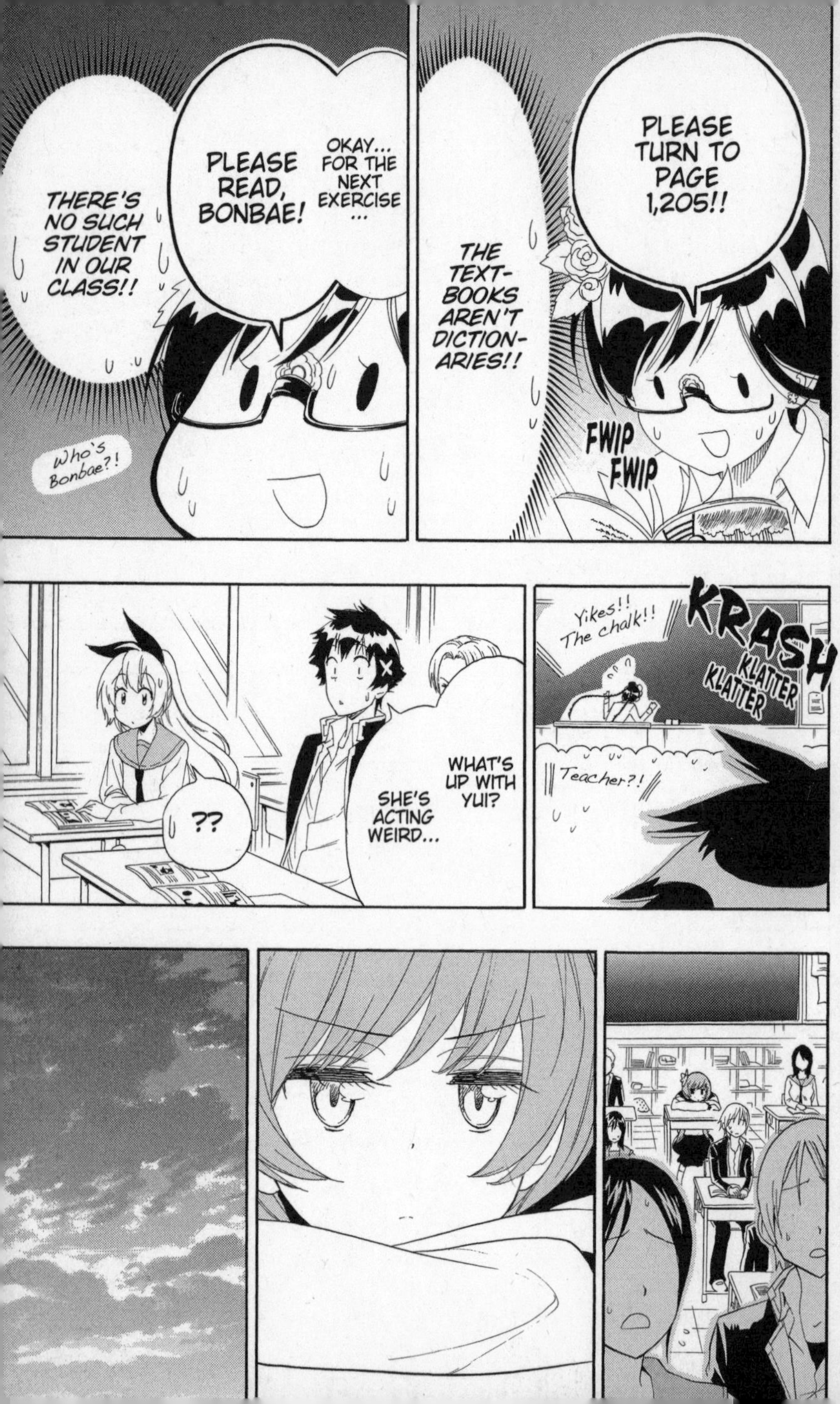
PLEASE TURN TO PAGE 1,205!!
THE TEXT-BOOKS AREN'T DICTION-ARIES!!
FWIP FWIP
OKAY... FOR THE NEXT EXERCISE...
PLEASE READ, BONBAE!
THERE'S NO SUCH STUDENT IN OUR CLASS!!
Who's Bonbae?!
KRASH
KLATTER KLATTER
Yikes!! The chalk!!
Teacher?!
WHAT'S UP WITH YUI?
SHE'S ACTING WEIRD...
??

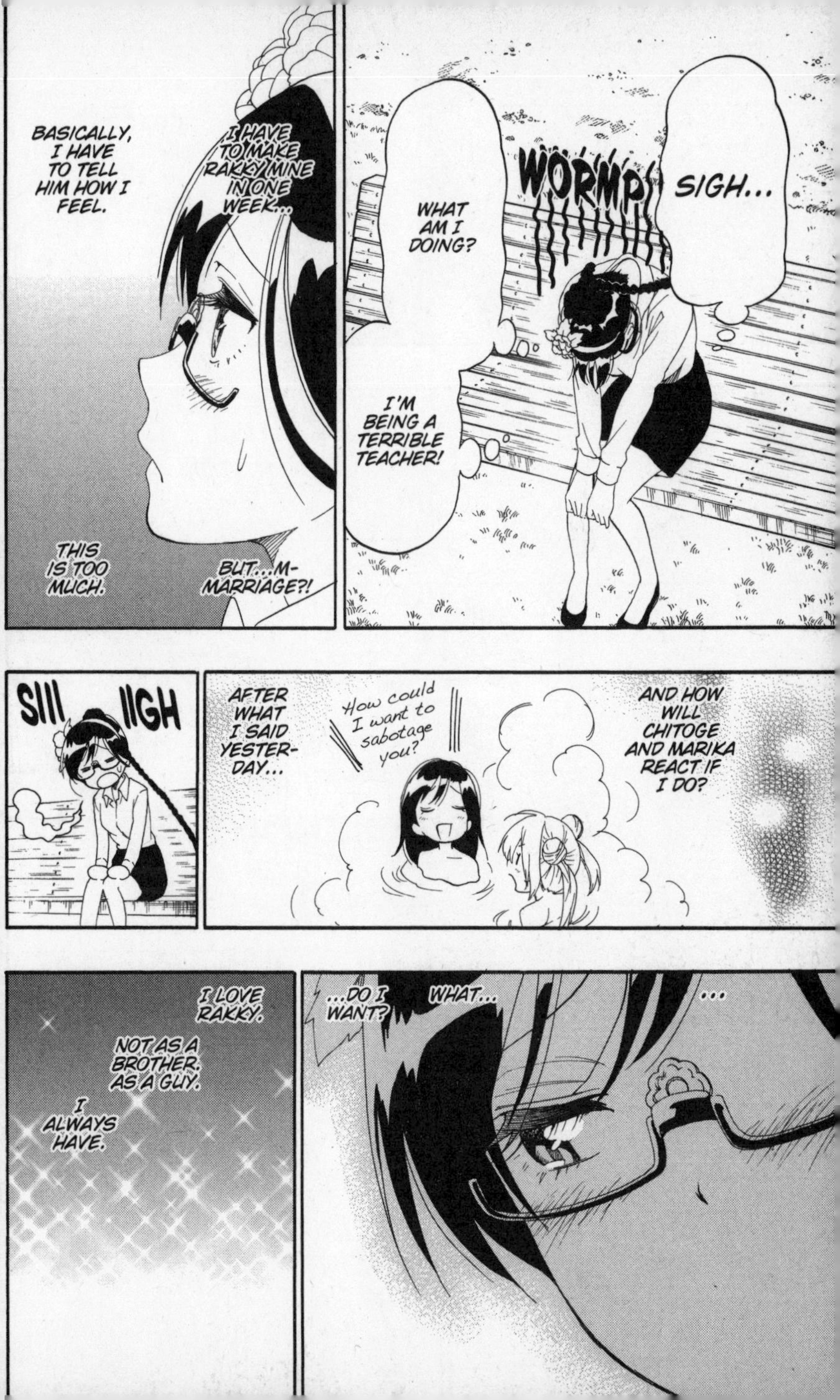
SIGH...
WORMP
WHAT AM I DOING?
I'M BEING A TERRIBLE TEACHER!
I HAVE TO MAKE RAKKY MINE IN ONE WEEK...
BASICALLY, I HAVE TO TELL HIM HOW I FEEL.
BUT...M-MARRIAGE?!
THIS IS TOO MUCH.
AND HOW WILL CHITOGE AND MARIKA REACT IF I DO?
How could I want to sabotage you?
AFTER WHAT I SAID YESTERDAY...
SIIIIGH
...
WHAT...
...DO I WANT?
I LOVE RAKKY.
NOT AS A BROTHER. AS A GUY.
I ALWAYS HAVE.

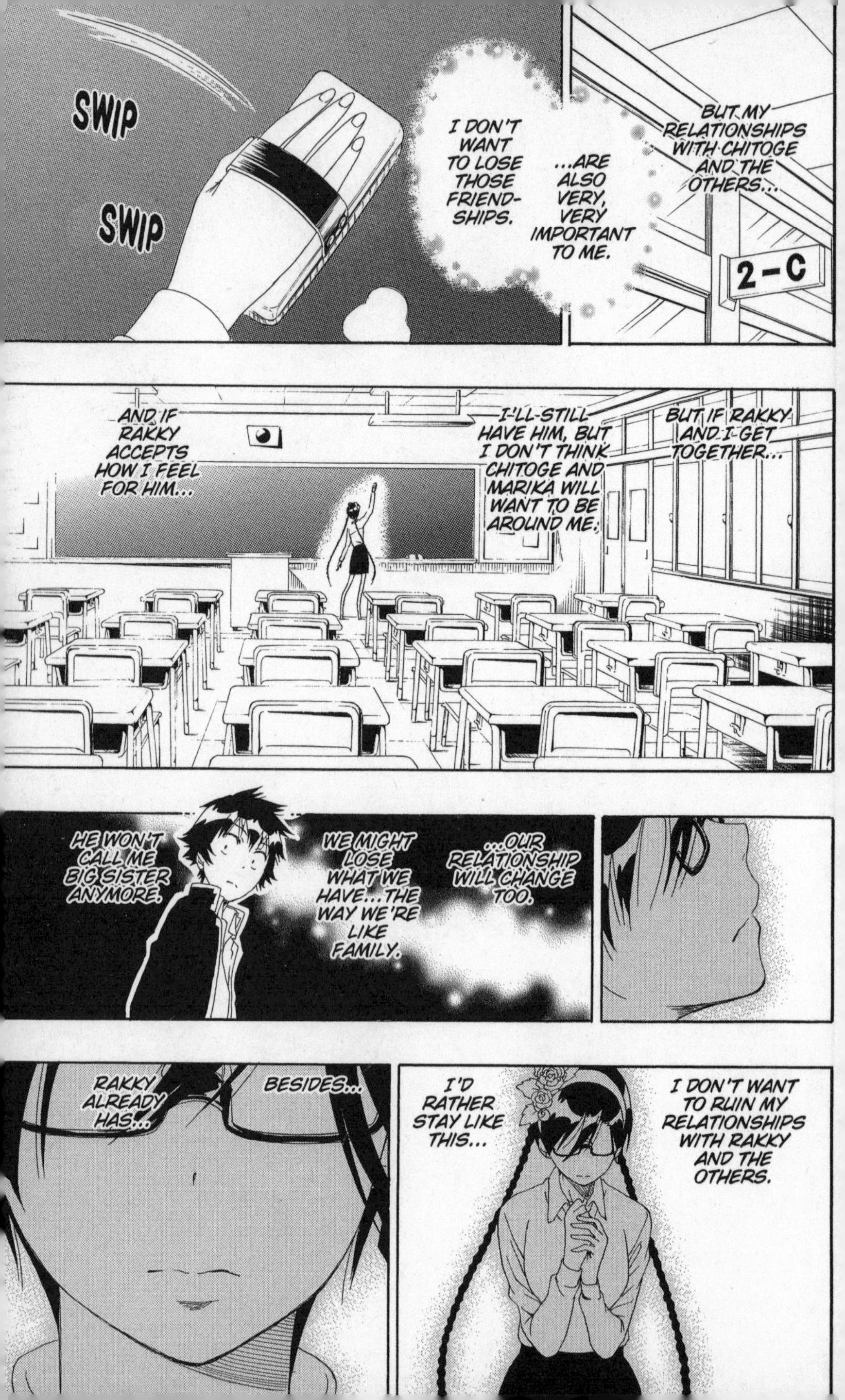
BUT MY RELATIONSHIPS WITH CHITOGE AND THE OTHERS...
...ARE ALSO VERY, VERY IMPORTANT TO ME.
I DON'T WANT TO LOSE THOSE FRIENDSHIPS.
SWIP
SWIP
BUT IF RAKKY AND I GET TOGETHER...
I'LL STILL HAVE HIM, BUT I DON'T THINK CHITOGE AND MARIKA WILL WANT TO BE AROUND ME.
AND IF RAKKY ACCEPTS HOW I FEEL FOR HIM...
...OUR RELATIONSHIP WILL CHANGE TOO.
WE MIGHT LOSE WHAT WE HAVE... THE WAY WE'RE LIKE FAMILY.
HE WON'T CALL ME BIG SISTER ANYMORE.
I DON'T WANT TO RUIN MY RELATIONSHIPS WITH RAKKY AND THE OTHERS.
I'D RATHER STAY LIKE THIS...
BESIDES...
RAKKY ALREADY HAS...

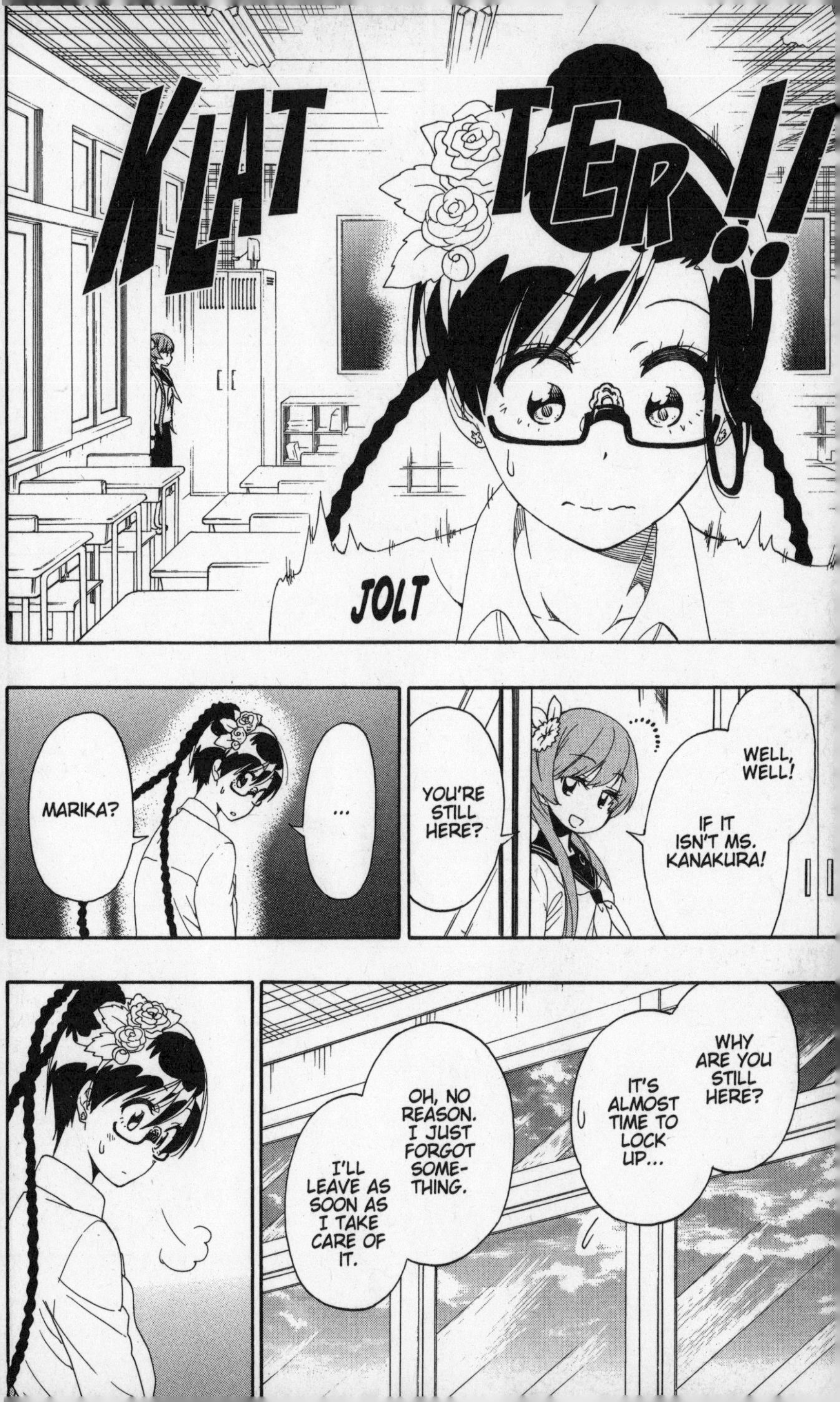
KLATTER!!
JOLT
WELL, WELL!
IF IT ISN'T MS. KANAKURA!
YOU'RE STILL HERE?
...
MARIKA?
WHY ARE YOU STILL HERE?
IT'S ALMOST TIME TO LOCK UP...
OH, NO REASON. I JUST FORGOT SOME-THING.
I'LL LEAVE AS SOON AS I TAKE CARE OF IT.

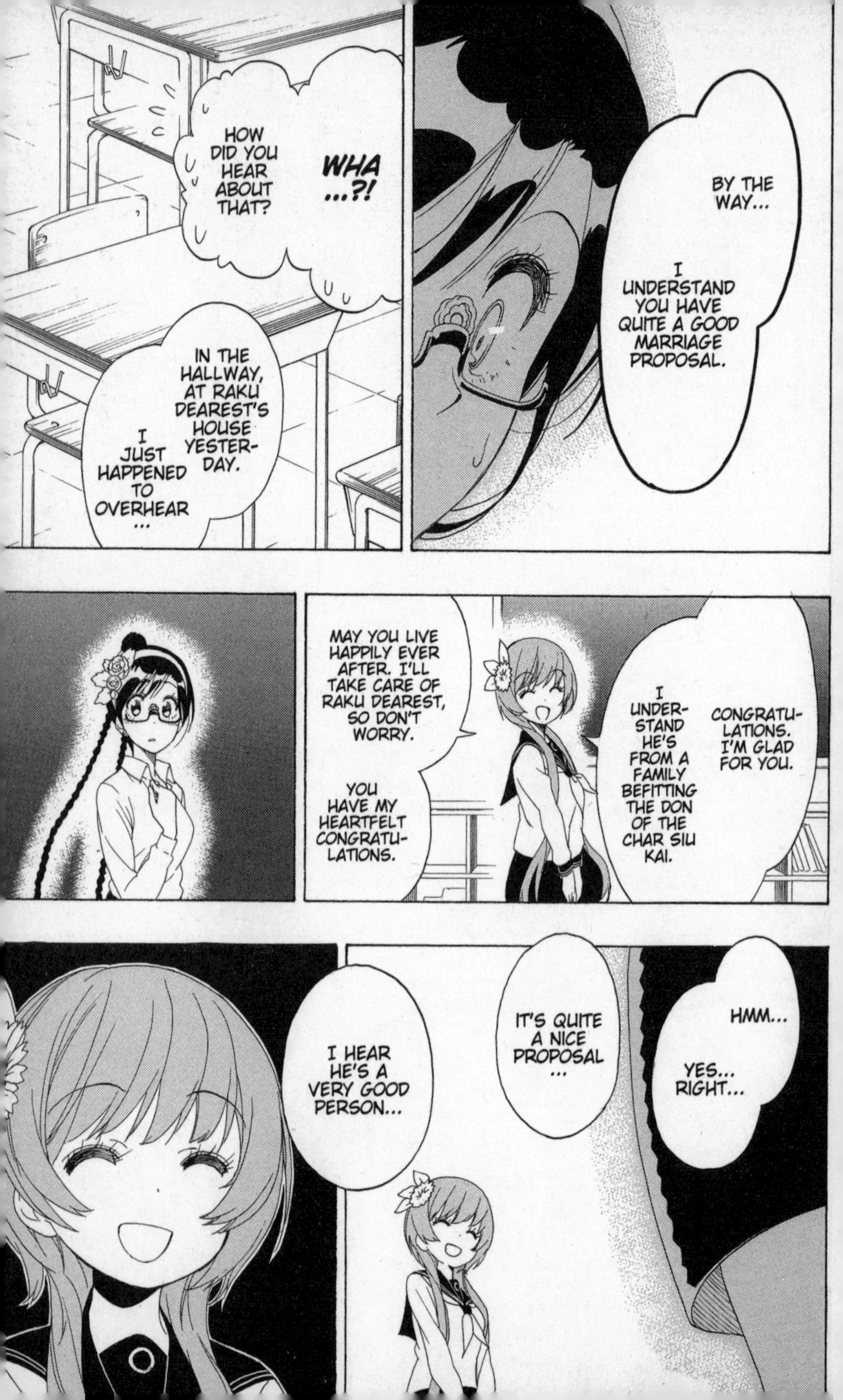
BY THE WAY...
I UNDERSTAND YOU HAVE QUITE A GOOD MARRIAGE PROPOSAL.
WHA...?!
HOW DID YOU HEAR ABOUT THAT?
IN THE HALLWAY, AT RAKU DEAREST'S HOUSE YESTERDAY.
I JUST HAPPENED TO OVERHEAR...
CONGRATULATIONS. I'M GLAD FOR YOU.
I UNDERSTAND HE'S FROM A FAMILY BEFITTING THE DON OF THE CHAR SIU KAI.
MAY YOU LIVE HAPPILY EVER AFTER. I'LL TAKE CARE OF RAKU DEAREST, SO DON'T WORRY.
YOU HAVE MY HEARTFELT CONGRATULATIONS.
HMM...
YES... RIGHT...
IT'S QUITE A NICE PROPOSAL...
I HEAR HE'S A VERY GOOD PERSON...

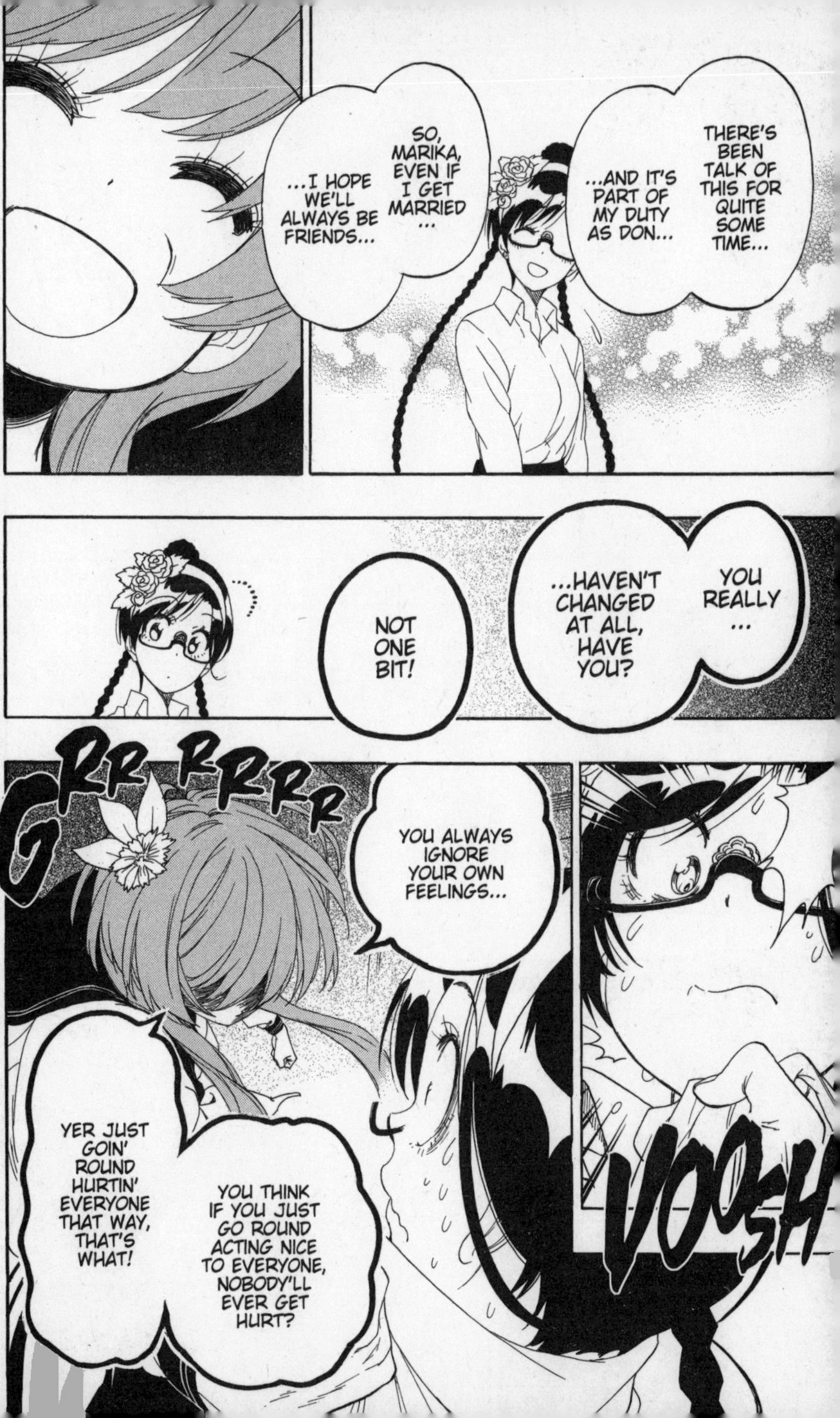
THERE'S BEEN TALK OF THIS FOR QUITE SOME TIME...
...AND IT'S PART OF MY DUTY AS DON...
SO, MARIKA, EVEN IF I GET MARRIED...
...I HOPE WE'LL ALWAYS BE FRIENDS...
YOU REALLY...
...HAVEN'T CHANGED AT ALL, HAVE YOU?
NOT ONE BIT!
VOOSH
GRRRRRRR
YOU ALWAYS IGNORE YOUR OWN FEELINGS...
YOU THINK IF YOU JUST GO ROUND ACTING NICE TO EVERYONE, NOBODY'LL EVER GET HURT?
YER JUST GOIN' ROUND HURTIN' EVERYONE THAT WAY, THAT'S WHAT!

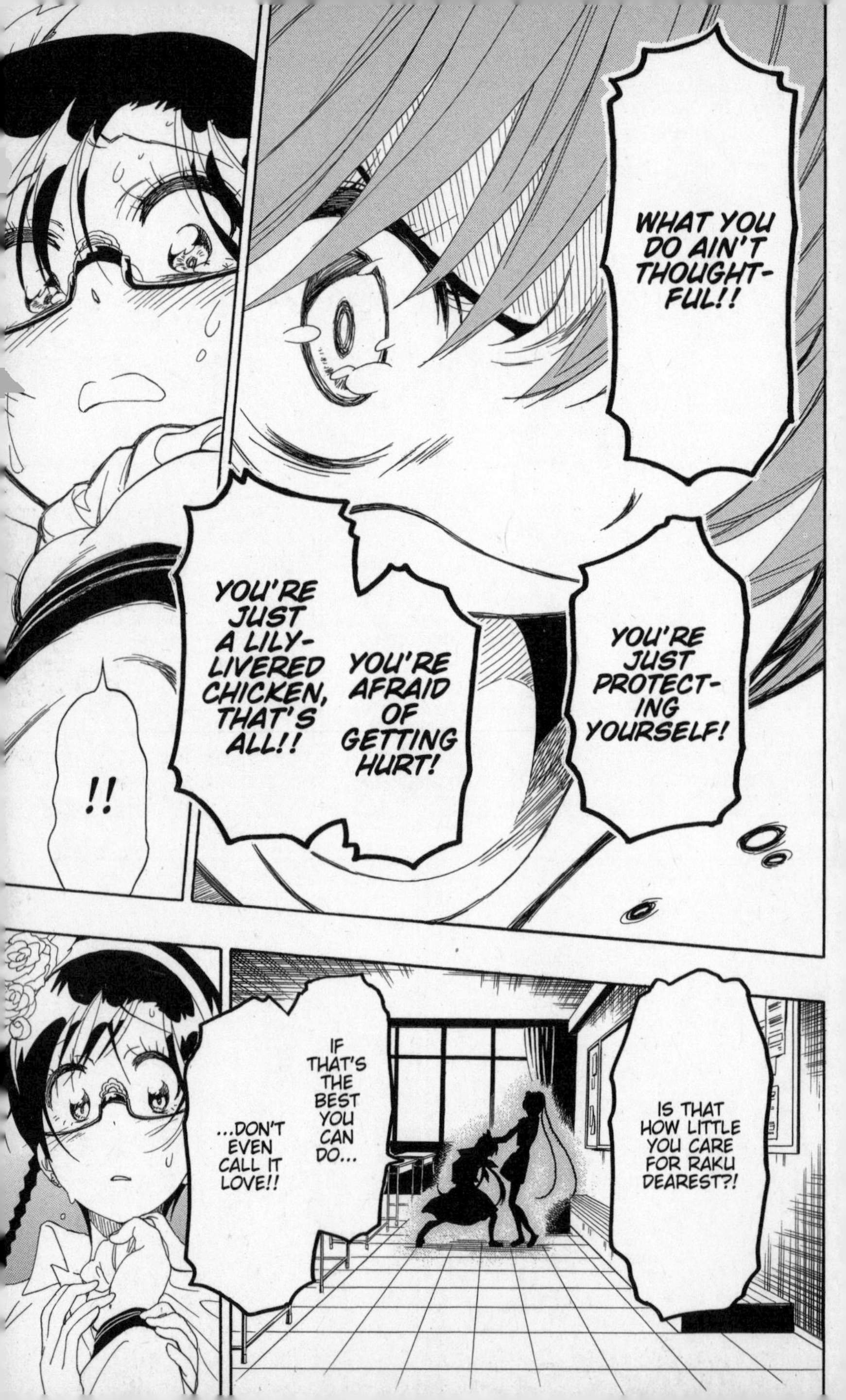
WHAT YOU DO AIN'T THOUGHTFUL!!
YOU'RE JUST PROTECTING YOURSELF!
YOU'RE AFRAID OF GETTING HURT!
YOU'RE JUST A LILY-LIVERED CHICKEN, THAT'S ALL!!
!!
IS THAT HOW LITTLE YOU CARE FOR RAKU DEAREST?!
IF THAT'S THE BEST YOU CAN DO...
...DON'T EVEN CALL IT LOVE!!

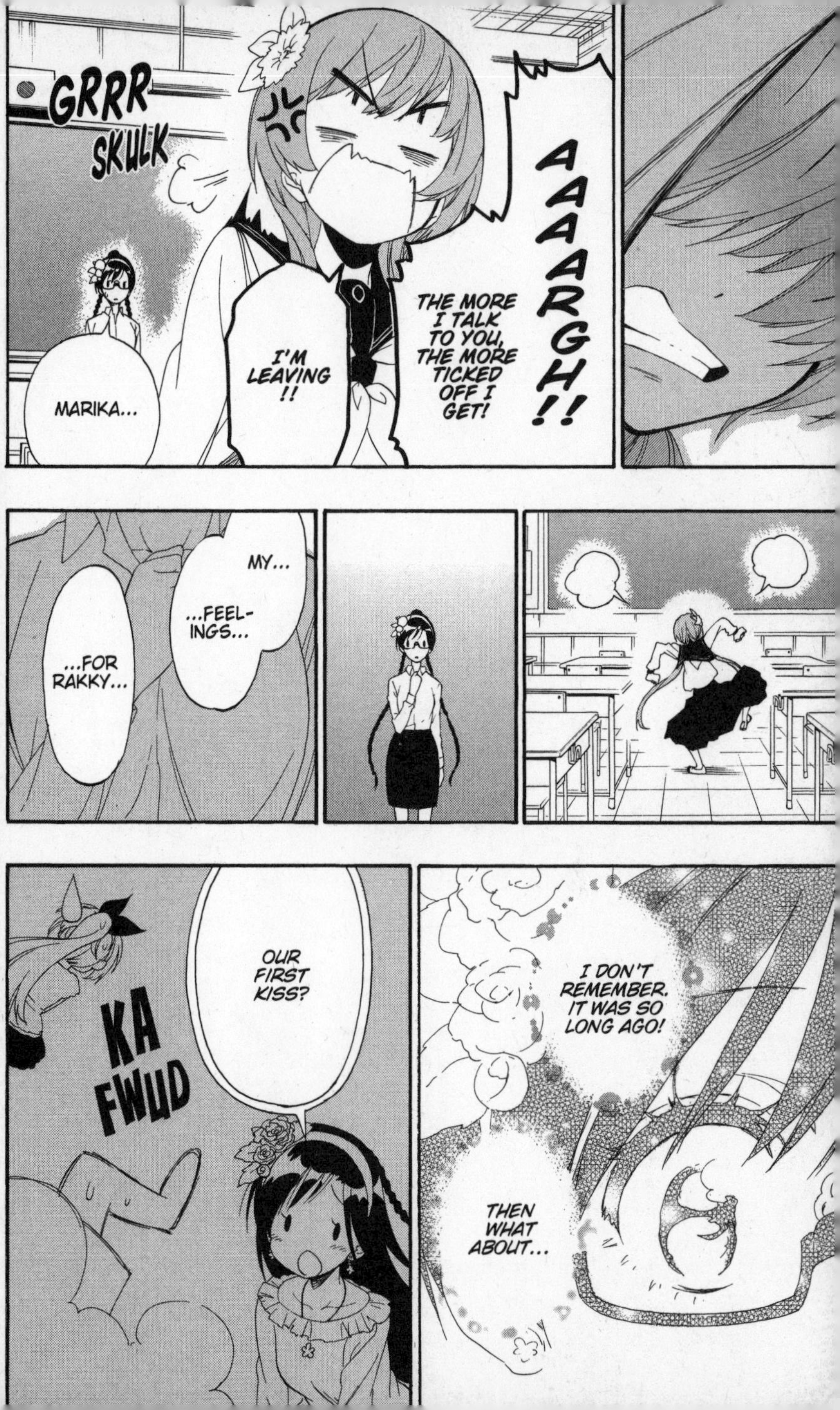
AAAARGH!!
THE MORE I TALK TO YOU, THE MORE TICKED OFF I GET!
GRRR
SKULK
I'M LEAVING!!
MARIKA...
MY...
...FEEL-INGS...
...FOR RAKKY...
I DON'T REMEMBER. IT WAS SO LONG AGO!
THEN WHAT ABOUT...
OUR FIRST KISS?
KA FWUD

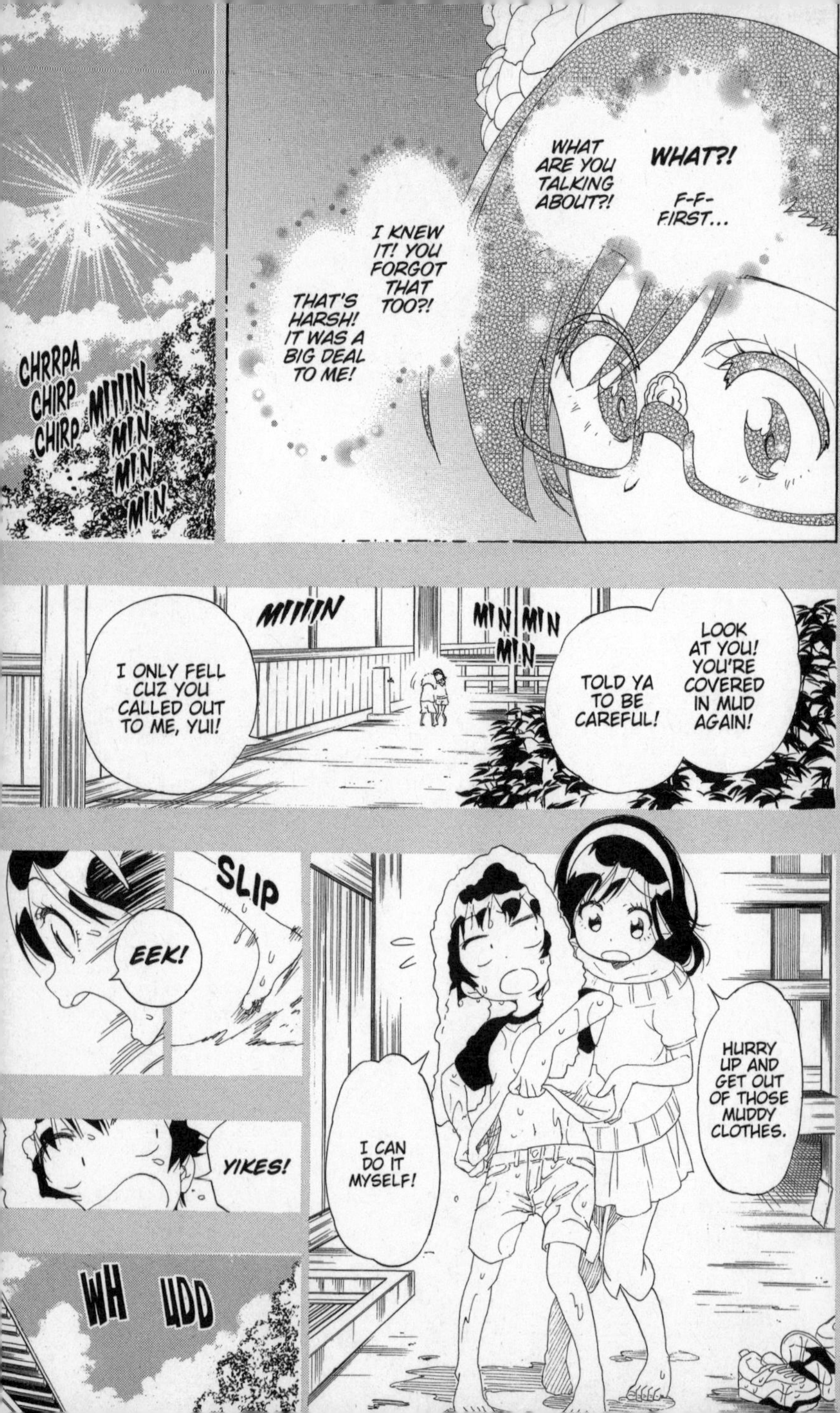
WHAT?!
F-F-FIRST...
WHAT ARE YOU TALKING ABOUT?!
I KNEW IT! YOU FORGOT THAT TOO?!
THAT'S HARSH! IT WAS A BIG DEAL TO ME!
MIIIIN MIN MIN MIN
CHRRPA CHIRP CHIRP
LOOK AT YOU! YOU'RE COVERED IN MUD AGAIN!
TOLD YA TO BE CAREFUL!
MIN MIN MIN
MIIIIN
I ONLY FELL CUZ YOU CALLED OUT TO ME, YUI!
HURRY UP AND GET OUT OF THOSE MUDDY CLOTHES.
I CAN DO IT MYSELF!
SLIP
EEK!
YIKES!
WH UDD

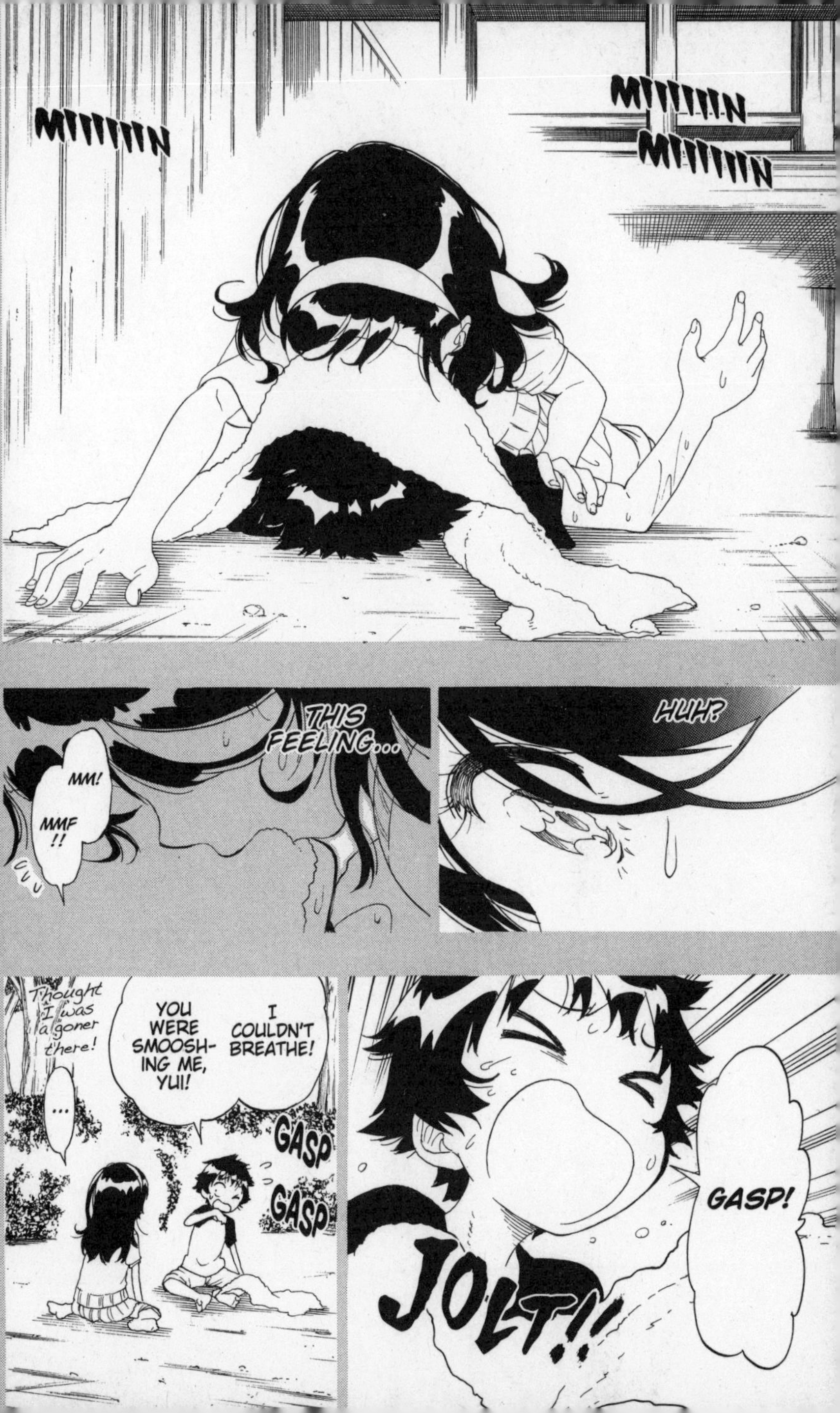
MIIIIIIN
MIIIIIIN
MIIIIIIN
HUH?
THIS FEELING...
MM! MMF!!
GASP!
JOLT!!
YOU WERE SMOOSH-ING ME, YUI! I COULDN'T BREATHE!
GASP GASP
Thought I was a goner there!
...

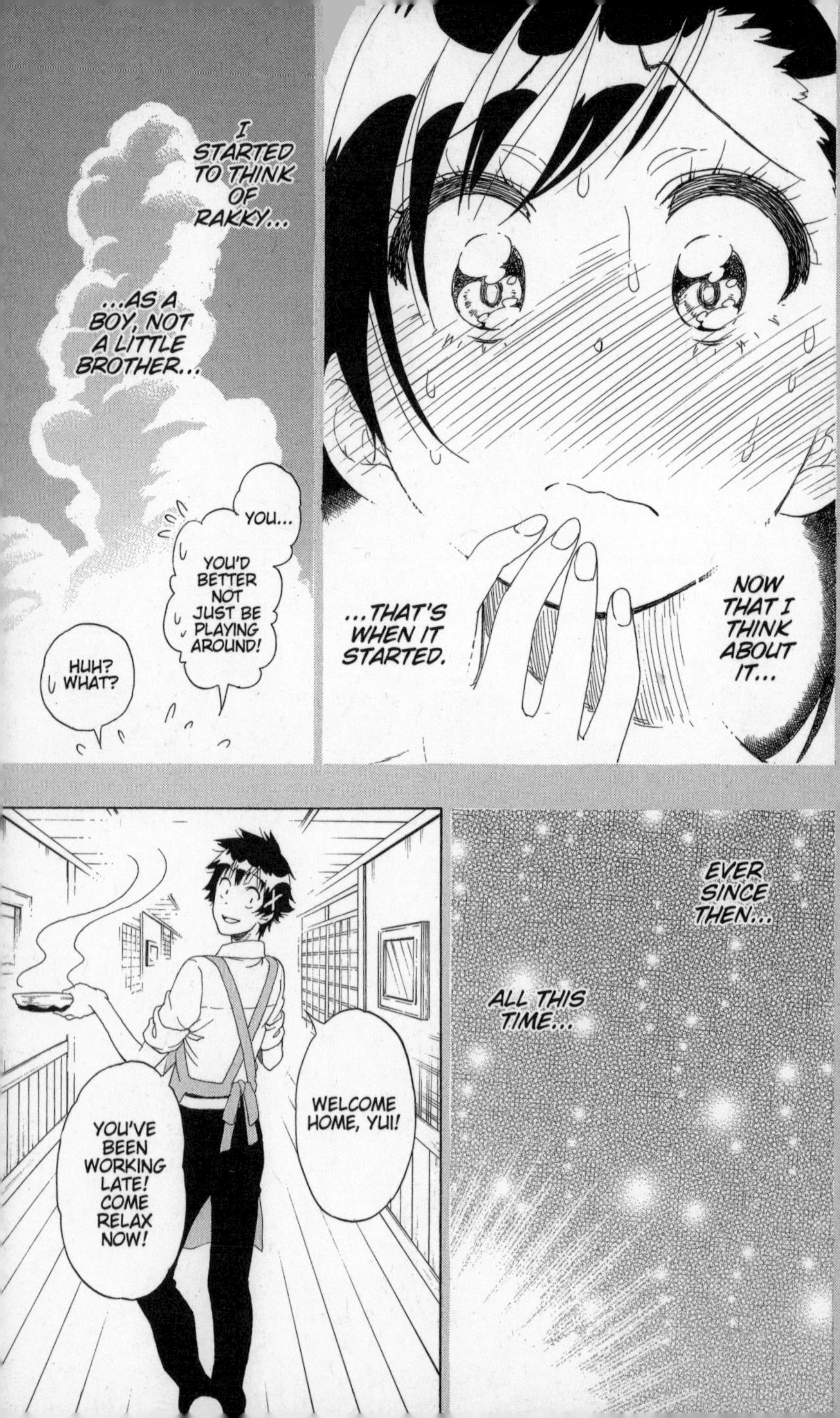
NOW THAT I THINK ABOUT IT...
...THAT'S WHEN IT STARTED.
I STARTED TO THINK OF RAKKY...
...AS A BOY, NOT A LITTLE BROTHER...
YOU...
YOU'D BETTER NOT JUST BE PLAYING AROUND!
HUH? WHAT?
EVER SINCE THEN...
ALL THIS TIME...
WELCOME HOME, YUI!
YOU'VE BEEN WORKING LATE! COME RELAX NOW!

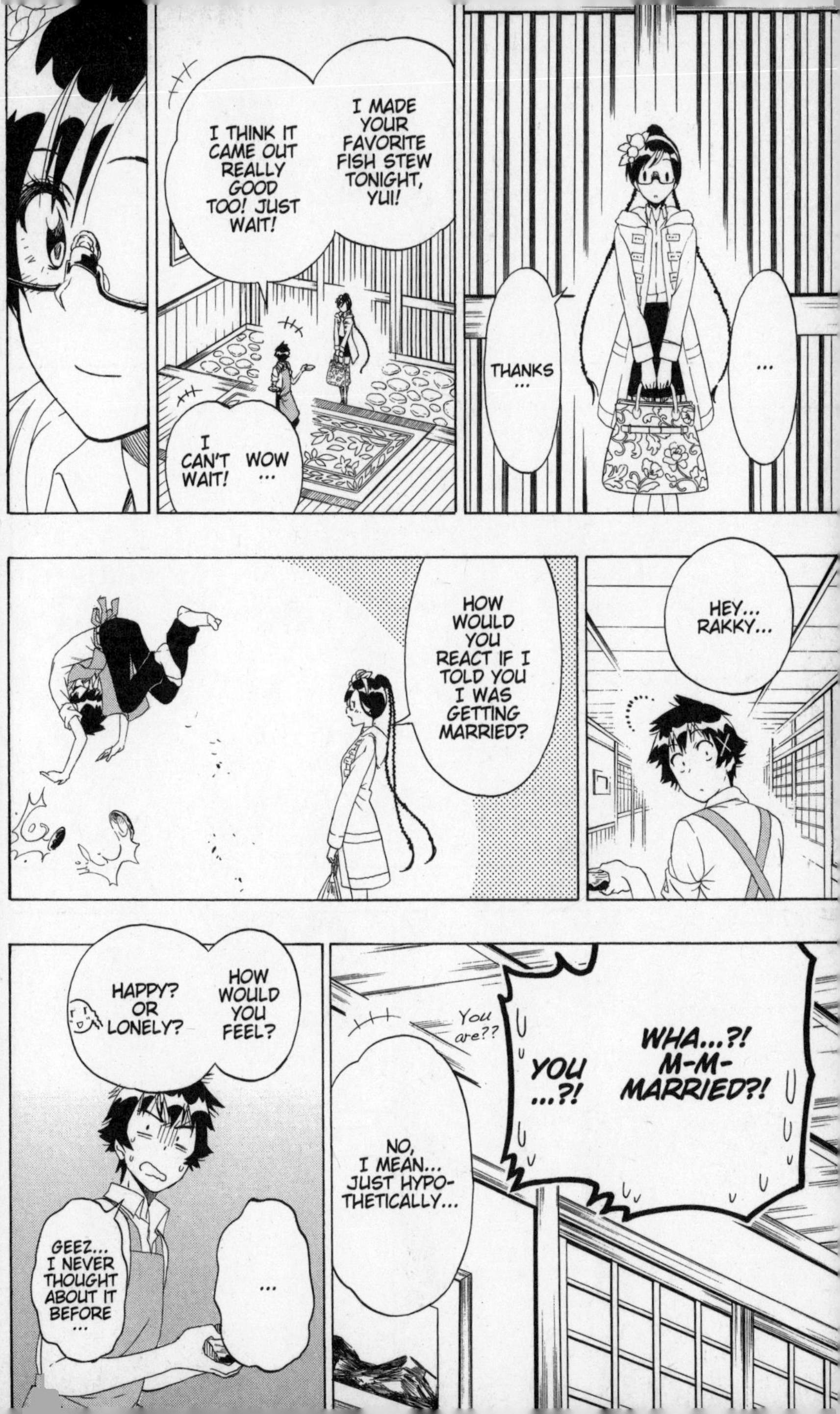
...
THANKS...
I MADE YOUR FAVORITE FISH STEW TONIGHT, YUI!
I THINK IT CAME OUT REALLY GOOD TOO! JUST WAIT!
WOW...
I CAN'T WAIT!
HEY... RAKKY...
HOW WOULD YOU REACT IF I TOLD YOU I WAS GETTING MARRIED?
WHA...?! M-M-MARRIED?!
YOU...?!
You are??
NO, I MEAN... JUST HYPOTHETICALLY...
HOW WOULD YOU FEEL?
HAPPY? OR LONELY?
...
GEEZ... I NEVER THOUGHT ABOUT IT BEFORE...

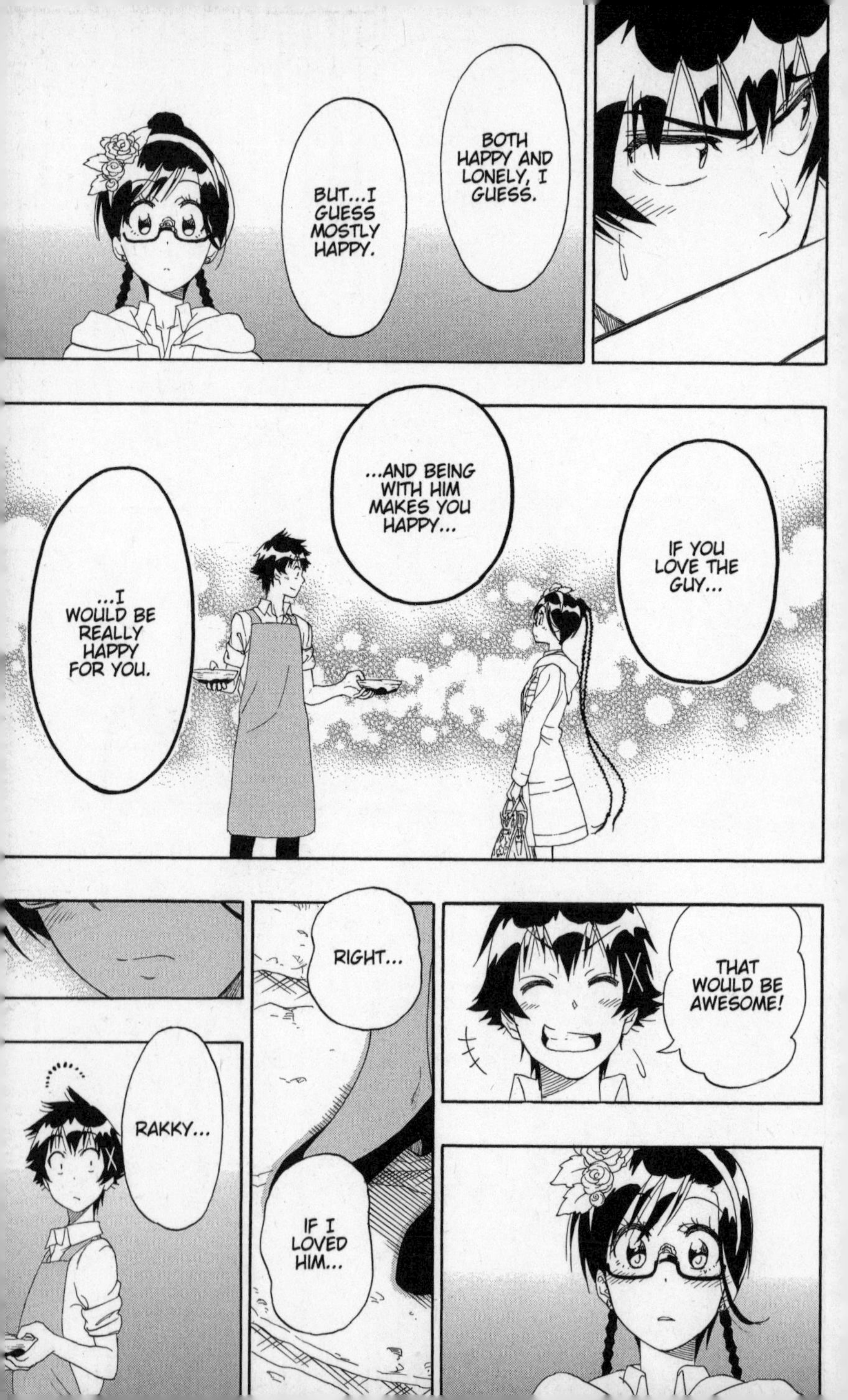
BOTH HAPPY AND LONELY, I GUESS.
BUT...I GUESS MOSTLY HAPPY.
IF YOU LOVE THE GUY...
...AND BEING WITH HIM MAKES YOU HAPPY...
...I WOULD BE REALLY HAPPY FOR YOU.
THAT WOULD BE AWESOME!
RIGHT...
IF I LOVED HIM...
RAKKY...

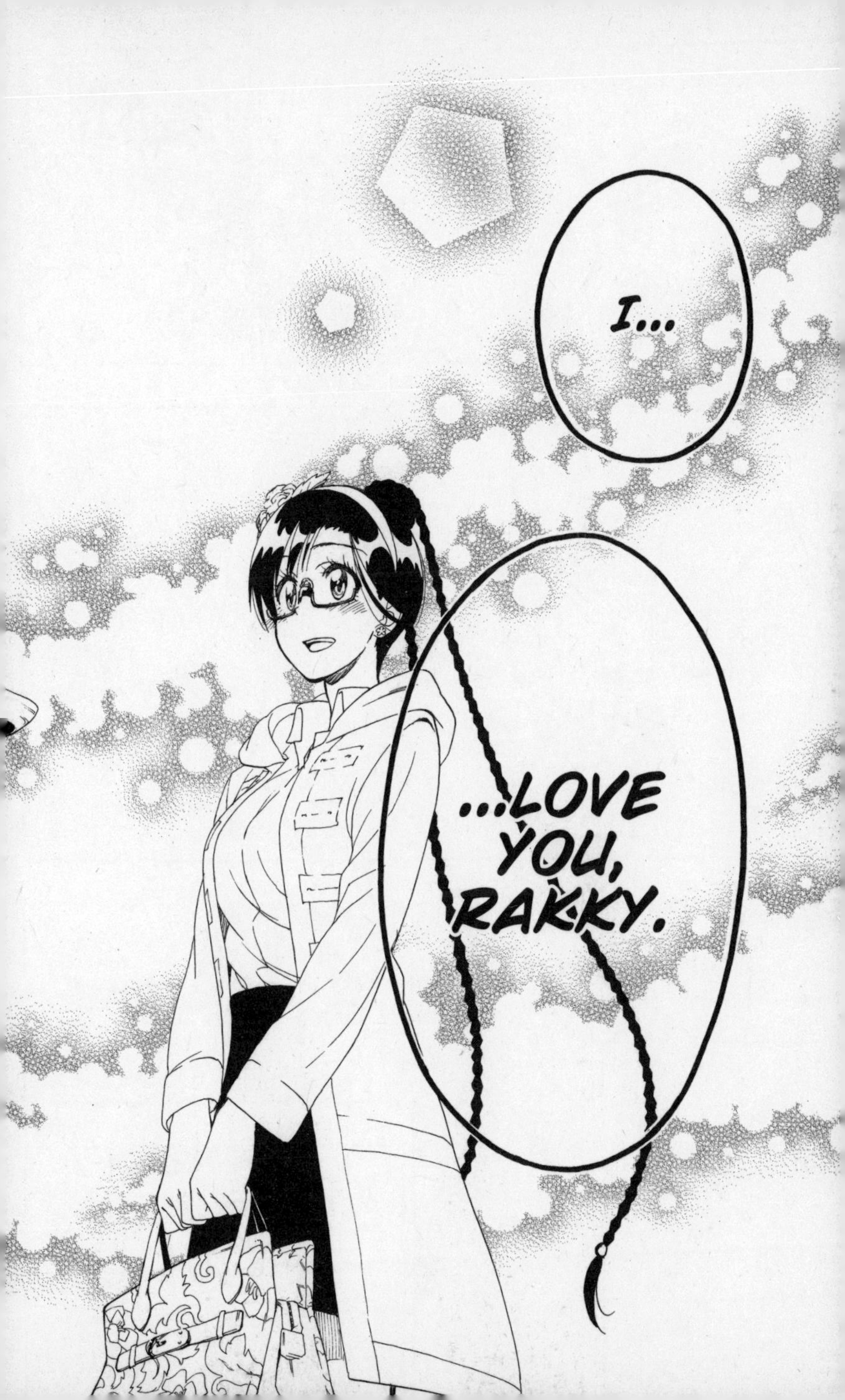
I...
...LOVE YOU, RAKKY.

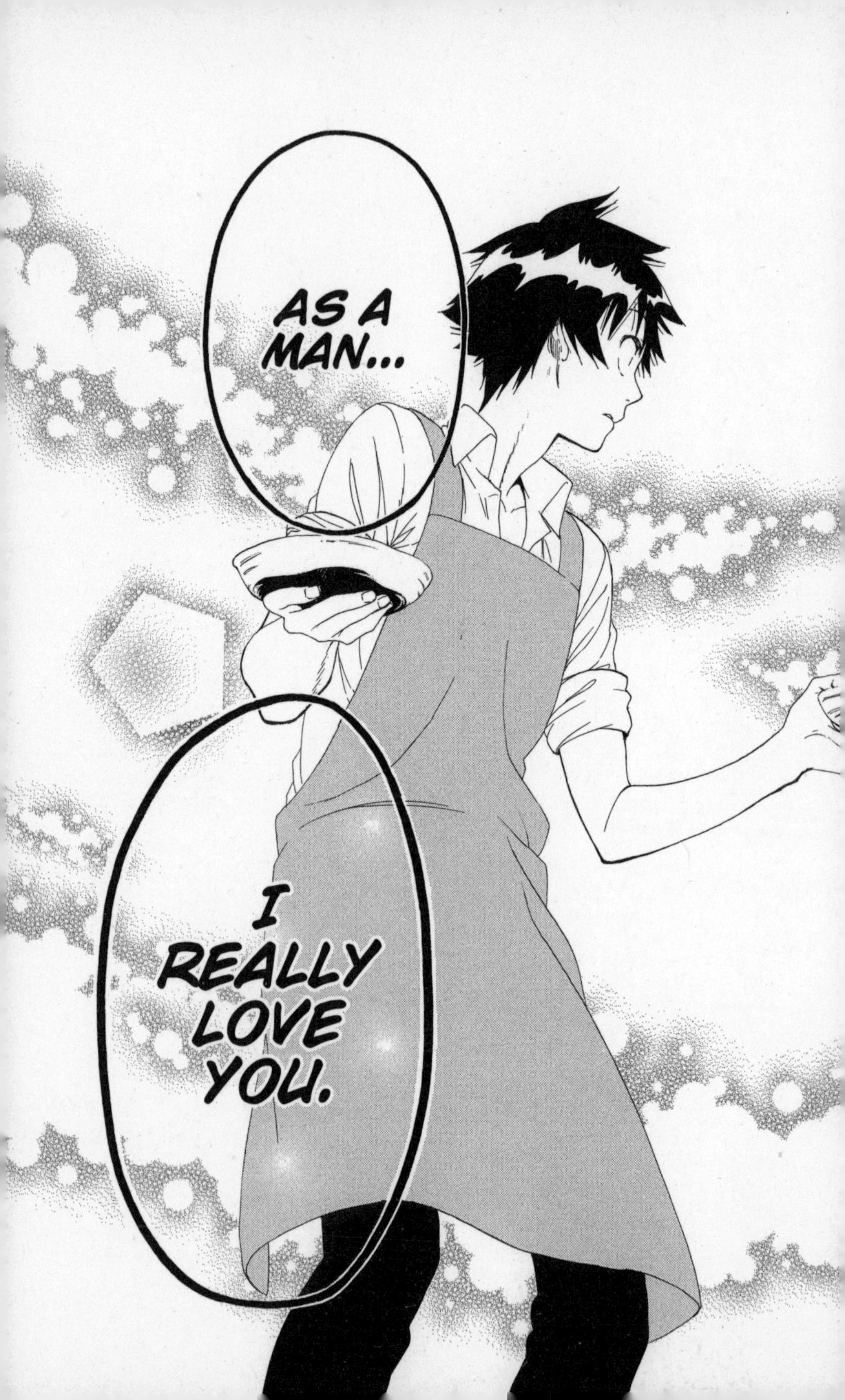
AS A MAN...
I REALLY LOVE YOU.

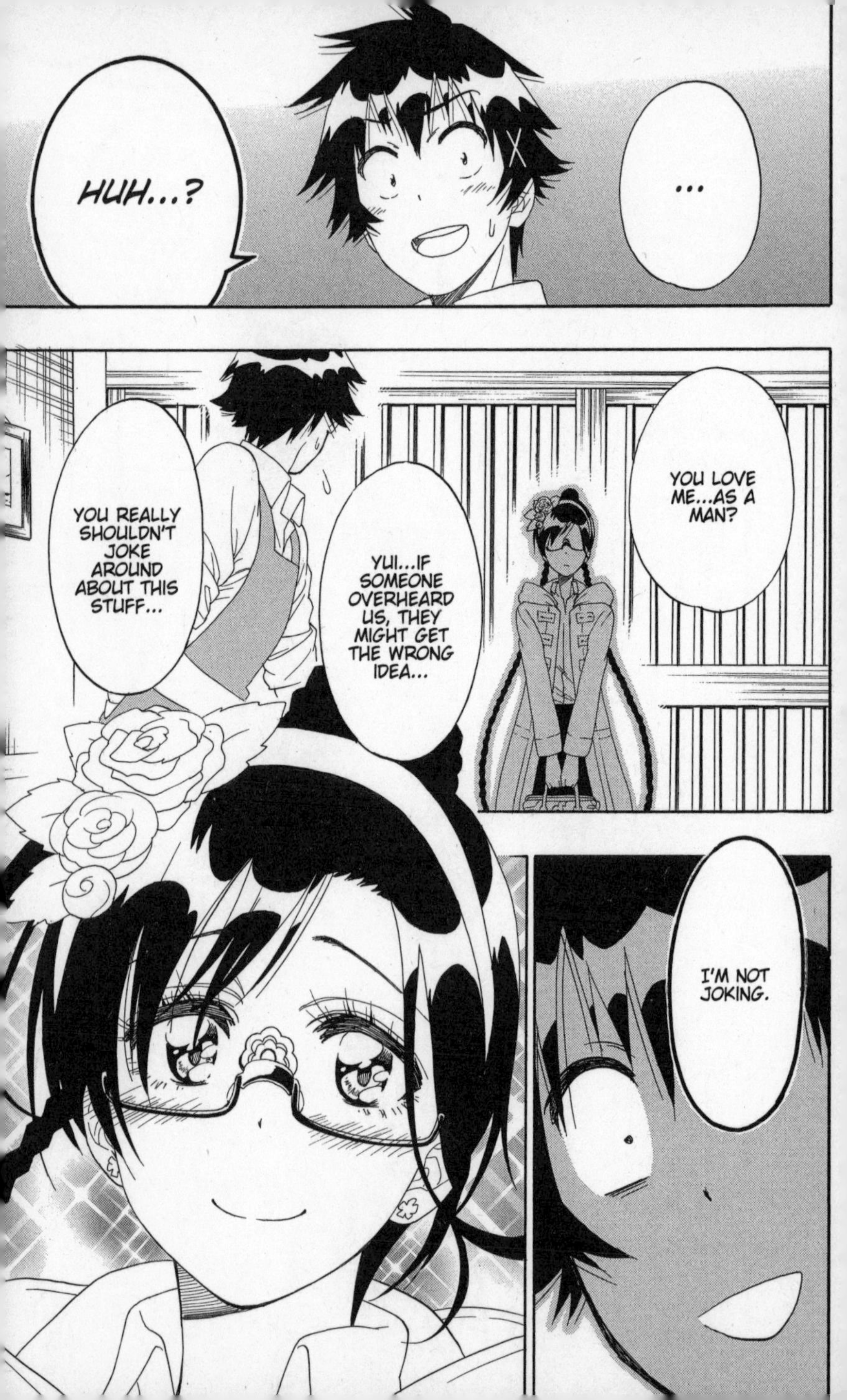
...
HUH...?
YOU LOVE ME...AS A MAN?
YUI...IF SOMEONE OVERHEARD US, THEY MIGHT GET THE WRONG IDEA...
YOU REALLY SHOULDN'T JOKE AROUND ABOUT THIS STUFF...
I'M NOT JOKING.

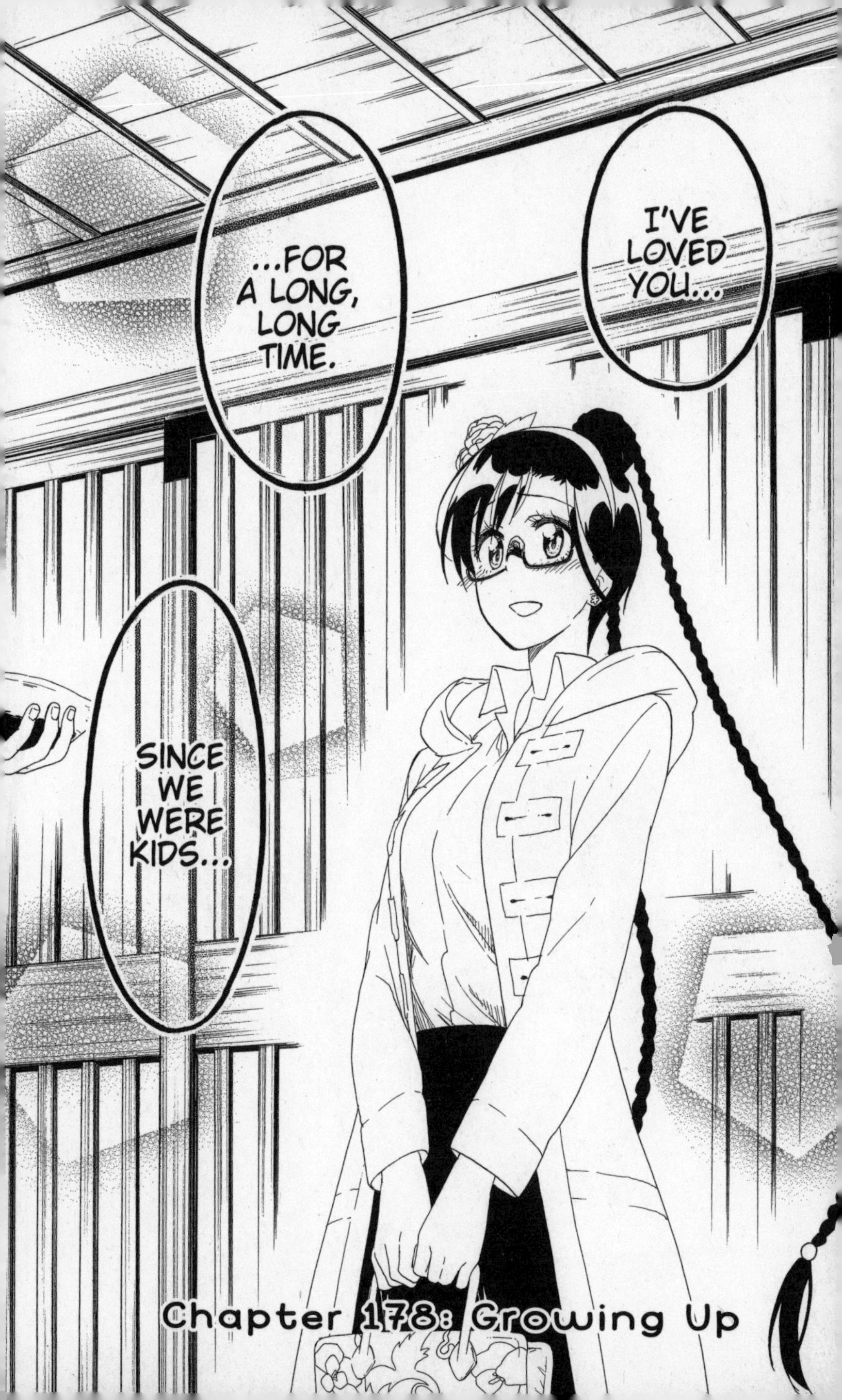
I'VE LOVED YOU...
...FOR A LONG, LONG TIME.
SINCE WE WERE KIDS...
Chapter 178: Growing Up

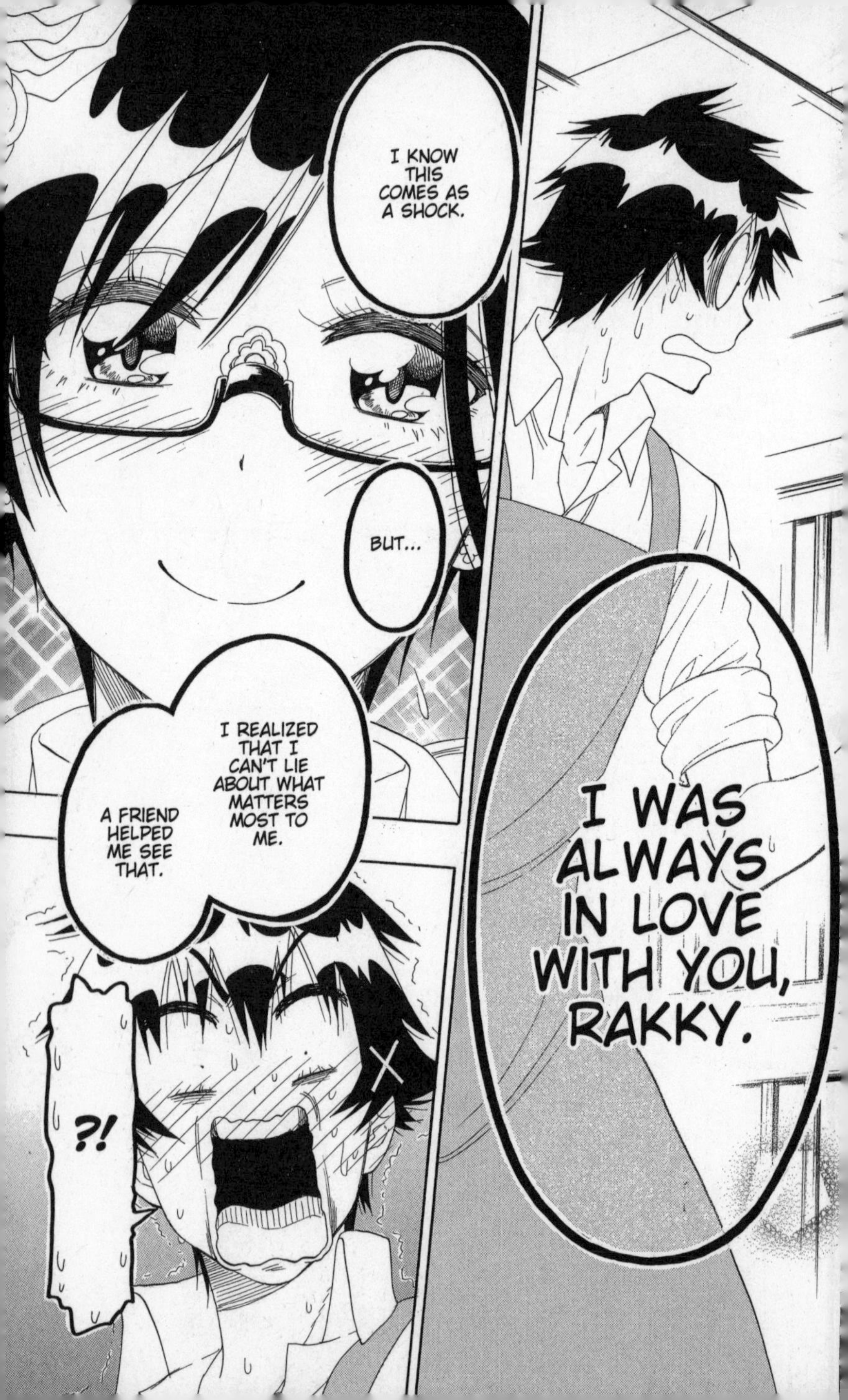
I KNOW THIS COMES AS A SHOCK.
BUT...
I REALIZED THAT I CAN'T LIE ABOUT WHAT MATTERS MOST TO ME.
A FRIEND HELPED ME SEE THAT.
I WAS ALWAYS IN LOVE WITH YOU, RAKKY.
?!

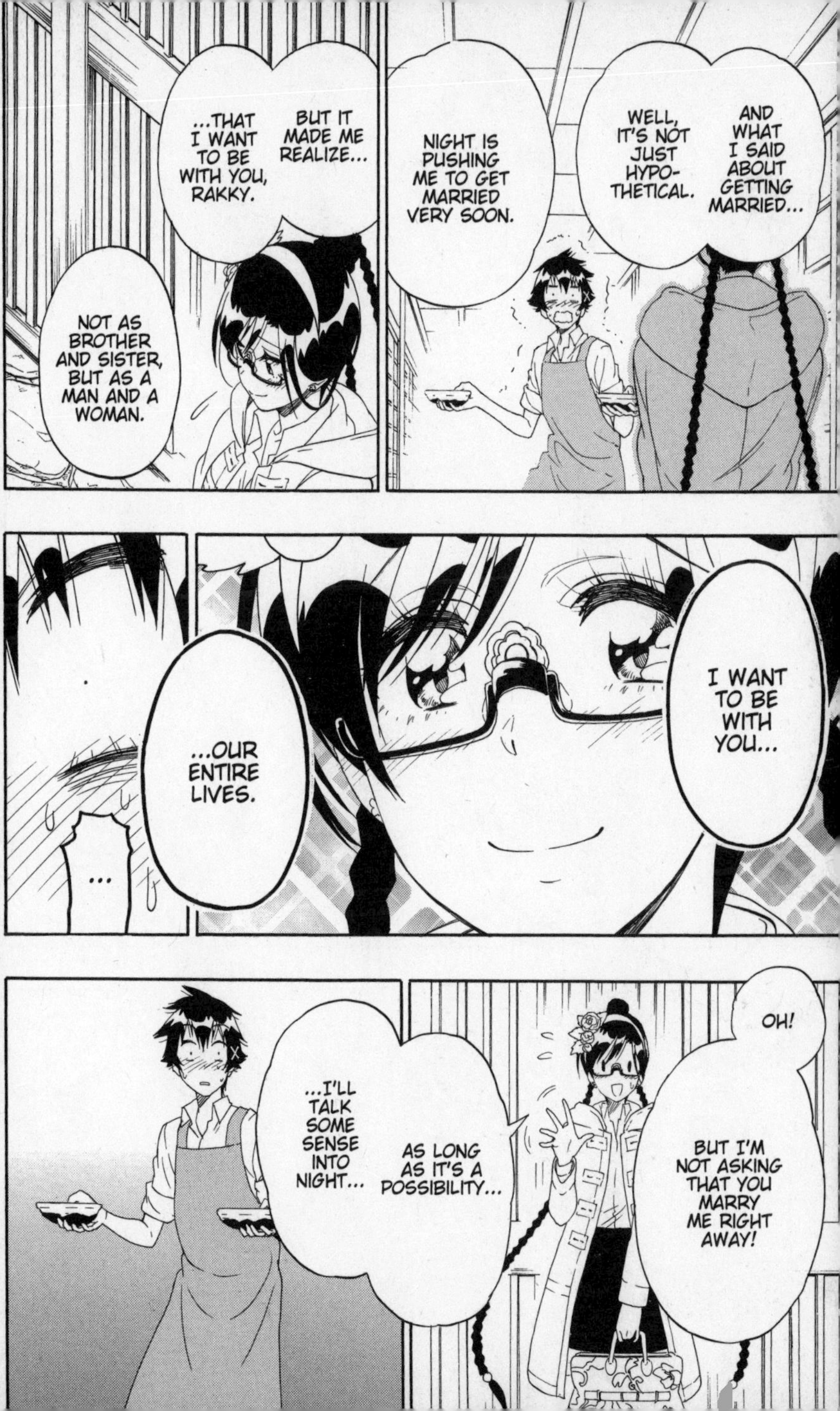
AND WHAT I SAID ABOUT GETTING MARRIED...
WELL, IT'S NOT JUST HYPO-THETICAL.
NIGHT IS PUSHING ME TO GET MARRIED VERY SOON.
BUT IT MADE ME REALIZE...
...THAT I WANT TO BE WITH YOU, RAKKY.
NOT AS BROTHER AND SISTER, BUT AS A MAN AND A WOMAN.
I WANT TO BE WITH YOU...
...OUR ENTIRE LIVES.
...
OH!
BUT I'M NOT ASKING THAT YOU MARRY ME RIGHT AWAY!
AS LONG AS IT'S A POSSIBILITY...
...I'LL TALK SOME SENSE INTO NIGHT...

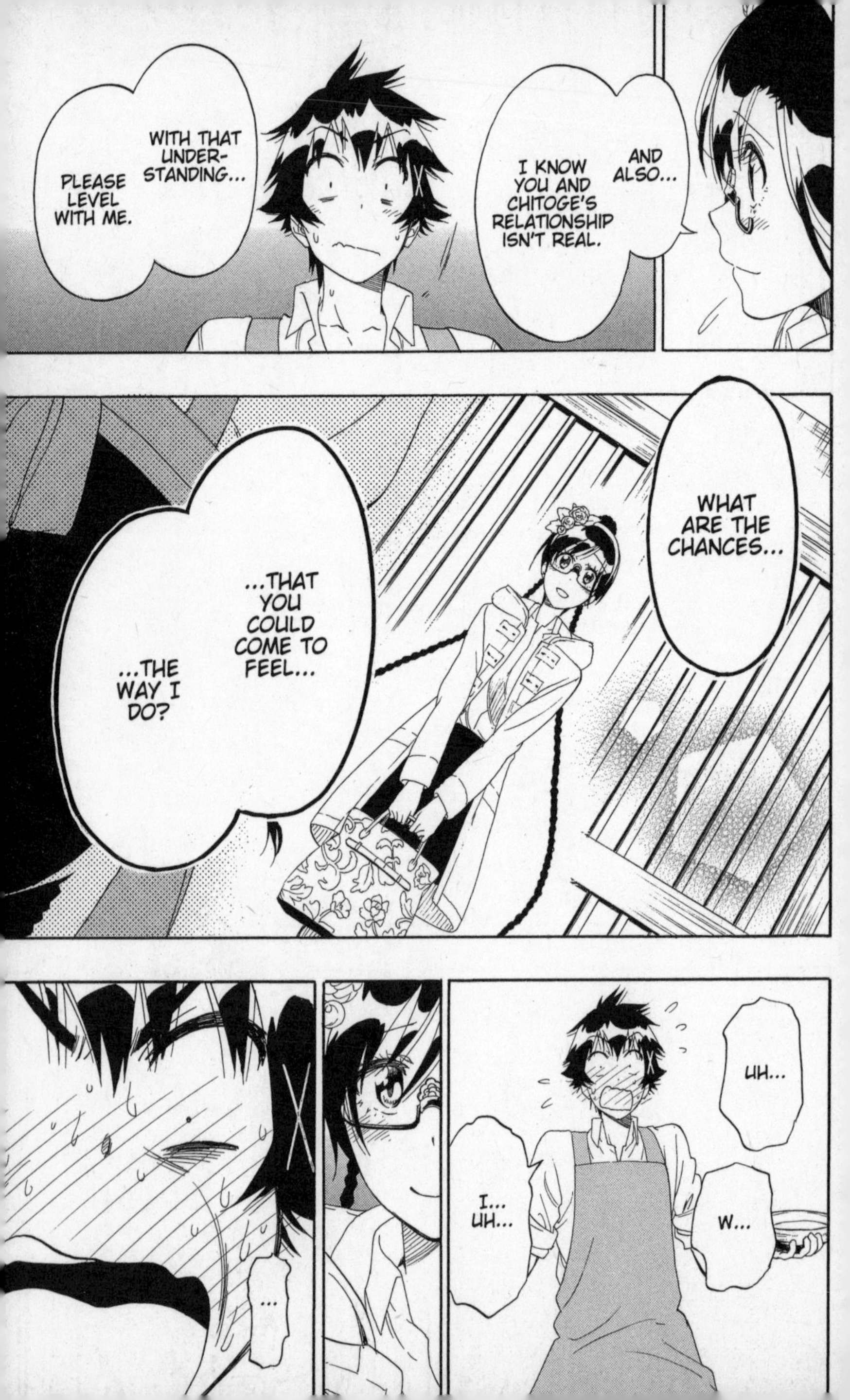
AND ALSO... I KNOW YOU AND CHITOGE'S RELATIONSHIP ISN'T REAL.
WITH THAT UNDER-STANDING... PLEASE LEVEL WITH ME.
WHAT ARE THE CHANCES...
...THAT YOU COULD COME TO FEEL... ...THE WAY I DO?
UH...
W...
I... UH...
...

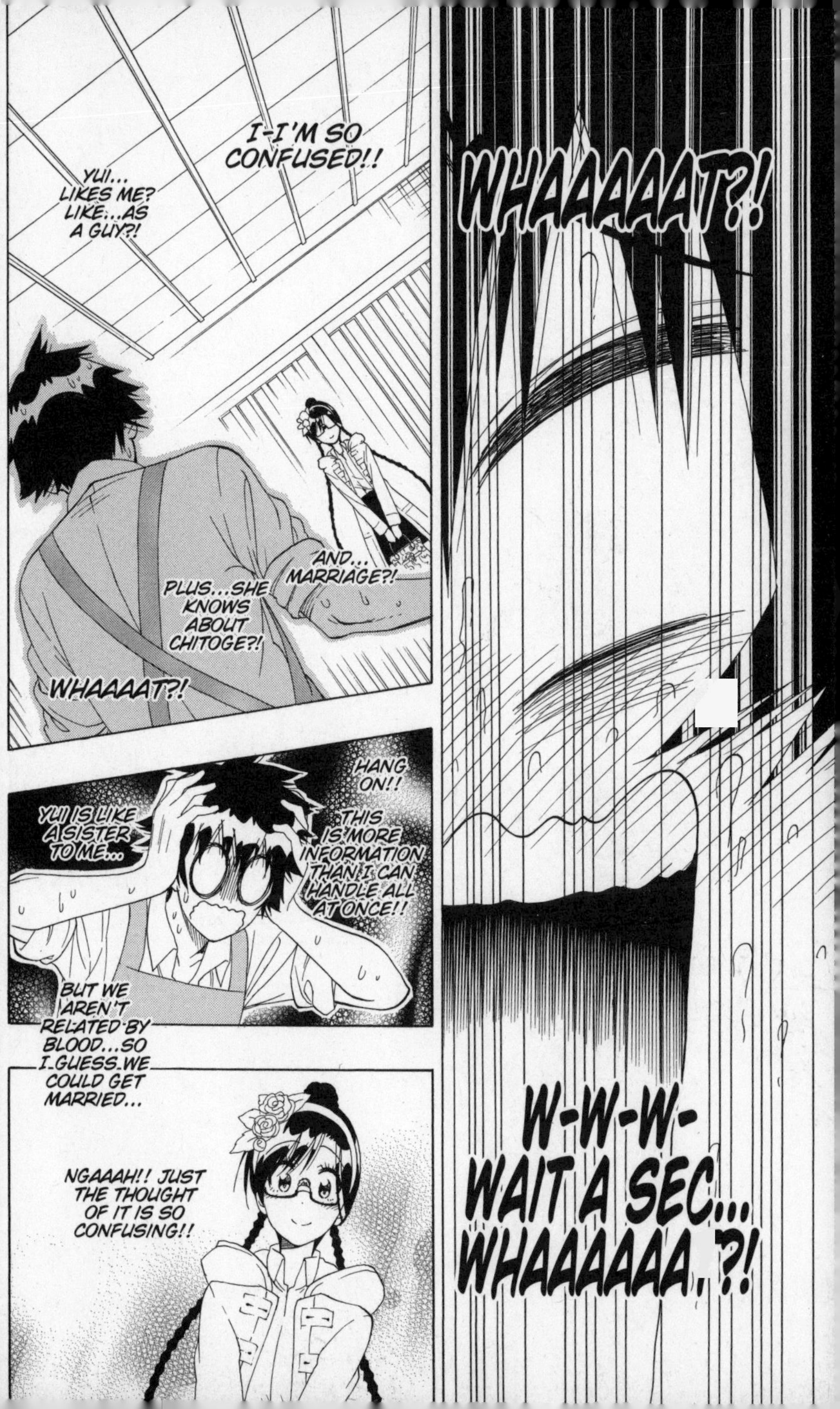
WHAAAAAAT?!
W-W-W-WAIT A SEC... WHAAAAAA ?!
I-I'M SO CONFUSED!!
YUI... LIKES ME? LIKE...AS A GUY?!
AND... MARRIAGE?!
PLUS...SHE KNOWS ABOUT CHITOGE?!
WHAAAAT?!
HANG ON!! THIS IS MORE INFORMATION THAN I CAN HANDLE ALL AT ONCE!!
YUI IS LIKE A SISTER TO ME...
BUT WE AREN'T RELATED BY BLOOD...SO I GUESS WE COULD GET MARRIED...
NGAAAH!! JUST THE THOUGHT OF IT IS SO CONFUSING!!

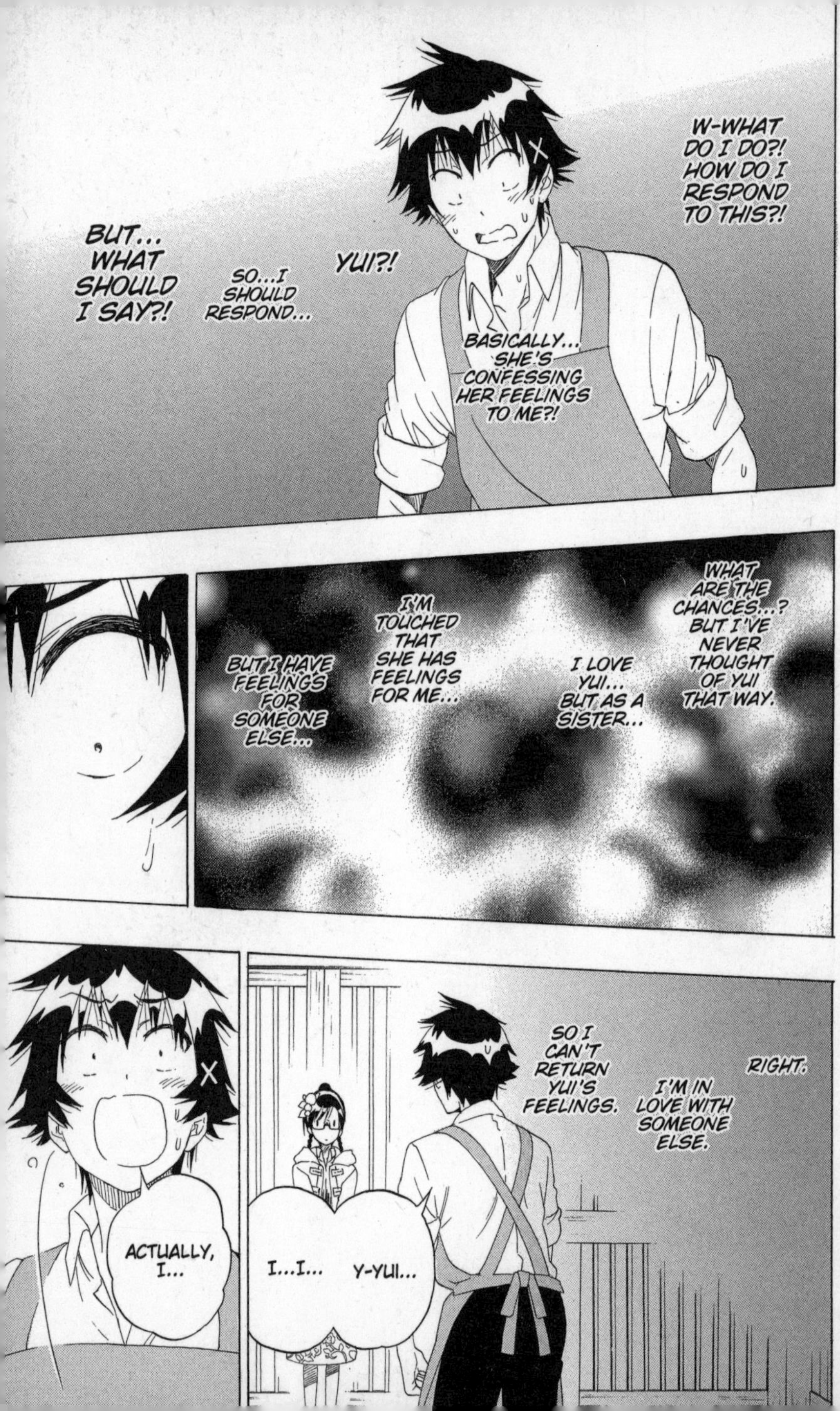
W-WHAT DO I DO?! HOW DO I RESPOND TO THIS?!
BASICALLY... SHE'S CONFESSING HER FEELINGS TO ME?!
YUI?!
SO...I SHOULD RESPOND...
BUT... WHAT SHOULD I SAY?!
WHAT ARE THE CHANCES...? BUT I'VE NEVER THOUGHT OF YUI THAT WAY.
I LOVE YUI... BUT AS A SISTER...
I'M TOUCHED THAT SHE HAS FEELINGS FOR ME...
BUT I HAVE FEELINGS FOR SOMEONE ELSE...
RIGHT.
I'M IN LOVE WITH SOMEONE ELSE.
SO I CAN'T RETURN YUI'S FEELINGS.
Y-YUI...
I...I...
ACTUALLY, I...

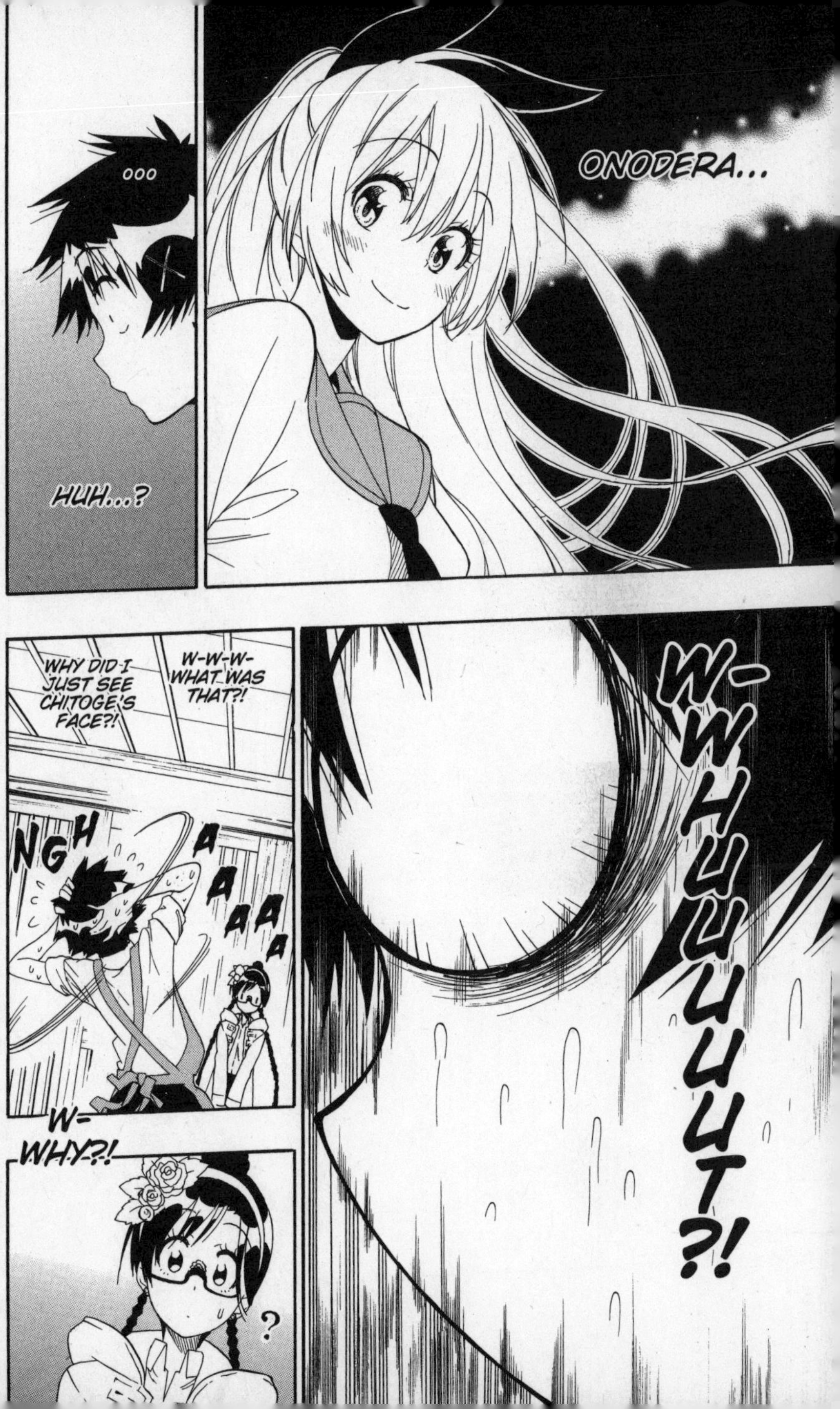
ONODERA...
ooo
HUH...?
W-WHUUUUUT?!
W-W-W-WHAT WAS THAT?!
WHY DID I JUST SEE CHITOGE'S FACE?!
NGH
AAAAAAA
W-WHY?!
?

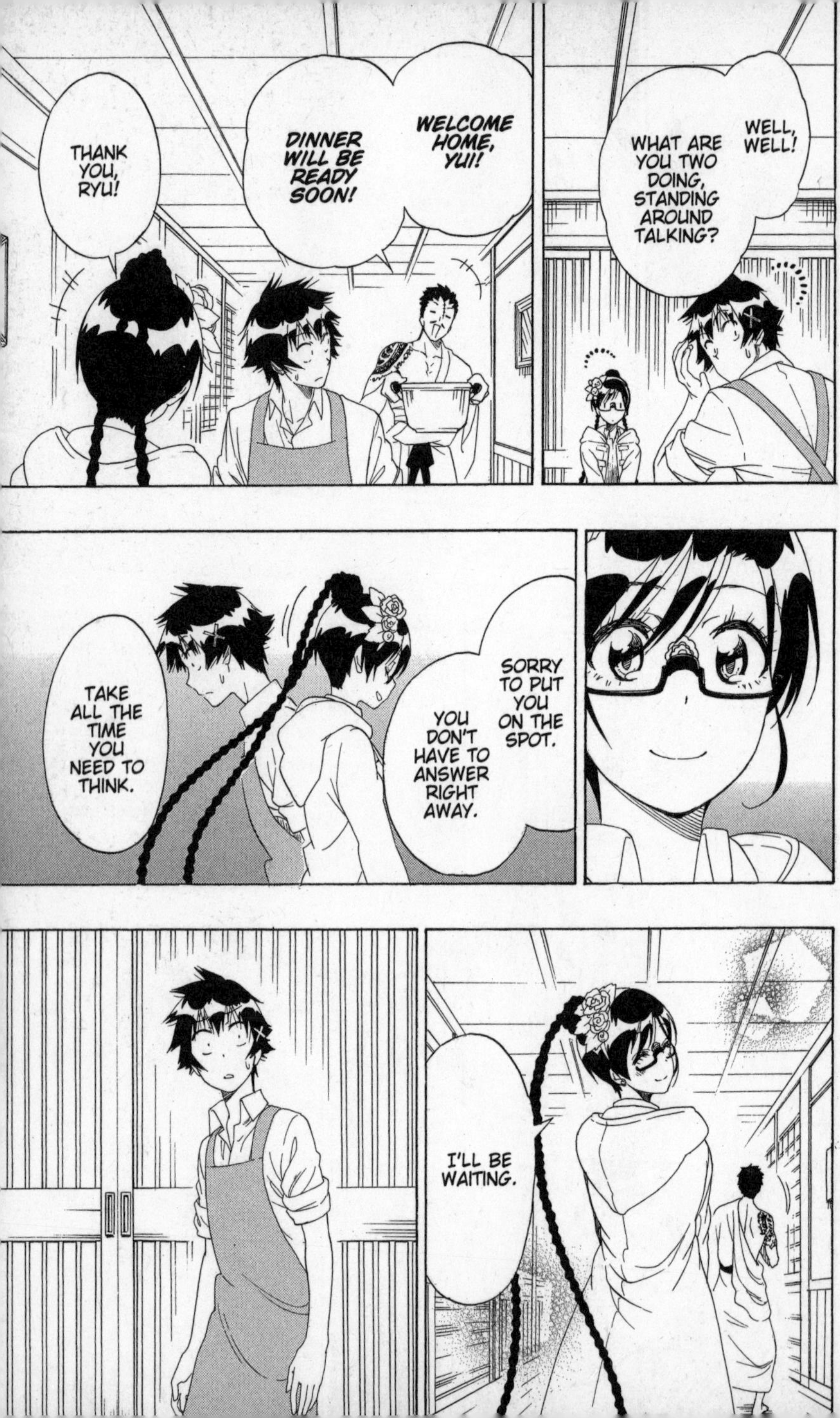
WELL, WELL!
WHAT ARE YOU TWO DOING, STANDING AROUND TALKING?
WELCOME HOME, YUI!
DINNER WILL BE READY SOON!
THANK YOU, RYU!
SORRY TO PUT YOU ON THE SPOT.
YOU DON'T HAVE TO ANSWER RIGHT AWAY.
TAKE ALL THE TIME YOU NEED TO THINK.
I'LL BE WAITING.

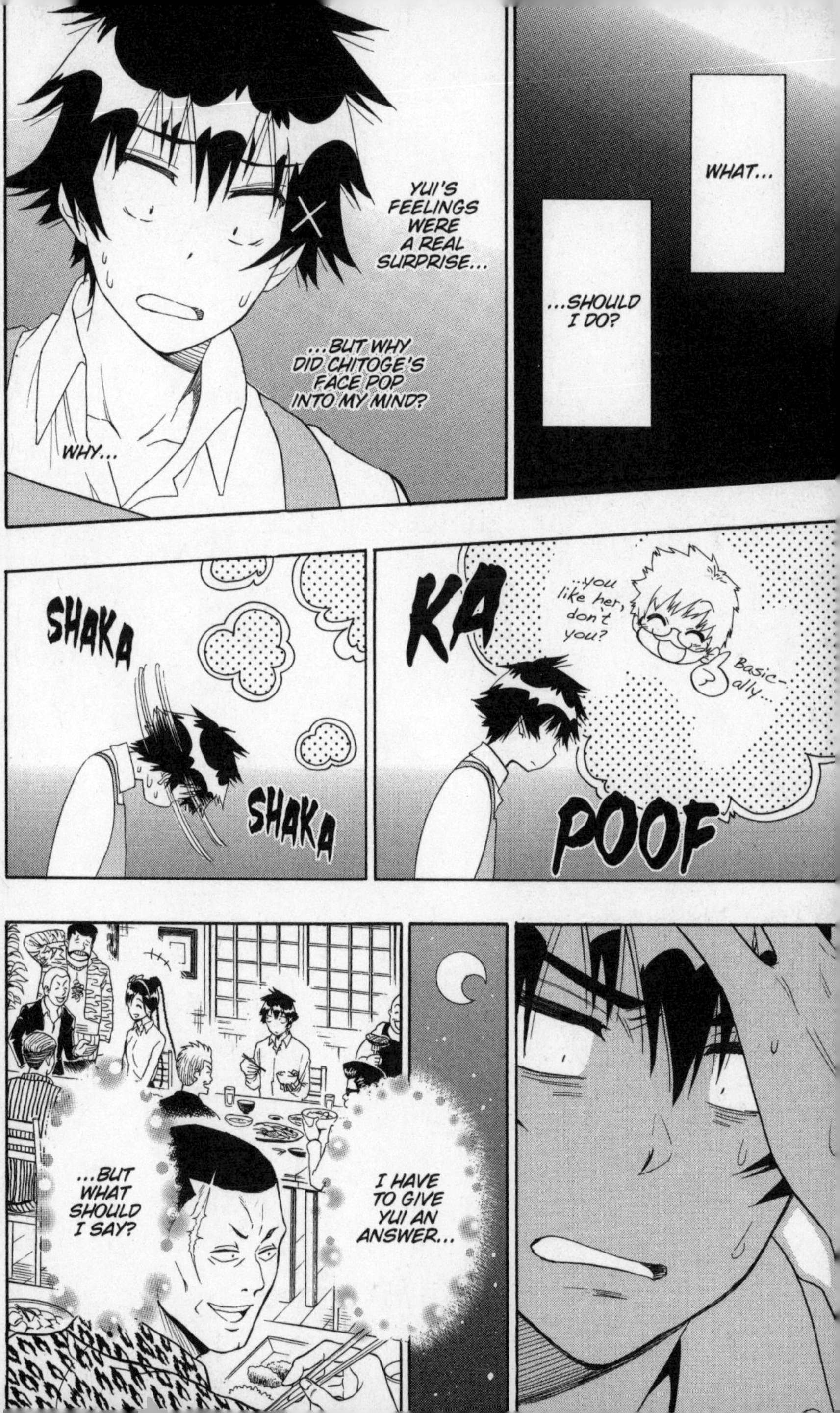
WHAT...
...SHOULD I DO?
YUI'S FEELINGS WERE A REAL SURPRISE...
...BUT WHY DID CHITOGE'S FACE POP INTO MY MIND?
WHY...
KA
Basic-ally...
...you like her, don't you?
POOF
SHAKA
SHAKA
I HAVE TO GIVE YUI AN ANSWER...
...BUT WHAT SHOULD I SAY?

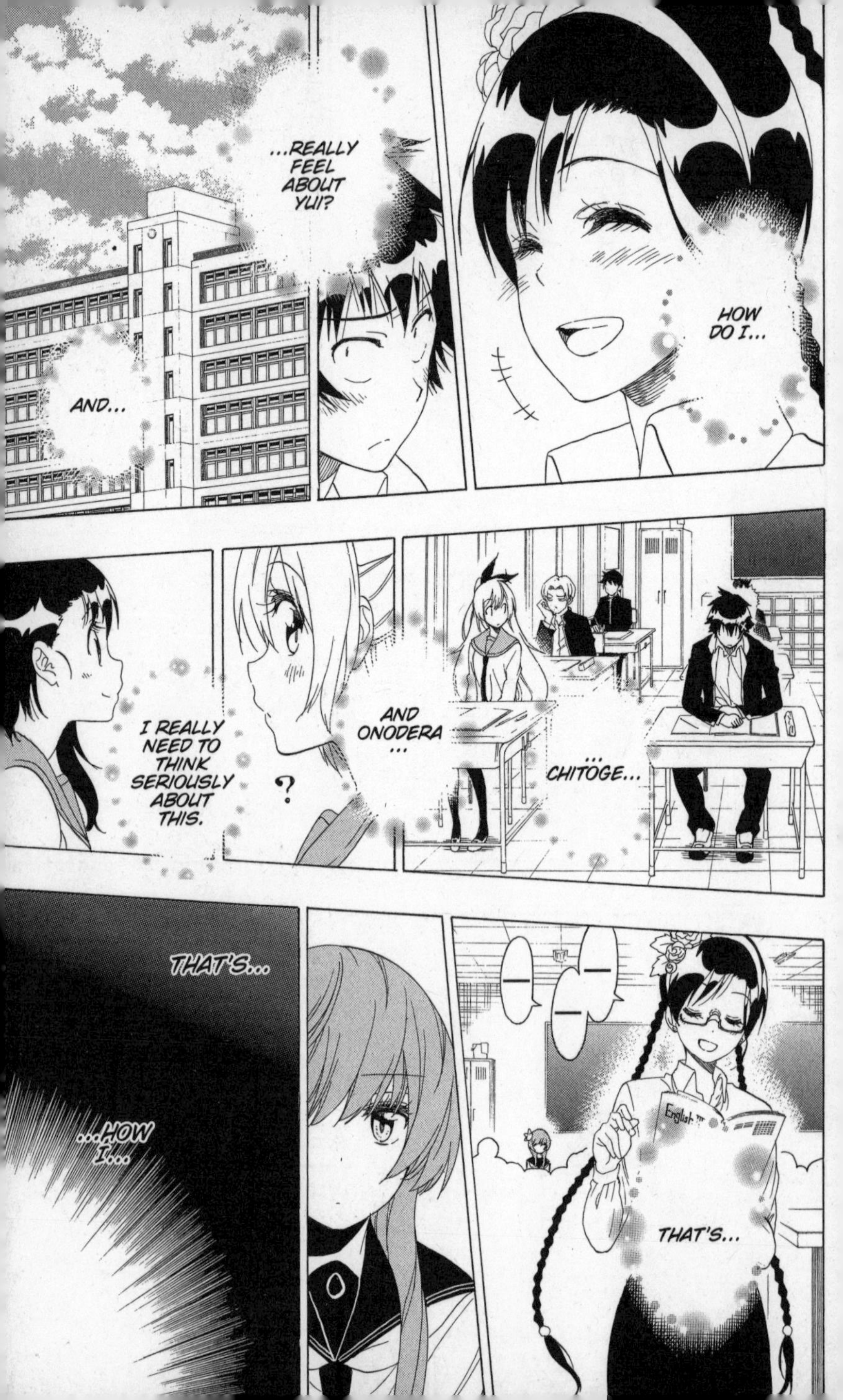
HOW DO I...
...REALLY FEEL ABOUT YUI?
AND...
...CHITOGE...
AND ONODERA ...
?
I REALLY NEED TO THINK SERIOUSLY ABOUT THIS.
—
—
—
THAT'S...
English
THAT'S...
...HOW I...

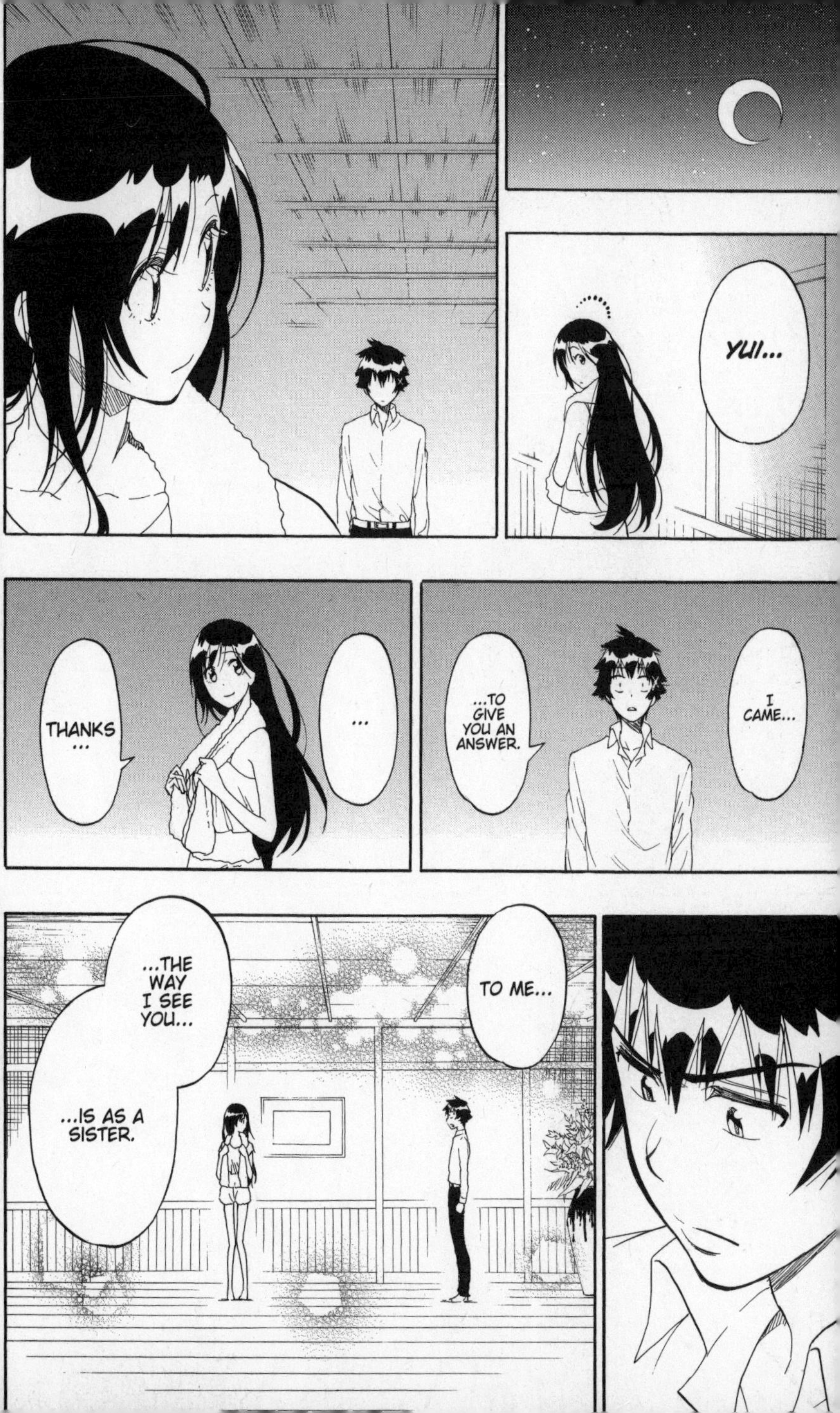
YUI...
I CAME...
...TO GIVE YOU AN ANSWER.
...
THANKS...
TO ME...
...THE WAY I SEE YOU...
...IS AS A SISTER.

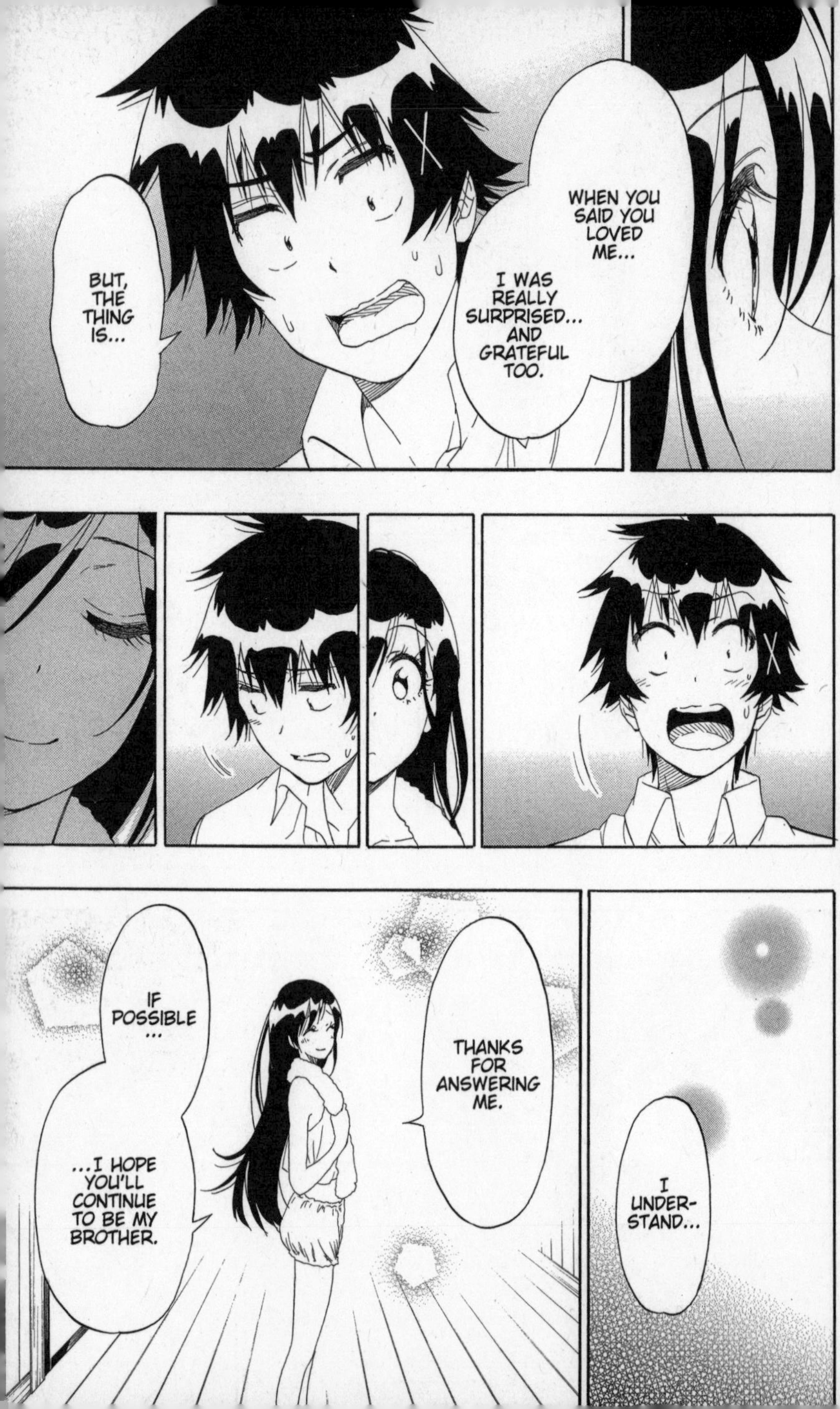
WHEN YOU SAID YOU LOVED ME...
I WAS REALLY SURPRISED... AND GRATEFUL TOO.
BUT, THE THING IS...
I UNDER-STAND...
THANKS FOR ANSWERING ME.
IF POSSIBLE ...
...I HOPE YOU'LL CONTINUE TO BE MY BROTHER.

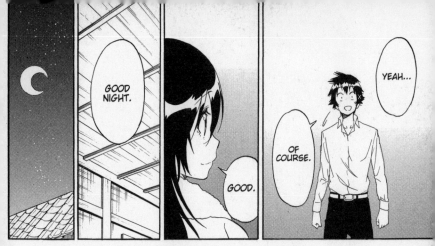

YEAH...
OF COURSE.
GOOD.
GOOD NIGHT.
DID I SAY...
...THE RIGHT THING?
DID I HURT HER AS LITTLE AS POSSIBLE?
MAYBE I COULD'VE DONE BETTER.
HOW...
HOW DOES YUI FEEL RIGHT NOW?

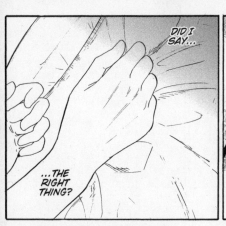

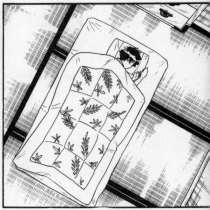

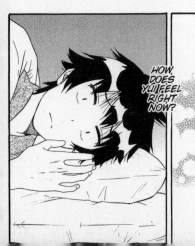

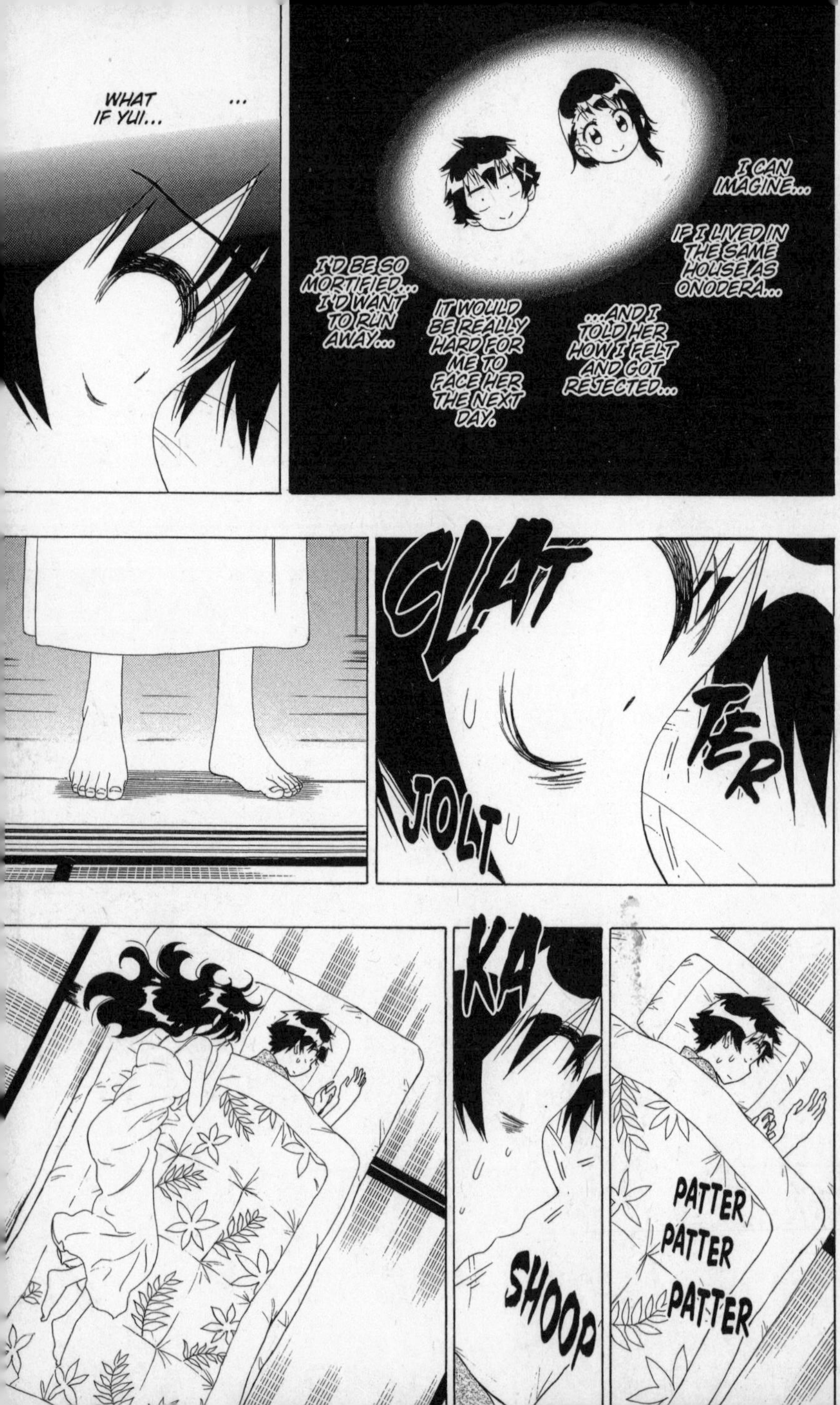
I CAN IMAGINE...
IF I LIVED IN THE SAME HOUSE AS ONODERA...
...AND I TOLD HER HOW I FELT AND GOT REJECTED...
IT WOULD BE REALLY HARD FOR ME TO FACE HER THE NEXT DAY.
I'D BE SO MORTIFIED... I'D WANT TO RUN AWAY...
...
WHAT IF YUI...
CLATTER
JOLT
PATTER
PATTER
PATTER
KA
SHOOP

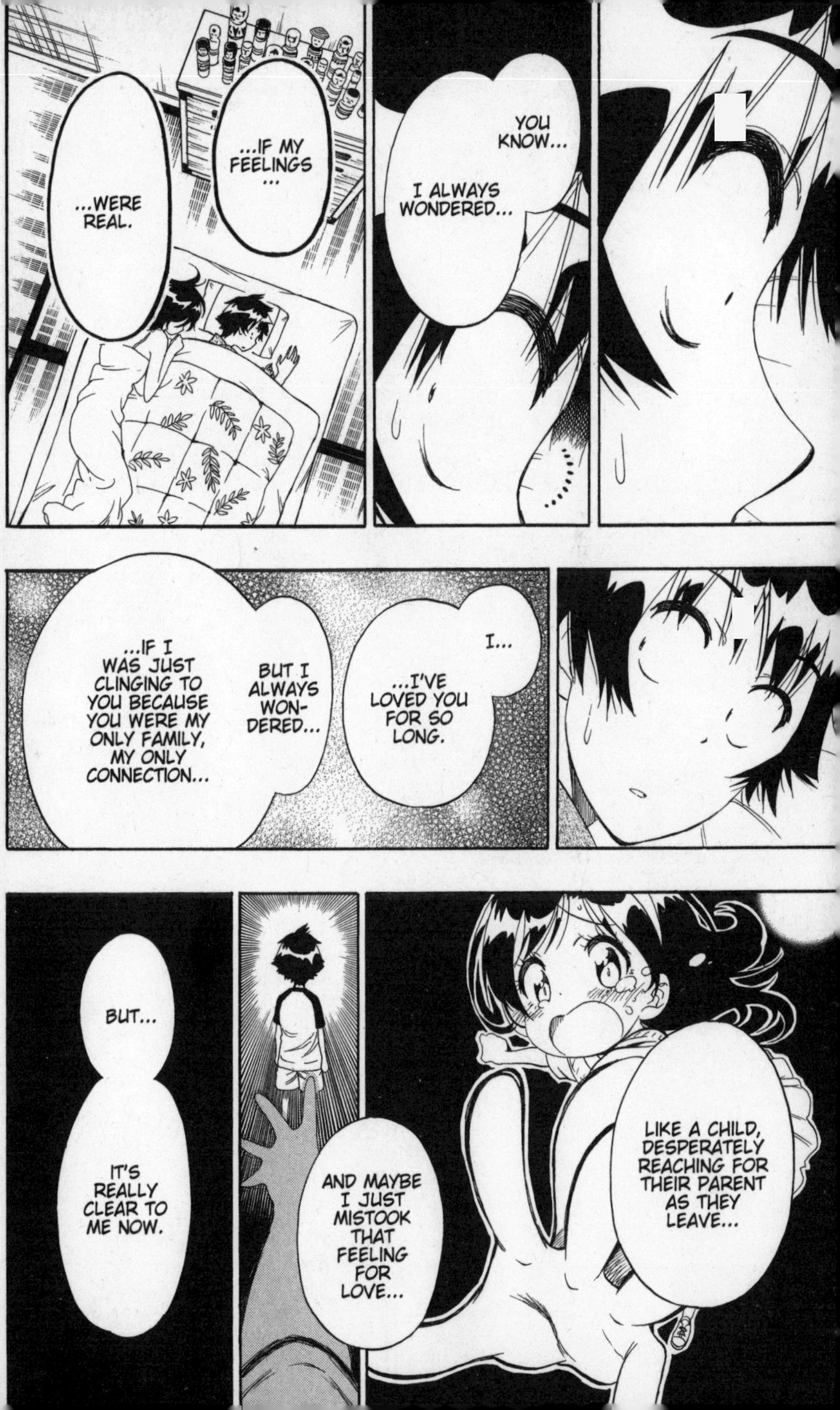
YOU KNOW...
I ALWAYS WONDERED...
...IF MY FEELINGS ...
...WERE REAL.
I...
...I'VE LOVED YOU FOR SO LONG.
BUT I ALWAYS WON- DERED...
...IF I WAS JUST CLINGING TO YOU BECAUSE YOU WERE MY ONLY FAMILY, MY ONLY CONNECTION...
LIKE A CHILD, DESPERATELY REACHING FOR THEIR PARENT AS THEY LEAVE...
AND MAYBE I JUST MISTOOK THAT FEELING FOR LOVE...
BUT...
IT'S REALLY CLEAR TO ME NOW.

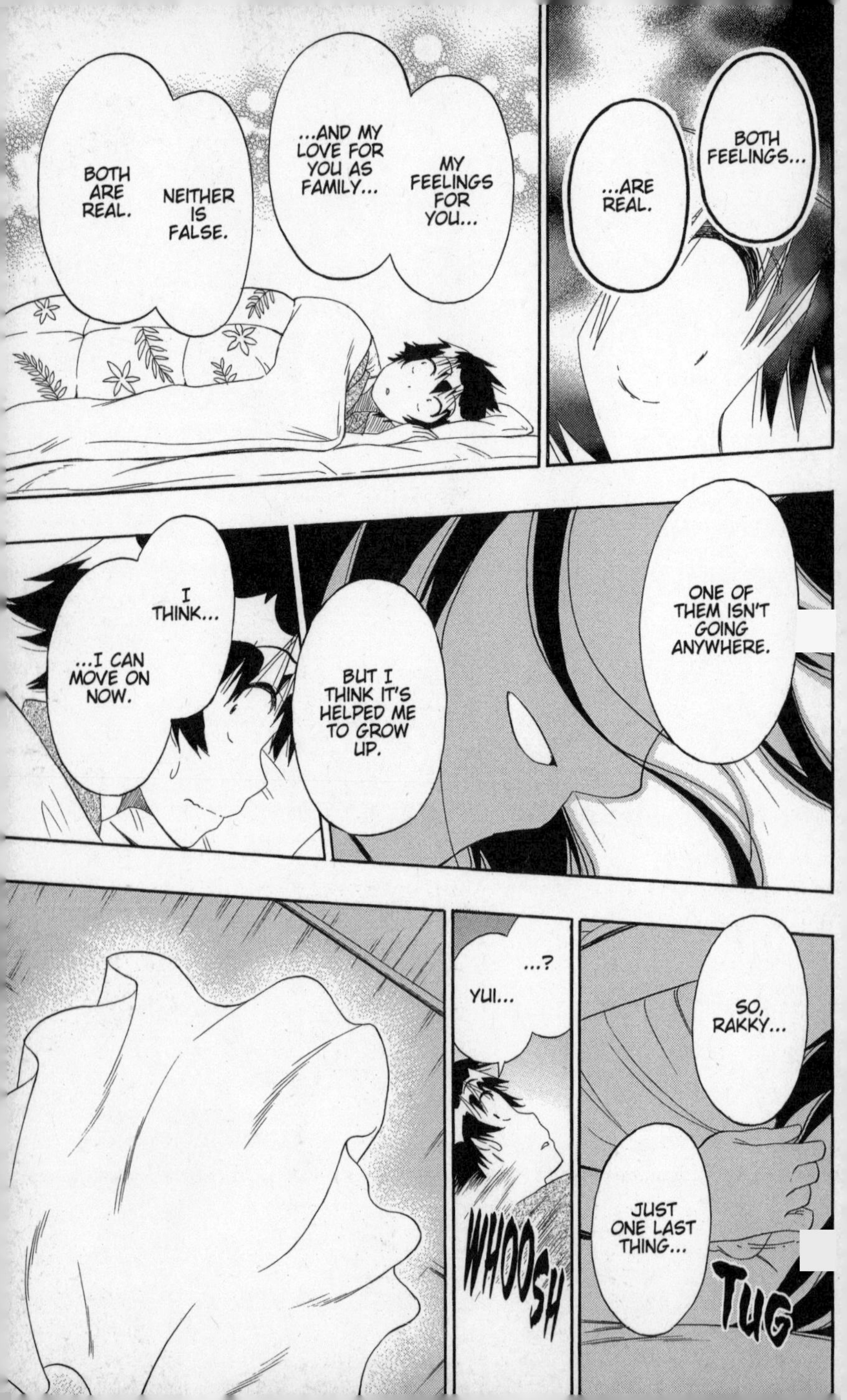
BOTH FEELINGS...
...ARE REAL.
MY FEELINGS FOR YOU...
...AND MY LOVE FOR YOU AS FAMILY...
NEITHER IS FALSE.
BOTH ARE REAL.
ONE OF THEM ISN'T GOING ANYWHERE.
BUT I THINK IT'S HELPED ME TO GROW UP.
I THINK...
...I CAN MOVE ON NOW.
SO, RAKKY...
JUST ONE LAST THING...
TUG
...?
YUI...
WHOOSH

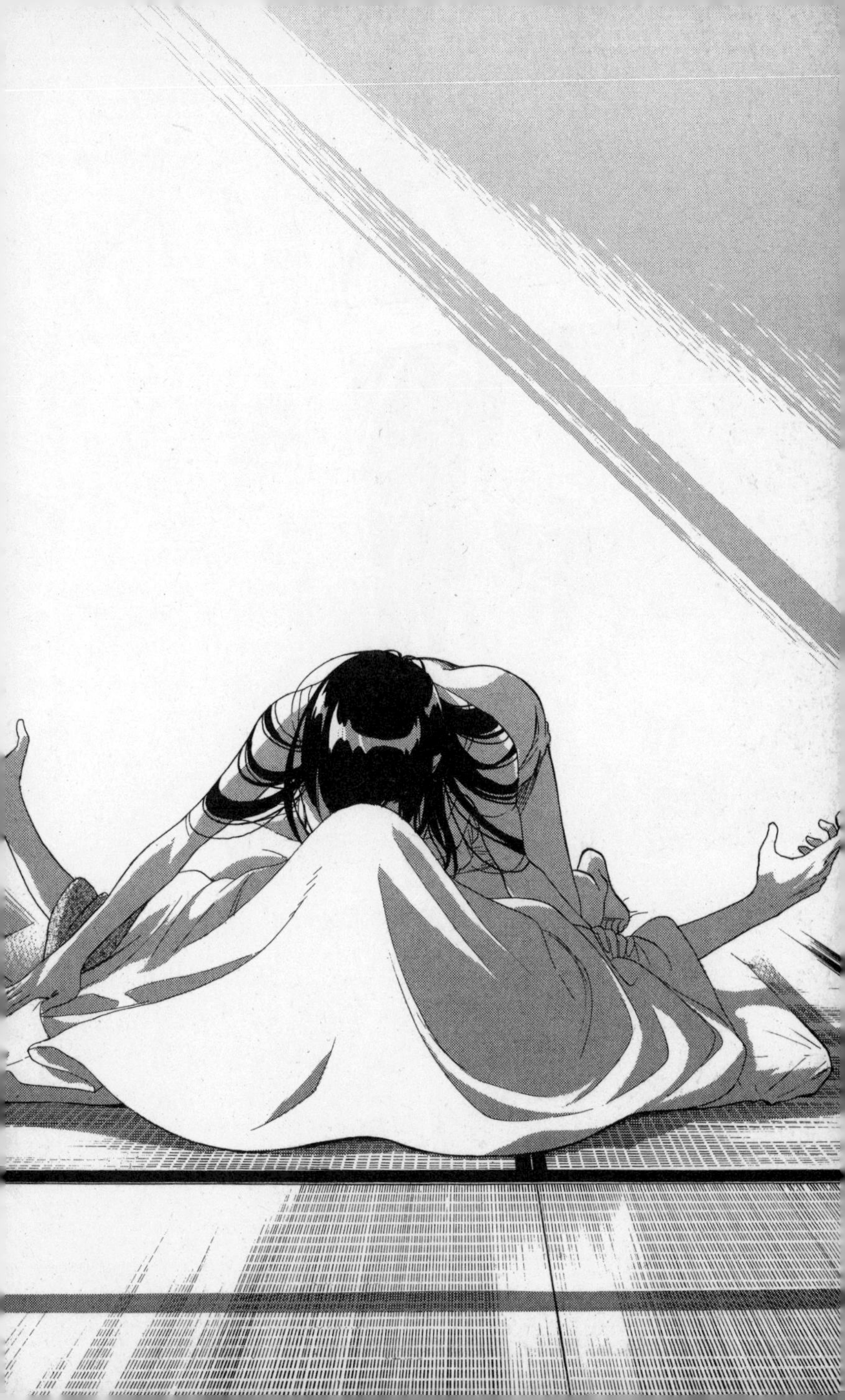

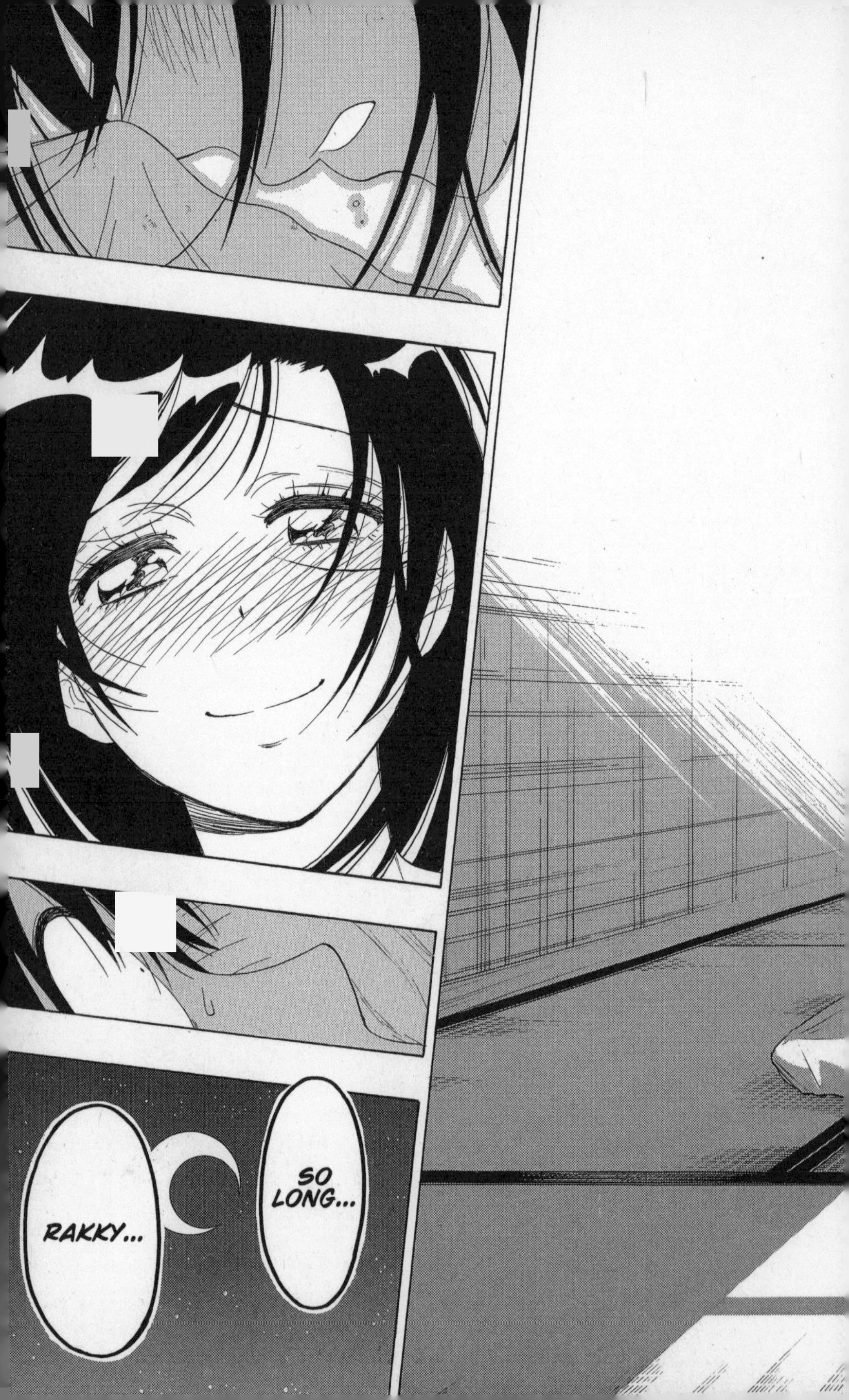
SO LONG...
RAKKY...

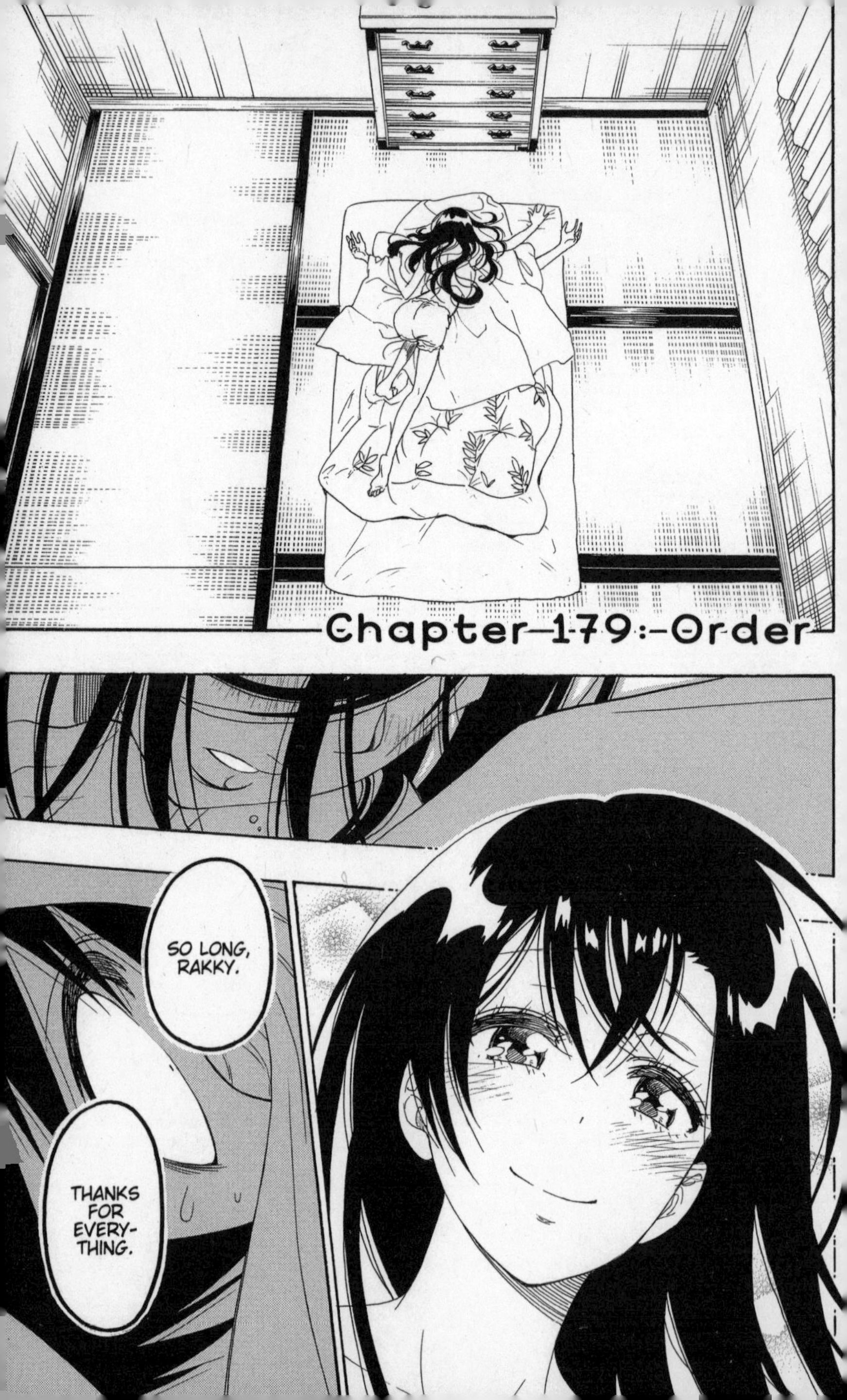
Chapter 179: Order
SO LONG, RAKKY.
THANKS FOR EVERY-THING.

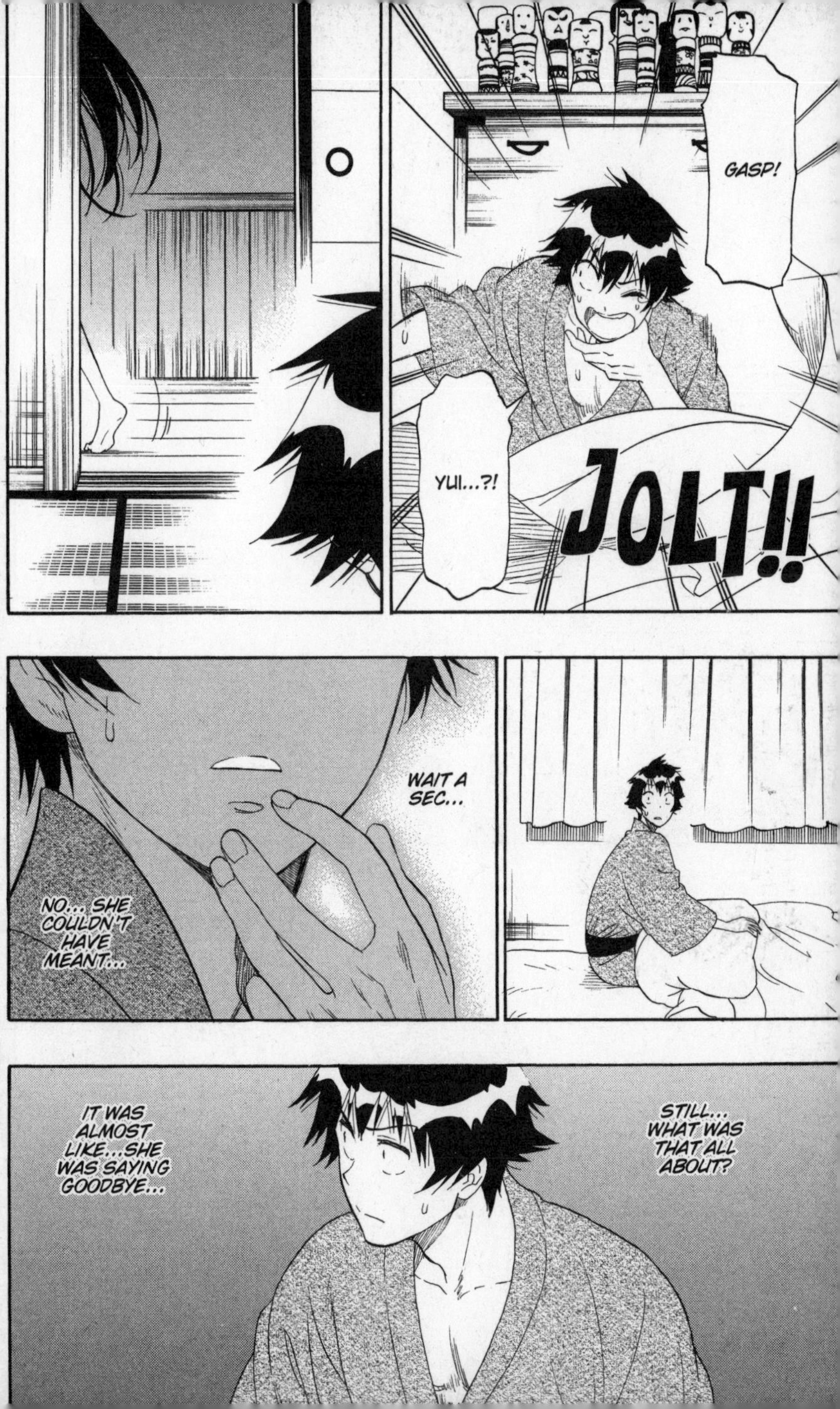
GASP!
YUI...?!
JOLT!!
WAIT A SEC...
NO... SHE COULDN'T HAVE MEANT...
STILL... WHAT WAS THAT ALL ABOUT?
IT WAS ALMOST LIKE...SHE WAS SAYING GOODBYE...

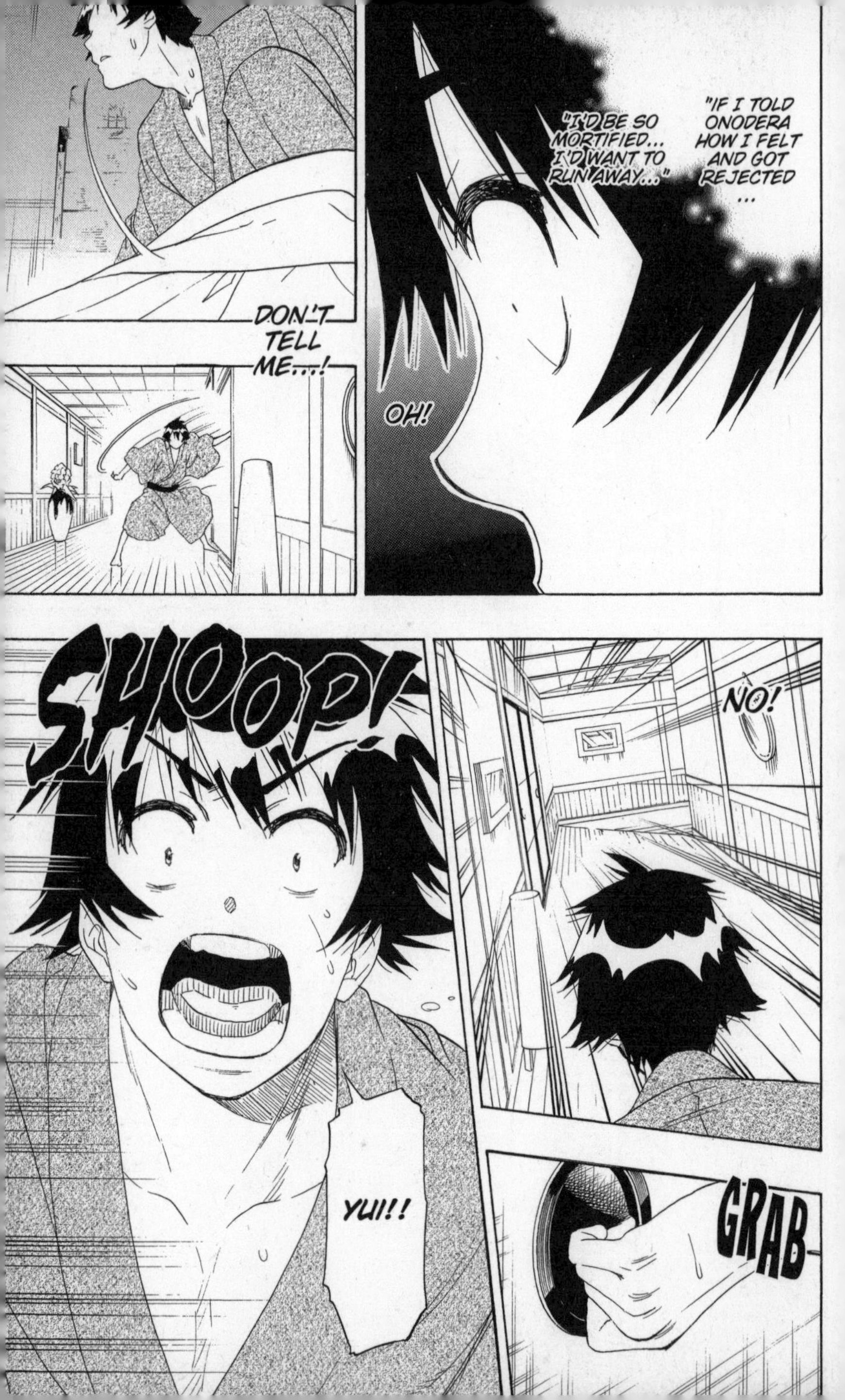
"IF I TOLD ONODERA HOW I FELT AND GOT REJECTED ...
"I'D BE SO MORTIFIED... I'D WANT TO RUN AWAY..."
OH!
DON'T TELL ME...!
NO!
GRAB
SHOOP!
YUI!!

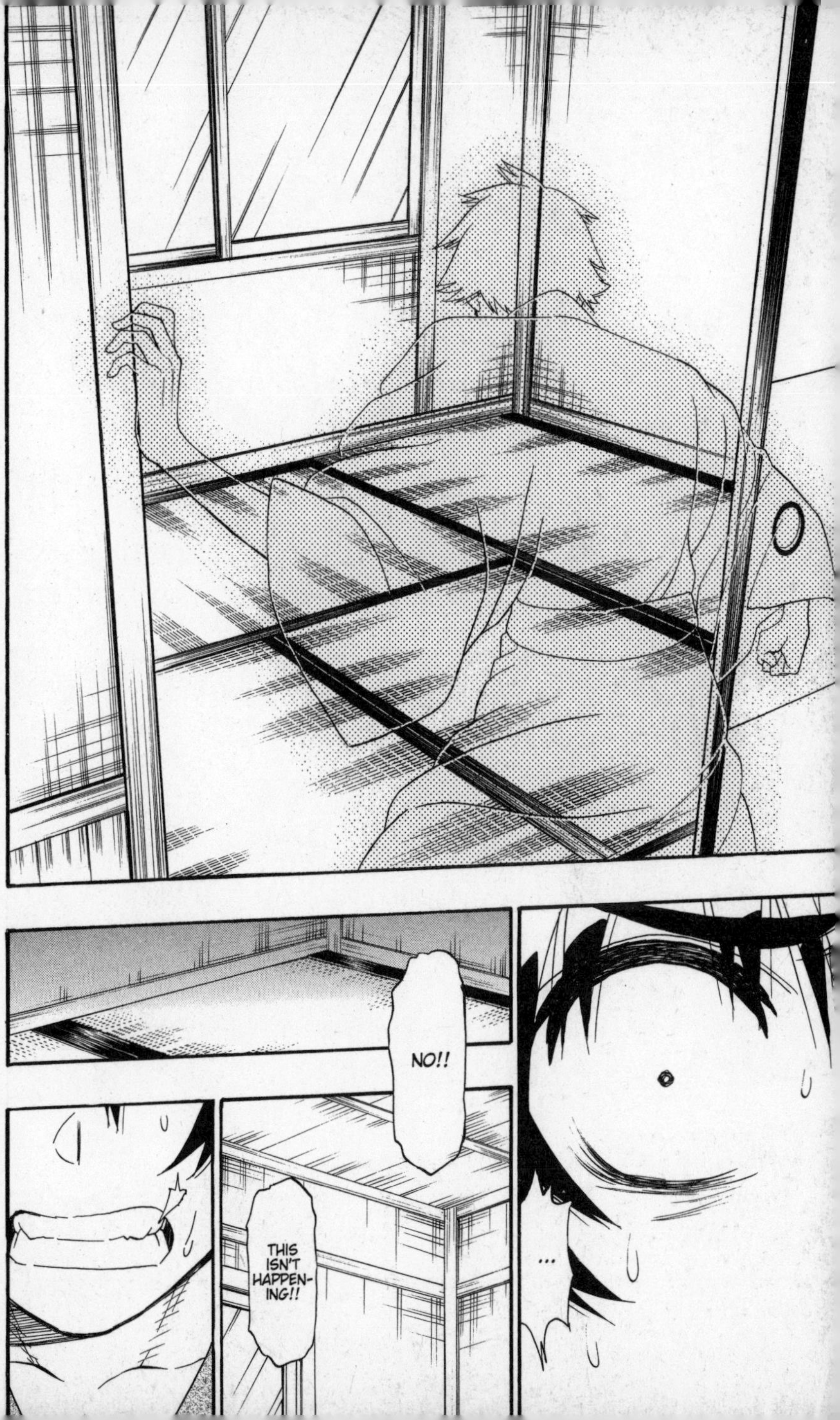
...
NO!!
THIS ISN'T HAPPEN-ING!!

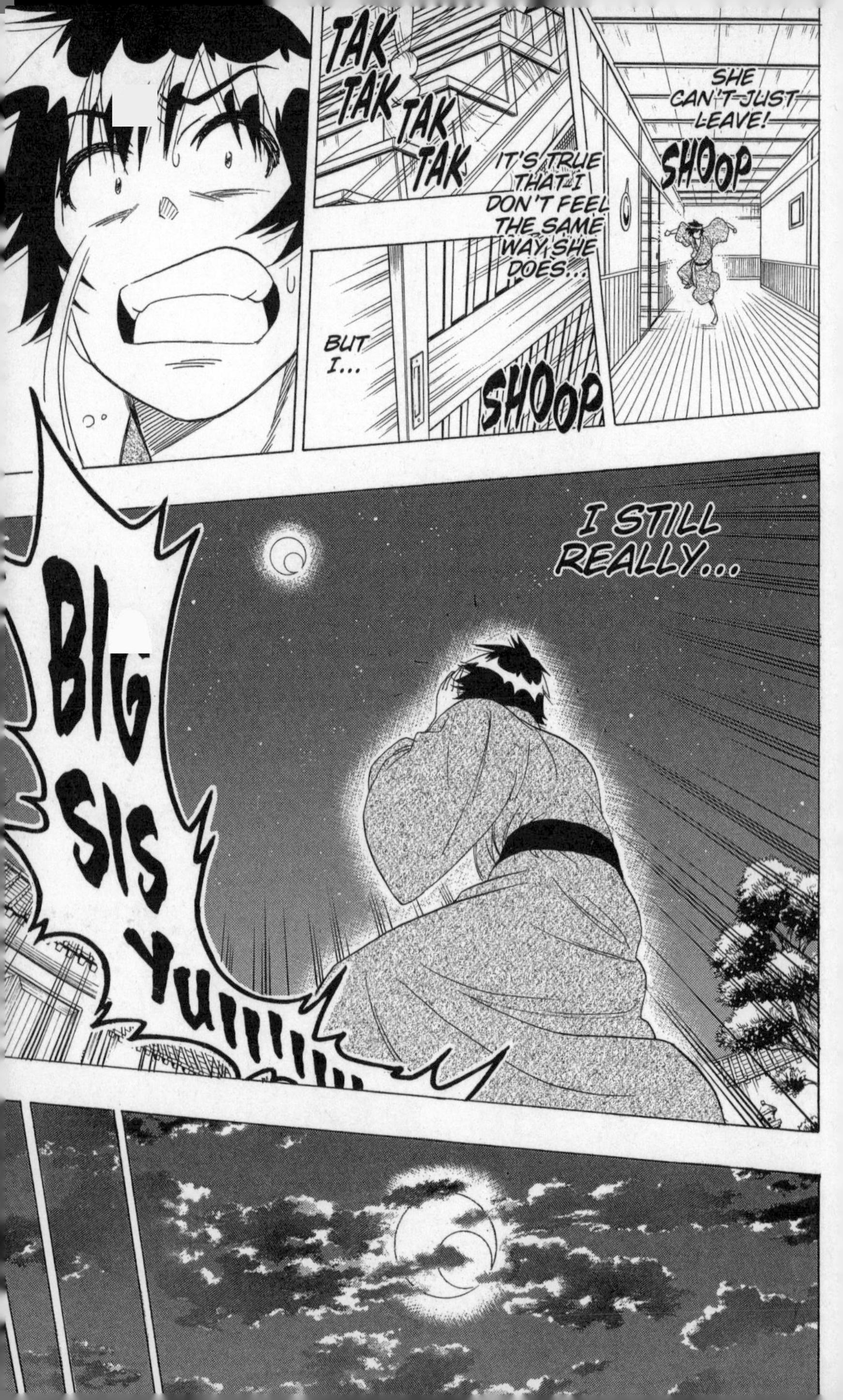
SHE CAN'T JUST LEAVE!
SHOOP
TAK TAK
TAK TAK
IT'S TRUE THAT I DON'T FEEL THE SAME WAY SHE DOES...
BUT I...
SHOOP
I STILL REALLY...
BIG SIS YU!!!!!!

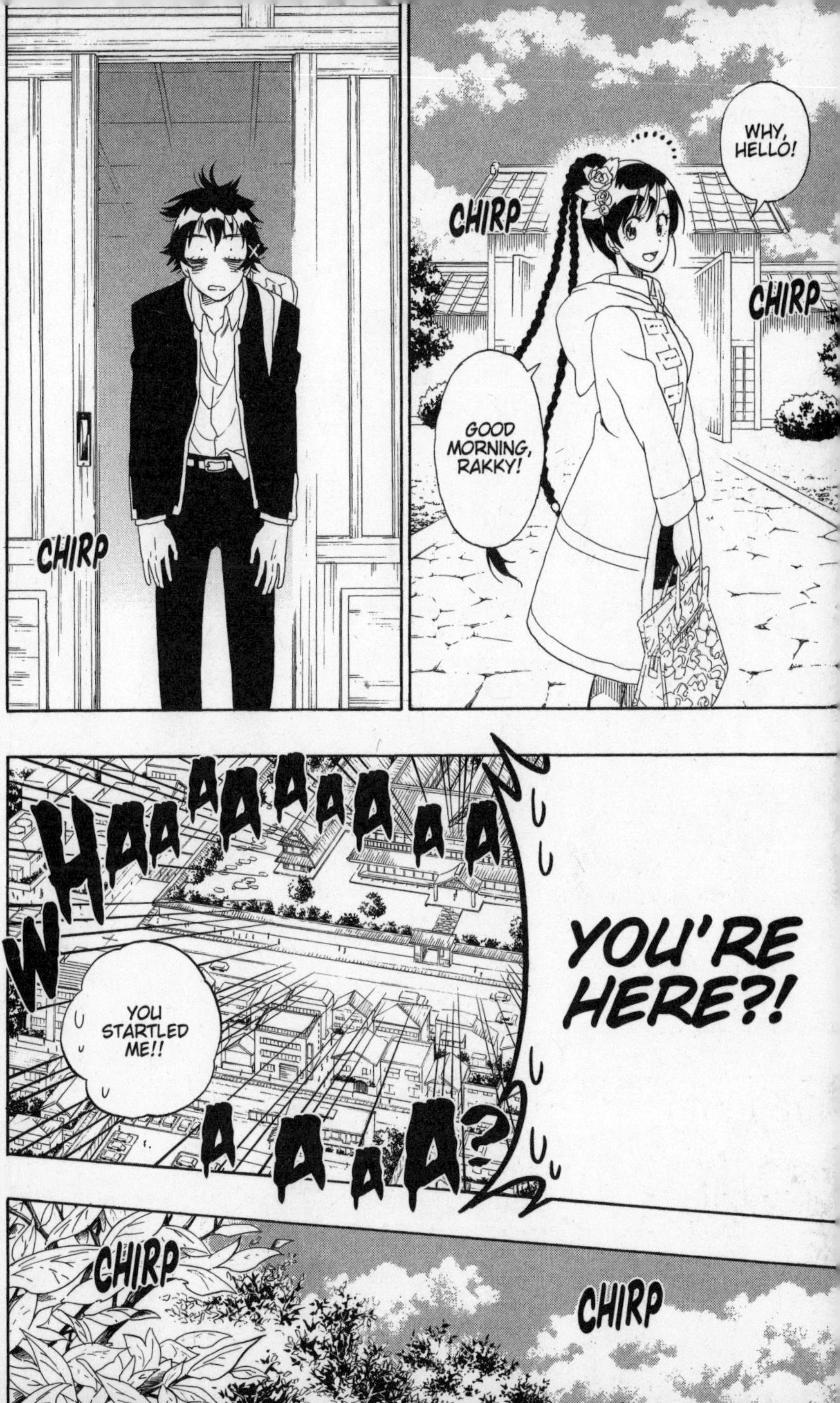
WHY, HELLO!
CHIRP
CHIRP
GOOD MORNING, RAKKY!
CHIRP
YOU'RE HERE?!
WHAAAAAAAAAAAAA?
YOU STARTLED ME!!
CHIRP
CHIRP

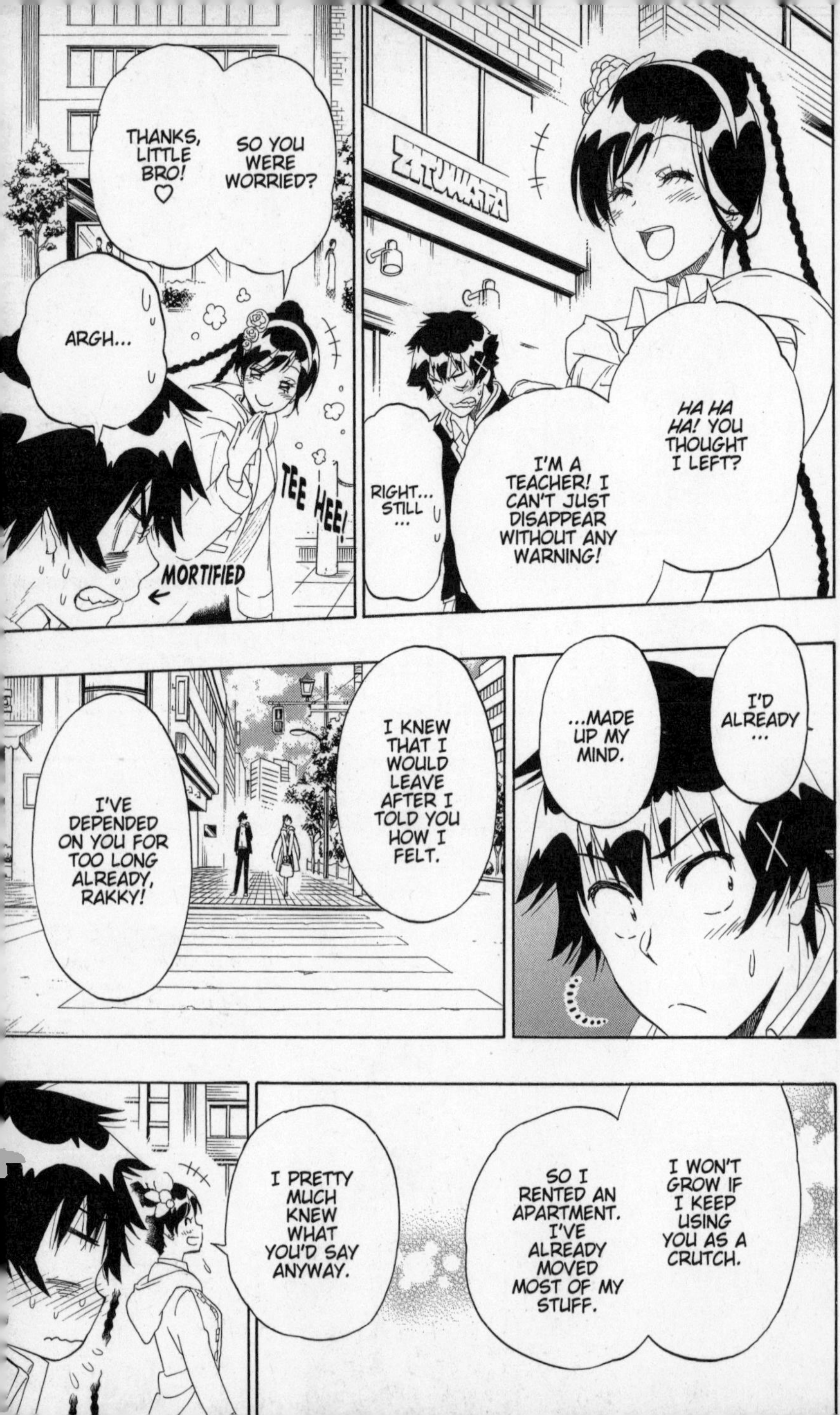
HA HA HA! YOU THOUGHT I LEFT?
I'M A TEACHER! I CAN'T JUST DISAPPEAR WITHOUT ANY WARNING!
RIGHT... STILL ...
SO YOU WERE WORRIED?
THANKS, LITTLE BRO! ♡
ARGH...
TEE HEE!
MORTIFIED
I'D ALREADY ...
...MADE UP MY MIND.
I KNEW THAT I WOULD LEAVE AFTER I TOLD YOU HOW I FELT.
I'VE DEPENDED ON YOU FOR TOO LONG ALREADY, RAKKY!
I WON'T GROW IF I KEEP USING YOU AS A CRUTCH.
SO I RENTED AN APARTMENT. I'VE ALREADY MOVED MOST OF MY STUFF.
I PRETTY MUCH KNEW WHAT YOU'D SAY ANYWAY.

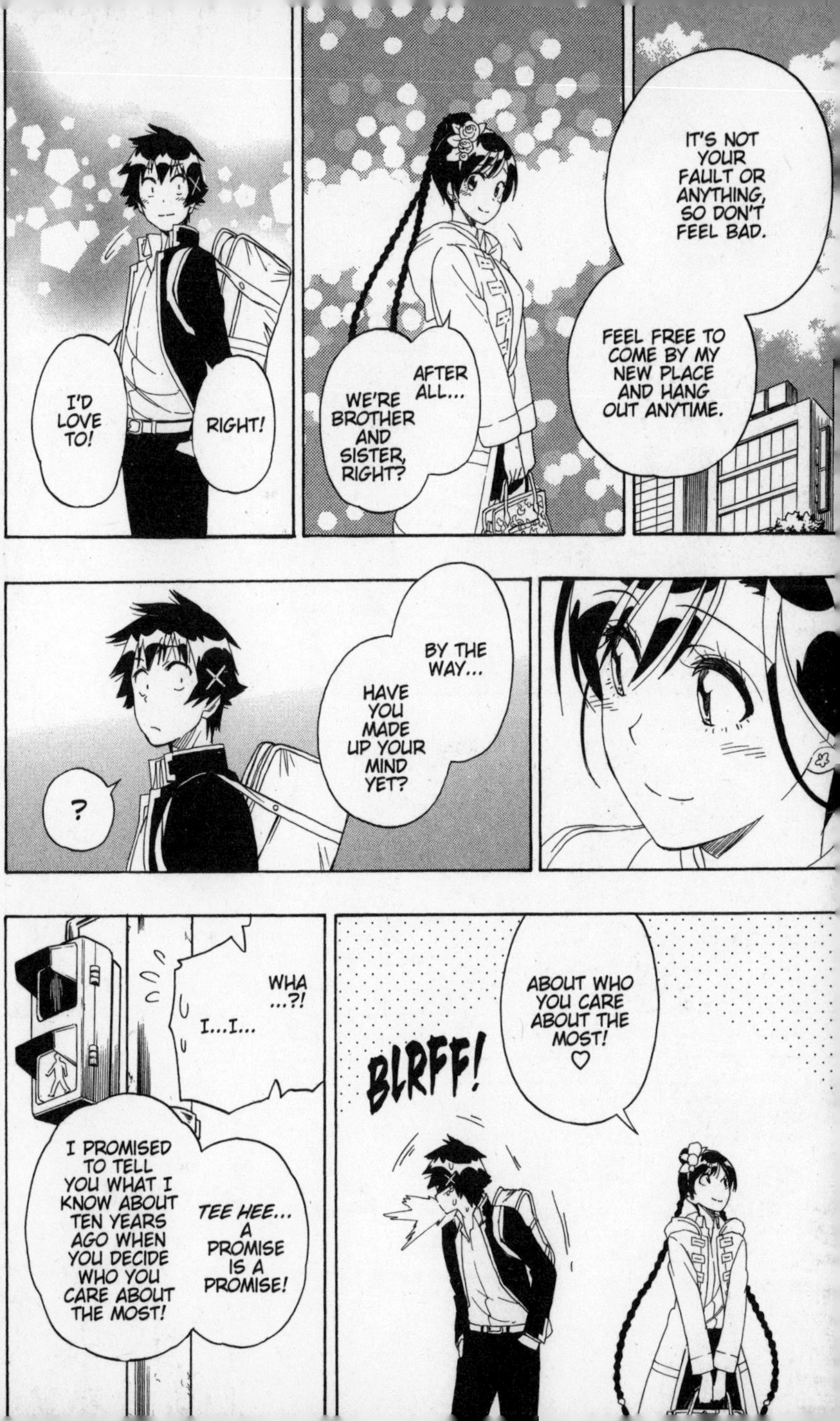
IT'S NOT YOUR FAULT OR ANYTHING, SO DON'T FEEL BAD.
FEEL FREE TO COME BY MY NEW PLACE AND HANG OUT ANYTIME.
AFTER ALL...
WE'RE BROTHER AND SISTER, RIGHT?
RIGHT!
I'D LOVE TO!
BY THE WAY...
HAVE YOU MADE UP YOUR MIND YET?
?
ABOUT WHO YOU CARE ABOUT THE MOST! ♡
BLRFF!
WHA ...?!
I...I...
TEE HEE... A PROMISE IS A PROMISE!
I PROMISED TO TELL YOU WHAT I KNOW ABOUT TEN YEARS AGO WHEN YOU DECIDE WHO YOU CARE ABOUT THE MOST!

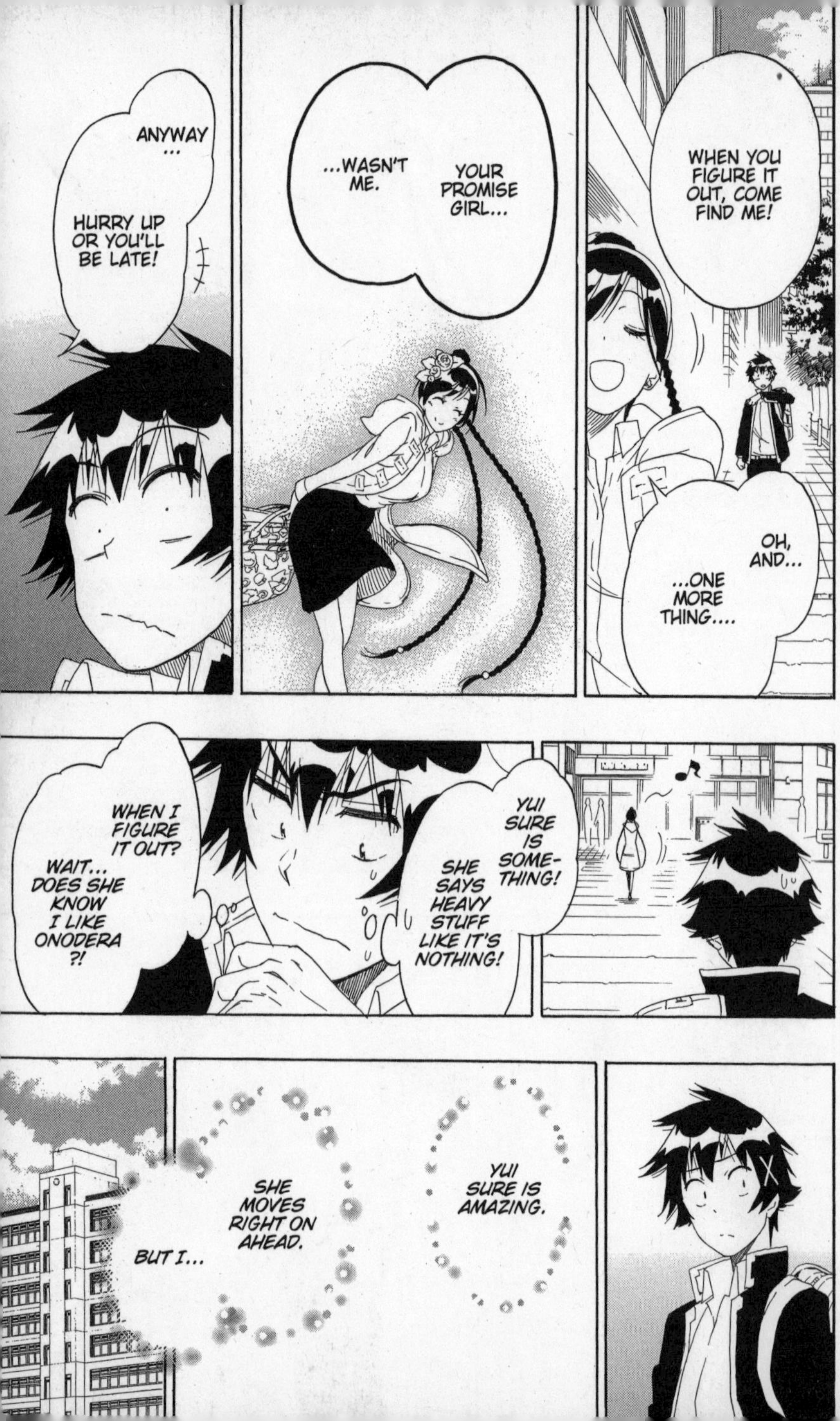
WHEN YOU FIGURE IT OUT, COME FIND ME!
OH, AND...
...ONE MORE THING....
YOUR PROMISE GIRL...
...WASN'T ME.
ANYWAY...
HURRY UP OR YOU'LL BE LATE!
YUI SURE IS SOME-THING!
SHE SAYS HEAVY STUFF LIKE IT'S NOTHING!
WHEN I FIGURE IT OUT?
WAIT... DOES SHE KNOW I LIKE ONODERA?!
YUI SURE IS AMAZING.
SHE MOVES RIGHT ON AHEAD.
BUT I...

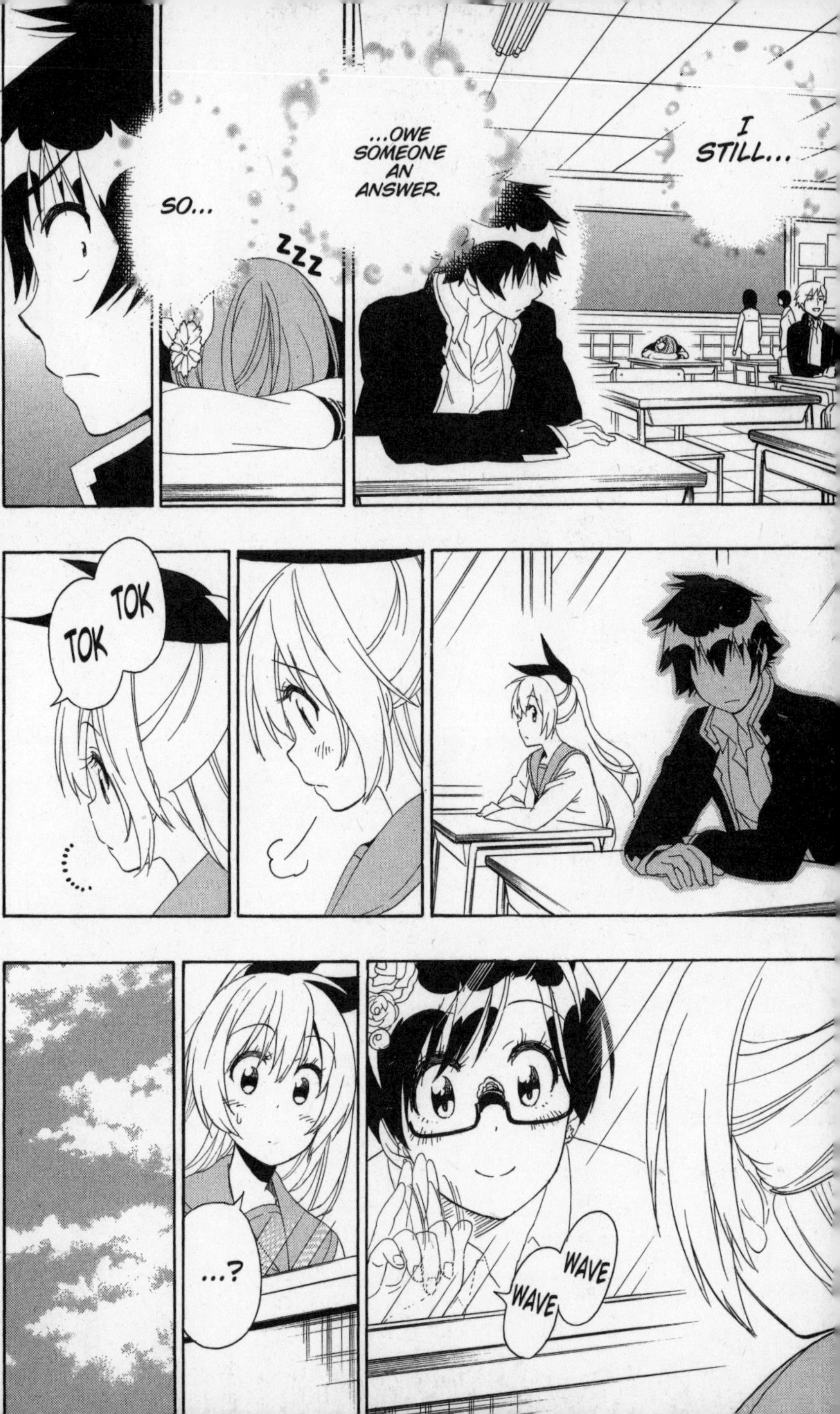
I STILL...
...OWE SOMEONE AN ANSWER.
ZZZ
SO...
TOK TOK
......
WAVE WAVE
...?

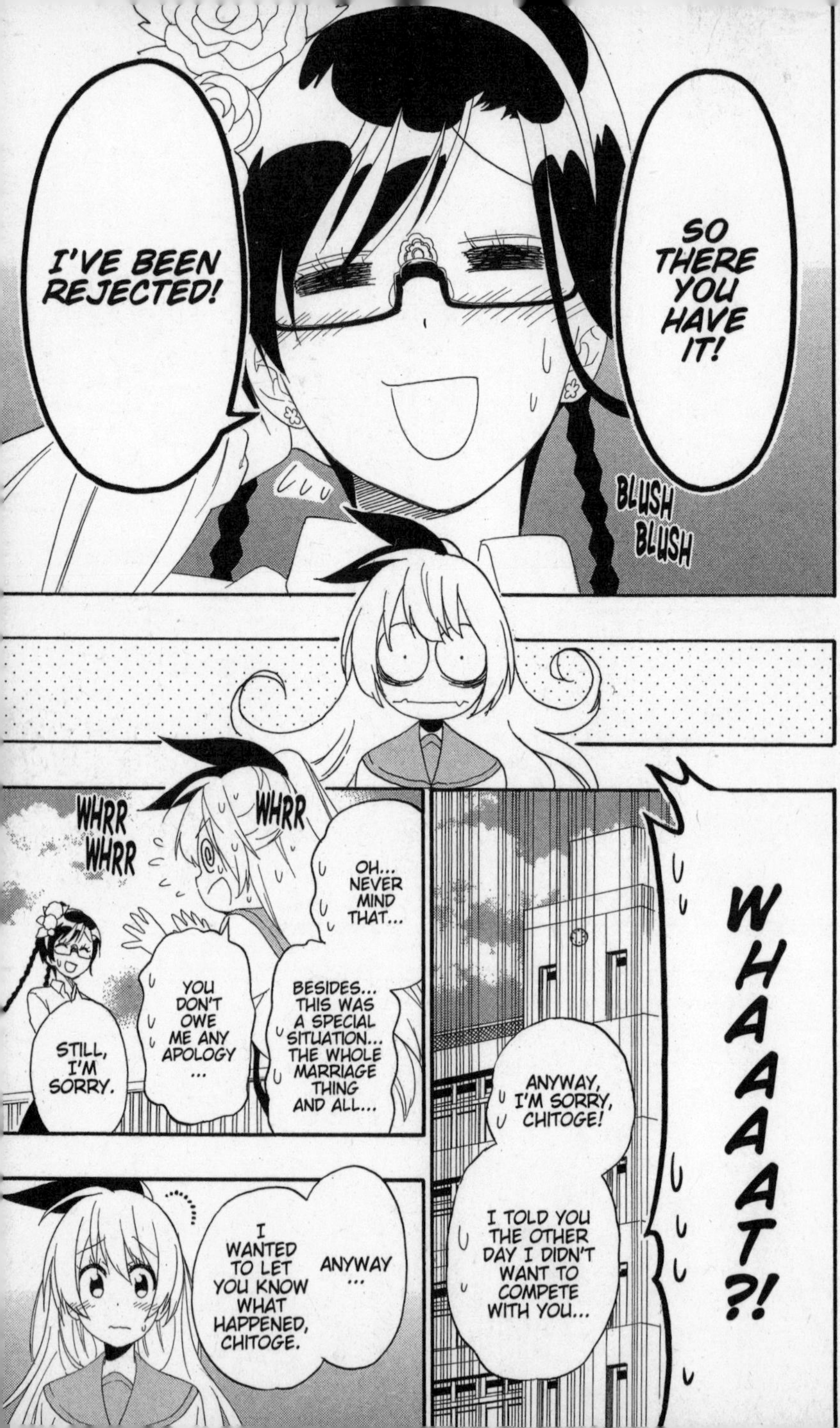
SO THERE YOU HAVE IT!
I'VE BEEN REJECTED!
BLUSH BLUSH
WHAAAAAT?!
ANYWAY, I'M SORRY, CHITOGE!
I TOLD YOU THE OTHER DAY I DIDN'T WANT TO COMPETE WITH YOU...
WHRR
WHRR WHRR
OH... NEVER MIND THAT...
BESIDES... THIS WAS A SPECIAL SITUATION... THE WHOLE MARRIAGE THING AND ALL...
YOU DON'T OWE ME ANY APOLOGY...
STILL, I'M SORRY.
ANYWAY...
I WANTED TO LET YOU KNOW WHAT HAPPENED, CHITOGE.

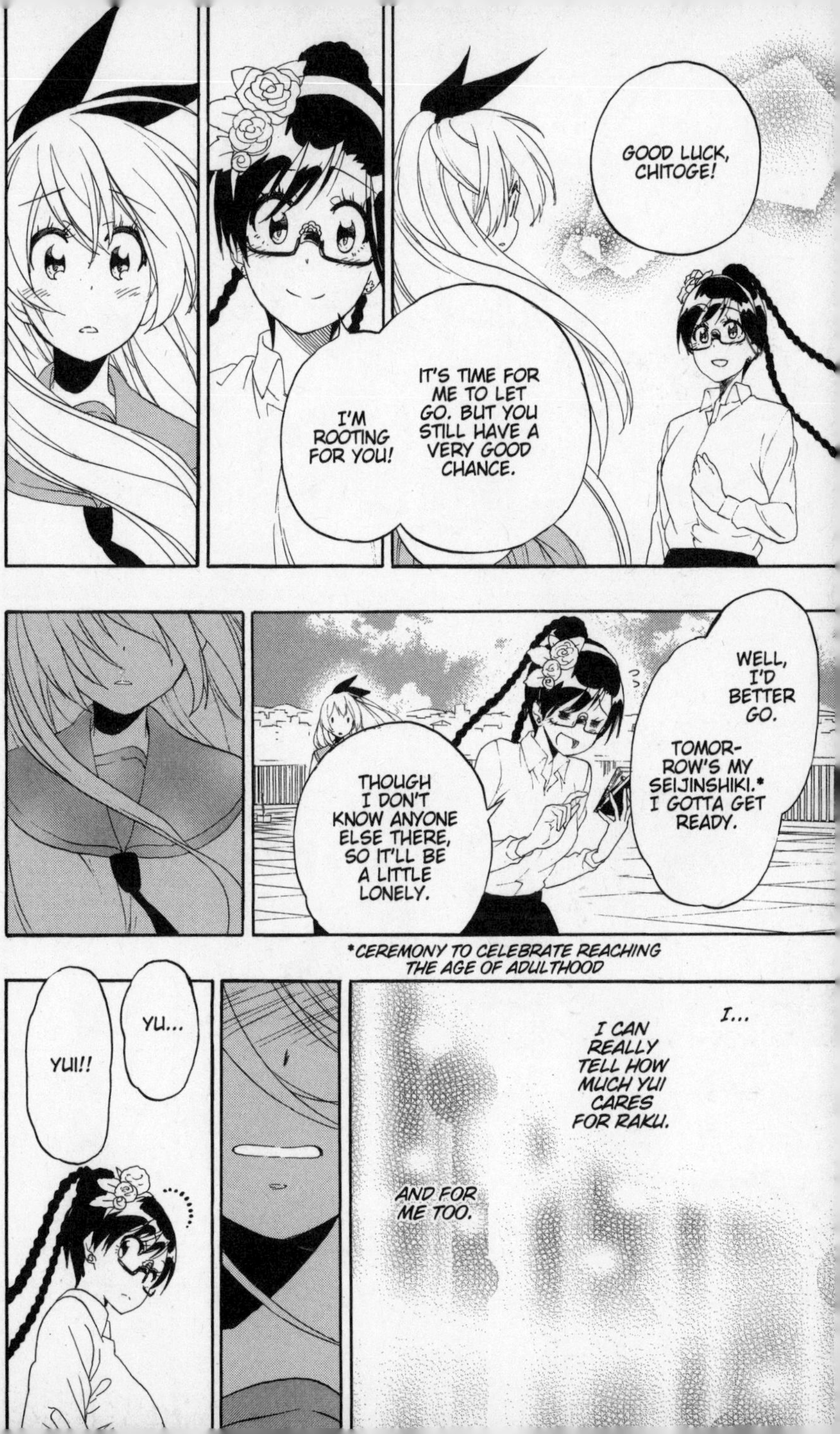
GOOD LUCK, CHITOGE!
IT'S TIME FOR ME TO LET GO. BUT YOU STILL HAVE A VERY GOOD CHANCE.
I'M ROOTING FOR YOU!
WELL, I'D BETTER GO.
TOMOR-ROW'S MY SEIJINSHIKI.* I GOTTA GET READY.
THOUGH I DON'T KNOW ANYONE ELSE THERE, SO IT'LL BE A LITTLE LONELY.
*CEREMONY TO CELEBRATE REACHING THE AGE OF ADULTHOOD
I...
I CAN REALLY TELL HOW MUCH YUI CARES FOR RAKU.
AND FOR ME TOO.
YU...
YUI!!

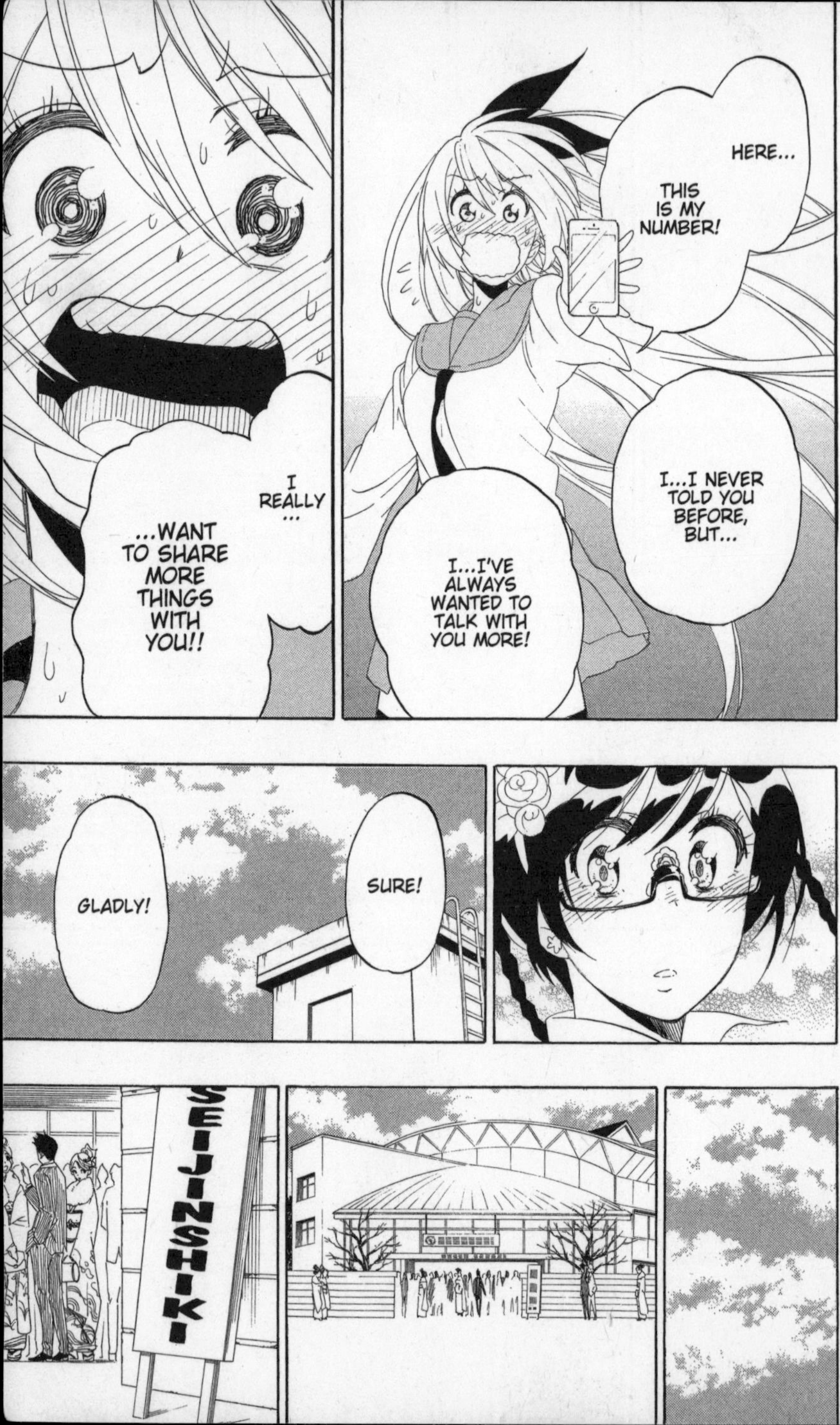
HERE...
THIS IS MY NUMBER!
I...I NEVER TOLD YOU BEFORE, BUT...
I...I'VE ALWAYS WANTED TO TALK WITH YOU MORE!
I REALLY...
...WANT TO SHARE MORE THINGS WITH YOU!!
SURE!
GLADLY!
SEIJINSHIKI

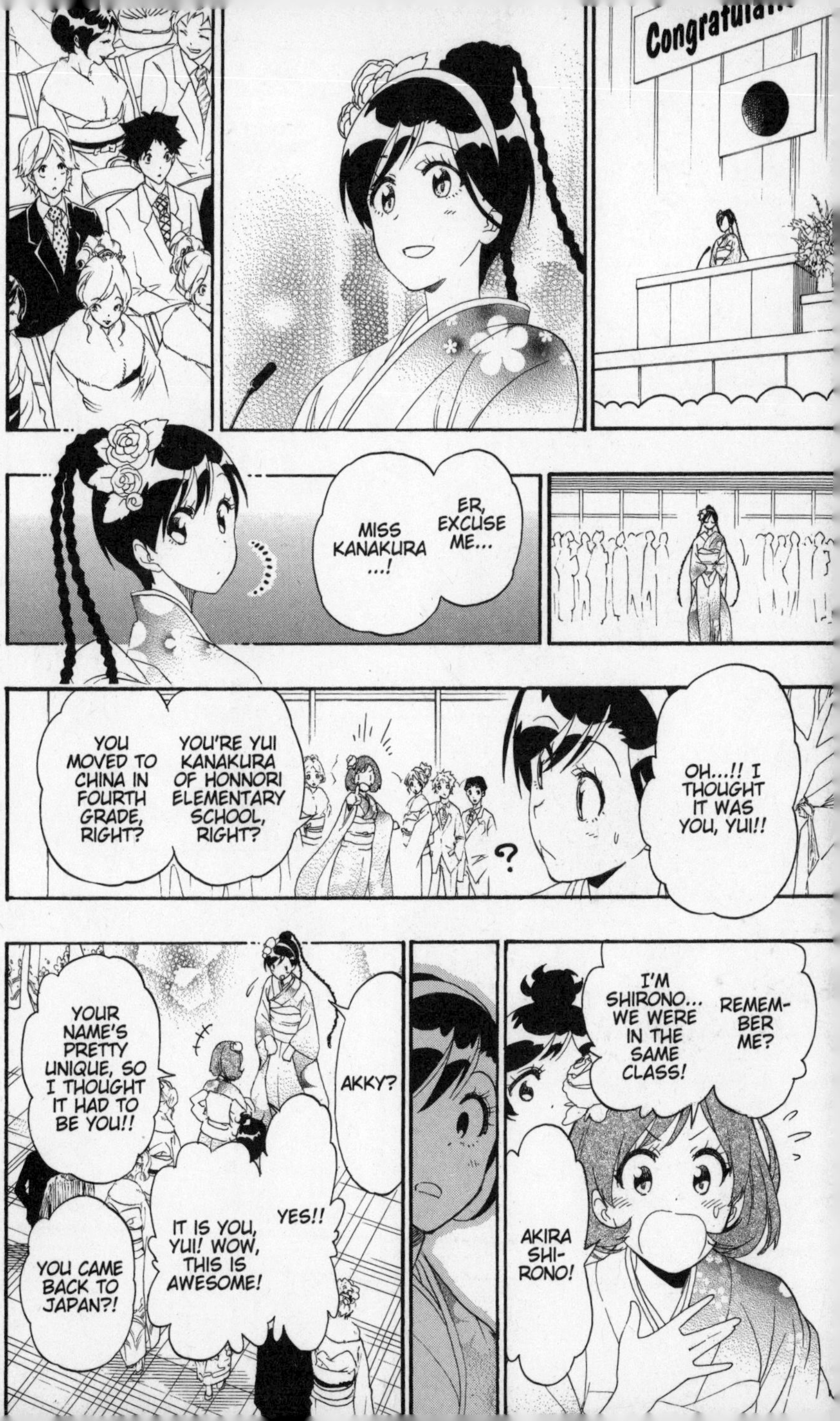
Congratula
ER, EXCUSE ME...
MISS KANAKURA ...!
OH...!! I THOUGHT IT WAS YOU, YUI!!
YOU'RE YUI KANAKURA OF HONNORI ELEMENTARY SCHOOL, RIGHT?
YOU MOVED TO CHINA IN FOURTH GRADE, RIGHT?
REMEM-BER ME?
I'M SHIRONO... WE WERE IN THE SAME CLASS!
AKIRA SHI-RONO!
AKKY?
YES!!
IT IS YOU, YUI! WOW, THIS IS AWESOME!
YOUR NAME'S PRETTY UNIQUE, SO I THOUGHT IT HAD TO BE YOU!!
YOU CAME BACK TO JAPAN?!

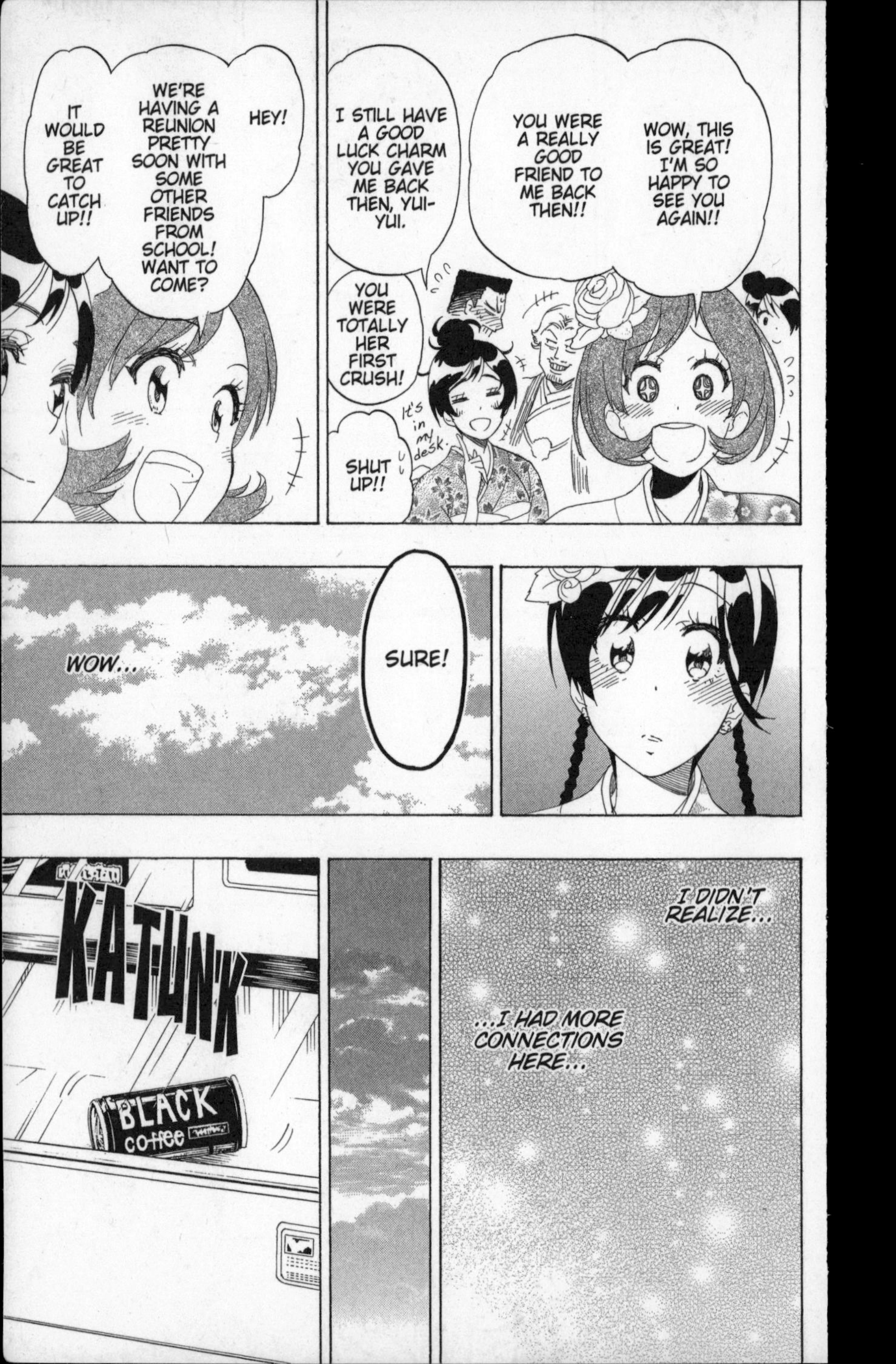
WOW, THIS IS GREAT! I'M SO HAPPY TO SEE YOU AGAIN!!
YOU WERE A REALLY GOOD FRIEND TO ME BACK THEN!!
I STILL HAVE A GOOD LUCK CHARM YOU GAVE ME BACK THEN, YUI-YUI.
YOU WERE TOTALLY HER FIRST CRUSH!
It's in my desk.
SHUT UP!!
HEY!
WE'RE HAVING A REUNION PRETTY SOON WITH SOME OTHER FRIENDS FROM SCHOOL! WANT TO COME?
IT WOULD BE GREAT TO CATCH UP!!
SURE!
WOW...
I DIDN'T REALIZE...
...I HAD MORE CONNECTIONS HERE...
KA-TUNK
BLACK
coffee

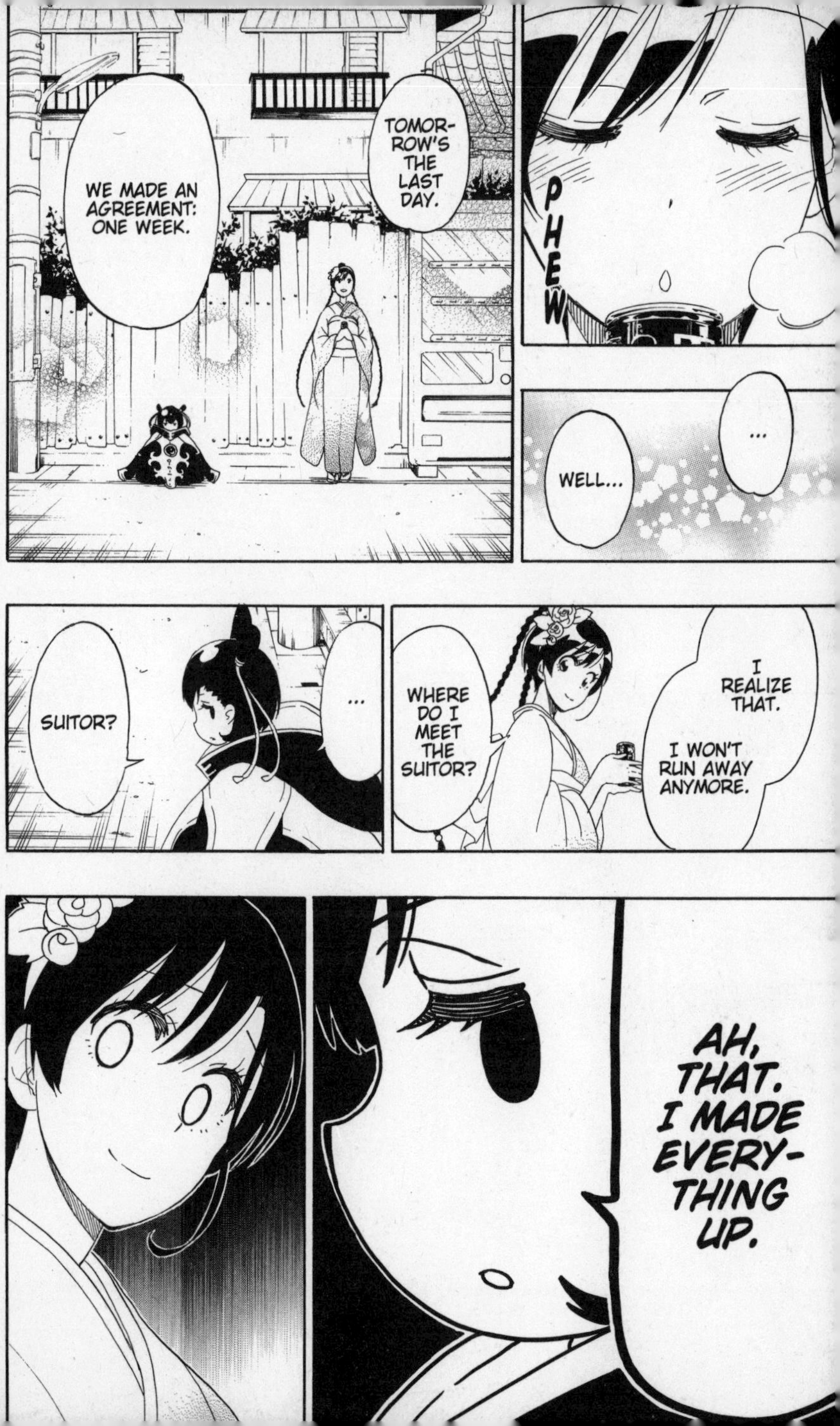
PHEW
...
WELL...
TOMORROW'S THE LAST DAY.
WE MADE AN AGREEMENT: ONE WEEK.
I REALIZE THAT.
I WON'T RUN AWAY ANYMORE.
WHERE DO I MEET THE SUITOR?
...
SUITOR?
AH, THAT. I MADE EVERYTHING UP.

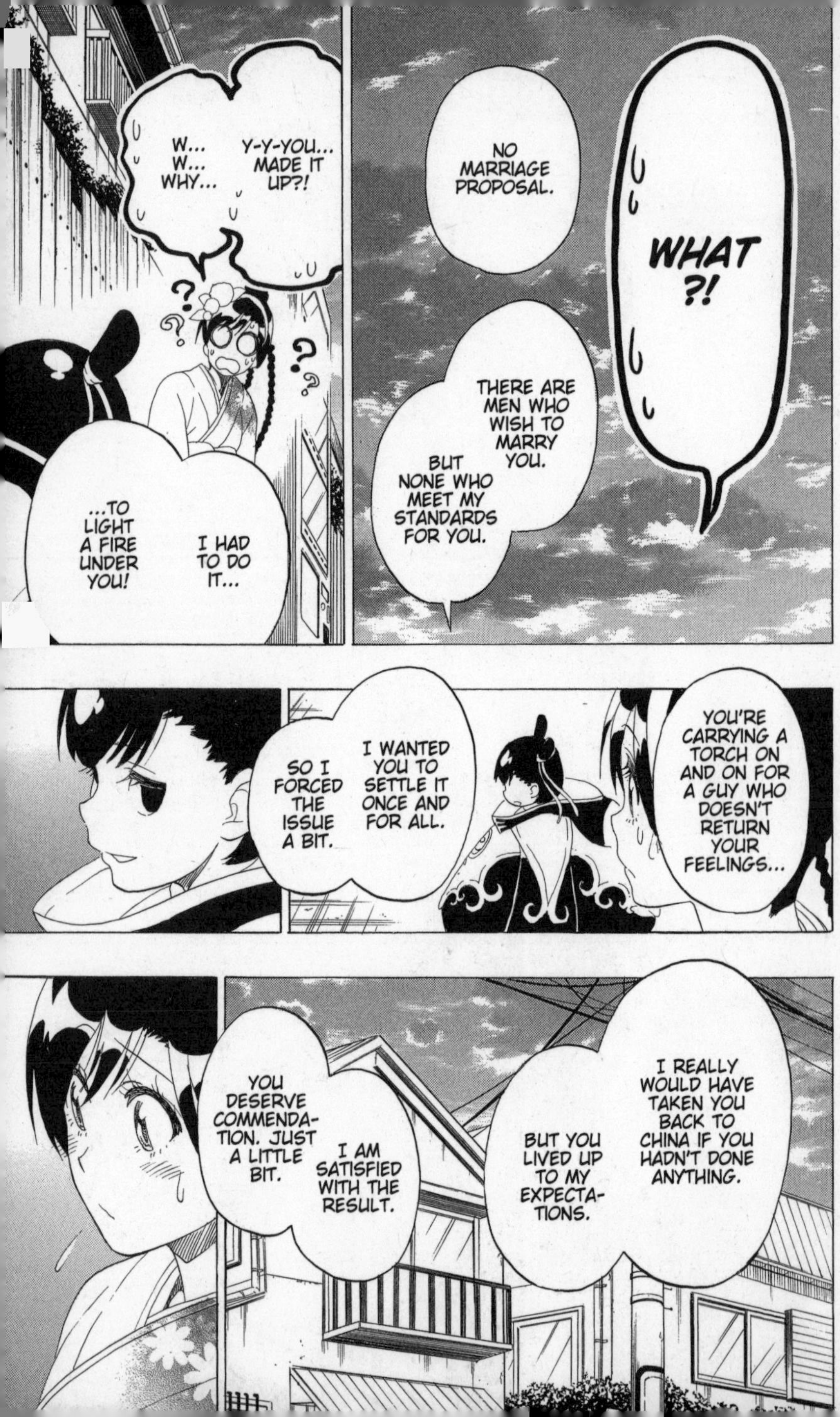
WHAT?!
NO MARRIAGE PROPOSAL.
THERE ARE MEN WHO WISH TO MARRY YOU.
BUT NONE WHO MEET MY STANDARDS FOR YOU.
Y-Y-YOU... MADE IT UP?!
W... W... WHY...
I HAD TO DO IT...
...TO LIGHT A FIRE UNDER YOU!
YOU'RE CARRYING A TORCH ON AND ON FOR A GUY WHO DOESN'T RETURN YOUR FEELINGS...
I WANTED YOU TO SETTLE IT ONCE AND FOR ALL.
SO I FORCED THE ISSUE A BIT.
I REALLY WOULD HAVE TAKEN YOU BACK TO CHINA IF YOU HADN'T DONE ANYTHING.
BUT YOU LIVED UP TO MY EXPECTATIONS.
I AM SATISFIED WITH THE RESULT.
YOU DESERVE COMMENDATION. JUST A LITTLE BIT.

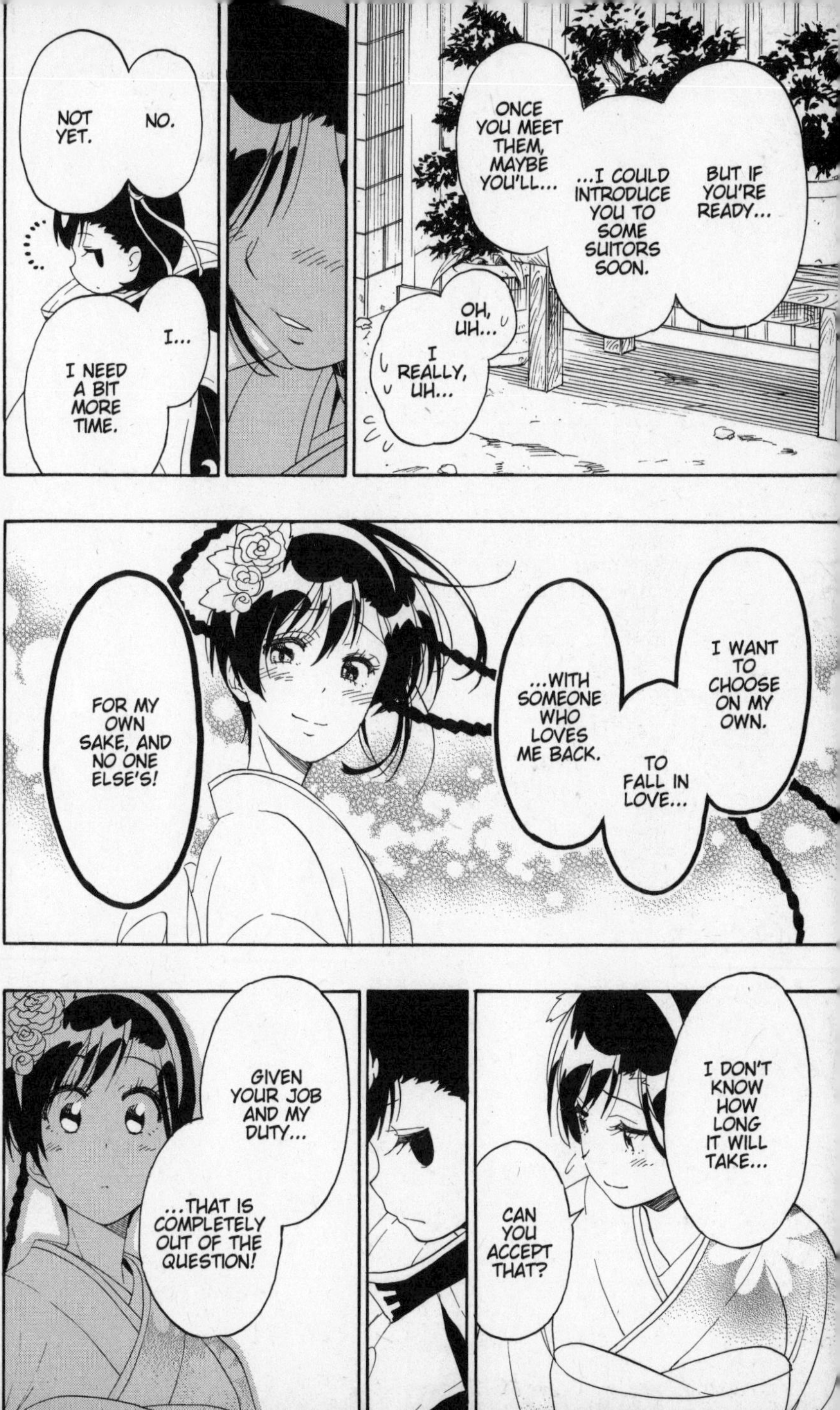
BUT IF YOU'RE READY...
...I COULD INTRODUCE YOU TO SOME SUITORS SOON.
ONCE YOU MEET THEM, MAYBE YOU'LL...
OH, UH...
I REALLY, UH...
NO.
NOT YET.
I...
I NEED A BIT MORE TIME.
I WANT TO CHOOSE ON MY OWN.
TO FALL IN LOVE...
...WITH SOMEONE WHO LOVES ME BACK.
FOR MY OWN SAKE, AND NO ONE ELSE'S!
I DON'T KNOW HOW LONG IT WILL TAKE...
CAN YOU ACCEPT THAT?
GIVEN YOUR JOB AND MY DUTY...
...THAT IS COMPLETELY OUT OF THE QUESTION!

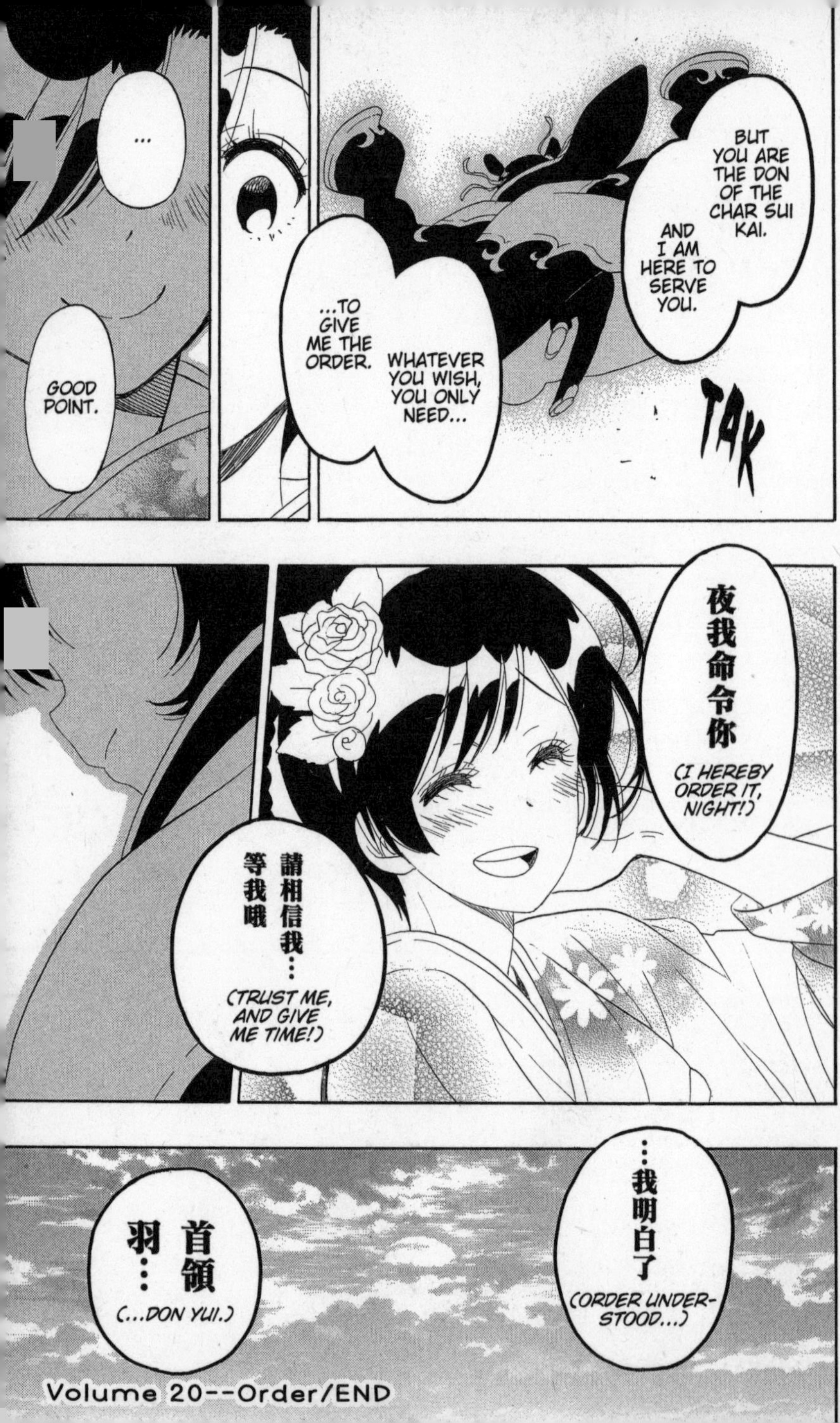
BUT YOU ARE THE DON OF THE CHAR SUI KAI.
AND I AM HERE TO SERVE YOU.
TAK
WHATEVER YOU WISH, YOU ONLY NEED...
...TO GIVE ME THE ORDER.
...
GOOD POINT.
夜我命令你
(I HEREBY ORDER IT, NIGHT!)
請相信我…等我哦
(TRUST ME, AND GIVE ME TIME!)
…我明白了
(ORDER UNDER-STOOD...)
首領羽…
(...DON YUI.)

Volume 20--Order/END

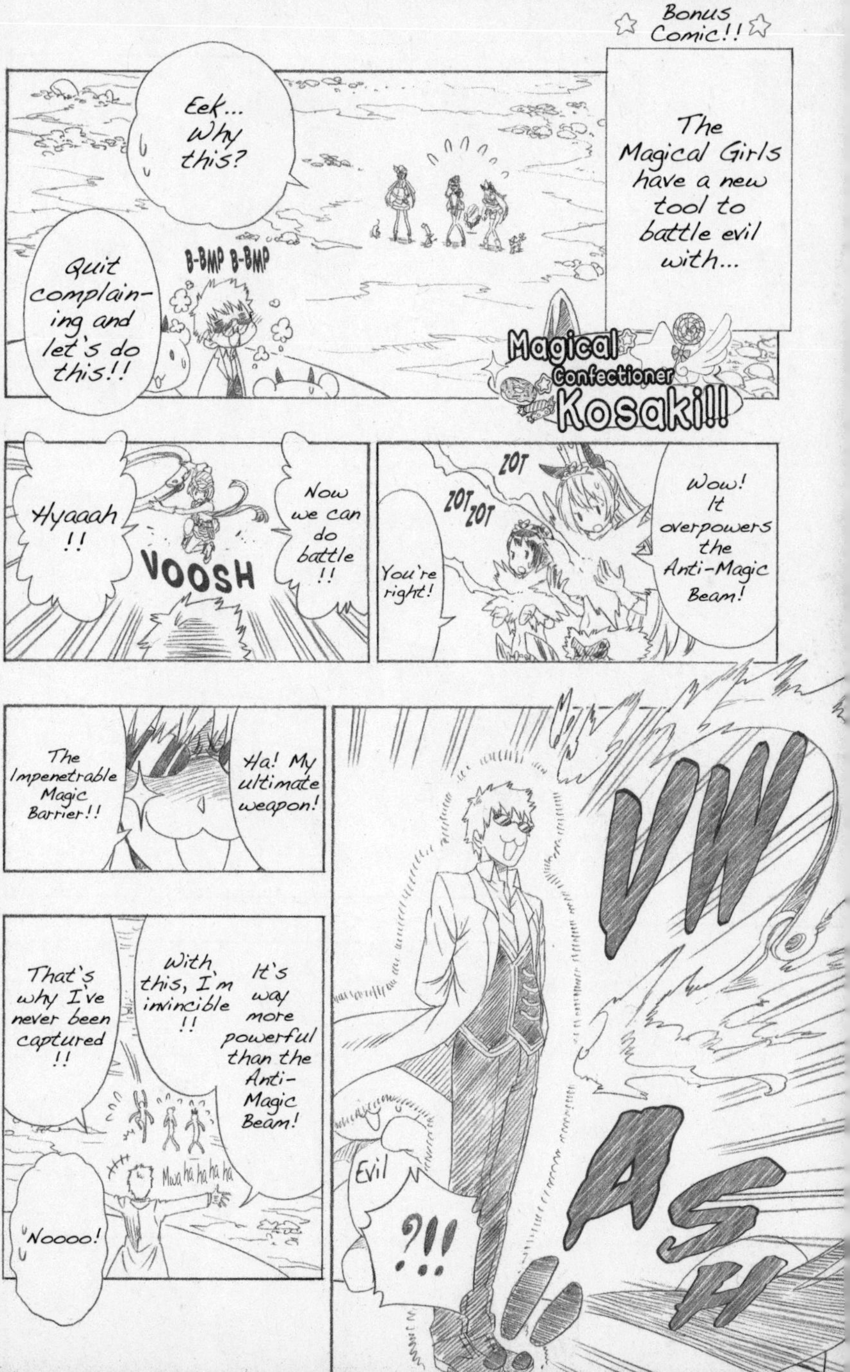
Bonus Comic!!
The Magical Girls have a new tool to battle evil with...
Magical Confectioner Kosaki!!
Eek... Why this?
B-BMP B-BMP
Quit complaining and let's do this!!
Wow! It overpowers the Anti-Magic Beam!
ZOT
ZOT ZOT
You're right!
Now we can do battle!!
VOOSH
Hyaaah!!
VWAASH
Evil ?!!
Ha! My ultimate weapon!
The Impenetrable Magic Barrier!!
It's way more powerful than the Anti-Magic Beam!
With this, I'm invincible!!
That's why I've never been captured!!
Mwa ha ha ha ha
Noooo!

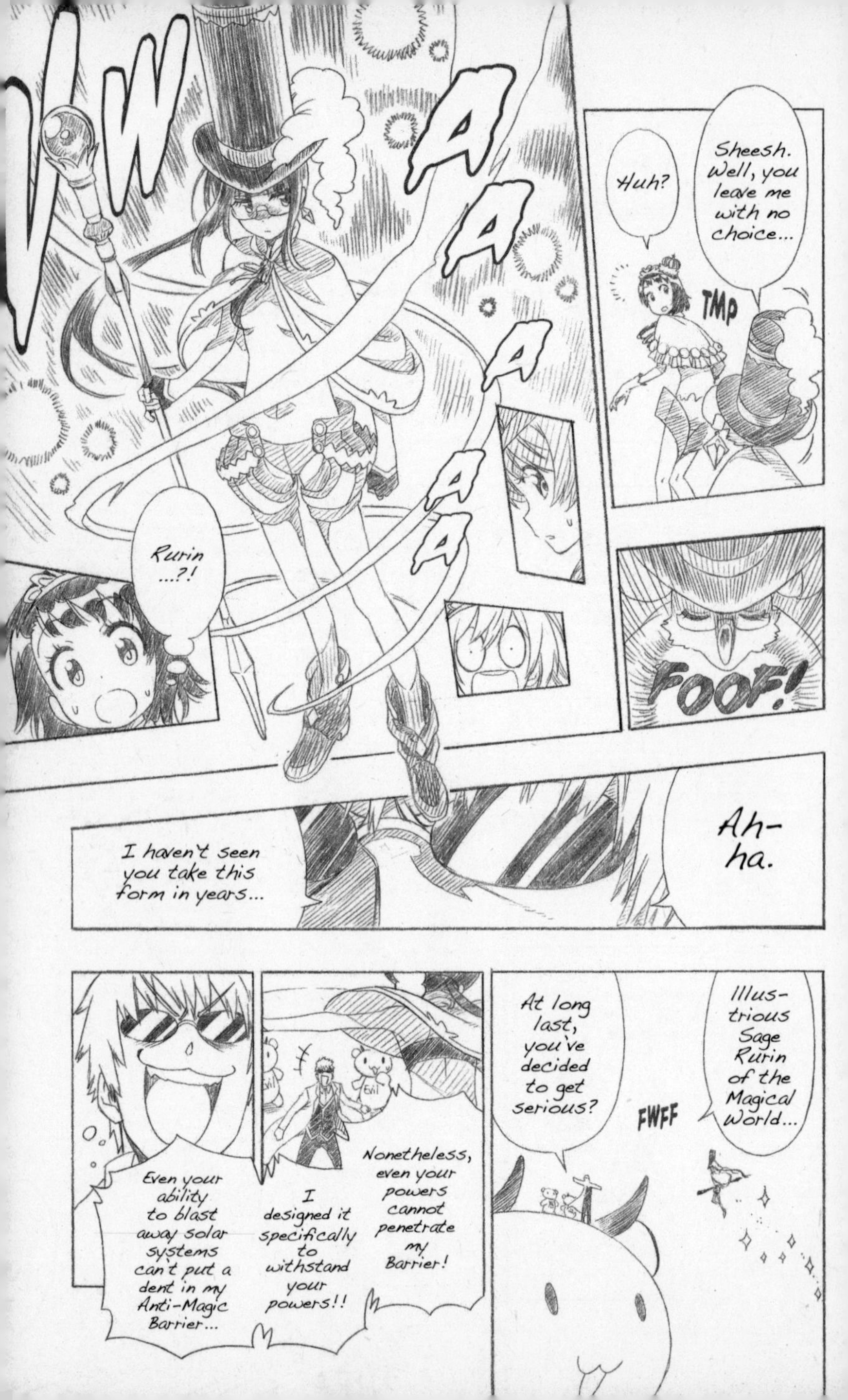
Sheesh. Well, you leave me with no choice...
Huh?
TMP
FOOF!
WAAAAA
Rurin ...?!
Ah-ha.
I haven't seen you take this form in years...
Illustrious Sage Rurin of the Magical World...
At long last, you've decided to get serious?
FWFF
Nonetheless, even your powers cannot penetrate my Barrier!
I designed it specifically to withstand your powers!!
Even your ability to blast away solar systems can't put a dent in my Anti-Magic Barrier...

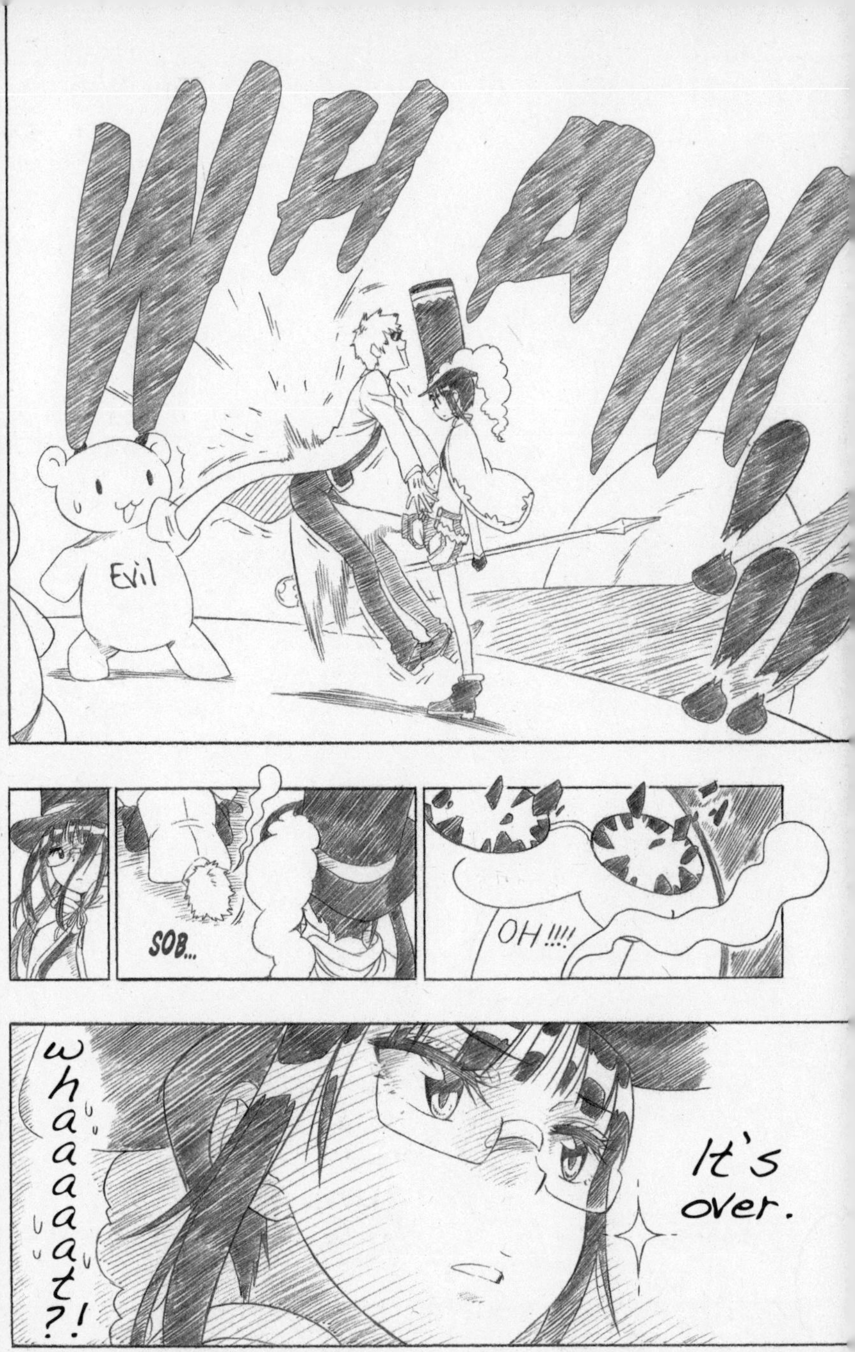
WHAM!!
Evil
OH!!!!
SOB...
It's over.
whaaaaaat?!

To be continued!! One final chapter!!

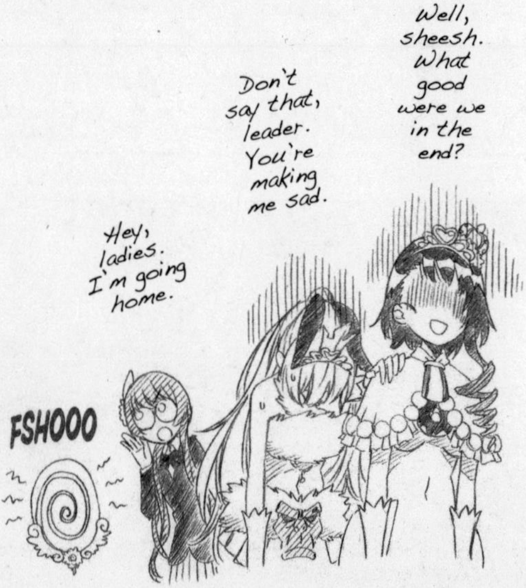
Well, sheesh. What good were we in the end?
Don't say that, leader. You're making me sad.
Hey, ladies. I'm going home.
FSHOOO

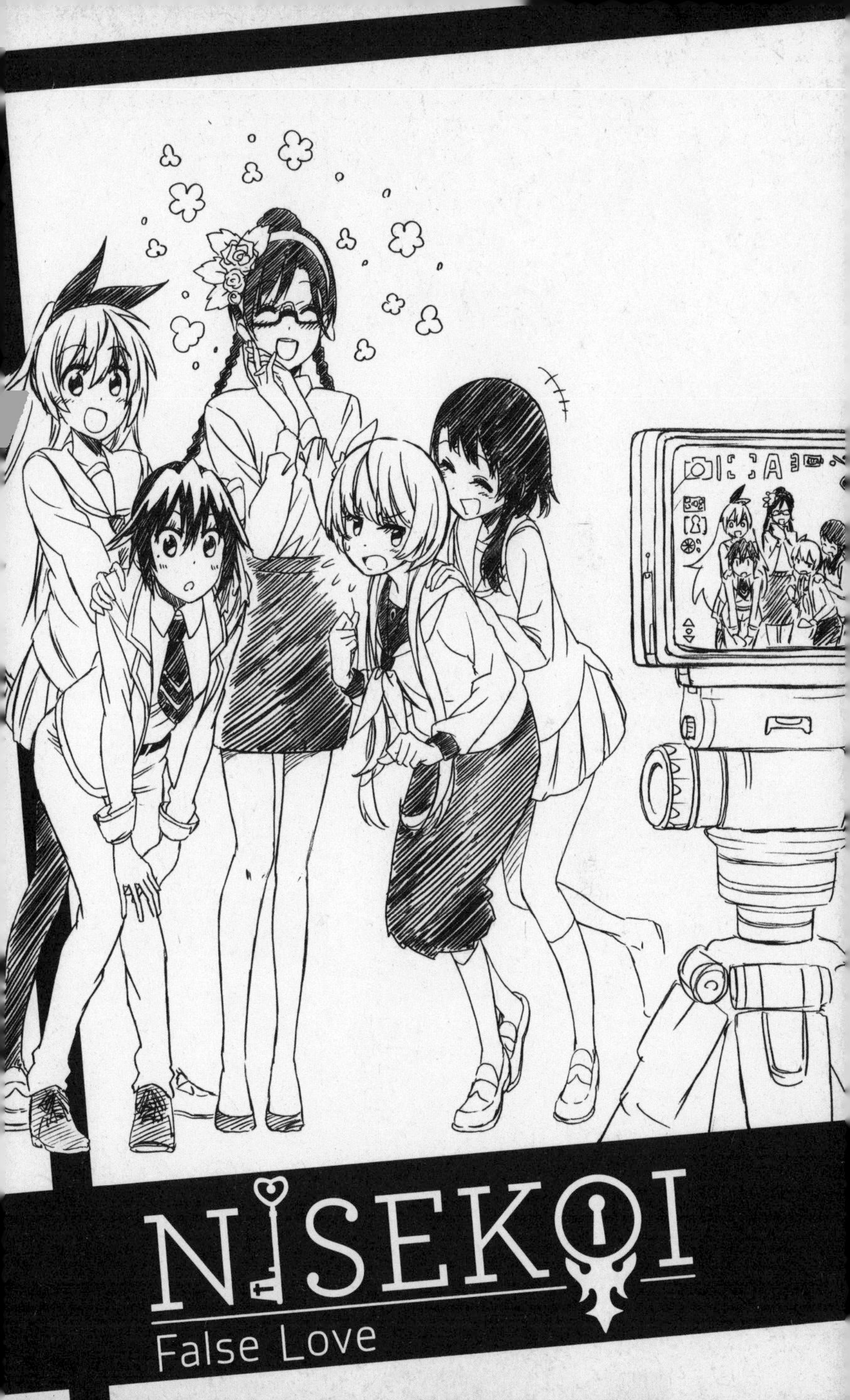

NISEKOI

False Love